SOCIOLOGICAL
THEORY:
INQUIRIES
AND PARADIGMS

SOCIOLOGICAL THEORY: INQUIRIES AND PARADIGMS

Edited by LLEWELLYN GROSS

State University of New York at Buffalo

A HARPER INTERNATIONAL EDITION

jointly published by

HARPER & ROW,   New York, Evanston, and London

and JOHN WEATHERHILL, INC.,   Tokyo

This Harper International Edition is an unabridged, photo-offset reproduction of the American edition. It is for sale in Japan by JOHN WEATHERHILL, INC., 50 Ryudo-cho, Azabu, Minato-ku, Tokyo; in the United Kingdom and on the continent of Europe by HARPER & ROW, LTD., 69 Great Russell Street, London W.C. 1; and in other designated countries by HARPER & ROW, PUBLISHERS, INCORPORATED, 49 East 33rd Street, New York, N.Y. 10016 / Copyright © 1967 by Llewellyn Gross / All rights reserved; no part of this book may be used or reproduced in any manner whatsoever without written permission except in the case of brief quotations embodied in critical articles and reviews. For information write Harper & Row at the New York address given above / Library of Congress catalog card number 67-10794 / Printed in Japan / First printing, May, 1967.

Contents

PART III: SOCIAL CAUSATION

PART IV: THEORY FORMATION

PART V: THEORY AND SOCIAL PROBLEMS

PART VI: THEORY AND VALUES

Foreword

The strain toward consistency of which Sumner wrote in describing the folkways is applicable to the methods and objectives of modern sociological theory. The norms of science place great stress upon the production of a coherent product, one that is cumulative and, within its own idiom, as nearly conclusive as possible. Although indeterminism and uncertainty are generally acknowledged in scientific attempts to order experience, they are usually underplayed in the interest of achieving the kind of closure that is intellectually satisfying.

How much questioning of well-founded ideas can the professional sustain without seriously disrupting the scientific enterprise? What ideas must he support, given his own professed demand for scientific criticism? Each professional's reply to these and similar questions depends, ultimately on what he accepts from his predecessors and on how he assesses contemporary claims for authenticity. That the sociological product is, in our day, not only importunate but contingent and controvertible in its account of reality is the principal burden of the introductory essay. The

degree to which succeeding essays illuminate this theme must be left
to the reader's judgment. Nevertheless, sensitivity to the diversity and
interplay of conceptual alternatives is visible in the writings of each
author. Meadows notes, for instance, that much of man's life has been a
dialogue between chaos and cosmos. Organization theory rests on order
and the analogical way in which it is shaped by models. It is, accordingly,
committed to a metaphysical orientation. Models of fixed relations are
contrasted with models of variable relations as modes for building patterns
of order. In Harrell's essay, the problem of social order is examined
through the relationship of values to behavior and of language to perception. His primary concern is with the basic issue of whether symbols
conceptualize order or can correctly be said to determine it.

No treatment of social order would be complete without considering
the role of causality and its modern alternatives, sociological empiricism
and sociological functionalism. With this thought in mind, Theodorson
discusses unicausality, multiple and mechanical causation, and proposes a
limited conception of causality applicable to cross-cultural research. The
problem of social order in current evolutionary studies is then discussed
by Goldstein who examines the role of causal conceptions in developmental theories. As Goldstein suggests, all conceptions of causal development rest upon the way in which historical events are read and logically
arranged. Numerous possibilities may be seen to follow, one of which
points to the use of logically tight but empirically bogus accounts of
historical explanation, another to historical explanations which are
empirically genuine but logically loose. The subtleties of this dilemma are
explored by Dray in addressing himself to issues arising from Donegan's
attempt to escape its consequences. A not dissimilar procedural dilemma
is explored in Rose's perceptive analysis of the relation of theory to
empirical subject matter. Rose finds that method is not universal but
varies with the "image of reality" which the scientist projects. As a
result some researchers employ a circular logic in which method produces conclusions rather than independent tests of findings. In Schrag's
essay some of the preceding issues are catalogued by placing them within
a framework of system-forming procedures. Drawing from numerous
theoretical terminologies, including those of description and explanation,
observation and classification, postulates and theorems, an elementary
paradigm for theoretical analysis is offered.

Theories more substantive but, nonetheless, methodologically informed, are presented in essays by Etzioni and Roach. Searching for pathways to a peaceful world society, Etzioni develops a multifaceted theory of how international conflict can be contained. To this end he discusses the shift from duopoly to pluralism, the role of buffer states, of an international floating vote, and the bases in psychology and sociology for the upward transfer of powers, rights and sentiments to centralized international organization. Roach, aware of the complexity and tangential character of all theory, orders a wide range of research pertinent to the genesis of lower-class cultural, social, and personality deficiencies. In doing this he challenges viewpoints neglectful of those etiological determinants of human behavior commonly known as "material conditions." The essay by Gross on applied theory attempts to locate the general features of social problems within a transactional scheme which is, at one and the same time, both logical and pragmatic.

The volume closes with two papers in the sociology of knowledge. Both Walter and Horowitz deal with the role of the human factor, including the place of objectivity and perspective, in sociological writing. Walter argues that social scientists can select problems dispassionately and furnish objectively warranted explanations of social events since denial of this would place them in a paralyzing contradiction. Horowitz, on the other hand, views the problems selected by sociologists as responses to such conditions as formal organization, scientific status and community expectations, including serviceability to purchasers. He presents a profile, in diagram and prose, of professionals and occupationalists together with anti-sociologists and unsociologists.

A dialectic of persistent issues, ever incomplete of final resolution, stand like crisscrossed beacons in the essays of each author. The diverse referential groundwork upon which symbols rest and symbol-users respond are weighed by Meadows, Harrell, Theodorson, Dray, Rose, Roach, and, indeed, by all contributors. If values, along with problems of human freedom and choice, are included as viable elements in theory, the essays by Dray, Goldstein, Horowitz, Etzioni, and Walter may be prominently mentioned—but only at the risk of seeming to exclude similar implications searchingly explored in the other essays. Assumptions about what is to be taken as ideal or material, causal or functional, wholistic or partial, are among the volume's most pervading concerns. By means of approaches imaginatively conceived, each essay uncovers roads to reality, signposts for guiding the student who, if he possesses ingenuity, may use them to discover fresh avenues of meaning.

LLEWELLYN GROSS

September, 1966

PART

I Orientation

Sociological theory:
LLEWELLYN GROSS
questions and problems

In the opening paragraph of *Modernity and Liberty* Horace Kallen writes:

> Every so often, when I come upon the word "problem" in a work of philosophy or social science, I experience wonder. The works, as a rule, evince no more genuine curiosity than a catechism nor are more given to doubt than a multiplication table. Their "problems" seem to follow from their solutions, not their solutions from their problems. The answers are all known in advance, so that the questions they settle seem to be rhetorical and the reasoning which leads to them but the dialectics of a foregone conclusion. Their argument moves in a circle, the self-confirmation of dogmatic certainty. Yet they repeat the word "problem" as automatically and as frequently as a personal pronoun, with the consequence that the natural or common meaning of the word is stood on its head, the "problem" designates the formal or systematic elaboration of the unproblematical. Seeking the causes of this paradox, I can find no more satisfactory explanation than our spontaneous aversion to the problematical. Innately we prefer belief to doubt and certainty to uncertainty; we feel safer with ordered sequence than with indeterminate change; repetitive "necessary connexion" gives us assurance; innovative spontaneous variation does not.[1]

Kallen's remarks may be taken as background for what seems on

[1] The University of Buffalo Studies, Vol. 18 (March, 1947), p. 73.

3

reflection to be a strange situation. Apparently most social scientists believe their own work approximates certainty. Yet no two of them provide the same analysis of similar problems and none ever writes that another's work is entirely acceptable. When unsolved problems are mentioned they are offered as afterthoughts to a finished product.

The individual social scientist writes as if each item in his analysis fell into its proper place. Selecting information from widely diverse sources, his presentation suggests that every phrase and citation is part of a well-rounded, fully integrated whole. On this assumption there is little room for doubt or uncertainty. However, when the presentations of social scientists are examined as a body, differences of interpretation are seen to outnumber similarities. Social scientists cite one another but seldom admit to incorporating more than a few ideas from any one. The practice of citing ideas from many authors and few from any one nurtures a threefold belief: that discoveries in social science are necessarily cumulative, that one's own writing contributes to this end, and that the offerings of others are open to doubt and uncertainty. But if attitudes of doubt and uncertainty are justified when considering the work of another, why shouldn't they be justified when considering one's own work?

Were individual researchers willing to credit as little certainty to their own work as they do to the work of others, they might more nearly fulfill the norms of science. Scientific norms can be realized only by avoiding dogmatic closure on the one side and skeptical license on the other. To achieve such norms, solutions to current problems should be used to project unsolved difficulties. Then each social scientist's contribution would be seen as but a small addition to that of his predecessors. Scientific writings would be devoted to the perplexities, doubts, and uncertainties encountered by their authors. The professor would, in A. N. Whitehead's words, "exhibit himself in his own true character— that is, as an ignorant man thinking, actively utilizing his small store of knowledge." He would agree that the undefined, the infirm, and the precarious are more intrinsic to the realities of sociological knowledge than is commonly supposed.

METHODS AND OBJECTIVES

This essay is an open invitation to pose questions which clarify significant problems. A variety of perplexities are presented, each designed to enrich sociological theory. As intellectual sketches they cannot presume to be objectively correct or true. At best they are counters for venturing novel queries and claims, original proposals, and fresh judgments. Their principal purpose is to stimulate inquiry, which may be elicited as quickly by opposition as by acceptance. Even the assumption that knowledge should be liberated does not entail its acceptance—if one can dispute it without being a party to it!

We assume that inquiry may follow a variety of styles—literary discourse, statistical analysis, logical reconstruction, prose elucidation of alternatives—indeed, any form deemed suitable by interested partic¡pants. We assume, moreover, that the central concepts of modern science —data, hypotheses, theory, causation, verification, etc., are meant to express relative degrees of certainty, qualitatively or quantitatively graduated. Such concepts attempt to draw from the infirmities of human experience approximations of knowledge grounded on reasonable belief. Studies of the kind found in our *Symposium on Sociological Theory*[2] may be taken as representative. But modern social science has a nether vocabulary which seeks degrees of certainty through the indirect route of discordant principles and claims. Doubt is brought to the fore and sureness of belief is won by confronting obstacles glossed over in the premature closure of "scientific results." Such an approach is nearer to the socratic method than it is to system building. Its stock in trade includes the language of dialogue and inquiry, conflict and controversy, dialectic and dilemma, paradox and conjecture, ambiguity and antinomy. The two approaches differ in emphasis, in what is assumed as starting points, since all of science must come to terms with competing viewpoints, or it is nothing. It must seek some version of consistency, truth, or probable use, and for this reason cannot avoid epistemological assumptions. A passage by Karl Popper accents this standpoint.

> It is necessary for us to see that of the two main ways in which we may explain the growth of science, one is rather unimportant and the other is important. The first explains science by the accumulation of knowledge: it is like a growing library (or a museum). As more and more books accumulate, so more and more knowledge accumulates. The other explains it by criticism: it grows by a more revolutionary method than accumulation—by a method which destroys, changes, and alters the whole thing, including its most important instrument, the language in which our myths and theories are formulated.[3]

Whether the primordial roots of science are conceived as the accumulation of hypotheses or the development of critical methods, the questioning process is ubiquitous. Without questions there can be no subject for research since then there is no articulated uncertainty or difficulty, no point worthy of dispute—nothing unsettled. Without questions there can be no sense of the problematic, no curiosity about the unknown, no engagement with hidden sources of understanding. Things

[2] L. Gross (ed.), *Symposium on Sociological Theory* (New York: Harper & Row, 1959).
[3] Karl R. Popper, *Conjectures and Refutations* (New York: Basic Books, 1962), p. 129.

which are "beyond question" are beyond deliberation, proposal, and critical judgment. Paradoxical though it may seen, respect for the contours of the unknown is a necessary condition for appraising what is known. This, it would seem, is the most urgent requirement of science.

CONTEXTS OF QUESTIONS

Word questioning

All words give rise to questions because their threads of meaning are intertwined with the developing senses of other words, whose various constituents either move in unison or emerge as clashing symbols, eluding clear analysis. The patent consideration that words cannot be detached from either their users or the changing things they signify implies that they are governed by shifting connotations. And are not all connotations conditioned by the imagery through which experience and idea are cast?

Assumptions of questions

All questions, other than rhetorical ones, assume that something unknown may happen, be brought about, or be the case, unless circumstances are shown to limit possible outcomes. They assume that intellectual alternatives are open until restricting situations are set forth or until proof is believed to obtain without serious doubt or error. In some instances, they ask for the probability that decisions can be subscribed to or construed in specific ways under specific conditions. To estimate probabilities, explicitly and unambiguously, some things must remain unquestioned—facts, premises, beliefs, values—for without them no idea can have an intelligible degree of specificity. Hence a distinction must always be maintained between what is taken in question and what is not taken in question.

Questions and conjectures

Bound as they are by insufficient evidence, all questions give rise to conjectures, imaginatively conceived outcomes, speculative or calculated estimations, for which the questioner seeks some indication of truth. Anticipations of truths to be discovered in the phenomenal world presuppose the contingency of things. The reduction of contingency rests upon such elementary questions as, "What is the object X?" "What is the word for X?" "What does one think about X?" Apart from the many usages of the verb "is," no conjecture joined to the triumvirate of word, thought, and object can be advanced without recourse to additional words. The choice of prepositions alone alters the texture of language: What is the idea *of* culture? What is culture *about, above, against, for, within*? Where is culture *at*? As long as words are subject to social contingencies, no thing is inviolable to conjecture or immune from questioning.

Alternative replies to questions

When the full range of alternative replies to a many-sided question is reduced to the simplest possible choices the respondent is confronted with a series of yes and no judgments. For every calculi, personal or logical, yes and no judgments are required by the demand for definiteness (i.e., unambiguous designation). Nevertheless, new discoveries in science have been found to follow negative replies to questions which have logically or conventionally received positive replies. To escape fixed alternatives, methods of inquiry which challenge familiar lines of assertion and denial must be developed. Such methods would minimize the force of traditional thoughtways in the determination of positive and negative conclusions.

Pseudo-questions

The process of questioning may be viewed as either interrogation or inquiry when it is systematically ordered for purposes of obtaining evidence. The issue of "pseudo-questions" arises when interrogation is designed to persuade or catechize. "Pseudo-questions" are subterfuges for assertions intended to convey a preconceived belief or socially defined creed. Replies to such questions are scrutinized for their usefulness in indoctrinating beliefs and discrediting doubts.

THE QUESTIONING PROCESS

Questioning attitude

The questioning attitude is ubiquitous for two reasons. First, it is an implicit condition, a necessary posture, for extracting the meaning of such categories of thought as adjustment, change, choice, norm, person, equilibrium, group, criticism, hypothesis, probability, relativity, theory, and utopia, to mention but a few. Secondly, it takes cognizance of the fact that no word can retain univocal meaning for very long. The image of every word is changed by events and experience, by conflicting beliefs and doctrines, by contrary styles which both affirm and deny its suitability for ordering things. Harmony and discord, action and reaction are as omnipresent in the realm of ideas as they are in the realm of social phenomena.

Import of questions

A liberalized view of the character of questions attributes to all some degree of import. In a manner of speaking, every question asks about possible existence. The skeptical Hume declared, "It is an established maxim in metaphysics that whatever the mind clearly conceives includes the idea of possible existence or, in other words, that nothing we imagine is absolutely impossible." Eternal life is possible for some people because they can imagine themselves existing in the indefinite future. Eternal life is improbable for science but to rule it out, absolutely and irrevocably, complete knowledge of every being in the universe must be presumed. In the absence of complete knowledge, science resolves the issue of immortality by reference to problems of proof and confirmation, to criteria for testing empirical claims. Within the spatial temporal limits of empirical confirmation the question of "eternal life" is "meaningless." But to hold this conclusion with decisive finality is to challenge the scientific premises upon which it rests. Disconfirmation must be shown by acknowledged precedures and, if shown, cannot be regarded as established for the indefinite future.

Necessary questions

Questions of attribution, relationship, proportionality, variation, contradiction, and negation are necessary for understanding physical and social nature in their scientific, moral, and historical manifestations. No doubt, every question requires extremes and intermediates to fix its coordinates and define its regions of application. Questions are understood in terms of their likenesses and differences, their similarity to others, to which they are perceived as related. Yet perceived relations cannot be identified without comparing their unities and diversities. One must question the respects in which the sameness and difference of a relation is itself like or unlike the sameness and difference of other relations before one can approach an unambiguous judgment. Only through an orderly process of inquiry can one come near to knowing how the "same" concepts can have "different" meanings and "different" concepts the "same" meaning.

Fruitful questions

Perhaps the most fruitful questions are those from which it is impossible logically to elicit either an indefinite number of contradictory interpretations or an indefinite number of indeterminate observations. If every possible interpretation or observation follows from a given question, proposed replies are not restrictive of useful, valid, or true knowledge. A minimum of nine concepts is contained in the question, "Is technological innovation the primary cause of cultural change?" Each concept varies in observational and interpretative meaning. If every possible meaning were equally probable, the question could hardly contribute to understanding. But if each concept contains a meaning whose sense can be indicated by reasonably precise criteria there is gain in knowledge. Some proposed replies can be said to be "true" and others can be said to be "false." Of course, care must be taken not to restrict possible meanings by "loading" questions with implicit premises. Sociological inquiry could be biased by asking, "What are the *valid* reasons for believing that technological innovation is the primary cause of cultural change?" "What is the most recent illustration of the *fact* that technological innovation is a primary cause of cultural change?" "*Since* technological innovation is the primary cause of cultural change, what is the role of belief systems?" Such statements are biased insofar as they deny the need for open inquiry.[4] To ask what could be the case though it may not be the case, is to direct oneself beyond what is necessary, inescapable, or inevitable—to what is, in the preview of the future, partly contingent. As long as what usually happens in some sphere of events is not everywhere the same, there is room for growth and novelty. When atypical or exceptional occurrences are not ruled out, man is free to reshape a larger portion of his world.

QUESTIONS ABOUT QUESTIONS

Where should questions begin

Where should the questioning process begin? Presumably the meaning of every question depends upon the usage attributed or accredited to each word within it. Word usages must be specified through identifying categories—class, type, property, or relation—before relevant replies can be joined to them. Since identifying categories are not usually made explicit, respondents must look for ways of assigning form and content to them. In the absence of precise clues to the meaning of categories, a minimum body of principles for gauging replies is a basic necessity. But where is such a body of principles to come from and what should be its

---

[4] Nevertheless, the challenge of every question lies in the quest for the actual through the possible, for "a disjunction of answers" in the realm of controlled imagination.

characteristics? Should it reflect universal kinds of human responses, not unlike the ubiquitous concern for the what, where, when, and why of things? If so, how does one get from such responses to those used by science—data, definition, measurement, causality, order, etc.? Are they brought in from sources outside of science or are they the outgrowth of developments within each field of specialization? Are there any responses unique to sociology itself? Where do such typical sociological categories as sex, age, income, education, class, and ethnic membership belong with reference to this problem?

Where should questions lead

Around what circle of ideas, through what lines of inquiry, toward what empirical probabilities should the questioning process proceed? If the questioning process is continuous and unremitting to the end of doubting all assertions, decision becomes impossible without fostering contradiction between word and deed. On the other hand, if the questioning process takes some assertions as beyond doubt, on what grounds can it claim to do so? Does every assertion worthy of expression rest on grounds of justification designed to preclude alternative claims? But in this case, does not every assertion become entrapped in an infinite regress to sources of justification which, though they add one claim upon another, elude the ultimate firmness of meaning? On what basis, then, is one to decide among things to doubt and things not to doubt? Should one begin by questioning much on the assumption that by doing so one will come to achieve a larger measure of certainty? Should one begin by questioning little and later question more on the assumption that one will then be able to distinguish the falsely certain from the truly certain? Should one view all questions of certainty and doubt as relative to contexts, separating assertions *within* contexts from assertions *about* contexts? For instance, does the question, "Who has legitimate authority" take as indisputable ideas that are not so taken in the question, "Do we have legitimate authority"? Does the question, "What is culture?" raise doubts not assumed by the question, "Is there a middle-class culture?"

How are counter-questions chosen

At any point in discourse or dialogue how does one choose among counter-questions and counter-replies? Is there a social drift toward patterns of converging and diverging replies? Is there always a contest between questions and replies wherein each attempts to contain the other, the force of replies containing the limits of skepticism and the force of questions containing the limits of dogmatism? Can or should a clear distinction be made between questions of fact and questions of counter-fact, between the actual and the possible? Are some questions of counter-fact more subject to identification and appraisal than others, more within the bounds of scientific, pragmatic, ethical, or esthetic endeavor? Can the scientist, through the art of compounding questions, produce the freedom of mind from which original discoveries arise? How is he to break the finality of authority and achieve objectivity without resort to discordant questions?

When should questions end

At what time and place should the questioning process be brought to a provisional halt? Are there tentative degrees of conclusiveness or certainty which can serve as points of reprieve from persistent doubt? Do the certainties assumed by some questions constitute the doubts assumed by others? In the sequential interchange between questions and replies can consistency be assessed? Can forms of orderly progression be catalogued? If decisive social action requires the presence of indisputable premises, how do we recognize them or how may they be best understood? Can rules of regression to "fundamentals" be logically formulated which are at the same time compatible with diverse paths of scientific inquiry?

When are questions significant

On what grounds, if any, should a question be judged significant? Are tautological questions altogether devoid of meaning? For instance, is the question "If all men seek status do all men seek status?"—entirely without new sense? Does such a question call to issue the universality of the class of all men together with the allegation of status as a universal property? Should the question be altered slightly to ask, "If all men seek status, are all men status strivers?"—Can it be conceded that inconsistency is not implied on the grounds that a reasonable claim can be made for the possibility that though all men may be status seekers, not all men may be status strivers?

The issue of whether the conditions stated or implied by a question are so logically redundant as to render replies meaningless is comple-mented by conditions which seem to have no logical connection with the questions which follow from them. For instance, is the question "If all men seek status, what are the mineral resources of the United States?"—an altogether meaningless one? Cannot a context be supplied to render even this an intelligible kind of query? Do not most men assume un-expressed but intelligible contexts when raising questions of this kind?

A PARTIAL INVENTORY OF QUESTIONS

The phrasing and expansion of questions is beset with nearly limitless possibilities. The plenitude of questions, conventional and unconventional, are as endless as the outermost reaches of human intelligence. While inquiring into the question of what ought to be questioned, the sociologist must presume to know something about inquiry. But since every inquiry is constantly undergoing change—else it would not be inquiry—there is no way of fixing its limits. To restrict inquiries to the principal preoccupations of sociology is to assume that future inquiry must be limited by past inquiry, a condition which would lead to the foreclosure of free intelligence.

From the welter of possible categorizations we have elected "language," "history," "cause," and "value" as guides to theoretical questions. Language is the symbolic vehicle or expressive medium through which ideas are cast. By shaping observations it provides the lineaments of how we know what we know. History is the substance or groundwork to which sociology must ultimately reply. As the surviving records of man, it returns us to that which underlies our subject. Concepts of cause (reason, or purpose) reflect attempts to speak to the why of social phenomena. They represent the infusion of form and order within the substance of language and history. Concepts of value bring the language of history and cause or the cause in language and history to the platform of the person, role, group, class, or society from whom and for whom the order of language, history, and cause is justified.

QUESTIONS ABOUT LANGUAGE

Sources of language

From what sources are forms of language derived: the structure of the world, the immutable features of the human mind, or the contrivances of culture? Can sociological theory depict the relation between language and the rest of the world? Does sociological language depend upon pictures (copies) or images of pictures of the world? Are social events, whether pictured or not, logically and empirically independent of one another? (A plurality of independent items or elements?) Are social events known through causal inference from sense-data or through hypothetical restatements (reductions, reconstructions) of such data, in which the question of illusion is central? Are social events more like the constructions of social theorists, or are they "more like the passage in a law court from the presentation of evidence to the pronouncing of a verdict?" Can sociological language only draw attention to but not say anything about the world?

Conduct of words

Can talk about how words are used be separated from the unwitting use of words? Can decisions be made on how words may be used to describe things before committing oneself to some standard of comparison? If thinking is a taking care of and keeping account of the conduct of words, is a notation needed to study and control their resourcefulness? Does thinking depend upon polar words (e.g., before and after, high and low) with doubtful middle zones where evaluations lapse into obscurity and nothingness? Does thinking depend upon some compromise between what is routinely settled and what is to remain unsettled? Is the probability of compromise greater or less as thinking moves from the less abstract and hypothetical to the more entire and actual?

Comparison of words

Upon what bases can two words be said to have something in common? Can one compare words which share the same situations? Can one speak of a network of transactions pertaining to partially similar words in partially similar situations—with words and situations partially co-varying? To what extent are the discriminations and connections (dividings and combinings) which arise in the development of meaning a result of reflection or of deliberate analytic scrutiny? Under what headings should the sociologist arrange the similarities and differences which occupy his attention? Does the comparison of words always call for an examination of the respects in which they:

1. indicate the same things
2. talk about or characterize these things in the same way
3. accent, or actualize the same characteristics (refer to the same structural or metaphoric detail)
4. rest upon the same decisional or valuational grounds
5. produce changes or happenings of the same type and in the same direction
6. presume or suppose the same conditions and consequences?

What are the feed forwards and feedbacks among the parts of comparative analysis? Wherein, whereby, whereof, and wherefore do they serve?

Misunderstanding of words

Is it true that "words could not do their work unless they could rightly mean many more things than any one man in any one view can see them as meaning"? (Richards.) Is it possible then to make a "systematic study of the inherent and necessary opportunities for misunderstanding which language offers?" Must there be a common concern for the diplomacy of the divided mind, for conflicts between opposing tendencies and for the resolutions that generate intelligibility and consensus? Are the most resourceful and indispensable words in any language those that give structure to thought, words like being, whole, part, same, different, some, all, etc. Must one reject certain words because they suggest others, which though not used, do mislead on meanings?

Conditions of meaning

What are the conditions under which words and sentences have meaning or make sense? What weights can be given to correlation with experience, reduction to elementary terms, translation into necessary truths, analyses of contradictions, criteria of conventionality, commitments to analytical or empirical discoveries, etc.? What are the implicit rules of scientific language, those governing the use of such words as true, false, right, wrong, acceptable, uncertain, mistaken, and so on, within that language? How may the sociologist judge the truth of statements of the following kind: "What the sociologist sees when he looks at society is part of his own socialization"? (Cf. Russell's statement: "What a physiologist sees when he looks at a brain is part of his own brain.")

Definitions

Is the search for definitions to encompass word usages misguided because many words cannot be related to one another? Can most words be formed into families, each of which is united "by a complicated network of similarities overlapping and crisscrossing; sometimes overall similarities, sometimes similarities of detail"? (Wittgenstein.) If words have meaning only in contexts, must their contexts be examined in order to trace their family resemblances? Must one study the meaning of a word in many classes of contexts, each of which is taken as a standard? For any given word, are there many formulae, no one of which is better fitted than any other to stand for *all* its possible shades of meaning? Are there some respects in which the meaning of a word cannot be put into words? What meanings, then, must sociologists take into account when engaged in research?

Word mappings

Does sociological theory need several kinds of word mappings taking into account the complexities of speaker, subject matter, time, place, audience, and circumstance of utterance? Which of our most problematic words can be fruitfully reconstructed and which must be left as problematic? Which technicalities are avoidable and which are not? What distinctions are worth drawing and what connections are worth making? Do problems always arise when one states who says what apart from whens, whys, and wherefores?

Theoretical concepts

Do questions about theoretical concepts imply some form of dualism, and if so, what are their strengths and limitations? Should one separate languages into descriptive (or signalizing) functions and expressive (or argumentative) functions? Should one make distinctions between the meaning of statements and the method of their verification, between dispositions and occurrences, between "knowing-how" and "knowing that," between cognition and affect, between understanding man and explaining his behavior? Can a case be made for sociologies being under or overdeveloped in respect to "observationalism," "scientism," "positivism," "phenomenalism," "existentialism," "objectivism," "unobservables," "hypothetical constructs," "theoretical contexts," or other forms of higher-order symbolism?

Philosophical distinctions

What are the grounds for maintaining or obliterating certain standard philosophical distinctions when engaged in the process of forming sociological theories: mind-body dualisms, conditionals (counterfactuals) and categoricals, induction and deduction, probability and certainty, analytic and synthetic, logical and factual, intension (sense, synonymity) and extension (reference, class of things)? Can two terms be different in sense yet identical in reference?

Sociology of symbols

To what extent can the key terms of sociological relations (status, class, reference groups, etc.) be applied to relations between symbols? Do sentences have types of unity similar to groups? Is it intelligible to say that symbols interact, conflict, cooperate and assimilate syntactically and semantically? Is what is said through metaphor the same as what is acted out in ritual and ceremony? Is what is said without metaphor (naked seeing) the same as what is acted out in technology? Are some metaphors like some rituals, ornamental rather than functional?

Ordinary language

Does ordinary language describe precisely enough the events and relations its users intend to describe? Can a more precise language say everything that can be said in ordinary language and more? Can a phrase of ordinary language be ascriptively correct in a given situation (others will receive empirically true information) without being syntactically correct? Can it contradict rules of sentence formation and yet be meaningful? Can syntactical rules be applied to nonlogical situations? Should the concepts of sociology be explicated by ordinary language? Does the use of ordinary language confuse professional language by introducing or embodying considerations that spring from everyday thought? Are deliberately constructed (artificial) languages freer of metaphysical commitments, idiomatic constructions, grammatical vaguenesses (or ambiguities) and non-empirical imputations?

Normative language

Are there identifying properties of "goodness," characteristics that identify the necessary and sufficient conditions of goodness? Are there constitutive properties of "goodness," characteristics that define the ingredients of goodness? What are the primary properties of goodness— the greatest possible balance of hedonic effects (pleasures over pains), coordination and fulfillment of expectations, need reduction and need augmentation, realization of self-directed performance, the greatest happiness of the whole, the maximization of human values, the exclusion of arbitrary inequalities in respect to welfare, justice, liberty—or others?

Procedural language

Can sociology achieve sharper meanings by placing old words in novel juxtapositions or by using certain neologisms? Are there conferring properties such as prudential maxims, rules of social policy, technological recipes, and methodological formulae which may be called "good-making" or "ought-making" properties? Can it be said that if any word has certain conferring properties defining the conditions of its employment, it is good? Are such properties empirical generalizations based on calculation from practical experience?

Logic and fact

Even though logic does not entail the existence of that to which it refers, does it presuppose reference to the existence of true and false attributes? If so, should logical usage (expressing correspondence with facts) be separated from logical meaning (expressing correspondence with propositions)? Does the statement, "All A's are B's" presuppose the existence of things? Does the statement, "If anything is A it is B" presuppose nothing about the existence of things? Is the assertion that "A is true" anything more than the economical reiteration of other words and sentences that its speaker presupposes and endorses. For instance, does "A is a culture" endorse the use of (applicability of) the word "culture" in a family of sentences?

General statements

Can general statements be completely verified by reduction to immediately observed objects, or must they be verified by reduction to terms having incomplete specifications of meaning? Are some general statements neither analytic nor empirical and yet necessary (truths)? (For example, "No man can be both cultured and unlearned in every respect.") Are there any statements that are wholly convincing, that are incorrigible and thus immune from revision? Can a statement be tested "by itself," apart from its position in the whole of science, or indeed, the whole of experience including the entire body of human discourse? Must abstract frameworks correspond with or include some kinds of existing things to be useful?

Conditionals

On the assumption that general conditionals (if anything is A it is B) are merely empirical, how can they be used to account for unobserved connections? If they are not empirical then are their counter-factual (or subjunctive) antecedents false and on this account all true (since true consequences follow from both true and false antecedents)? But if one dispenses with conditionals how is one to distinguish natural laws from coincidental general statements? How is one to account for ordinary reasoning of the type, "If such and such a thing were done this would happen." To what extent are general conditionals implicit (if not explicit) in promises, threats, injunctions, wagers, requests, counsels, games, etiquette, scientific regularities, morals, technology, and grammatical styles (cf. Ryle). Aren't these categories patterns or products of social interaction and thus relevant to sociology?

Probability

Under what conditions can probability be interpreted as a logical relation between evidence and hypotheses? Under what conditions can probability be interpreted as the frequency with which one class of things is generally another class of things? How can both be consistently distinguished from the philosophical problem of justification and the psychological problem of discovery? Is the meaning of probability statements confused with the grounds on which they are made? When should sociological statements be verified by direct descriptions of private experience and when by intersubjective descriptions of publicly observable things? Should complete verifiability be expected or is some degree of testability (confirmation) sufficient?

Rules of induction

Are rules of induction based on logical or empirical justifications? Do they implicitly define the concept of confirmation in the way rules of deduction implicitly define the concept of logical consequence? Or are they governed by their truth frequency, by the proportion of cases in which they have led from true evidence to true conclusions? Or do rules of induction simply codify existing inductive practices?

Notations

Can a better understanding of sociological language be achieved without an improved system of notations? Are all notational systems destined to be expressions of the necessities of logic and mathematics, of hypothetical statements rather than of categorical statements, and thus not *about* phenomena? Is it possible to achieve a foolproof language, one that does not admit of being misunderstood?

Certainty

Is the statement that one knows something with certainty an indication of confidence in what one believes, an authorization to one's hearers to hold one responsible for what is said, an invitation to take what one says for granted, a ritual act the performance of which meets some kind of social expectation, or a statement grounded on sufficient reasons including those of immediate experience?

Sociological criteria

Are sociological criteria largely a matter of comparing the meanings of certain words and deciding upon their relevance for the solution of a problem? How many relevant criteria can sociologists conveniently handle in making comparisons? Can the question of criteria be examined without stating the respects in which they are both relevant and irrelevant? Can one class of cultural meanings be compared without reference to a related class of cultural meanings? Can a full understanding of ordinary (or scientific) language be obtained through a sociological analysis which uses sociological prose? (Cf. "Sociologies of science" and "Mass communication.") Can sociological prose be fully understood by using a scientific (or ordinary) language? Can logical theory supply what is lacking in sociological prose? Is a logical account of prose preferable to a prose account of logic? Are such words as scientific, ordinary, sociological, and logical, debunking terms? How can a language about languages be purified of the complexities and confusions that characterize all languages?

Sociological problems

Is sociological language like a game with tailor-made rules for each sociological problem? Does each sociological problem, no matter how general, vary in the kinds of data held to be relevant for its "solution"? Is there any stable property that can be defined as the descriptive element in every sociological problem? Should distinction be made between the meaning of a sociological term and its criteria of application, between what it chooses to say and how it is used to indicate the presence of something? Are criteria of application always commendatory or prescriptive with reference to their defining or instrumental properties and their kinds of preferred objects? Do such criteria sometimes serve as signals to release action in accordance with choice?

Criticism and inquiry

Is there a fundamental difference (ethical, methodological, etc.), between the objective of maintaining convergent purposes (by persuasion or compromise rather than coercion), the objective of maintaining divergent purposes, and the objective of maintaining both convergent and divergent purposes? May an inquiry be of value, even though its goal be obscure, because of things encountered on the way? May an inquiry, valueless in itself, be of value for suggesting other problems that may be approached with more probable outcomes? Can one understand (know) the meaning of a result without being able to give a correct analysis of it?

Dialectic and inquiry

Is dialectic "a process of criticisms wherein lies the path to the principles of all inquiries"? (Richards.) What are the alternative devices of language? Are there more venturesome forms of analysis, more fruitful forms of verbal conduct than are now used? Must one ask of every inquiry what kinds of replies it asks him to look for, what kinds of evidence or claims it directs him toward? Is it more useful to look for what is common in all concepts than to attend to shifting differences among families of concepts which possess subtle variations and inter-connections of meaning? Is the latter analysis far removed from either the construction of a calculus or the determination of empirical fact? Are strictly logical deductions (implications) not open to questions of attitude, belief, or other forms of social and psychological contingency? Must every analysis contain a hidden grammar? If certainty is never pos-sible, can the word "perhaps" be applied as an indefinite term to every written claim?

Reconstruction of sociological theory

Is sociological theory a study of how social events are related (or how social actions occur) or is it the result of common expectations (rules?) governing languáge usage in the profession? Is it that professionals, fascinated with their forms of expression, receive therapeutic release from communicating shared words and neologisms to one another? Do such communications relax tensions in the same way that language games do? Should a rational reconstruction of social action include a rational reconstruction of the action of sociologists? Do they together constitute a rational reconstruction of sociological knowledge? Is the distinction between social action and sociological action similar to the distinction between the logic of the discovered and the logic of discovery? (Cf. Reichenbach.)

QUESTIONS ABOUT HISTORY

Understanding history

Can present generations of social historians understand past genera-tions of people whose experiences were unlike their own? In most cases, how valid is the testimony of eyewitnesses and of second or third person accounts? Is something akin to imaginative reconstruction required to interpret the records and documents of the past? If so, are there cannons of scientific imagination definite enough to be transmissible to others? What is history good for: to pay tribute to honor, faith, and courage; to vindicate the principles of democracy, liberty, and order; to show the triumph of right over wrong; to express the inspiration of statesmen and poets and the allusions of theologians and pedagogues; to provide a source of livelihood for many? What are the consequences of scholarly contemplation over the possibility that "government might logically be anarchial, that law might be lawless, that history might be reduced to an obituary notice." (Cf. Commager.)

Unity and diversity in history

Is the basic historical question, "How has this come out of that," or "How has this postwar state of affairs come out of that prewar state," or "How has the transit come to be made from an antebellum dispensation to a postbellum one that is strikingly unlike its predecessor"? (Cf. Toynbee.) Does reality pass through different orders of being without losing its continuity or identity? (Smuts.) Does history, like Faust, enable one to understand the good of evil? Can history by unified through a single but many-faceted principle, such as "Thought makes the whole dignity of man; therefore endeavor to think well—that is the only morality" (Pascal.) Is it futile to search for a historical formula that will satisfy the need to "fix a necessary sequence of human movements"? (Cf. Adams.) Is there a drift from unity to multiplicity in history? Is there a drift from asymmetry to symmetry or the reverse? Is society exhausted, the universe chaotic, and man a fallen being? What is traditional and permanent in history: What is experimental and ephemeral? Are moral integrity, kindness, loyalty, charity, honesty, largely literary values or are they also historical values? If the word *scientia* means no more than knowledge can history be regarded as science?

Historical categories

Is historical relevance determined by the appropriateness of certain categories of analysis or interpretations, such as biographical, geographical, chronological, and functional (person, place, time, and organic unity)? To what extent do key words or phrases descriptive of a single exclusive characteristic lead to historical distortions or misrepresentations (e.g., Age of Faith, Baroque Period, Englightenment, Industrial Revolution, Century of Progress)? What form of historical arrangement should be emphasized for various scientific purposes—the highlighting of personalities, group associations, institutional changes, temporal periods, or cultural localities?

Causation in history

Do major historical changes sometimes hinge on incidental events; results which are grossly disproportionate to their causes? (Consider the introduction of grass seeds and clovers, the absence of which lead to soil exhaustion and the decay of empires [Simkhovitch]; the conquest of the Aztec empire with gunpowder and a handful of men.) Is it that nature loves the imponderable and incalculable rather than the simple and that it is man alone that loves the simple? Does history more often provide clues to the possible rather than the probable, the ability to anticipate rather than to predict, the capacity to take precautions rather than to take control? (Gottschalk.) If the problem of historial causation is unsolved is there any other course, short of nihilism, but to express our notions of historical causation in subjective terms?

Reason in history

Is "reason" identifiable in terms of grammar, meaning, coherence, normality, or morality as opposed to vagrant impulses, restless instincts, haphazard desires, and conditional reflexes? Are decadent civilizations those which express primitive emotions and appetites (drinking, loving, and fighting) or those which reject conventions and conformities and the futility, degradation, and annihilation of man? What is the place of obscurity and erudition, intricacy and simplicity, nihilism, and poetic vision, humility, and renunciation in historical writing? What kinds of historical contexts favor irrationalism, evolutionism, pragmatism, determinism, romanticism, intuitionism, and humanitarianism? Are these all species of antirationalism?

Time and design in history

Is history the only source of our identity since in the eternal present, apart from the momentary present, the past is all we know? Is not the present forever slipping into the past? Is true history always contemporary history—history that has a vital meaning for those alive today? (Cf. Croce, Zimmern, Toynbee.) Does a changing society need a changing conception of history in which the past is continuously reinterpreted to fit the shape of the present, just as a stable society looks for stability in ancestral wisdom? Is there any evidence for or usefulness in the idea of decline from a golden age or pristine stage of existence? (Cf. Spengler, Sorokin, and Toynbee.) Is this basic theme built on the analogy of birth, growth, old age, and death or on that of ignorance, selfishness, fear, and hate? Does history have any kind of plot or drama, grand design, or final meaning?

Historical influence

What is the relationship between frequency of literary referrals (including citations) and the historical influence of a person or event? What is the relationship between both and the assessment of the person or event as good or bad (eminence and notoriety)? Is cultural similarity between successive ideas or events an adequate criterion of historical influence, even when literary referral is given for rhetorical effect? What is the meaning of "scholarly indebtedness" to one's predecessors or contemporaries? To what extent are reactions against antecedent persons or developments a major cause of historical influence (for example, Ana-baptists, English Chartists, American Abolitionists, Russian Anarchists, etc.)?

History and impersonal forces

Is history "little more than the register of the crimes, follies and mis-fortunes of mankind" (Gibbon) or is it "advancing rapidly to destinies beyond the reach of mortal eye" (Jefferson), to the tune of impersonal forces (Brooks Adams)? Have the historians of the last century concerned themselves largely with forces rather than with persons, with science rather than with ethics, with analysis rather than with narrative? If the law of history is the law of the concentration of force, should a country adapt its policies to that law by seizing power? (Cf. Brooks Adams.)

History and sentiment

Have most writers of the last two or three decades shifted their attention from the economic to the social, from indignation and re-bellion to derision and estrangement, from public outrage to private repudiation, from satire of the rich to satire of the middle classes? Are recent writers lacking in sympathy and respect for the dignity of man? Is historical (journalistic) criticism futile because public notoriety is honored? Is criticism interpreted as good sport or humor, erotic titilla-tion or escape from life? Is it a kind of verbal passion (or surface descrip-tion) and thus devoid of personal immediacy?

Tragic view of history

Is the highest achievement of man a "program for discontent"? (Whitehead.) Are the most creative elements in human history con-spicuous for their instability? Are the stablest elements the most primitive and formless (e.g., Periclean Athens, Renaissance Italy, Elizabethan England)? Is it the forms of evil rather than its presence or absence that history may accept as expository goals for itself and remedial goals for society? How enlightening is it to say that the root of evil in human history is pride (Toynbee), the universal nemesis, idolatry? Do cultural heroes and the achievements of their civilization spring from pride even though pride "goeth before a fall"? Are faith and self-respect dependent upon pride? Must all learning come through suffering? If so, is not ob-jectivity bought at the price of an emotional experience?

Historical change

What is the role of the following in assessing both the immediate and underlying causes of historical changes: (a) the search for recognition, fame, and glory (Greece and Barbarians), (b) the will and prowess of great leaders (Hebrews to Carlyle and since), (c) the interplay between providence or fate and the drives and impulses of men (Hebrews, Greeks, and Romans), (d) the conflict of emotional and dramatic imagery— the literary face of history (Greek), (e) the theological intervention of God in human affairs; the course of man's career according to a divine plan (Christian), (f) the balance between competition and its control (Hobbs), (g) the tendency toward reason and the preservation of freedom, rights, and privileges (Locke), (h) the perfectibility of man in the face of obscurantism (Voltaire and other French philosophers), (i) the conflict between likes and dislikes, pains and pleasures (materialism of La Mettrie and Helvetius), the opposition between selfishness and altruism, vice and virtue (romanticism of Rousseau), (j) the idea of progress (Hegel, Saint-Simon, Comte), (k) the struggle for existence and the survival of the fittest (Darwin, Spencer, Marx) or the condition of economic scarcity (Malthus), (l) the expressions of national character (Herder, Michelet, Macaulay, Treitschke), (m) the scientific descriptions of particular historical sequences (Ranke and others), (n) the pluralistic or manifold development of civilization (J. H. Robinson and the New School), (o) a monistic principle of growth and decay with reason the seed of destruction (Spengler, Toynbee, Bergson, Gasset, Croce)?

History and objectivity

Must we say that "history is neither written nor made without love or hate"? (Mommsen.) Are great historians distinguishable by their imaginative reach and grasp and not necessarily by the soundness of their conclusions (cf. Herodotus, Gibbon, Toynbee), or does the very poetry of history consist in its literal truth? (Cf. Trevelyan.) Should history be more concerned with the commonplace, every day events such as economic and family affairs or should it give greater attention to political or military events? Can there be pure history—history recorded from nobody's point of view, for nobody's sake? Is not the most objective history necessarily governed by special interests and beliefs? Are Jefferson's words, "I have sworn upon the Altar of God eternal hostility against every form of tyranny over the mind of man" a strike for or against historical objectivity?

Subjectivity in history and historians

Is historical man motivated by self-interest, the belief in predestination or inner grace, good works' competition, altruism, the desire for perfection, unconscious dispositions, myths, and legends, the external factors of race, culture, and milieu or dominant characteristics and ideals (e.g., the "inconsistency" of Rousseau, the "truthfulness" of Washington, the "atheism" of Paine, the "democratic" fervor of Lafayette)? Must all social historians find what they are looking for (e.g., "Dictatorship always follows revolution"; "Wars are more likely to occur between evenly balanced alliances"; "Protestantism" contributed heavily to the growth of Capitalism"? (Sombart, Weber, Tawney.)) To what degree are historians dependent upon psychological analogies between their own experiences and the actions of those they are interpreting? To what extent do new experiences of present events (e.g., war) permit of new analogies for understanding earlier events? Is the principle method of history that of temporal analogy: the deduction of similar consequences from similar antecedents ("the lessons of history")?

Credibility of history

If the most credible type of historical document is an instruction or a command, what are the implications of this fact for an adequate description of social events? What are the most prevalent distortions to be found in letters, diaries, biographies, public reports, and "official histories"? Are social laws and regulations "the expression of the hopes, fears, commands, threats, or expectations of some individual or group of individuals"? (Cf. Gottschalk.) Should we apply Veblen's dictum: "The first requisite for constructive work in modern science, and indeed for any work of inquiry that shall bring enduring results, is a skeptical frame of mind."

History and language

Has language been used by the aristocracy to cultivate primarily decorative, honorific, esoteric, or sacred knowledge, and by the anonymous masses to defeat injustice, famine, deprivation, and suffering? Could orthodoxy be standardized, prejudices spread, and oppressive political power and privilege consolidated without the embalming of written forms in codes of law and social ritual? Is not language, the major means of human communication, intellectual growth, and cultural achievement, also the primary barrier to free inquiry? If free inquiry is essential to a rational and responsible morality and dialectical interchange essential to free inquiry, is the latter not thereby fully justified?

History and democracy

What processes brought about the change from a transcendental idea of good and true in history and religion to its identification with democracy (the social welfare of the common people)? Is American democracy linked to the acquisition of property as a "vocational calling" in which individualism and conscience are invested as natural rights? Has America turned away from the practical concern for democratic (mass) values to a new kind of transcendentalism, the concern for the socially possible? If so, does this change come from the need to consider more fully the autonomy and integrity of free men or from the desire to escape from the immediate struggles of society? (Cf. Hutchins and Niebuhr, Freud, Peirce, James and Dewey.)

History and natural law

Have the premises of a preexisting and fundamental natural law been used to explain the maintenance of slavery and industrial capitalism, of checks and balances, of separation of powers, of states of nature, of social contracts, of inalienable rights, of immutable constitutions and judicial reviews? Were such images based on static premises and deductions? Does government resemble a machine, or is it more like the dynamics of organic life, a living process? Is the mechanical view of government vested in homilies and incantations rather than in diagnosis of underlying processes? What are the fundamental differences between starting with a series of abstract principles and deducing some ideal course of action, and starting with a concrete situation and seeking some pragmatically workable solution? Was the formula of natural law extending from Greek and Roman philosophy through medieval Christianity and the English and American revolutions a formula expressive of the certainty of Euclid and the permanence of God, a manifestation of man's great need for security and repose? Did it provide order in a world of disorder, a conservatism that most reform movements have had to attack before they could be effective? (Cf. Commager.)

History and sociological language

Can sociologists account for the changes in American thought from single-factor to multiple-factor determinism, from an idealistic and religious viewpoint to an empirical and secular viewpoint, from focusing on ultimate goals to focusing on means, from absolutism to pragmatism, from a reformist to a conservative mood toward life? To what extent can Thoreau's doctrine of "civil disobedience," Brooks Adams' theme of "centralization and decay," and James' view of a "pluralistic universe" be rediscovered in the new language of sociology?

Sociology of literature

Is a main function of the sociology of literature to bridge the gap between the value words of literature (through *their* implicit empirical referents) and the descriptive words of sociology (through *their* implicit value referents)? How can the literary caricature be a model and replication of life if it does not join with sociological observation—unless the sociologist is in error? Were the novelists of the twenties and thirties as alienated from their society as Edmund Wilson, Lewis Mumford, Bernard De Voto, and Alfred Kazin contend? Were they more sensitive than others to ugliness and the amenities of life? Were they by social inheritance idealists and thus protestants? Were they engulfed by the transformation of a rural into an urban economy? Were they consciously seeking to strike a blow for the freedom of man? What is the meaning of "the tragedy of man's inhumanity to man"?

QUESTIONS ABOUT CAUSE

Meaning of causality

Is causality a category describing the character of the causal bond in respect to (a) a general connection between events, or (b) a particular connection between events? Is causality as a general connection equivalent to the statement "The same cause always produces the same effect"? Is causality as a particular connection equivalent to the statement, "Under conditions $c_1 \ldots c_n$, X invariably causes Y"? Is causality a doctrine asserting the universal validity of the causal principle, "Everything (every event, occurrence, happening) has a cause"? Is causality an epistemological category referring to the description of experience (to reasoned knowledge of things) or is it a trait of the things themselves? Is it verified in experience but not derivable from it? Is causality a necessity of thought (the product of a synthetic faculty of the imagination) or an *a priori* regulative principle or presupposition? Does causality function as a maxim or vague rule for directing the course of inquiry? Is nature ruled by "laws of cause and laws of chance in a certain mixture" (Born)? Are the laws of causality theoretical probabilities or empirically found statistical correlations? Is the attempt to disentangle simple, linear, cause-effect bonds from universal patterns of (organic) independence an artifact of abstraction? If causality is a mental construct should it be regarded as a produced connection or as an experienced association? If causality is an objective form of interdependence obtaining among real events should it be taken as representing determinate connections within the world? May diverse categories of causality concur in one and the same process?

Causality and constant conjunctions

Does the constant conjunction formula express a relation of correlation rather than of connection? Are all constant conjunctions symmetrical?

Do correlations of qualities in biology, of numbers in mathematics, and of physical properties in mechanics allow for the genesis of one thing by another? Do some forms of causality express timelessness and lack of self-movement as in mathematics and logic? Is absence of causality assumed by Humean empiricists and then proved from this assumption, viz., that since impressions are momentary entities unconnected with past and future events, causality is absent? Do empiricists make the mistake of identifying the truth of causality with the *criterion* of causal truth, the meaning of a proposition with its (reduced) basis of verification? If every criterion of material existence is reduced to sensing, acting, and judging, is one to conclude that the existence of everything is dependent entirely upon these responses?

Causal interpretations and sociology

Which of the following causal (or lawlike) interpretations of, "If C, then E" are most suitable for sociological analysis? (1) Where C and E designate particular properties belonging to any undifferentiated class of concrete objects (events, processes, conditions). (2) Where C and E designate particular properties belonging to differentiated classes of concrete objects. (3) Where C and E are quantified propositions with definite truth values; sentences capable of verification and holding always, or some of the time. Thus we have, "If C, then E always" or "If C then E sometimes." (For all [most] C and E, if C is the case, then E is the case.) But doesn't this formulation emphasize sameness of C and E rather than the constancy of their relation? (4) Where when C happens E occurs regularly (ensues invariably) as contrasted with E's occurring under varying conditions (i.e., not unconditionally). (5) Where C is existentially prior to E but need not precede it in time (or E is asymmetrically dependent upon C). (6) Where the connection between C and E is conditional and asymmetrical as well as constant, unique and necessary (When necessity is not identified with unconditional occurrence, but with lack of exceptions, the linkage of constancy with uniqueness). (7) Where there is a one-to-one correspondence between C and E (uniquely or unambiguously) *or* a one-to-many correspondence of C to alternatives of E (statistical or not). (8) Where C and E express not a constant conjunction, external association, or invariable coincidence between antecedent and consequent, but a genetic connection or process of change; "A world of mere *withness*, of which the parts were only strung together by the conjunction 'and'" (James.) (9) Where C and E are never taken to be identical on the grounds that no event ever happens more than once. On the principle of the identity of indiscernables, causes and effects cannot be the same in all respects. Can this principle be modified and expressed as "If similar causes happen under similar conditions, then similar effects are always produced by them"? Moreover, are not variations in individual instances admitted by the proviso that causality applies to events of the same classes or kinds and thus to the relation between them?

Continuity of cause and effect

Is there continuity of action between cause and effect? How can continuity of action be distinguished from spatial contiguity (action through adjacent contact)? Does the hypothesis of contiguity require an infinity of observations between any two events at different points in space? What would "action by contact" mean in sociology: direct conflict or coordination of responses between people; propagation of authoritative commands through continuous media of communication; a field of social power measured directly or inferred from individual response? If the hypothesis of continuity were abandoned, would all field theories (gravitational, electromagnetic, Gestalt, Lewinian, social interactional, etc.) have to be ruled out? Are the principles of causality and contiguity (as nearby action) logically independent? Is contiguity consistent with the reversal of the causal connection (here effects appear before their causes)? Is the time priority of cause over effect essential to causality or may this linkage be instantaneous?

Causal constancy

Does causal constancy include (a) numerical equivalence or proportionality, (b) immutability or invariance, and (c) identity of structure? Does invariance imply that a term or part of a chain of causes (e.g., forces) and effects (e.g., velocities) is indestructible or conserved and thus can never be lost? Does immutability imply that "nature is prodigal in variety but niggard in innovation"? Does identity of structure imply bi-unique correspondence, i.e., coordination of non-arbitrary sets (kinds) of elements? Does identity imply that the same mathematical form can be correlated with an infinity of concrete objects having the same structure? If causality cannot explain novelty (newness) does the failure of causal laws serve as a criterion for disclosing the emergence of newness, or does the latter serve as a criterion for disclosing the failure of causal laws?

Causal chains

Must all causal chains either have or have not a beginning; do they require either a first cause or infinite regress? What kind of opposition, if any, occurs between the idea of a first cause or prime mover and the requirement of sufficient reason? Which of the following maxims has widest application to sociology: "small causes have small effects"; "small causes have great effects"? Does the latter apply primarily to chance phenomena or to unstable social situations where change does not move from one unique state to another? What is the bearing of a perturbation or interruption in a sequence of social changes on the assumption of causal chains?

Isolation of causal chains

Is the causal chain, interpreted as a situation in which every effect is also a cause, an isolated abstraction since every link in the chain is produced by several determiners of which the chief one is singled out? In short, is the causal chain a one-sided singling out of a rich network of interconnections? Is isolation, though fictional, a methodologically necessary hypothesis for tracing out connections? Are interposing influences small enough to cancel one another? Does the possibility of isolating causal connections imply the absence of universal interdependence? If universal interdependence implies universal causal connection, how is isolation possible? Is the isolation of causal chains whether unilinear, multilinear (parallel and non-parallel), divergent, or convergent, a necessary scientific fiction because all things are engaged in a process of limitless complexity? Do the divergent chains of biological evolution and the convergent chains of cultural evolution both lead to the development of emergent levels (or qualities)? Are causal chains useful approximations for limited domains and for short periods of time? Can the logical figure known as sorites be taken as a model of a causal chain? Does not such a chain require an explanatory hypothesis?

Mechanical causality

Does the mechanical concept of matter define the latter as purely passive with motion elicited by agents external to material things (as summarized in the concept of force)? Is the principle of the mechanical self-movement of matter—the principle of inertia enunciated by Galileo, Descartes, and Newton—openly non-causal? (Cf. Bunge.) (For example, the motion of a billiard ball is not only the resultant of the initial blow but also of the previous state of the ball which existed in the absence of causes.) If, on the other hand, inertia is a cause of motion, then are not all qualities causes? By analogy, are many alleged sociological causes no more than conditions of cultural inertia? Is the principle of the equality of action and reaction in Newtonian mechanics noncausal in that it rejects unidirectional actions beyond a first approximation? Are there any passive material systems in sociology (cf. cultural products) which do not react on the social actor?

Mechanical and dialectical theory

Is the concept of inner stress within the mechanical theory of continuous media (fluids and elastic solids) noncausal in focusing on the combined action of external and inner (intermolecular) forces? Is the mechanical principle in accord with the principle of dialectic which asserts that stresses on material objects may develop to the point of producing qualitative changes in such objects? In short, can it be said that since the mechanical principle asserts not only the force concept but the importance of self-movement and inner stress, it contains some of the ingredients of the dialectical theory of social change?

Mathematical causality

If mathematical equations are devoid of empirical content, can they be taken as the mirror image of causality or other forms of determination? Are the multiplicity of social means and ends the opposite of the uniqueness of process asserted by causality and assumed in certain mathematical solutions? Is the causal problem a semantic and not a syntactical one, dealing with the interpretation rather than the representation of theories?

External and internal causes

Does every cause indicate the presence of an efficient agent acting extrinsically upon the subject? Can the efficient agent be separated from the internal cause (or inward principle) of things? Do most effects arise from a combination of external action and internal conditions? (For instance, in socialization, does something new occur in the child activated to respond to his parent? May different social stimuli produce the same effect, depending on the response organs, feeling states, or predispositions, perceptual, affectional, etc. of the child?) Are certain reactions triggered but not produced by external stimuli? Is spontaneity (self-movement) justified on the evidence that every bit of matter is buzzing with activity? Is spontaneity limited by the intrinsic character of other objects? Does freedom consist of the lawful self-determination of actors? Is the thesis of external causation abused when authors trace a line of thought from one writer to another without allowing for the influence of social and environmental determinants all along the line, any one of which could be taken as the partial or total (but fictitious) originator? Are concepts of extension and duration relational properties which have nothing to do with causality attributed to external action?

External causes and self-sustaining processes

In what types of social phenomena does the continuance of process depend upon the persistence or maintenance of the cause? (Does "The effect cease after the cause has ceased"?) Are there sociological instances of self-sustaining processes analogous to the way in which free association is caused by a sequence of words, each of which is viewed as the cause of the next? Do some intrinsic causes unchain an internal process that is thereafter not only self-sustaining but amplified to effects enormously larger than the triggering cause (consider nuclear chain reactions and nerve pulses which are more than conductors of sensations, images, and ideas). Does the notion of self-sustaining processes allow for voluntarism and the noninevitability of future events? In general, are external causes effective solely to the extent to which they trigger, enhance, or dampen inner processes? Is complete self-determinism (total freedom) as insufficient as external determinism when both are conceived as unchainers of inner processes or as agents molding passive materials)?

Social process

Is social process reducible to invariable (uniform) succession of states in time? Is succession shown in experience (or observation), or can active production and reproduction be acknowledged? Would precedence enable the sociologist to distinguish relevant antecedents from all others? Is it useful to add to the notion of succession that of the uniqueness of states in a closed system? Can the notion of uniqueness of continuity (necessary and sufficient causes) include all cultural determiners (social constraints and symbolic directives)? Are states of social objects systems of qualities which cannot act as agents of causal efficacy? If the latter is true, perhaps causality is not reducible to invariable, unique, and continuous succession of states? Is it then reducible to social prediction?

Social substance and attribute

Is the relation between social substance (or substratum) and social attribute (or predicate) so accidental that it allows for the circulation rather than the authentic appearance (or emergence) of novelty? Are substance and attribute contingently related and thus neither necessarily associated nor deducible from one another? What are the implications for sociology of the empiricist view that things are unorganized aggregates of sense data lacking an inner, necessary, or genetic connection; the view that "Everything we see could also be otherwise"; the view that experiences and methodological rules might have been different? Can one speak intelligently of "occasional causes"?

Social causality, summation, and equilibrium

Does social causality refer to the summative character of causes and effects? In other words, do social causes act independently of one another but additively to produce summative effects? Is social analyis the decomposition of a complex determinant into a sum of causes or the separation of a given result into individual components? Does the hypothesis of causal summation follow logically from the isolation of causal lines, the neglect of reciprocal action, and the fact that the nonadditive action of joint causes may produce noncausal entities? Does nonlinearity entail nonadditive connection and thus noncausality? Is randomness an illustration of the nonadditivity of causal factors? Does social equilibrium result from the canceling out of nonadditive forces in which no opposing trend prevails overwhelmingly? Are status, norms, and other group properties more stable the larger the number of elements which cancel out individual deviations? Can totalities or wholes arise without the systematic integration of individual elements, without a constant relation between any two elements within them? Is it true that no unidirectional cause-effect bond can be inferred from the mutual repulsion of two interacting groups? Is it true that social causality cannot be regarded as a particular case of interaction because the latter lacks the essential component of irreversible productivity? Can the interaction of individual entities produce supraindividual entities having qualities of their own that behave as self-contained units? Would this mean that the independence of causal factors entails the independence of their effects?

Social stability and instability

Does the principle "small causes, small effects" define or describe stability in social systems (where, after small departures from equilibrium, there is a return to stability)? Does the principle, "small causes, large effects" define or describe departures from stability or transitions from one unstable state to another (where the cause only triggers a process it does not entirely control)? Is instability a source of causal discontinuity in social phenomena? Can a cause be small enough to have no effect? Can qualitative jumps occur at critical points in the process of social change? Is a principle of discontinuity inherent in all classifications since they are based on qualitative differences? Is discontinuity dependent upon (the continuity of) contexts and levels? Is the difference between social consensus and social conflict (or stress) merely the difference between focusing on the whole phenomena and focusing on a part of it? Is the basic aspect of social conflict that of action-reaction (as seems to be true of particle mechanics)? Is a system of self-correcting devices (feedback) an illustration of social consensus? Are conservative ideologies instances of positive feedback since they reinforce the conditions that elicited them? Are revolutionary ideologies instances of negative feedback? If the direction and intensity of change in one system is entirely defined by that of another is the latter the cause of the former?

Causality and novelty

If causal agents act on passive things that are incapable of self-activity—of adding something of their own to the causal bond—does it follow that effects must preexist in their causes? Would causality prevent genuine novelty? Can causality give rise to objects new in number and quantity but not in kind? Can the effect include less than, more than, or sometimes less and sometimes more than the cause? Are all forms of newness repetitions of what was given from the beginning, merely unfoldings of preexisting capacities? If one assumes that the effect contains nothing which was not contained in the cause, then is change ultimately reduced to permanence and variety to identity? Is the definition of new properties relative to the context of analysis? Must some new properties occur for the first time in the universe and if so how do we identify them? Can new properties emerge without entailing the emergence of new laws? Can new laws be added to old laws? Can new laws emerge from old laws? If old laws change does this mean that the same cause may no longer produce the same effect (the connection is altered)? Does causality apply to the laws of phenomena (regarded as absolute) rather than to the phenomena themselves (regarded as events which are relative to space-time contexts)? Could the constants of nature change while the laws of nature remain unchanged? If the latter happened would the regularity between cause and effect be unbounded by time?

Determinism

Does determination refer to the presence of definite properties (characterized unambiguously, precisely, and clearly)? Or does determinism refer to constant and unique connections among things or events including their states or qualities such that they are fully predictable (that is, not open to new and unexpected outcomes)? Does determinism refer to the definite ways (actions or processes) whereby an object acquires a property? Can events develop out of preexisting conditions and happen in one or more definite ways without being unique or well defined? In other words, can things have definite characteristics but acquire them in a lawless, unpredictable way (consider, for instance, the acquisition of qualitative characteristics through continuous evolution)?

Determinism and lawfulness

Is determinism synonymous with lawfulness or may the former obtain without the latter? Can any one type of determinism be assigned a territory (area or sector of reality) where it operates to the complete exclusion of other types of connection? What are the essential characteristics of a principle of lawfulness or orderliness? Can one say that "every single event is determined in accordance with a set of objective laws"— whether he knows these laws or not? Are facts determined by laws or are laws merely the forms or patterns by which facts are characterized? Is a statement of universal lawfulness consistent with individual exceptions among occurrences subsumed under the law? Are exceptions nothing but the least frequent alternatives? Are infrequent alternatives due to statistical variations or the intersection of separate laws or both? Is individual irregularity consistent with social regularity?

Determinism and chance

Are the "laws of chance" instances of one form of determinism? Is the appearance of "heads" in coin throwing the determinate result of a determinate operation and thus dependent upon certain kinds of pre-existing conditions (coins of certain sizes and dimensions in a gravitational field of certain properties)? Would a completely random result of throwing coins include arms, legs, and feet or any other thing, actual or imagined? If statistical laws are not statistically determined, what are they? Can an identifiable behavioral complex be followed by a large to infinite number of different responses and still be determined in the same way that individual behavior is conditioned along one of numerous possible paths by culture, family interaction, and unique experience? In judging questions of determinacy-indeterminacy are objects of observation dependent upon an observer who is free to "conjure up" (with or without measuring devices) the bonds that connect the successive states of a social system?

Determinism and social science

Which of the following categories of determinism are applicable to social science? (a) quantitative self-determinism: continuous determination of the consequent by the antecedent in the spontaneous unfolding of states that are precisely calculable, (b) interactional determination: reciprocal causation or functional interdependence, (c) statistical determination: the result of joint action by independent or quais-independent entities, (d) structural (or wholistic) determination: composition of whole by parts and parts by whole, (e) teleological determination: direction of means by ends or goals which need not be purposefully planned, (f) dialectical determination: the qualitative self-development of a process by the "inner" strife and eventual synthesis of its essential characteristics, (g) combinations of the above genetically connected with one another in such a way that the higher types are dependent upon the lower but not entirely reducible to them.

Indeterminism and sociology

Which of the following statements are most useful for sociology: (a) Some things or properties may appear out of nothing. (b) Some things or properties cannot appear out of nothing. (c) Out of nothing comes nothing. (d) There are neither absolute beginnings nor absolute endings. (e) Everything (some things) may be the outcome of conditions or processes which do not occur in a lawful way. (f) Events may uniformly follow one another without being produced by one another. (g) Certain events may result from the operation of a transcendental agent, regardless of prevailing conditions? If there are no infallible rules for making scientific discoveries and no scientific procedures for ensuring success, can one be certain that scientific research (creation) is not partially lawless?

QUESTIONS ABOUT VALUE

Value judgments

Are value judgments claim-making assertions of what a speaker feels, believes, or intends to do? Do value judgments differ from "authoritative" verbal exercises such as approving, refusing, forbidding, etc.? Do they involve giving correct answers under difficult conditions (without reliable instruments)? Do they differ from factual statements in being less methodic and foolproof and from guesses or intuitions in being based on a skill or gift which can be developed by practice? Are they, rather than commands, answers to the question, "What shall I do?" Can value judgments be either comparisons or ranking of properties (or properties defined by other properties)? Are value judgments no more arbitrary than the standards of science since they involve reference to future purposes (e.g., desirable conditions)? Can value judgments guide us to truth and falsity (or, be true and false)?

Ethical terms

Are definitions of ethical terms an expression of personal stipulations —linguistic reconstructions of how such terms should be used—or reportive definitions of how people actually use such terms? Is an adequate definition of ethical terms dependent upon professed intentions about actual behavior (choices) in specific situations? Can it be decided whether two expressions of intention are synonymous by noting whether they are always applied without doubt to the same actual or imaginary situations? But then will any two terms ever mean the same thing in all possible contexts?

Value judgments and factual claims

If value judgments can be transformed into verifiable statements do they differ from factual claims in respect to the purposes they serve? Are factual claims always based on descriptive reproductions, word pictures, or narrative substitutes for witnessing? Are not some factual claims comparatively ambiguous and vague? Is the purpose of value judgments to say something about the appropriateness of acting in certain ways when certain things or properties are available and the purpose of factual claims to describe things and correlate their properties? Granting this distinction, is a change in criteria of less consequence for factual claims than for value judgments on the assumption that the latter amounts to giving different advice about the right course of action? Are value judgments like factual claims in that they must be not only verified but also validated? In other words, must it be shown that verified value judgments (e.g., a thing is good to a certain degree when selected criteria are employed) can also be validated (e.g., that selected criteria are the right ones and ought to be employed)?

Valuational and factual statements

Is the valuational meaning of a statement synonymous with the set of facts that could be offered in support of it, were it challenged? If so, are not valuational statements informative of what facts are likely to be offered and which are likely to be challenged? Is not knowledge of what a sociologist advises, favors, or approves, a key to how he uses facts? Cannot the words he chooses to use in describing facts contain both valuational and referential meaning—without which he could not hope to alter perception, thought, or imagination? Can one assess the factual character of a sociological statement without assessing the author's valuational utterances? (except for sociologists who assert they *never* make valuational utterances?)

Distinction between desired and desirable

Can the usual distinction between the desired (as an empirical *is*) and the desirable (as a valuational *ought*) be taken as equivalent to the distinction between the inductive generalization of values and the hypothetical reconstruction of them? Of course, it may be said that inductive generalizations are based on factual observations whereas hypothetical reconstructions are based on factual judgments, but does not this view neglect the role of judgment in factual observations?

Reasons for action

Must each person who has reasons for a given action be aware of his subjective intentions and thus be able to express the grounds on which he chooses to act? When a person cannot give reasons for his action is it still possible for him to apply criteria of right and wrong to his choices? Must the expert's interpretation of another person's reasons for action rest on more than an analogy with his own introspective experience? (Cf. Freud and Weber.) Are not Freudian explanations acceptable to the therapist only when they are acceptable to the agent undergoing therapy? Are Weber's and Parsons' conception of tradition as normative midway between reasons for action and purely reactive habits? Do all reasons for action depend upon the extension of words into the future and thus upon some constancy in usage; in short, upon the application of a rule acceptable in a social context? Can continuity of experience have any relevance without this requirement?

Cognitive and emotive aspects of reason

What is the relation between the cognitive and the emotive side of reason: causal, conflicting, or of unknown mixture? Can people have full knowledge without acting in accordance with reason and act in accordance with reason without full knowledge? Can a person waver over an alternative that is not consciously known to him? Is it true that no factor can be the reason why someone did something unless he was moved to act by it? May a fact be a reason for doing something even though no one is moved to do that thing? What is meant by explanation of an act in contrast to deliberation and justification of an act? Are deliberation and justification kinds of explanations when they move a person to action? Does deliberation differ from justification in that the first attempts to determine the best course open to one and the second to show that one has taken the best course (the difference between what action is right and why an action is right)?

Attitudes, beliefs, and reasons

Are all disagreements in attitude rooted in disagreements in belief? Are disagreements in attitude toward who should be privileged, for instance, rooted in beliefs about class and ethnic superiority? How are modes of reasoning about beliefs elaborated and interwoven to result in effective changes of attitude? Which modes of reasoning are ineffective when allowance is made for background conditions and interpersonal contexts? Do some reasons hold for everyone (all persons) except when contravened by limited rules involving particular persons, facts, or contexts? How are reasons weighed to determine their superiority or priority? Are universal reasons always superior to particular reasons when they apply to the "same" circumstances? Are legal reasons always superior to reasons of self-interest? How useful are *prima facie* reasons, those that presume "other things being equal"? What gives rise to the presumption of a *prima facie* reason?

Non-rational methods for changing attitudes

What are the most effective non-rational methods for changing attitudes toward ethical judgments: persuasion that "depends on the sheer direct emotional impact of words—on emotive meaning, rhetorical cadence, apt metaphor, stentorian, stimulating, or pleading tones of voice, dramatic gestures, care in establishing *rapport* with the hearer or audience, and so on"? (Stevenson.) What are the effects of sleeping metaphors, epigrams, declaratory prose that suggest interpretations rather than describe or picture meanings; of phonetic expressions and appeals to daydreams, supernatural images, and other classes of un-verifiables? What are the effects of such words as "duty," "ought," and "should," and of appeals to prudence, respect, or caution? Do not all agreements exemplify a mixture of persuasion and rationality, there being no immaculate conception of ideas?

Normative statements as prescriptions

Should normative statements be viewed as types of prescriptions and, thus, as possessing qualities common to commands, requests, sermons, and cookbooks? Does "prescribing, in general, tell us to do something in contrast to statements which tell us that a certain thing is the case"? Can one, for every prescription, find a corresponding factual description of what would be the case if the prescription were fulfilled? (Hare writes "The door being closed, please" for the prescription and "The door being closed, yes" for the fact statement.) Does a universal normative prescription state that everyone in all conditions *ought* to do a certain thing by virtue of the meaning or definition of "ought"? Does the speaker wish or prefer that his maxim hold for all logically possible situations (cases) including those in which he himself would be bound if he were in such situations?

True ethical utterances

Can agreements about beliefs be used to cause ethical utterances to appear true rather than to be proven true? Can agreements which support or attack an ethical utterance bring about a situation which later judgments (attitudes) describe as social fact? Is it possible that the same utterances made by different people will always have different descriptive meanings unless their inferences are tabulated and agreed to be the same? Is ethical truth anything more than specification of the reasons one resolves to accept in support of an ethical judgment, anything more than the grounds upon which one is psychologically disposed to induce others to accept a belief? How do decisions about valid induction and deduction in science differ from this process? (Consider Hume's view that decisions regarding valid and invalid methods reflect habits of belief and disbelief.)

Generality of ethical statements

Is generality an essential standard for assessing an ethical statement? Are particular ethical statements valid only when supported by a valid general principle defined as a statement about the abstract properties of every case of a particular kind? Does the conjunction of a valid general principle (containing only variables and properties) with a true statement of fact (containing reference to particular persons and events) logically imply a particular ethical statement? Does the validity of a particular ethical statement require the possibility of specifying a valid general principle? Does justification of the standard of generality depend upon the following principle: "If something has an ethical property ("wrong," "desirable," "good") then anything else exactly like it in all other respects must have the same ethical property"? (Brandt.) Is it true that if two things (acts) do not have the same ethical properties (e.g., one is "good," the other "bad") then it must be that they differ in at least one other abstract property? Is it true that under the same circumstances what is right for one person must be right for every other person? If not, could one assert moral principles with the intention of making an exception of himself? But, then, how does one know that any two things have the same abstract properties if such properties are infinite in number? And if one cannot speak of abstract properties must one refer to particular persons or things with all the prejudices to which such referrals are heir? Are some principles narrower in scope than others and for this reason easier to defend but less universal? Are some principles invalid or implausible and if so which ones? For example, is the principle, "Everyone has a right to become a sociologist" invalid unless qualified by the phrase, "as long as a need exists relative to other professions"? Which general principles are then the most valid?

Principles of consequences

What is the applicability of the following principles of consequences: (1) "If the consequences of *A*'s doing *X* would be undesirable, then *A* ought not do X"; (2) "If the consequences of everyone's doing X would be undesirable then A ought not do X"; (3) "If the consequence of no one's doing X would be undesirable then A ought to do X"? Does it follow from any of these principles that "A ought to (or ought not to) do X"? Is there a dissimilarity of circumstance between the consequences of A's performing an action and the consequences of everyone's (no one's) performing that action? Is the principle, "If the consequences of A's doing X would be desirable, then A ought to do X" logically invalid but morally valid? What follows from interpreting "undesirable" as "wholly undesirable" on the one hand, or as "undesirable in some respect" on the other hand? Is the weighing of consequences necessary in the latter case? What reasons or justifications are required for the conclusion that "A ought to do X"? (Cf. Singer.)

Justification of actions

If a sociologist is to justify his actions must he (1) correctly describe the facts of the situation and (2) show that these facts are good reasons for his actions? If a sociologist is to explain his actions must he show that he (1) deliberated on the facts of his situation, (2) knew the determining facts, and (3) believed that the determining facts were reasons for his action? Can a person be said to have explained his actions if he thought he had reasons even though he was mistaken (factually wrong) in one or another respect? Can one explain a person's actions by reporting his deliberations and their outcome? Can a person's actions be said to be justified even though the above characteristics may not apply? Does justification depend upon facts that *anyone* would take as right reasons for a course of action (or reasons for the best course of action?)

Justification and generalization principle

Must the justification of all actions be derived from some principle of generalization? Is the justification of a moral rule ("lying is wrong") equivalent to explaining why a certain kind of action is generally right or wrong (why lying is wrong)? Is it irrelevant (or false) to answer, "Lying is wrong because most people disapprove of it"? Is the act wrong even though it is widely and strongly approved? Is it wrong because of what would happen if everyone lied? If everyone had a right to lie would contradiction and conflict be unrelenting and life impossible? Would communication be so difficult that eventually no one could speak and human existence would be unreliable? Would the survival of any kind of normative social order be possible without such rules? If it is undesirable for everyone to lie then must it be said that no one has a right to lie without a reason? Is it possible for the rule to have an exception? If so, then is it contradictory to say of any moral rule that it can hold without exception (i.e., without qualifying circumstances)? Does the generalization principle provide criteria for deciding or mediating between particular cicumstances? When particular circumstances are at issue can an action be shown to be right by showing that it would be right for everyone in similar circumstances to so act (or by showing that the consequences would not be undesirable)? In resolving conflicting claims is a generalization principle always appealed to even though not explicitly invoked? Does the fact that a principle is not mentioned mean that it is not used or presupposed?

Assessment of ethical principles

What are the essential standards for identifying an ethical statement or principle? Is consistency such a standard on the premise that its absence precludes a coherent notion of what is right or desirable? Is definiteness impossible in the presence of contradictory standards? Is it necessary to supplement all universal statements by a principle of priority in accordance with which they can be ranked? Are comparative rankings always transitive and if not how can one formulate a clear ethical directive? Without comparative rankings may not general principles have clashing implications for particular cases? Under what circumstances do particular cases disagree with general ones and how can this kind of inconsistency be reduced?

Values and scientific objectives

If the objectives of science are to maximize social adjustment or human welfare how can they be affirmed without a scientific definition of their properties? If the maximizing of human welfare requires the correlation of science with extrascientific conceptions, how can science achieve this correlation without reconstructing the non-scientific environment including the extrascientific conceptions of what ought to be? If the justification of scientific activity is to be found in its objectives then shouldn't (ought not) one engage in scientific activity if and only if there is reasonable probability that it will achieve these objectives? Is not this concern the implicit *ought* in all scientific reasoning? More specifically, if description, explanation, and technical assessment of modes of human adjustment are the objectives of science isn't it the case that one ought to engage in scientific activity only when these objectives are likely to be achieved? And if certain objectives *ought* to be achieved must not the scientist insist that certain means *ought* to be used, namely those that are scientifically adequate, proper, or effective? Is a scientific objective a causal (probability) statement that justifies a valuational statement? Are additional premises required for the transition from causal to valuational statements?

Imperatives in sociology

Must sociology subscribe to a set of imperatives, without which it could not proceed in accordance with method or reason? Is not all method an expression of what something is to become and thus a desire (or, less subjectively, an expression of the desirable)? Can the relation of one desired method to another be found in factual propositions that link them together? How can scientists deliberate and select among imperatives without grounding them in factual reasons? What are the basic methodological imperatives? (e.g., "Be consistent, in valuation and in thought and action." (C. I. Lewis.)) Does one establish an imperative by justification or explanation or the conjunction of both? Is an empirical reason an elliptical explanation or justification of an imperative? (e.g., is the empirical reason that methods X, Y, and Z contribute to ("explain") scientific truth also a justification of why (of the imperative that) sociologists should use these methods)? What are the different imperatives, suppressed or expressed, by the sociologist; their premises, priorities, and relationships to the "facts" of society? On what authority are they valid or sound? Are they like metaphysical claims, axiological ideals, rules of gamesmanship, dominant action tendencies, semantic appraisals, methodological resolutions, or dispositional predicates, extracted from society or human nature? Can imperatives be validly appraised as successful when the manner in which they are executed determines the desired outcomes?

Sociology and ethical premises

If ethical premises are so ubiquitous that ethics must be used in sociological thinking and sociology in ethical thinking, how does one certify such premises? Are the premises of ethics comparable to the premises of science? Is observation and logical reconstruction in science similar to observation and logical reconstruction in ethics? Are value judgments and methods of certification clearly on the side of any one discipline? Are the resources of all disciplines necessary to adjudicate among those principles that should be taken as unquestioned for the duration of any given study (problem)?

Ethical principles and social problems

Must not every citizen who shares a social problem be guided by ethical principles which are not only definitive of that problem but productive of it? If all social problems result from group adherence to ethical principles how can the former occur without the latter? To resolve a social problem, must not some end (desire, value, goal) be taken as unproblematic (given) and used to evaluate it? Is it the case, then, that ethical principles obtain at every state in the resolution of a social problem, that there are no descriptive premises without accompanying ethical premises? Does not every society, scientific or humanistic, have a set of unquestioned ethical premises in terms of which its members evaluate the work of their peers? Are not descriptive means and ends always linked to consequences that contain ethical predicates? In any event, are there any premises or predicates which are exempt from fallibility or doubt?

Values in sociological inquiry

Is it possible to have inquiry without the motivation of curiosity or practical interest? Can the sociologist safely proceed with an inquiry without being prepared to defend it against those who hold opposing attitudes, and in doing so must he not use rational or persuasive methods which require evaluative (normative) judgments? Can one pursue the truth in full detachment from the attitudes and values of those who may support or disrupt that pursuit? Are description and clarification the sole achievements of sociology and if so how do we prevent these achievements from being used as reasons for affecting attitudes that make a difference in ethical judgments?

Ethical judgments and the sociologist

If sociologists have no criteria for distinguishing ethical judgments from nonethical ones, are they bound to mix the two indiscriminately in their written discourse? If sociologists do not search for criteria by which ethical judgments can be identified, how can they conclude that ethical judgments are an expression of culture or majority opinion? Are there, then, at least two versions of scientific objectivity? Do sociologists have any basis for knowing whether they make ethically wrong judgments within the operation of scientific institutions?

Disagreements in sociology

Are disagreements in sociology caused by differences in opinion, attitudes, or beliefs that are in some respects always emotional? How can the same "facts" or properties elicit different viewpoints when they "speak for themselves" or are implied by the same conceptual frameworks? Does not every sociologist find occasion to disagree with his colleagues and can such disagreement ever be expressed without affirming what should or ought to be done? Are not critical assessments offered as invitations to the reader to announce himself in favor of the declared viewpoint? Is not the vocabulary of criticism always comprised of words which attract or repel the reader? Is not the purpose for mentioning facts of observation to influence attitudes and establish ethical convictions? In scientific discussion, is not the interplay between ethical convictions, beliefs, facts, and attitudes such that "reasoning" may incorporate some mixture of each at almost every point? How does one know which facts should be rehearsed as either relevant or persuasive unless one holds normative considerations in mind?

Dilemmas, paradoxes, and questions

Dilemmas and paradoxes stand midway between the declarative sentence which characterizes most of sociological writing and the interrogative sentence which characterizes so little of it. The declarative sentence asserts and denies but since it rarely does both in the same context it cannot compel the thinker to weigh his certainties and doubts while confronting opposing ideas. Interrogative sentences leave decision open to a wide range of possible senses, relations, and references. They prompt an indefinite number of others which must be answered before they can themselves be answered. Dilemmas and paradoxes, on the other hand, are constrained by lines of closure which do not apply to true interrogatives. They constitute a partially bounded universe, in which each question turns upon others for further information. Insofar as they generate a family of questions they provide a meeting place for soliciting a cluster of intellectual claims.

On sociological dilemmas

In common usage a dilemma appears when we have only two courses of action open to us and both are attended by unpleasant consequences. Stebbing defines a dilemma as "a compound argument consisting of a premise in which two implicative propositions are conjunctively affirmed, and of a premise in which either the implicants are alternatively affirmed or the implicates alternatively denied." Described more fully, a dilemma is an argument composed of (a) the conjoint affirmation of two or more hypothetical premises, (b) the affirmation of the antecedents of the hypotheticals as an alternative (disjunctive) premise, and (c) the affirmation of the consequences of the hypotheticals as an alternative (disjunctive) conclusion. Each of these steps may be illustrated in the following dilemma:

a. If there is a state authority then political liberty will be denied.
   If there is not a state authority then self-seeking will prevail.
b. But there must be either a state authority or not.
c. Therefore either political liberty will be denied or self-seeking will prevail.

Other forms of the dilemma do occur but back of each is a situation consisting of a forced option between alternatives which are equally welcome or equally unwelcome.

At least three principal ways of escaping a dilemma have been established by tradition. First, one may deny that the antecedents of the hypotheticals are in fact the only alternatives and thus exhaustive. One might, for instance, claim that a limited state authority is possible by public consent, by special qualification, or by balance of power, all welcomed alternatives. Secondly, one may deny that the conclusion of the dilemma is a necessary consequence of the hypothetical premises. Thus, it may be claimed that under a state authority liberty will be subject to the rule of law, conscience, reason, or custom. Finally, one may rebut the dilemma by posing a counterdilemma. The latter can be offered by negating and interchanging the implicates of the original dilemma. For example, it may be claimed that the presence of a state authority implies that self-seeking will not prevail, whereas its absence implies that political liberty will not be denied.

Dilemmas are pervasive features of every kind of written work; indeed, they are latent in all forms of symbolic expression. Nevertheless, certain standard types represented by characteristic forms of sentence structure are classic. Familiar cases include the Caliph Omar's justification for destroying the library at Alexandria, a lawsuit between Protagoras and Eulathus, and a famous argument between an Athenian mother and her son over the advantages and disadvantages of entering politics. In the modern era, numerous dilemmas have arisen from the controversies between science and theology, science and humanistic ethics, and theology and humanistic ethics. Witness, for instance, the implications of evolutionary theory for the theistic origins of man, the antinomies of conscience and mechanism in the mind-body problem, and the conflicts of morality and social practice in science, religion, and popular fiction.

The dilemmas listed below are, at best, hints of what may be uncovered in future research. Nothing can now be said about their typicality, genuineness, or professional significance. Some approximate commonsense statements on widely popular issues. Some are couched in familiar styles of sociological writing; others possess the appurtenances of logical ordering. A few turn on surprising alterations of conventional viewpoints. They differ from one another in level of abstraction and degree of elaboration. Each favors certain perspectives at the expense of others and, for this reason, all are incomplete.

SOME APPARENT DILEMMAS

1. . . . Though it is nearly impossible to be without, it is often uncomfortable to be with a group. The burden of loneliness is assuaged—perhaps nearly overwhelmed—by the presence of others. Yet the demands they make and restraints with which their presence must be purchased are an almost equal burden. One lives in the tension between society and solitude. The deprivations imposed by each group differ, as do the psychological and material satisfactions offered. But some are universal: Group members always must inhibit aggressiveness against other members and tolerate some aggression from them. They must give up some personal preferences, habits, ideas, and gratifications and indulge their fellows! For the sake of support of the remainder they must surrender not a little of their original nature. At times, all human beings might ask with Lord Byron: "Is it not better thus our lives to wear/ Than join the crushing crowd, doom'd to inflict or bear?" But it is a rhetorical question. We have no choice. Still we are responsible for not surrendering too much, for remaining ourselves. . . .[5]

2. . . . Communism is an extreme form of democracy, and it is totalitarian: but equally the totalitarian state in the form of fascism is an extreme form of democracy. All forms of socialism, whether state socialism of the German kind, or democratic socialism of the British kind, are professedly democratic: That is to say, they all obtain popular assent by the manipulation of mass psychology. All are actually majority governments. It has often been pointed out that in some ways the organization of society in Nazi Germany is much more thoroughly democratic than the organization of society in Great Britain or the United States. The German army is more democratic than the British army; the German industrial system is more democratic than the capitalist industrial system; German finance is more democratically controlled than finance in a plutocracy like ours. In Germany power and responsibility are not the prerogatives of birth or wealth, but are delegated to the holders of office in a party organization; and though such a system is strongly oppressive of individual freedom and therefore not democratic in the libertarian sense of the word, it is at least as democratic as a system which delegates the symbols of authority to a parliament and leaves the real power in the hands of those who control the financial system. National Socialism relates justice to service and group loyalty, which may not be defensible from an abstract ethical point of view; but it is at least an improvement on a system which confuses justice with competitive struggles of the jungle. It is mere hypocrisy on the part of democratic propagandists to pretend that Great Britain or the United States enjoy some mythical happiness or freedom which is denied to the Germans, the Russians, or the Italians; we "enjoy" chaos just as they "enjoy" order; we "enjoy" license, they "discipline"; the choice is in each case equally democratic. . . .[6]

[5] Ralph Ross and Ernest Van den Haag, *The Fabric of Society* (New York: Harcourt, Brace & World, 1937), p. 73.
[6] Herbert Read, *The Politics of the Unpolitical* (London: Routledge & Keegan Paul, 1943), p. 3.

3. . . . The representatives of our several disciplines are well aware that we find ourselves constantly confronted by these unhappy alternatives: greatly insightful and perceptive work tends to be difficult to check and difficult to build upon: on the other hand, work that is methodologically rigorous tends to lose significant problems and bog down in trivialities. Even in this form, this is perhaps too absolutely stated, but it sets out a dilemma familiar to all of us. It is in connection with this dilemma that I am eager to stress the values of an honest self-knowledge. Spurious claims to being "scientific," and scientific rejections of significant problems, can be avoided only if we first recognize them fully and clearly for what they are. I would submit that if we scrutinize our work carefully and represent its character accurately to ourselves and others, we will at least have a chance to create more satisfying alternatives than the "literary"-without-proof or the "scientific"-without-importance. . . .[7]

4. . . . Arguments about relevance within a framework of discussion are not possible because (1) in cases where the subject is clearly defined the notion of relevance is redundant, and (2) in cases where the subject is not clearly defined any argument about relevance amounts to an argument about the subject itself. Why do we then incline to believe otherwise?[8]

5. . . . More specifically, our dilemma is this: We must usually choose between (1) studying many variables in one or a few societies, or (2) studying and comparing many societies in terms of a few variables. Given the traditional methods, it is usually impossible to do both. Consequently, research, even at its best, commonly tends to take one of two courses. In one of these there is an intensive ethnographic account of a single society, with either an implicit or an explicit backdrop of impressionistic comparison to one or two other societies. In the other, there is a comparison of many societies in which, at most, two or three variables are treated simultaneously.[9]

6. . . . Today at last we are able to formulate the dilemma that unconsciously has puzzled men for centuries. Should we state scientific facts at all levels of human growth and in all manner of social situations irrespective of their educative and psychological effects? Should we always formulate facts in the language of instrumental thinking, irrespective of the circumstances that man is used to thinking in terms of images, and that destruction of this imagery destroys the appeal value of our ideas and the human element in them? Or else, should we tell stories that have educative value and humanizing power, but do not correspond with what our fact finders present as tested truth? . . .[10]

7. . . . The perennial problem of free speech, for example, plagues every generation of Americans. One of the major perplexities in the maintenance of this value is that it is self-contradictory. Shall the person who does not believe in the value of "free speech" be allowed to speak freely in a way that will undermine this value? If so, then this great goal is being abandoned to possible self-elimination. If, on the other hand, free speech is to be denied to those who, if given power, would eliminate this goal, then the goal itself is being limited, at least partially. Some people have tried to solve this dilemma by asserting that it will do no "Harm" to let people who detest

[7] Louis Schneider, "Discussion," in Francis L. K. Hus, ed., *Aspects of Culture and Personality* (New York: Abelard-Schuman, 1954), p. 228.

[8] Gilbert Ryle, *The Concept of Mind* (New York: Nelson, 1962), p. 490.

[9] Alvin W. Gouldner and Richard A. Peterson, *Notes on Technology and the Moral Order* (Indianapolis: Bobbs-Merrill, 1962), pp. 12–13.

[10] Karl Mannheim, *Freedom, Power, and Democratic Planning* (New York: Oxford University Press, 1950), pp. 291–292.

free speech utilize this freedom to undermine it. But such a solution is logically fallacious, because it implies that speech itself is harmless, a proposition which, if true, means that it makes no difference whether speech is free or not.[11]

8. . . . In these paragraphs we have been saying that prejudice is a normal phenomenon, that in one sense it is little more than a form of preference, and that prejudice "for" entails almost inevitably prejudice "against." It is doubtful if there is such a thing on earth as a wholly unprejudiced person. Such a person would be devoid of conviction, devoid of opinion, devoid of preferences—in short, a cipher. Even those who take pride in being, as they think, unprejudiced are prejudiced against the prejudiced.

Sociologists, for example, who as a rule are both personally and professionally as unprejudiced a group as it is possible to be, are nevertheless prejudiced against the keepers of concentration camps, the masters of slaves, oppressors of the poor, usurers, religious fanatics, totalitarians, tyrants, racists, and chauvinists. And they are prejudiced against them as types, not only as individuals. The types, in fact, are also stereotypes and in this respect the "unprejudiced" sociologist is no different from anyone else.[12]

9. . . . In their efforts to aid the underdeveloped areas the Western powers, but especially the United States, are confronted with a basic ideological dilemma. In responding to their own changing beliefs, as well as to the challenge of nativist movements, Americans have sought to administer aid in the spirit of help and guidance, which respects the different cultural traditions of native peoples and seeks to enlist their willing cooperation. But in order to give maximum effectiveness to technical aid and managerial guidance the United States becomes the advocate of individualism and a spirit of enterprise abroad, partly as a result of her own traditions (though the strength of this appeal has been declining at home), and partly because individualism and enterprise are very important factors in economic development. Thus, there is a double ideological dilemma. The obsolescence of the entrepreneurial ideology at home is accompanied by its recrudescence abroad. Yet this recrudescence has not occurred directly and unequivocally, for it runs counter to the genuine respect for different cultural traditions and it is jeopardized by being turned into an anti-Western and especially anti-American slogan.[13]

10. . . . This is not the place to consider in detail the relations between the socially plausible, in which appearances persuade though they may deceive, and the true, in which belief is confirmed by appropriate observation. It may be enough to suggest that the independence between the two confronts the sociologist with some uncomfortable alternatives. Should his systematic inquiry only confirm what had been widely assumed—this being the class of plausible truths—he will of course be charged with "laboring the obvious." He becomes tagged as a bore, telling only what everybody knows. Should investigation find that widely held social beliefs are untrue—the class of plausible untruths—he is a heretic, questioning value-laden verities. If he ventures to examine socially implausible ideas that turn out to be untrue, he is a fool, wasting effort on a line of inquiry not worth pursuing in the first place. And finally, if he should turn up some implausible truths, he must be prepared to find himself regarded as a charlatan, claiming as knowledge what is patently false. Instances of each

[11] K. Davis, H. Bredemeier, and M. Levy, *Modern American Society* (New York: Holt, Rinehart and Winston, 1949), pp. 23–24.

[12] Robert Bierstedt, *The Social Order* (New York: McGraw-Hill, 1957), p. 441.

[13] Reinhard Bendix, *Work and Authority in Industry* (New York: Wiley, 1956), p. 445.

of these alternatives have occurred in the history of many sciences, but they would seem especially apt to occur in a discipline, such as sociology, that deals with matters about which men have firm opinions presumably grounded in their own experience.[14]

Together with logical considerations sociological dilemmas pose questions of the following kind:

1. Is the argument as a whole scientifically sensible, inductively true, or factually correct in some clearly specifiable way? In what respects is it trivial or marginal to the sociological universe of discourse?

2. Does the minor premise (the disjunctive) exhaust all the possible alternatives? In what respects are its grounds adequate or unassailable? Is the dilemma unsound because of oversimplification?

3. For whom are the consequences of a dilemma acceptable or unacceptable—for what group, policy, or plan; for which principle or empirical result?

4. Do counterdilemmas apply to the same range of cases under the same sets of conditions? In many instances a counterdilemma may only appear to be inconsistent with the initial dilemma. When different conclusions reflect different ways of viewing the same facts both may be correct and there may be no refutation.

5. What combinations of hypothetical and disjunctive propositions, of antecedents with consequences appear most frequently in the sociological literature?

6. Are there social-psychological criteria of "valid" inference, and if so, what is their possible relationship to logical validity? What are the outcomes of the affiliation of logical dilemmas with rhetoric and debate for the development of a viable social science?

7. With what freedom can premises be reconstructed to produce or avoid (credit or discredit) consistency, paradox, intelligibility, and fruitfulness? What questions arise from the possible variations in premises, from ways in which they may be combined, and from the kinds of consequences which may be drawn from them? What are the characteristics of those patterns of linguistic expression in which the resolution of one dilemma creates other dilemmas?

ON SOCIOLOGICAL PARADOXES

Any proposition contrary to received doctrine which appears to be founded on evidence as conclusive as that doctrine is said to be paradoxical. Thus, when two or more incompatible propositions appear to be equally "true" in the light of impartially applied criteria, a paradox

[14] Robert K. Merton, "Problems and Prospects," in R. Merton, L. Broom, and L. Cottrell, Jr., eds., *Sociology Today* (New York: Basic Books, 1959), pp. xv–xvi.

arises. To resolve a paradox evidence must be found which will add credibility to one proposition at the cost of others. In some cases, new interpretations (postulates, hypotheses) must be sought which, if factually confirmed, would eliminate the paradox.

The paradoxes of language, of perplexing contradictions in theory and fact, are troublesome because they give rise to ideas which seem both correct and incorrect when judged by indispensable standards of meaning. When some situation is so strongly believed that supporting evidence is deemed unnecessary, and at the same time it cannot be described without appearing incredible, a serious intellectual problem arises. Attempts to express difficulties produce confusion while attempts to avoid difficulties prevent understanding. Faced with apparently incorrigible combinations of premises and conclusions, the reasonable course is to accept all aspects of a conflicting experience and seek to resolve what seems irresolvable by devices more effective than arbitrary verbalizations. Such devices cannot be promoted without attributing scientific significance to human predicaments.

Perhaps the most persistent source of paradoxes in sociology arises from the many levels of language vaguely distinguishable within it. Sprinklings of ordinary language may or may not be interspersed with the terminology of statistics and mathematics. Preferred kinds of formal or technical language are presumed to describe the realities mentionable in prose English, yet analytic comparisons of language levels have not been offered by sociologists. At least no language has been developed which appears to be as free from bias as the "neutral" rules of metatheory in mathematics and logic. Without standards of linguistic reference, differences in usage cannot be distinguished. This limitation would not be so serious if sociologists could make their meanings clear by direct reference to physically tangible things. But in the absence of highly visible objects how can they know when they are evaluating rather than predicting, or persuading rather than informing? What clues can they use to disentangle the multiple categories of meaning that enter into the typical sociological expression? Are the concepts of "institution," "status," and "role" primarily semantic or syntactical? In what respects are they observational, abstract, or hypothetical? To cope with these questions sociologists must do more than *use* the language of sociology; they must write *about* it. Common usage must be examined on a level as nearly independent of that usage as a reconstructed language will allow. But when one contemplates the problem of where a reconstructed language is to come from, of how to think about it without resorting to ordinary language, he is caught in a paradox. The best way to exhibit the obscurities of ordinary language is to construct a precise language which is clearly independent of the typical meanings of ordinary language. But then if the two languages are independent how can one be translated into the other? Will tests of their correspondence require the construction of a third language and if so how is this to be done without embracing the same difficulties that arise from a twofold language?

Perhaps the paradox of a twofold language may be resolved if elements in both can be found which will permit translation from one to the other. Thus if some of the categories and rules of ordinary language prove to be identical with some of the categories and rules of logic the latter can be used to systematize ordinary language. But, paradoxically again, the analogy must not fit too well. If two languages become nearly identical in every respect there is little advantage in using one over the other. And if they differ greatly one cannot be used effectively to interpret the other. Beyond these methodological difficulties are the numerous problems which arise from attempts to write within the scope of a single language. Prelinguistic and extralinguistic meanings (thought patterns) are readily projected into the simplest contexts. A host of allusions and counter examples, unintended by the writer, creep into the reader's responses to shape his interpretation of things and their qualities. Entities and properties may be confounded by personalized analogies which provide no more than fleeting reference to the writer's purposes. In many cases a reader cannot know how a writer means to use familiar words. Moreover, if he knew how to avoid misapplications he would have no assurance that others would follow suit by adapting the writer's meanings. Thus the question of whether a given language is appropriate to its subject matter becomes, in itself, a question of language usage.

The discovery of paradoxes in language has lead to extensive efforts at reconstructing the foundations of thought. By bringing incompatible concepts and rules within the same universe of discourse, mathematics, logic, and philosophy of science have answered old problems and posed new ones. No doubt, some sociological problems resemble logical paradoxes in compelling scholars to choose between an acceptable rule of reasoning productive of absurd conclusions and the abandonment of such a rule in favor of less absurd conclusions. However, since "sociological paradoxes" contain theoretical terms laden with empirical content, they differ from logical paradoxes in respect to analytical rigor. A sociological paradox arises when "empirically true" premises together with "empirically derived" processes of inference lead to "empirically false" consequences. The paradox is more complete when "empirically false" consequences are seen by processes of inference to require reinterpretation of empirical premises, previously believed to be "true." Should it follow that when these premises are taken as "false" their consequences must be taken as "true," the paradoxical circle of reasoning is complete.

The following paradoxes represent a preliminary attempt to bring accepted ways of reasoning in close proximity, thereby exposing their regions of uncertainty and contradiction. They are meant to set the stage from which an analysis of the structure of sociological paradoxes may begin. Though limited in variety, they reveal a few of the perplexing puzzles which arise when disparate lines of interpretation are joined together. In some cases the consequences of a premise appear to negate that premise. In other cases the contrary consequences of a premise appear to negate it if, indeed, they do not seem to lead to the same conclusion. When sociological paradoxes are catalogued, the difficult issue of whether they can or should be restated in strictly logical form may be susceptible to analysis. Questions concerning their fictional and factual character may also be subject to intensive inquiry.

SOME APPARENT PARADOXES

1. It has been said that sociologists should be tolerant of everything but intolerance. Does this mean that sociologists should not be tolerant of those who are intolerant of social intolerance?

2. We are told that objectivity requires emotional sensitivity of the interviewer to the social situation. We are also told that objectivity requires intellectual detachment of the interviewer from the social situation. Finally we are told that objectivity requires "participant observation" of the interviewer in the social situation. What does objectivity require?

3. According to sociology, the explanation of individual behavior is to be found in the group. According to psychology, the explanation of group behavior is to be found in the individual. But sociology usually leaves the explanation of the individual to psychology and psychology usually leaves the explanation of the group to sociology.

4. A complete sociological analysis of society would begin with the role of the sociologist analyzing society and since this analysis is itself data for further sociological analysis there should be analyses by sociologists of sociologists analyzing society. Indeed, since each new analysis requires in its turn another analysis an infinite number of analyses is necessary for a complete account of society.

5. An exact science of society is impossible for the following reasons: All science depends upon the law of excluded middle, "Nothing is both A and non-A." But to apply this law, every element of social action must remain unchanged for more than one instance of time and no element of social action must have contradictory properties at one instance of time. Since no element of social action meets these conditions, an exact science of society is impossible.

6. ". . . The principle of rebellion is the same as that of conformity. It is the true nature of society that is conformed to when the traditional morality is obeyed, and yet it is also the true nature of society which is being conformed to when the same morality is flouted. . . ."[15]

7. ". . . The early Christians knew very well that the world is full of devils, and that he who enters politics, e.g., the realm where alone power and violence as means are valid, concludes a pact with devilish powers, and that from good may only come good, from evil only evil is not true; but very often the contrary. Who does not see this is politically a child. . . ."[16]

8. ". . . Conquering the physical world, (man) fails to conquer himself. That is the tragic paradox of this atomic and sputnik age. The fact that nuclear tests continue, even though it is well recognized that they are very harmful in the present and in the future; the fact that all kinds of weapons of mass destruction are being produced and piled up, even though it is universally recognized that their use may well exterminate the human race, brings out this paradox with startling clarity."[17]

9. ". . . Many industrial social scientists have put themselves on auction. The power elites of America, especially the industrial elite, have bought their services—which, when applied to areas of relative power, have restricted the freedom of millions of workers. Time was when a man knew that his freedoms were being curtailed. Social scientists, however, are too sophisticated for that. The fires of pressure and control on a man are now kindled in his own thinking. Control need no longer be imposed. It can be encouraged to come from within. Thus the faith that if ' people develop propaganditis' the effectiveness of control would be weakened seems to miss the point. A major characteristic of twentieth-century manipulation has been that it blinds the victim to the fact of manipulation. Because so many industrial social scientists have been willing to serve power instead of mind, they have been themselves a case study in manipulation by consent."[18]

To circumvent the constraints laid down by paradoxical formulations, modes of linguistic clarification unfamiliar to the social science should be sought. Perhaps considerations of the following kind would advance understanding.

[15] Emile Durkheim, *Sociology and Philosophy*, trans. D. F. Pocock (New York: Free Press, 1953), p. 66.
[16] Max Weber, *Max Weber and German Politics*, trans. J. P. Mayer (London: Faber & Faber, 1944), p. 89.
[17] Jawaharlal Nehru, "The Tragic Paradox of our Age," from *The New York Times Magazine*, September 7, 1958, p. 110. Reprinted in Edgar A. Schuler *et al.*, *Readings in Sociology* (New York: Crowell, 1960), p. 857.
[18] Loren Baritz, *The Servants of Power* (Middletown, Conn.: Wesleyan University Press, 1960), pp. 209–210.

1. The likelihood that the assumptions, inferences, and conclusions derived from paradoxical statements depend upon multiple usage within the same universe of discourse. Thus, specific claims for empirical truth and valid reasoning would be subject to fresh inquiries.

2. The likelihood that paradoxes may be eliminated by restricting the unguided application of concepts. In some instances a paradox may refer to trivial cases only or to empirical items which have little significance for sociological theory. Nevertheless, empirical items which do not appear to support a coherent body of theory should be shown to be irrelevant before being declared inconsequential.

3. The possibility that concepts and principles may be redefined to escape difficulties imposed by their acceptance. As the history of paradoxes reveals, this may be done by introducing new assumptions including new meanings at new levels of analytic transformation. Thus the meaning of the term "meaningless" and the possibilities of the word "possibility" have been frequently subject to logical and empirical exploration.

4. The probability that circular reasoning and infinite regress is implicit in much of social science. No doubt revelations of circularity are obscured by the informal styles of exposition which characterize present-day social science. Though circular reasoning may not involve logical contradiction it often fosters conceptual isolation and empirical equivocation.

5. The probability that intellectual obstacles arising from the apparent opposition of logic and experience, reason and fact, would repay closer scrutiny. A nest of difficulties surrounds much social science writing because arguments over what is conceivable are not clearly separated from arguments over what is actual. Confusions of this kind cannot be resolved until the grounds of antinomous principles are used to refute or invalidate one another. Of course, a major gain occurs when contradictory principles can be retained through revision of the fundamental conceptions upon which they rest. A striking example is the attempt by Singer to resolve the controversy over Mechanism and Vitalism in biology by changing the laws of logic. In the briefest terms, he showed that although logical classes may be contradictory, the inclusion of existing things in contradictory classes may not lead to logical inconsistency.

In sum, the analysis and resolution of paradoxes are aided by the application of criteria for determining consistency and contradiction; by definitions of both literal and metaphorical meanings, and by exploration of the ladders on which terminological interpretations may hold. Some terms interpenetrate, some are incomplete, some cancel each other out, and some shift in usage from one sentence to another. If a paradox is expressed in a bundle of sentences, intersentence comparisons may have to be made before the paradox can be disentangled. This is the problem of determining the respects in which a word, sentence, or thing is comparable to another word, sentence, or thing. In some instances, relevant likenesses are not explicitly mentioned but only suggested. In other instances, likenesses are stated incompletely and must be either supplied or restricted by altering contexts. But to approach precision, examination of contexts, together with estimations of the respects in which qualities and relations correspond, is essential. Through contextual analysis the practical limits of moving from observed resemblances to inferred resemblances may be understood. Through the use of analogy and figurative language, of similes, parables, and myths, old illustrations may be clarified, new principles revealed, and fresh hypotheses brought to life.

THE PROTEAN CHARACTER OF SOCIOLOGY

We have written of the probability that many of the problems which arise in sociology are generated by the forms of language we are accustomed to using. Prose language is the principle instrument of sociology and insofar as it cannot be eliminated, the non-linguistic phenomena with which it deals must be articulated in terms of that language or some other language (formal or informal) to which it is accountable. We have indicated that every word in sociological usage is a potential item of interpretation, of diverse analyses, and of varied critical evaluations. Since no set of symbols can be completely separated from the intentions of its users, no language fully exhausts the meaning of the ideas it represents. For this reason, all languages are subjective to a greater or lesser degree. Of nearly equal significance, because it often goes unnoticed, is the likelihood that strains toward conceptual invariance (constancy) systematically minimize the real variability (inconstancy) of social phenomena.

That sociology is handicapped by restrictions of language frames and facilities, by the persistent tendency to overdetermine referential usage, and by the inability to shape clearly in words the ideas to which it is heir and the things to which it would respond, is evident from earlier portions of this essay. Indeed, the following words are burdened with these same difficulties. To explicate fully the shifting connotations of language we would have to add phrases without end, each designed to elucidate what went before until no one felt it necessary to dispute our conclusions! With practical considerations in mind, we shall hedge against premature closures by staging verbal arrangements in such a way as to permit of the widest possible latitude of interpretation. Since we freely reconstruct previously contrived categories, the adventuresome critic is free to contrive his own. Indeed, the critic may, if he wishes, take as his point of departure the assumption that what we offer are little more than implausible hypotheses.

Propositions asserted for purposes of examining the respects in which they can be proven or disproven may be called *theses* and *countertheses.* Although frequently limited to capsule expressions of belief, estimations may be made of their factual and logical support. When such estimations are scaled and weighed they can be seen as *claims, proposals,* and *considerations. Claims* are imperative demands for the recognition of a logical circumstance or the maintenance of a state of affairs, as the claimant views it. They are founded on what is believed to be a proper or fitting requirement for the situation or objective under review. *Proposals* are equivalent to suggestions offered for exploration by others with the admission that they may be accepted or rejected at the discretion of the recipient. In their strongest form they are kin to propositions propounded for purposes of discussing, arguing, or testing some task, policy, or condition. *Considerations* refer to the process of groping after or casting about for means to comprehend the possibilities of some idea. To raise a line of thought for consideration is to invite reflection on some object, or aspect of it, for the sake of clarifying a principle, assessing a situation, or choosing a course of action. As such they are less decisive than claims and proposals.

Admittedly, all propositions are *problematic* in the sense that they are forever subject to change. Procedures of revision and resolution are themselves theses and countertheses, claims, proposals, or considerations which rest on a wide variety of categories and criteria, most of which are never completely articulated. Nonetheless, any category or criterion of language can, to some extent, be turned about and examined through the spectrum of meaning implied or suggested by the others. This principle pertains in full to the aforementioned sentences and to those which follow. Since most sentences are as broad in their implications as the full complement of language, all conceptual possibilities are enlarged by tracing the growth and formation of changing contexts.

CONSIDERATIONS PERTAINING
TO SCIENTIFIC COMMUNICATION

Thought and communication

The thought behind every conceptual scheme, image or argument is only partially dependent upon language. If this were not so, human discriminations could not be carried in thought without being expressible in language. If this were not so, new vocabularies could not be invented or explained. If thought had no preverbal basis, it could not be stimulated by autonomic, visceral, and skeletal responses. Do not deaf mutes and probably animals distinguish and choose, without using language? Undoubtedly, language and thought are only partially dependent upon concrete experience. Many conceptions are not testable by sensations and their implementing apparati; they describe no "handling action" and they have no phenomenal (physical) counterpart. Thus, the meaning of sex and age in a particular society cannot be fully understood without a social assessment of their volitional and anticipatory dispositions—as often a function of grammatical gender as of pictorial representation.

Language and communication

To interpret one language scheme in terms of another without claiming the ontological priority of either, a methodology must be developed which does not require large sacrifices of crucial idiomatic meanings. The fault of many methodologies is that they offer language schemes which are heir to the very difficulties they hope to surmount. To view any scheme with maximum objectivity its potential usefulness must be assumed. Such an assumption amounts to a willingness to tamper with its central concerns, to design exploratory procedures for overcoming impediments. Rather than refutations it means proposals for the consideration of one's colleagues; the use of conciliatory devices for achieving mutually corrective results. It means a relativization of absolutistic positions but not the complete relativism that precludes all judgments of significance. Though certain language schemes may be more useful, more reasonable, or more fruitful than others, sociologists cannot yet present criteria which will convince the multitude of scholars. This is the job of methodology, and sociologists should concede that defensive postures in favor of one clarified language over another are inimical to this job.

Academic conventions and communication

Sociologists rarely write as if they understand the restrictive influence of academic conventions. Too often they foster research which stands in close continuity with preferred traditions. Too often publishing practices are not regarded as open to innovation. Too often, it seems, sociologists take the quantity of a colleague's writings as a measure of his academic worth. Do not sociologists mirror their culture? Are fads in choice of research governed by official and unofficial status systems? Is professional advancement unduly weighted in favor of colleague and institutional accommodations? How often is academic identification based on the substitution of an atypical characteristic for the total person in the same way that skin color elicits racial stereotypes? For these reasons sociologists should reexamine with fresh curiosity the place of "values" in the scientific enterprise. Many sociologists agree that values enter science through the door of their presuppositions. Do values also pervade lines of reasoning and the conclusions drawn from them? The fact that different interpretations are often drawn from the same data necessitates consideration of the role of private and public values in science.

CONSIDERATIONS PERTAINING TO OBJECTIVITY

Objectivity and expert consensus

Upon analysis, the question of who qualifies as a scientific expert appears to be reducible to the question of who or what group is in position (or power) to define scientific truth effectively. But is acceptance by a sizable body of experts a sufficient guarantee of scientific truth, or does the latter depend on other considerations? If scientific truth depends solely on expert consensus then it will vary with different professional communities. "Today's truths are tomorrow's lies." If scientific truth depends upon methods of rational proof—types of evidence, the intersubjective weighing of diverse claims—how are they to be certified except through collective agreement in attitudes? (Cf. Barzun.) Can one avoid the claim that scientific agreement resides in the composition of individual (or group) beliefs deriving from private sources of judgment?

Is there a difference between proving a theory and getting it accepted, between settling a dispute by showing that one party is correct (or right) and settling it by showing that both parties have come to hold the same viewpoint? If it is possible to have objective proof without professional agreement or the latter without the former, can it be concluded that objective proof is independent of professional judgments?

Objectivity and subject matter

Do the following interpretations provide a valid or useful basis for distinguishing between objective and subjective judgment? (Cf. Paul Edwards.)

1. A statement is objective if its subject matter is something other than an event in somebody's mind. If it asserts the existence or describes the features of a mental event it is a subjective statement.

2. A statement is objective if its subject matter is something other

than an event in the mind of the author. If it asserts the existence or describes the features of an event in the author's mind, it is a subjective statement.

3. A statement is objective if its subject matter is something other than a biased event in the mind of the author. If it is greatly colored by the author's mind or emotions, regardless of the nature of the subject matter, it is a subjective statement.

In which combinations of these three senses of objectivity do various types of moral and scientific statements (or judgments) fall? Is such a statement as "I think Negroes are morally inferior" objective in sense (2) but subjective in sense (3)? Is Dr. Smith's "true" statement, "My intelligence score on the Stanford-Binet is 160" subjective in sense (2) but objective in sense (3)? Is the unconditional statement, "In my belief, Russia destroyed the Summit meeting," an objective or subjective claim? Should it be concluded that, despite the apparent objectivity of a description, when belief is taken as the point of consideration the claim is subjective? Is the truth (or falsity) of belief and of fact altogether independent of one another?

Objectivity and full understanding

Must the question be raised of how much objectivity is attended by the continuous repetition of concepts to the point where familiarity produces the subjective sense of authentic meaning? When each word is explained by other words regularly associated with it, and these are usually without empirical substantiation, is objectivity assured? Is it possible that one is caught in the dilemma of "having to get thoroughly into a subject" before he fully understands it, but once having understood it his commitments cause him to lose his objectivity? Is it possible that scholars cannot successfully criticize a work before learning it well, but that this emotional investment prevents them from being able to view it objectively?

CONSIDERATIONS PERTAINING TO SOCIOLOGICAL EMPIRICISM

Since professional sociologists commonly assume that the claims for empiricism are well established, the present remarks are directed to a brief summary of the claims against it. If these remarks have the brevity of dogmatisms others may welcome the opportunity to examine them with renewed vigor.

Limitations of empiricism

1. The principal limitations of empiricism stem from insufficient assurance that current observations will not be contradicted by new disclosures from other times and places. Always we are confronted with the hazards of interpreting past and future events which are not exposed to direct observation. Always we are dependent upon the deposits of memory and the fancies of prophecy, upon diagnostic and prognostic signs which are never more than partially illuminating. The obscurity surrounding attempts to discern with clarity, forces us to make our experiences congruent by stipulating meanings which will carry over from one situation to another. For this reason, all expressions of scientific regularity contain transcendental qualities, a consequence known to every scientist who attempts to define the empirical scope of social phenomena.

As sociologists we want to say more than that certain events have been observed in this place or that; unless we can state the "when" and "where" of past and future observations there can be no prediction or postdiction. But to anticipate the observation of events we must spell out the conditions required for their appearance. We must be able to indicate the possible circumstances, professional personnel, and states of preparedness (including operational equipment) in accordance with which new observations can be made.

In principle, science assumes that the conditions of observation sufficient for testing hypotheses are always incomplete. Therefore, any chosen class, property, or predicate is necessarily restricted in its radii of denotations. Verification is premised on the belief that events appearing in the present can sustain hypotheses referring to past and future events of the same general type. The belief is tested by requiring that the place and date of events furnishing evidence for hypotheses differ from the place and date of events used to confirm them. Since present events must be typical to or logically connected with non-present events, sociologists can assess the probabilities of hypotheses only by developing a methodology which extends beyond the literal interpretation of empirical phenomena.

Empiricism and objectivity

2. Observation is an experience of the individual scientist and refers to a specifiable set of results following from a specifiable set of human acts. In this process there is no guarantee that constant errors deriving from intersubjective consensus can be controlled or eliminated. Without such a guarantee, operationalism cannot assume that non-human responses to the external world are reducible to human responses or their

equivalents. Presumably the same non-human property is always measured by the same human operations. There is, then, no problem of relating operations to one another or of defining the generic features of an operational definition. Taking consensus as a sufficient test of objectivity, operationalism and empiricism have little use for metaempirical frameworks. But consensus is also a test of tradition and fashion in intellectual work. Thus, consensus may mean no more than a readiness to combine words in popular ways. It need not be based on verbally uncorrupted observations or on incorrigible human experiences. Groups of people as well as individuals are capable of systematic errors in perception and analysis.

Empiricism and theory

3. The logical or theoretical scheme within which a particular observational sentence is inserted or to which it is fitted determines judgment of its meaningfulness as well as of its meaninglessness. Per contra, the theoretical organization of science (premises, rules of inference, theorems) is not reducible to empirical or operational referents; it is above or beyond any collection of descriptive signs. To be scientific, sociology must use supersensory predicates which are not equivalent to the tangible objects and events to which they are applied. Note, for instance, the insufficiency of sensory referents for "social status," "cultural norms," or "group cohesion." These terms suggest meanings which cannot be confined to any existing body of empirically designated data or to any operationally defined series of behavioral acts. They are constructed out of an imaginative matrix derived, in part, from hypothetical possibilities. They depend upon simplifications, purifications, interpolations, and idealizations of descriptive materials. In a similar way, notions of truth and validity depend upon conceptual frameworks not entirely visible; upon inferences from sensory impressions which are often fleeting, fragmentary, discrete, and ideographic. Containing surplus elements of an extrainductive character, the theoretical claims of sociological hypotheses are always broader than the actual evidence upon which they rest.

As a consequence, isolated observations reported in a phenomenal language, simple or complex, can play but a small part in science. Through relational or coordinate schemes, observations are linked together and provided with more than momentary reality. Perhaps such concepts as "culture," "power," and "social role" are derived from logical reconstructions of observational indexes or by postulation of latent structures. But in any case, the significant problem of how empirical observations in sociology are to be systematically ordered, remains largely unexamined. With social events necessitating revisions of theoretical contexts, relations between discrete perceptions cannot be confirmed without more duplication of effort than now exists. For these reasons, many researchers should repeat similar processes within situations known to vary systematically and have the results checked by those of widely different orientations. Considerations of simplicity, esthetic appeal, and academic styles should also be recognized as viable elements in the scientific enterprise. Such considerations may have much to do with the vogue of operationalism and functionalism in sociology. No doubt the latter receive encouragement because they place arbitrary limitations on the infinity of possible observations.

Recapitulation

4. By way of summary and conclusion: All observations must be conceptually coordinated before they can be fitted into an intelligible framework. Since conceptual coordination depends upon assumptions regarding commensurability, spatial-temporal continuity and coherence—suppositions not directly testable—it rests upon metaempirical and metaoperational interpretations. In this sense, useful knowledge of observations requires reconstruction from above or outside of the observations themselves. The truths of theoretical relations are invisible and depend heavily upon linguistic forms that extend beyond any collection of observational materials. Their hypothetical features prevent them from becoming equivalent to any set of descriptive statements. Thus, the meaning of such concepts as "stratification" or "social mobility" cannot be exhausted by listing the sensory sources upon which they rest. If such a list were provided could the sociologist say that it specified a single concept and none other? To equate concepts with observations is to ignore the point that they have no precise operational or reductive basis. Being partly stipulative and transobservational they are not fully known through any kind of palpable experience. Ensuing therefrom, the range of actual evidence upon which hypotheses rest at any given time is narrower than the range of possible evidence—past and future—to which they are meant to refer factually. Hypotheses which do not transcend the circumstances of the immediately present to include both the events and relations of other times and places cannot speak to the problem of scientific order.

PROPOSALS PERTAINING TO STABILITY
AND CHANGE IN SOCIAL PHENOMENA

Toward stability

In reacting against the Aristotelian notion of fixed entities in nature, many students of human behavior could see only change and process. In the latter view nature was all of a piece—continuous and emergent—and such divisions as were found within it were believed to be humanly imposed. But both viewpoints easily present themselves as extreme positions. The scientific enterprise seems impossible without some minimum distinction beteewn things and their doings, or less crudely speaking, between behavior which is relatively constant and behavior which is relatively changeable. If all aspects of phenomena were changing at unknown rates and no aspect could be regarded as more stable than any other it would be impossible to discover or invent parameters which could serve as reference points for concept formation, generalization, and prediction. These key objectives depend upon some degree of constancy or recurrence within phenomena. How else would it be possible to derive knowledge from one space-time framework and apply it to another except for the presence of interchangeable similarities? If all were change with no differentiation in process or activity, human learning would be impossible. Without spatial-temporal selection and transference of human experience, there would be no basis for identifying one aspect of phenomena with another.

Neither absolute permanence nor absolute change seems to be reasonable. One must look for stability or persistence, for "thinghood" within the less changing aspects of each changing situation. In some instances, the more stable aspects will be manifested in the form of phenomena, in their tangible spatial outline. In other instances, they will appear as certain repeatable sensations manifested, naively, as descriptive features or qualities. Symbols representing permanence of process or mode of happening always reflect a particular stage of inquiry; the permanent characteristics of an earlier stage of inquiry frequently become the changing characteristics of a later stage of inquiry, at which point the problem under study is viewed in greater detail. Thus, what is permanent from the perspective of some limited context appears to be changing from the perspective of a wider context.

Toward change

The principal reason sociologists have difficulty assessing the conditions of social change and cognate ideas such as multiplicity, differentiation, diversity, severalness, proliferation, individuation, and conflict is that scientists and laymen are forever attempting to build into human affairs the kinds of constancy which will stabilize existence. Attempts to manage the incalculable and fortuitous mean that concepts of chance and accident, the uncontrollable and the irrational, the probable and the possible, are verbally formed into determinate qualities. Novel vocabularies of changing differences are transmitted into a language of stable things known through the substitution of one type of identity for another. Interchange, fluctuation, evolution, and permutation are translated into the persistence of underlying properties.

The necessity to see invariance in the most radical forms of variation produces a systematic distortion in the scientific enterprise. The necessity of widening universals at successively higher levels of abstraction together with the inability to comprehend and describe uniqueness, places a blanket on the discontinuity of concrete events. (Note how each of these words conjures up fixed elements of thought.) The sociologist finds countless items alike in being a part of culture, the institutionalization process, social norms, role expectations, etc. Moreover, variations of the concept of uniqueness cannot be communicated without joining the word to non-unique terms. As these similarities and commonalities are highlighted, discrete differences in experience are obliterated and all are seen as participating in some kind of uniformity or equilibrium. Simply because the mentality and language of men are what they are, over-generalization is a primary source of error and distortion in science. The principal means of correction, then, is to bring into discourse word variations which qualify or reduce word constancies, generalizations which limit or contradict one another, descriptions which stand in some form of opposition to each other. Against the contention that statements A, B, C, and D are coherent or connected we should indicate the respects in which they are incoherent or disconnected, functional or dysfunctional, consensual or dissensual. The risk of overemphasizing the second term in each of these pairs is not as great as the risk of over-emphasizing the first since all terms must be stated with the aid of symbolic constants.

The paradoxes of sociology (and all science) stem from the apparent fact that the reality of phenomenal differences is more evident than the reality of phenomenal identity.[19] Efforts should, therefore, be directed to demonstrating the many respects in which A is unlike B, B is opposed to C, and C is in conflict with D. Since language is inherently idealistic it tends to converge toward the articulation of phenomenal identities. To offset the imputation of excessive identities in the conceptualization process one should begin by seeking for similarities in phenomenal differences, (with emphasis on differences) and end by seeking for differences in phenomenal similarities (again with emphasis on differences). Such differences would constitute the more adequate grounds upon which enduring similarities are built.

[19] Identity is a limiting case of difference, as symmetry is a limiting case of asymmetry. Of course identities are never complete; if they were, no one could say that any two things are identical. They must at least be temporarily or spatially distinct.

Toward stability and change

All social phenomena (things, objects, events) can be dissected into permanent and transitory functions, powers, or dispositions. The *permanent* functions of a thing, its "essential" characteristics, are those properties which persist despite variations in surrounding conditions. Surrounding conditions are in turn synonymous with the functions of other things. It follows that things are known by what they do (i.e., by how they act) when confronted with other things known in the same way. When the permanent functions of a thing are destroyed it no longer exists or, more accurately, it is transformed into some other thing having dissimilar functions. The *transitory* functions of a thing are those powers or dispositions which are expressed or repressed (gained or lost) only under specific conditions, conditions which may appear frequently or only occasionally but never universally.

From permanent functions, concepts of stability and order and the notion of identifiable kinds arise; from transitory functions, concepts of change and disorder and the notion of evolutionary phases arise. Since specific conditions are required for the expression of transitory functions, functions which necessarily remain latent in the absence of these conditions, social changes cannot appear without them. The regular conjunction of a given permanent function with two transitory functions throughout a range of values is equivalent to a scientific generalization or law. Moreover, the conjunction of many permanent functions with many transitory functions is both possible and conceivable when viewed as expanding patterns or series of relata. Methodologically, first causes are no more than those permanent functions which "explain" the largest number of transitory functions relevant to the resolution of a problematic situation.

Application of the principle of permanent and transitory functions would alter the typical perspectives of the sociologist. To begin with, he must *assume* that things once believed to have autonomous powers are in fact continuous with other powers, coterminous with transitional phases from which they gradually grow. He must attempt to observe minutely, and with the aid of technical instruments, the details of those inchoate regions which are presumed to separate one thing from another. The more or less constant reference points which define frameworks must be subject to vigilant scrutiny so that gains derived from viewing them as dispositions can be fully realized. In this way the sociologist may discover extensional and durational occurrences, event-processes which bring together what before had been seen in separation. Rigidities derived from placing elements within a fixed and highly formal framework would be loosened and reshaped to the growing pattern of research.

If the descriptive character of old constituents is to be widened or narrowed into phases of events, they must be mixed, altered, and recombined in accordance with new specifications. This may best be done, not by shifting from one set of fixed concepts to another, as some sociologists seem to believe, but by delving through and under and across each of them, guided only by their use as external points of comparison. Then a vocabulary and system of reporting will emerge to describe the fluid phasic character of observations both as process and temporary terminus. Provisional locations of spatial-temporal coincidence, or the joint occurrence of neighboring actions, will be labeled in a manner which allows for both stable and shifting manifestations of phenomena.

As a simple illustration, note the research context in which status factors—occupation, income, education, etc.—are associated with patterns of social response. To observe this association in its transitory aspects verbal and somatic manifestations of status factors must be seen as continuous with those behavioral events which constitute the patterns in question. The apparent disjunctions between manifestations and patterns must be subject to especially close scrutiny, for in these regions dispositional aspects are most likely to be found. With detailed attention to ways in which separateness is fixed, events which bind permanent functions together will be open for renewed appraisal. With the aid of new linguistic tools, chasms of undifferentiated and unobserved phenomena may be logically spanned. By unfreezing established categories, fresh advances in observation and conceptualization may be forthcoming.

The preceding principle is consistent with the notion that there are no absolutely rigid cleavages in nature. It calls upon the sociologist to explore seriously existing distinctions between science and the scientist, structure and function, theory and observation, techniques (as means) and values (as ends), to say nothing of organism and environment, a distinction already subject to extensive appraisals.

CONCLUSION:

SOME THESES ON SYSTEMATIC SOCIOLOGY

Introductory note

The reader is reminded that the problems and issues of sociology can be expressed in sentences which represent varying degrees of assertive power. Most firmly stated are claims, patterns of mutually supporting beliefs which possess the aura if not the substance of certainty. Less definite are proposals, beliefs which admit of partially bounded areas of meaning. Least fixed are considerations, loosely phrased conceptual possibilities open to the freest kind of inquiry.

Since many of the theses contained herein run counter to the assumptions and conclusions of modern sociology, the principal task of the sociological critic is to assess each in the light of his theoretical allegiances. Believing that certain statements about sociology are both well established and contrary to the writer's judgment he may regard the following as highly improbable counterclaims, counterproposals or counterconsiderations. He may even find it convenient to view them as outrageous hypotheses which can be conclusively refuted through reasoned discourse or the fresh examination of empirical illustrations.

Contextal character of truth and falsity

1.1. Any statement in sociology can be regarded as either "true" or "false" depending on the sense conferred upon it by the context or scheme in which it is placed. Criteria of falsification can be construed as relative to specific premises and purposes, to the value coordinates that standardize conceptual schemes. These coordinates consist of general notions of what is relevant, reliable, or useful in the light of specialized interests, needs, or objectives.

1.2. No sociological scheme can represent more than a partial view of the universe. Schemes which claim to rest upon the reliability of sense perceptions apart from logical and other forms of metaempirical construction are cases in point. Similarly for schemes which reflect the operationalist's distrust of hypothetical terms and the theorist's belief in immutable categories. However, in the context of specific premises and objectives sociological concepts may have both permanent and transitory aspects.

1.3. In all classifications of sociological concepts, the terms used must not be regarded as fixed entities or "essences" but as analytic points of comparison transposable in such a way that new schemes of classification can be constructed. The manipulation and reassortment of such terms produces transformations in conceptual schemes which are productive of larger classes of categories and relations.

Relational character of concepts and methods

2.1. Every sociological concept can be joined through an indefinite set of relations with many others. For each concept there are others that resemble it in kind, quality, and degree. Research should therefore reveal the recurrence or conjugate correspondence of contrasting types of concepts, the specific ways or several senses in which they can be taken as the counterpart, correlate, or opposite of others and systematically joined with them.

2.2. All sociological concepts can be related by conceptual transitions or continuities. There are no sharp demarcations or disjunctions and no complete unities or identities that can be maintained in the face of every possible premise or objective. This principle applies to such dichotomies as structure-function, quality-quantity, real-ideal, individual-society, and many others.

2.3. All methodology is derived from the reciprocal interplay of question asking and question answering, in which every kind of query and reply has some claim for recognition. Thus the answers provided by inductive reasoning give rise to questions in the domain of deductive reasoning. The same process applies to the interplay between formal and empirical, pure and applied, necessary and probable, general and particular, mechanistic and teleological types of statements. In this interplay, apparently dissimilar problems are seen to be similar and vice versa.

Social character of conceptual meanings

3.1. Most co-relations of sociological concepts are due to historical chance or the probabilities of traditional association. Consequently the conformity of fact to hypothesis cannot be proved outside the premises and objectives of some conventional arrangement of words. Collective usage alone enables one to infer the "meaning" of a concept at one place in a scheme from the "meaning" of some other concept at another place in the same scheme. Connections between concepts are therefore not universal, necessary, or immanent.

3.2. No matter how concepts are formed it is possible to claim for them some degree of social validity. Concepts are embodied in ways of talking, and every way of talking has reference to somebody or something, real or imagined. Concepts symbolize the common disposition to respond "emotively," "heuristically," "intuitively," "analytically," or "descriptively", to some occurrence or event. Perhaps the expression, "uniformity of nature" can be regarded as a summarization of linguistic regularities apart from how the latter are established or justified. The statement, "All A's and B's" is acceptable only when many independent observers agree that each one's limited sample exhibits this regularity, a sample more accurately described as, "Some (all examined) A's and B's." Thus, whatever is repeatable in the communication of men everywhere must reflect the uniformities of their social nature. In this sense, authenticity is ubiquitous and language usage conditions "objective reality."

3.3. Conceptual schemes are the products of the same sources of motivation that give rise to other forms of linguistic expression—oral and esthetic gratifications, group identification and preservation, financial rewards and professional recognition. It is often these conditions and not the search for "objective" scientific truth that induces sociologists to adapt criteria of appraisal that are normative in their profession. Most forms of scientific expression are signals of agreement or disagreement, exhortations of what should or should not be done. Note, for instance, how frequently the word "empirical" is interjected into sociological writing without the slightest attempt to explore its possible meanings. "Truth," accordingly, consists of ceremonially determined equivalences between sentences or their constituent elements.

Ordered character of conceptual schemes

4.1. The objective of every conceptual scheme is to establish coherence, congruence, or concordance among its component elements. For this purpose, numerous vocabularies may be explored: subject-verb-object relations, typologies, growth and entrophy, information flows and networks, polarity-gradients and dominant-subordinate hierarchies, parametric complementarities and dispersions, correspondences of inner and outer forms, patterns of symmetry and reciprocal dependency, archetypes of stability and change, images (maps) and prototypes (territories).

4.2. The main task of sociological theory is to find ways of simplifying or reducing the diversity of language schemes, of ordering concepts in accordance with some principle of design: "analogical reconstruction," "homomorphic image," "epistemic correlation" or "axiomatic formalization." The conceptual schemes which most frequently incorporate one another's terms and relations are those which express some resemblance, correpondence, or consistency of formal structure. The notions of linear, cyclical, reciprocal, associative, and causal relationships are means of articulating such schemes.

4.3. The growth of knowledge and understanding is accomplished by attempting to place each conceptual scheme within the framework and perspective of some larger one. In certain cases, conceptual schemes are viewed through time as covering situations which move toward increasing similarity of form; toward common ends of adaptation and shared transactions. In other cases, conceptual schemes are viewed through time as covering situations which move toward increasing dissimilarity of form; toward opposing ends and conflicting transactions. Thus, most conceptual schemes require a wider framework within which their design may be incorporated. As a consequence, there is no complete, final, or totally consistent scheme.

Bibliography

Adams, Henry, *The Education of Henry Adams*, New York: Modern Library, 1931.

Barnes, Harry E. (ed.), *An Introduction to the History of Sociology*, Chicago: University of Chicago Press, 1948.

Bateson, Gregory, *Naven*, Cambridge: Cambridge University Press, 1936.

Becker, Howard, *Through Values to Social Interpretation*, Durham, N.C.: Duke University Press, 1950.

Becker, Howard, and Alvin Boskoff (eds.), *Modern Sociological Theory*, New York: Holt, Rinehart and Winston, 1957.

Black, Max (ed.), *The Social Theories of Talcott Parsons*, Englewood Cliffs, N. J.: Prentice-Hall, 1961.

Blanshard, Brand, *The Nature of Thought*, London: Allen and Unwin, 1940.

Brandt, Richard B., *Ethical Theory*, Englewood Cliffs, N. J.: Prentice-Hall, 1959.

Brinton, Crane, *Ideas and Men*, Englewood Cliffs, N. J.: Prentice-Hall, 1950.

Bunge, Mario, *Causality*, Cambridge: Harvard University Press, 1959.

Chisholm, Roderick, *Perceiving*, Ithaca, N.Y.: Cornell University Press, 1957.

Churchman, C. West, *Theory of Experimental Inference*, New York: Macmillan, 1948.

Creedy, F., *Human Nature Writ Large*, Chapel Hill: University of North Carolina Press, 1939.

Dewey, John, *The Quest for Certainty*, New York: Minton, Balch, 1929.

Durkheim, Emile, *The Rules of Sociological Method*, trans. Sarah A. Solovay and John H. Mueller, New York: Free Press, 1938.

Edwards, Paul, *The Logic of Moral Discourse*, New York: Free Press, 1955.

Fodor, Jerry A., and Jerrold J. Katz (eds.), *The Structure of Language*, Englewood Cliffs, N. J.: Prentice-Hall, 1964.

Frank, Phillip (ed.), *The Validation of Scientific Theories*, Boston: Beacon Press, 1955.

Feigl, H., and G. Maxwell (eds.), *Current Issues in the Philosophy of Science*, New York: Holt, Rinehart and Winston, 1961.

Goldenweiser, Alexander, *History, Psychology and Culture*, New York: Knopf, 1933.

Gould, Julius, and William L. Kolb (eds.), *A Dictionary of the Social Sciences*, New York: Macmillan, 1964.

Gouldner, Alvin W., *Enter Plato*, New York: Basic Books, 1965.

Gouldner, Alvin W., and S. M. Miller (eds.), *Applied Sociology: Opportunities and Problems*, New York: Macmillan, 1965.

Gottschalk, Louis (ed.), *Generalization in the writing of History*, A Report of the Committee on Historical Analysis of the Social Science Research Council, Chicago: University of Chicago Press, 1963.

Hanson, Norwood, *Patterns of Discovery*, Cambridge: Harvard University Press, 1958.

Hare, Robert M., *Freedom and Reason*, Oxford: Clarendon Press, 1963.

Hoijer, Harry (ed.), *Language in Culture*, Chicago: University of Chicago Press, 1954.

Hollander, E. P., and Raymond G. Hunt (eds.), *Current Perspectives in Social Psychology*, New York: Oxford University Press, 1963.

Horowitz, Irving L., *Philosophy, Science and the Sociology of Knowledge*, Springfield, Ill.: Charles C Thomas, 1961.

Horowitz, Irving L. (ed.), *The New Sociology, Essays in Social Science and Social Theory*, New York: Oxford University Press, 1964.

Kroeber, Alfred E., *Anthropology Today, An Encyclopedic Inventory*, Chicago: University of Chicago Press, 1953.

Ladd, John, *The Structure of a Moral Code*, Cambridge: Harvard University Press, 1957.

Lamont, Corliss, *Humanism as a Philosophy*, New York: Philosophical Library, 1957.

Lenzen, Victor, *Causality in Natural Science*, Springfield, Ill.: Charles C Thomas, 1959.

Lewis, Clarence I., *An Analysis of Knowledge and Valuation*, LaSalle, Ill.: Open Court Publishing Company, 1946.

Leys, Wayne, *Ethics for Policy Decisions*, Englewood Cliffs, N. J.: Prentice-Hall, 1952.

Lundberg, G. A., *Foundations of Sociology*, New York: Macmillan, 1939.

Lynd, Robert S., *Knowledge for What*, Princeton: Princeton University Press, 1946.

Madden, Edward H. (ed.), *The Structure of Scientific Thought*, Boston: Houghton Mifflin, 1960.

MacIver, R. M., *Social Causation*, Boston: Ginn, 1952.

Mannheim, Karl, *Man and Society in an Age of Reconstruction*, New York: Harcourt, Brace & World, 1940.

Martindale, Don, *The Nature and Types of Sociological Theory*, Boston: Houghton Mifflin, 1960.

Mehlberg, Henryk, *The Reach of Science*, Toronto: University of Toronto Press, 1958.

Merton, Robert K., *Social Theory and Social Structure*, Revised and Enlarged Edition. New York: Free Press, 1957.

Meyerhoff, Hans (ed.), *The Philosophy of History in Our Time*, New York: Doubleday, 1959.

Mills, C. Wright (ed.), *Images of Man*, New York: George Braziller, 1960.

Montague, William P., *The Ways of Knowing*, New York: Macmillan, 1925.

Muller, Herbert J., *The Uses of the Past*, New York: Oxford University Press, 1952.

Neurath, Otto, *et al.* (eds.), *International Encyclopedia of Unified Science*, Chicago: University of Chicago Press, 1955.

Niebuhr, Reinhold, *Faith and History*, New York: Scribner, 1949.

Popper, Karl, *The Logic of Scientific Discovery*, New York: Basic Books, 1959.

Quine, Willard V., *Word and Object*, New York: Wiley, 1960.

Rapoport, Anatol, *Science and the Goals of Man*, New York: Harper & Row, 1950.

Reichenbach, Hans, *The Rise of Scientific Philosophy*, Berkeley: University of California Press, 1951.

Richards, I. A., *Principles of Literary Criticism*, New York: Harcourt, Brace & World, 1961.

Russell, Bertrand, *Human Knowledge, Its Scope and Limits*, New York: Simon and Schuster, 1948.

Ryle, Gilbert, *The Concept of Mind*, New York: Barnes and Noble, 1949.

Scheffler, Israel, *Philosophy and Education*, Boston: Allyn and Bacon, 1958.

Simmel, Georg, *The Sociology of Georg Simmel*, translated and edited by K. H. Wolff, New York: Free Press, 1951.

Singer, Marcus, *Generalization in Ethics*, New York: Knopf, 1961.

Sorokin, Pitirim A., *Contemporary Sociological Theories*, New York: Harper & Row, 1928.

Taylor, Paul, *Normative Discourse*, Englewood Cliffs, N. J.: Prentice-Hall, 1961.

Teggart, Frederick, *Theory and Processes of History*, Berkeley: University of California Press, 1941.

Tönnies, Ferdinand, *Fundamental Concepts in Sociology*, translated and supplemented by C. P. Loomis, New York: American Book Company, 1950.

Toulmin, Stephen E., *An Examination of the Place of Reason in Ethics*, London: Cambridge University Press, 1950.

Toynbee, Arnold, *A Study of History*, abridged by D. C. Somerville, New York: Oxford University Press, 1945.

Weber, Max, *From Max Weber: Essays in Sociology*, translated and edited by H. H. Gerth and C. W. Mills, New York: Oxford University Press, 1946.

Williams, Robin M., Jr., *American Society*, New York: Knopf, 1960.

PART

II

Foundations of Theory

The metaphors of order:

PAUL MEADOWS *toward a taxonomy*

of organization theory

ROUTES TO THE METAPHORS OF ORDER

Chaos and cosmos: on the antiquity of the imagery of order

At bottom the problem of social organization is a function of the
problem of social order. Early cosmological accounts display the fact that
the universal human experience was confrontation and command of
chaos: the resulting order was thought to be a function of divinity: the
divine command of chaos is the source of cosmos. To this day in the
metaphysics of science we *discover* order, we do not *invent* it; we uncover
the orderliness of reality, its "connexity," in Whitehead's quaint phrase.
It is as though in the age-long ontological concerns of man cosmos has
been his destiny, chaos his evil genius; much of man's life has been a
dialogue between chaos and cosmos. And just as in the historic dialogues
cosmos triumphs over chaos, so in the sciences of the twentieth century
process triumphs over change, direction over motion. Thus, the very

nature of human experience created, or at least laid the foundations for, concern with the problem of social organization.

Organization is a function of the problem of order and orderliness; similarly, conceptualizations of social organization have been a function of the conceptualizations of the problem of order and orderliness. Very early in human experience order seems to have been a kind of inescapable and irretrievable empirical fact. The sun rises and sets; people are born, and they die; the seasons come and go; and there is the procession of the stars. The spatial patterning and temporality of man's experience established an imagery of order, forming a backdrop to the drama of cosmos rising out of chaos. In the slow incremental achievement of a substantial scientific stance with respect to the universe there had been built into man's semiotic of experience and into his traditional pieties the unquestionable assumption that this is an orderly universe. Before science and before philosophy, man was religious; and being religious, he put his trust and his prayerful hopes in what he felt to be the orderliness of the universe. In time he philosophized about this orderliness, fashioning great cosmological models to describe and explain this orderliness.

Thus, from the very beginning, organization theory has not escaped the tutelage, or possibly bondage, of analogy and therefore of metaphor. It is useful, therefore, to undertake this discussion with a quick excursion into the analogical character of organization theory as we find it in the cosmological setting of Greek theories of order, still powerful legacies in contemporary theory. Suppose we start, for example, with the notion, familiar today, that thought is patterned, that scientific and philosophical thought no less than mythological and folkic thought is shaped by implicit or explicit models—or forms, or patterns, or whatever the favorite word may be. This is indeed an old, a very old phenomenon. For example, Gomperz has shown that the early Greek philosophers did not throw off easily or completely the heavy mantles of analogy which so thoroughly dominated their mythological heritage. As Gomperz says: for them to explain a phenomenon means "to show that, even though at first sight it may appear very unfamiliar, yet, on closer scrutiny, it turns out not to be entirely unfamiliar, since it exhibits certain analogies with other phenomena familiar to us from common experience."[1] It is a fascinating thing in itself to trace and elaborate on the manner in which thought-patterns or models, or analogies, were selected by the early Greeks (and among contemporary writers, for that matter) from mythological imageries or from constructed imageries by means of which the less familiar has been explained by the more familiar. In an excellent study Ernest Topitsch has sorted out the basic types of models thus used

[1] H. Gomperz, "Problems and Methods of Early Greek Science," in *Philosophical Studies* (Boston, 1953), p. 76.

into the biological, the techno-morphic, and the socio-morphic.[2] His observations serve well at this point.

> Most of the basic concepts of Greek philosophy had originally a social or technical meaning. *Kosmos (mundus)* was the political and/or military order and organization but it had also the meaning of artistic beauty. *Nomos (lex)* was the custom and later the law, whereas *aitian (causa)* was changed from a concept of morality (guilt) into the main concept of the causal order. Not less important are the analogies taken from craftmanship and the arts. *Harmonia* meant originally the orderly adjustment of parts in a complex fabric, then the tuning of a musical instrument and finally the musical scale. In philosophy the word is used to denot the regularity, beauty, and justice of the universe. Substantially technomorphic are also both the Platonic idea and the Aristotelian entelechy. The idea, *eidos* and *morphe*, is the paradigm, the normative model of a thing. The realm of ideas contains the shapes of objects as their divine patterns or designs, to which they must conform in order to be perfect. Even more obvious is the use of analogies between certain natural events and purposeful human action in Aristotle. The living beings are conceived as products of superhuman craftmanship, which realizes "from within" pre-established forms in a given matter. The basic notions of potency and act are taken from human power and ability, which now remains latent and now becomes active (*ergon*), attaining its end (*entelechy*) only in its activity (*energeia*). Throughout technomorphic is also the Aristotelian concept of causality, the well-known theory of the four causes: *causa materialis, causa formalis, causa efficiens, causal finalis*. The underlying model is quite obvious. The working man has the aim (*finis*) to produce (*efficere*) an object of a preconceived and designed shape (*forma*) out of some matter (*materia*). This "artificialism" is still alive in the belief that the cause somehow "produces" the effect.

As elementary as these associations may appear, they are essential to our next theme, that the analogical mode of depicting and explaining organization precommits organization theory, and indeed theory in general, to a metaphysical orientation. This position has been stated very succintly by D. M. Emmett, who writes that "metaphysics starts from the articulation of relationships which are judged to be constitutive of an experience or experiences in a significant way. . . . A conceptual expression of such relationship is then extended analogically as a co-ordinating idea, in terms of what further ranges of experience may be interpreted; or it is used in making a judgment concerning the nature of 'reality.'"[3] Although metaphysical theories as coordinating analogies are different from scientific models which serve the same purpose,[4] both accomplish the same end: they become in Stephenson's perceptive phrase, "persuasive definitions."[5]

---

2 "Society, Technology and Philosophical Reasoning," *Philosophy of Science*, XXI (October, 1954), 275 ff.

3 D. M. Emmett, *Nature of Metaphysical Thinking* (London, 1945), p.v.

4 Cf. Emmett's description of the differences, *ibid.*, p. 215.

5 Cf. C. L. Stephenson, "Persuasive Definitions," *Mind*, XLVII (July, 1938), 331 ff. Writes Stephenson: "A 'persuasive definition' is one which gives a new conceptual meaning to a familiar word without substantially changing its emotive meaning, and which is used with the conscious or unconscious purpose of changing, by this means, the direction of people's interests."

Organization theory, then, may by virtue of its analogical matrix be seen as embedded in metaphysical theory, which performs for the theory of organization an informing, a shaping role. This relationship can be well observed in the major shifts in cosmological thinking as reported by R. G. Collingwood. There have been, he points out, three great periods of cosmological thinking, the Greek, the Renaissance, and the Modern. "Greek thinkers," he writes, "regarded the presence of mind in nature as the source of that regularity in the natural world whose presence made a science of nature possible. . . . Since the world of nature is a world not only of ceaseless motion and therefore alive, but also a world of orderly or regular motion, they accordingly said that the world of nature is not only alive but intelligent; not only a vast animal with a 'soul' or life of its own, but a rational animal with a 'mind' of its own."[6] The Renaissance view taking shape in the sixteenth and seventeenth centuries and antithetical to the Greek view, denied that, the world of nature, the world studied by physical science, is an organism asserting that it is devoid both of intelligence and life. The movements which it exhibits, and which the physicist investigates, are imposed upon it from without, and their regularity is due to "law of nature" likewise imposed from without. Both of these cosmological views are, it should be pointed out, analogical: The first sees the world as a macrocosm analogous to man himself as microcosm; the second sees the world as machine. Modern cosmology, Collingwood points out, owes something to both the Greek and Renaissance views; and like them it is based on an analogy, but a new analogy. Finding expression toward the end of the eighteenth century, this new view of the universe, writes Collingwood, is based "on the analogy between the processes of the natural world as studied by natural scientists and the vicissitudes of human affairs as studied by historians."[7]

The contemporary contrast between science as theoretical knowledge and history as empirical knowledge—between knowledge of natural structures and knowledge of particular events in space and time, between patterns of structure and patterns of historicity[8]—has become the focal point of severe and persisting clashes in the social sciences. The reduction of history to structure, often called historicism and often assailed as such,[9] represents basically the same analogical patterning and/or "strait-lacing" of events which has occurred in all formulations of organization theory from the beginning.

---

[6] R. G. Collingwood, *The Idea of Nature* (Oxford, 1945).

[7] *Ibid.*, p. 9.

[8] See the excellent study of this problem by Hugh Miller, *History and Science: A Study of the Relation of Historical and Theoretical Knowledge* (Berkeley, 1939).

[9] For example, cf. Karl Popper, *The Poverty of Historicism* (Boston, 1957); also W. Dray, *Laws and Explanation in History* (Oxford, 1957).

Some Greek legacies in organization theory

For that beginning we may turn, as so often in the history of thought, again to the Greeks. In that ancient setting this focal point of clash took the now familiar metaphysical form: namely, that the recognition of the presence, in Northrop's language, "of two extensive characteristics in the same universe"—i.e., that the physical is real and that it changes—"constitutes a problem."[10] Parmenides, who perceived this problem, held that these two characteristics can hold for the same universe only if nature is conceived as other than it appears to be. It is thus possible to distinguish between appearance and reality, to stipulate, in other words, a principle of being. The mathematical theory of nature appears at this point, replacing the thesis that the real is physical with the principle that the real is being and is rational.[11]

A third Greek legacy stems from the functional theory of nature, the work largely of Hippocrates of Cos, Empedocles, and Aristotle. The concept of the living organism as a mechanical system, the concept of birth, death, and structure of organic systems in terms of atomic constructs, these themes brought the theory of nature to the threshold of a third formulation, that reality is process. Confronting the phenomenal fact of organization in nature, Aristotle was led to the idea that "a living thing involves not only the stuff of which it is made, but the form which that stuff exhibits."[12] Both matter and form are causes. In the physical theory of nature, order is a function of the properties of matter. In the mathematical theory order is a function of relations. In the functional theory, both things and relations are causal. In the closing section of this discussion, on "Organization Theory and the Eschatons of Change," the forms and lineage of these intellectual legacies will be traced, particularly as they have found expression in primitivism, perfectionism, and evolutionism. At this point these legacies will be viewed in terms of the analogical matrix—the metaphoric character—of the theory of order.

This theme may be restated in terms of the Greek routes to an imagery of order. One route, as we have seen, held that order is inherent

---

10 F. S. C. Northrop, *Science and First Principles* (New York, 1931), p. 5.

11 Writes Northrop: "There are three consequences of the mathematical theory of nature which demands attention. The first is the primary causal importance which it gives to relations. . . . The second inevitable consequence. . . is epistemological in character. Plato stated it when he drew a distinction between the apparent world of sensation given in observation, and the real world of mathematical forms which is known only in reason. . . . The third consequence . . . is methodological in character. Since mathematical forms are not observed in nature and, as Plato said, are suggested by, but not contained in, the world of observation, it follows that one cannot proceed, as did the physical theory of nature, from the facts of observation to one's scientific principles by the necessary relation of formal implication. The facts merely suggest the mathematical forms; they do not imply or contain them. Hence, as Plato maintained, the fundamental scientific method in this theory is the method of hypothesis." *Ibid.*, pp. 15, 16.

12 *Ibid.*, p. 19.

and natural; it is "the way things are," as the phrase has it. Beyond the phenomenal lies the stable, essential, self-realizing autonomous and autocephalic noumenal; the idea-in-the-form. Equally persuasive, though vastly more disrupting in long transitional runs, was the argument that order is simply human habit, routine, convention, the pattern of the human observer's relation to the environmental complex, a pattern developed by human beings in time and through time, a space-and-time-binding custom. But since people have different as well as the same needs, since they have different conceptions of the same need, and since both conceptions and need change, the sophistic argument can become acutely uncomfortable, as it indeed did among the early Greeks. For when there are times which create powerful cravings for certitude, it is much easier, certainly much more reassuring, to find order in the nature of things, rather than in the uncertainties of highly unpredictable or variable or complex human reactions. Even today this sophistry prompts men to identify order as a function of the removal or reduction of uncertainty. Thus in current information and communication theory organization is identified as a function of uncertainty, and the problem of order is variously defined as a problem of the observer's membership in a particular environmental complex, of the observer's information about a given environmental complex, of his communication about an environmental complex, and of his control over it. For example, if the problem of order is regarded as one of information, then the establishment of order is held to be a function of the reduction of complexity, or of the formulation of probability statements about variability, or of the fuller adequacy of statements about events.

The Greeks fashioned two modes of building models of order: the *naturalistic* mode in which organization is a function of the way things are, and the *conventional* mode in which organization is a function of pattern-making experience. The first is a "fixed-relations" mode, in which essences and underlying structures are bindingly linked with traits of appearance in an established order. The second is experience- linked; it is a "variable-relations" mode which seeks to find in the probabilities and degrees of dependence, in repetitive sequences and in demonstrable co-variations, dependable organizations of reality. Stated incontemporary terminology and in greater comparative detail, the two modes of order are described in the following table.

Imageries of order and theories of organizations

Since organization theory is always rooted in the imagery of order, the development of theories of organization is a history of the metaphors of orderliness.

The oldest conceptualization of order, *hieratic* theory, faithfully reflects the ordered ranks of human beings themselves; it stipulates that order is a matter of hierarchy: There is a hierarchy of forms, of values, of authority—of reality. Obviously Aristotelian in source—though as a result of our developing cross-cultural perspective we may in time add some African and Asian cognate names—this theory images a total system

TABLE 1.   BASIC MODES OF BUILDING PATTERNS OF ORDER

Fixed-Relations Models: Focus on "Traits" (As in "Soft" Sciences)	Variable-Relations Models: Focus on "Variables" (As in the "Hard" Sciences)
A. Conceptual forms: classes, types, categories, maps	A. paradigms, equations, derivations
B. Reality orientation: external correspondence; iconic representation	B. internal coherence; symbolic representation.
C. Linguistic level: semantic (word-object); dependence on synechdoche	C. syntactic (word-word); dependence on symbol system and transformation rules
D. Pragmatic interest: didactic, illustrative, descriptive, representational	D. explanatory, predictive, interpretive, suggestive
E. Theoretical orientation: definitional definitive, codificational	E. postulational, exploratory, replicative
F. Major measure of validity: degree of "goodness of fit" with things, or with "structure" of things	F. degree of "goodness of fit" with primarily 1), accepted propositions and transformation rules and secondarily 2) with referential empirical system
G. Central logicizing activity: from *class* to event	G. from *system* to event
H. Historic tendency of major conceptual forms toward: congruence, closure, tradition	H. variance, openness, innovation, polymorphism

of reality moving toward, and being realized in, a final cause or end. Since the ultimate condition is indeed final, it is therefore more perfect. The imperfect present form—which Rudolf Bultmann characterizes as "the time-between" the "no longer" and the "not yet"[13]—is judged by

13 Cf. his *History and Eschatology: The Presence of Eternity* (Gifford Lectures, 1955), New York, 1957, Chap. IV.

its potential final perfection. This is not only a theory of order but of history, of orderliness-in-change. Reality is teleological; the end is contained in the beginning—in a closed-system, determinate process.

Another kind of imagery of order is *sequential*: One event, stage, or configuration uniformly or even typically follows another.[14] Both nature and culture exhibit a strain toward sequence, to paraphrase Sumner's famous dictum about the folkways. This sequential conception, historically always ambiguous at best, leaves many things unspecified. Are the sequences identical, invariant and dependent? Do they represent an unfolding entelechy—an homuncular pattern of orderliness— in change—or a functional emergence of one from the other? Are sequence patterns probability statements or structural statements about events? Historicisms of different varieties come up with answers which contrast sharply with the critical skepticisms of more jaundiced observers.

Configurational order conceptualization emphasizes that events typically occur together and belong together. There are concurrences in the universe as well as occurrences. The coexistential theme stresses familiar concurrences among events—markets, classes, institutions, situations, interactions. The theme is celebrated in such concepts as human nature, universal culture patterns, basic motivational structure, national character structure. Indeed, much of the descriptive task of the social sciences lies in the details and variety of coexistential order.

Covariant order invokes the imagery of variable relations models depicted above. Phrased in the more precise pattern of functional equations—it has at its command the rich language of mathematics—the imagery of invariant order holds: $X = f(Y)$, such that given a variation in Y there is variation in X; these may be given magnitudes so that precise prediction emerges. Closely allied is *probability* order, which postulates that an indeterminate reality can be reduced to calculations of occurrence and concurrence. A world of chance—even though an eventuated and eventful world—finds that in probability order the emotional liability "chance" becomes a powerful intellectual and technological asset; "probability" becomes the rich treasure of contemporary physical (and ultimately perhaps social) technology.

Finally, there is *syntactical* order, a linguistic imagery which evokes the rules of transformation of grammar, the syntax of language, as the basis not only for *symbolic* logic, with its codified transformation rules and procedures but also for *social* logic, as in parliamentary law, corporate finance, cost-accounting, game theory through which a social group functions and moves from one condition, form, phase to another. In this

---

[14] Cf. the recent exploration of this imagery of order in L. von Bertalanffy, *Modern Theories of Development* (New York, 1963).

metaphoric view of social reality "society" is seen as a complex, highly abstract syntax of social action whose transformation rules become codified in the grammar and rhetoric of institutions and of culture itself.

This brief excursion into the imageries of order was dictated by the conviction that many, if indeed not all, our theories of social organization are rooted in the fertile earth of historic metaphors of orderliness. Indeed, it may be argued that our theories of social organization are merely intellectualized and sophisticated efforts through conceptualization to render such imageries more precise, more formal and thus more certainly predictable.

Hieratic theories of social organization, beginning as ideologies of rank-ordered social existence and apologies for power, survive, for example, in current formal theories of public and private administration, despite contemporary embarrassment at the old-fashioned, interest-bound luggage which they carry along with them from the past. The task of the social scientist here is indeed herculean: how to mix hieratic order and functional analysis so as to produce a functional theory of organization. The always ingenious results are, not unsurprisingly, vulnerable to charges of inherent ideology, and they apparently cannot avoid the appearance or illusion of contrivance. The logical game here is clear: to utilize the currently popular (though besieged) rhetoric of functionalism in order to make negotiable and conventional what historically has seldom needed persuasive skills other than those of sacred tradition; and when that love has failed, the persuasive skills of sheer force have managed in the past to carry the day.

Marxist theory of social organization, based upon the theme of a natural and inevitable succession of social forms—social classes, social structures, political-economic systems—clearly embodies sequential imagery. Systematized by Aristotle, reported by Polybius, theologized by Joachim of Flora and by Vico, the conception of a necessary (and of course sufficient) succession of politico-economic forms moving toward a final goal-condition is, of course, one of the most authoritative, if controversial, theories of social organization today.

Configurational theories of social organization, typified in personality theory, psychiatry and abnormal psychology generally, have been revived in the social sciences, particularly anthropology, in the last three decades. The objective in this theorizing is the identification of "typical," "essential," "underlying," or "substratic" configuration of traits, themes, social habits and tendencies, value-orientations, dominant ontology. The "fixed-relations" models outlined above are being systematically explored in such studies. It requires little perception to note that the fondness for the concept "character structure" in culture and personality literature, to cite one example, suggests the prescientific and archaic character of much of this mode of theorizing. "Culture pattern," no less than national character structure, is not above censure on this score. Similarly, much of what we call the "war of the East and the West" is a "war," so to speak, between two configurational orders, vaguely but emotionally designated—after the manner of all dichotomous, two-valued and ethnocentric semantics—as "communism" versus "capitalism." Nineteenth century "characterology," it seems, though the butt of twentieth-century psychologists who scoff at its phrenological and other barnacles, has nonetheless vaulted into a position of monumental importance, mainly as a weapon in the ideological arsenal of the "cold war."

The more philosophical and mathematical imagery of covariance has sired a long line of organization theories: economic, geographic, biological, psychic, and sociological determinisms; and the end is not yet in sight. For an age which can engineer an *industrial* technology based on closed system theory has already demonstrated that it can engineer a similarly based *political* technology. Deterministic covariance is not fashionable among social scientists; but it is supported by some, who consider its primary and dependent variables the technological surrogates for early cosmological containments of chaos.

Having reviewed the basis of organization theory in the metaphors or imageries of order, it is now possible to switch to another perspective on the problem of organization theory, the level of conceptual organization in terms of which the problems of social organization are considered.

ORGANIZATION THEORY
AND THE GLOBAL TRADITION

The discussion of the analogical matrix of organization theory has sought to show that the nature of any theory depends heavily upon the perspective position of the observer. Indeed, theory may be defined as perspective organization of facts. Thus, one may withdraw a very great analytical distance from the grubby, empirical domain of the specific fact and develop what Merton has called a "global" perspective on social reality.

It is interesting, and very important, that in the history of social theory observers started with a kind of Olympian, long-view perspective on society as organization. The very choice of "society," a high-order, general abstraction, as the major focus of theory was significant in itself. Indeed, the great abstractions—"society," "mind," "mankind," "evolution," "process"—have been marched up'and down the mountains of historical, biological, physical, and psychological data. The theological traditions, looking at the universe *sub species eternitatis*, certainly reenforced this preference for the big-scale view. The first great theories of social organization were distant, detached, and cosmological. However, determined on a secular focus on the world, eighteenth- and nineteenth-century social theorists sought their explanatory models within the cosmos—for example, in the immanent processes of evolution or in the transcending but immanent processes of development (as in Hegelianism and Neo-Hegelianism). They wanted to explain the forms of reality through the structuralization of function, and many of them turned their inventive skills to the perfection of economic, political, social, cultural institutions and agencies which could and did provide increasingly complex structures for the emergent functions of a highly dynamic society.

But involvement in secularism was only one source of the development of a global perspective on social organization. As John Dewey pointed out in his classic volume during the 1920s, *Reconstruction in Philosophy*, great new perspective history has always emerged in periods of tremendous social, economic, and cultural change. Such change generates demanding and unsettling issues of order, public as well as private, personal as well as collective. This same point has often been made, for example, by Jewish scholars: The great phases or stages in the history of Judaism have been those periods when Jews, besieged from all sides, found it necessary and possible to develop a viable metamorphosis of the Jewish tradition. In other words, crisis in *culture* is the world-ground for crisis in *theory*! The emerging theory becomes a new map which not only pictures the whole scene but provides explanation of change and emergence. Thus, the first great theories of social organization stand as monumental pedagogical if not actual missionary efforts. They are also exercises in a secular homiletics and hermeneutics; and on occasion, as in the case of Comteanism, a polity, a litany, a liturgy, even a priesthood are devised to ensure that rhetoric bears fruit in social forms. The first sociologies were cosmologies: The part (man) is seen in terms of the whole (universe). This idealistic doctrine of continuity and essential identity, which views reality as organic unity, in which a part is part of all parts as well as of the whole, continues to this day in such various forms as culture-and-personality theory, national character theory, *Weltgeist* and *Volksgeist* theory, spirit of the system theory, universal dialectic process theory, and so forth.

It should be apparent that what we call "global" theory of social organization is really one which is intrasystem in character, or in fact systemic. The global theorist is explaining not merely one system but all systems. It is perhaps better to speak of it as "multiple system" theory, or a general systems theory. For it is of such scope and of such level of abstraction (in the semantic sense) and it has developed such comprehensive transformation rules (in the syntactic sense) that it moves with facility from one mode of theory construction to another.

Eighteenth-century rationalists and nineteenth-century romanticists found their bridge among systems in the recourse to a *universal substance* (a universal system-in-reality)—"God," "matter," "energy," and so forth. Later global theorists found their intersystem connexity in a *universal process*—"evolution," "progress," "entropy," and so on. Currently, global theory finds its intersystem connexity in a *universal dynamic*—"structure-function," "development," or "pattern variables." Thus, the earlier evocations of a peotic imagery of immanent or transcendent *tertium quid* have been pushed aside in favor of identifiable, measurable factors, co-varying, equilibrating, and integrating. At this level of abstractness the task of correspondence between intellectual model and empirical reality is rendered relatively simple: Reality has in fact been conceptually organized with expert internal consistency of parts and whole. Whether the ultimate terms of analysis are idealistic or materialistic, in global theory of organization the test of truth is not the familiar pragmatic one—"that which works"—but the truly intuitive one, "that which lurks" (beyond the phenomenological surfaces). Like all cosmological models, global theories of social organization stipulate the properties of the totality, such that any one thing exhibits all things; the properties of one instance of reality are comparable to the properties of all reality. If one knows the cosmos—the media of such grand-scale knowing have always varied, from sheer revelation to sheer lunacy—then one can predictably and reassuringly turn to any microsystem.

Organization theory universal process and universal substance

Few theorists working in the global tradition match Herbert Spencer, to whom we may turn at this point for illustration of intersystem connexity. For Spencer the problem of organization was not merely the fact of the unitary character of reality but the fact that it is organized in systems—biological, physical, psychological, social, cosmic systems. Since societies and all other forms of empirical social systems are very much alike, it is reasonable to adopt, as a model for understanding, the traits, tendencies, and variables of lower-level, even non-human systems. His heuristic model was the organism, which he used to explain the higher levels of reality. Assailed today as reductionism, this world view sees all levels of reality as interlaced by the same unifying properties, which in fact serve to describe the universe as a kinship system. Spencer sought to delineate and chart the metaphysical kinship structure of the universe, including man, especially man and his works. He identified process as the ultimate stuff of reality, though much of his vocabulary is shaped by the syntactical demands of one kind of process, evolution. Form is a function of process, and all forms are a function of the same process, or of its subvarieties.

Apparently aware of the fallacy of misplaced concreteness in his basic model, Spencer turned, in his examinations of the successive evolutionary structuralizations of function, to the "institutions" of human societies; he thus became one of the great institutional theorists of social organization. His institutional theory of social organization is oriented in terms of comparative study of systems, a study which holds that social systems, like all systems, evolve and must be studied in terms of the process of their evolution. Today we probably would prefer to say that social systems vary and like all systems they should be studied in terms of the process of their variation. The logical entailments of Spencer's institutional approach to organization theory include: (1) the conception that societies are definable, separate systems; (2) individuals as biopsychological creatures compose the system; (3) societies and individuals are organized into systems of behavior, a process occurring in and through institutions in conjunction with interactional processes internal and external to societies. Today we would probably say that organization occurs in and through culture and culture patterns. The "analogical ratio," as the medievalists would say, is clear—institutions : society = culture patterns : society.

Another kind of global theory stipulates not a universal process, as in the case of Spencer or Marx or Ward, but a universal substance as the matrix of organization. Substance views of organization antedate process views: The first cosmological and theological conceptualizations were substantial in character. "Time" occurred as a generational dimension (creation), as a moral dimension ("the Fall"), as a teleological dimension (the "millenium"). Time, in other words, is a turning point, a shifting of substance; it is a thing of crisis.

Substance theories of social organization have continued to be creatures of crisis. The source of the sense of crisis is multiple. Sometimes it emerges through the economic system, as in "the industrial revolution"; sometimes, in a political form, as in the overthrow of the "tyrants" in Plato's time; or as the result of the impact of scientific revolution. Here, indeed, are great grounds for important speculation about today. From generations of experience which we have had with theology, philosophy, psychology, one may say that a revolution in sociological theory of organization always seems to have come as the tail end of the procession of intellectual revolution. Theories of social organization arise out of major shifts in cultural and intellectual perspectives. Indeed, the very last thing man tries to rationalize is the new social environment in which he lives. His first intellectual considerations in a time of crisis center on his need to rationalize his new metaphysical world. A clear case in point is the historical emergence of the social science movement itself, which came only after the rationalists, the Encyclopedists and the romanticists had reworked a basic metaphysical theory for French society. Revolutionary French sociology came long after revolutionary French metaphysics, esthetics, epistemology, and ethics.[15]

The world of the nineteenth century was indeed a new world, its novelty sometimes described as industrial, sometimes as political, sometimes as urban, or as scientific, or as social. In what does the new society consist? Of what stuff is it? These were Saint-Simon's questions, and Sismondi's, and Proudhon's, and a host of other.[16] Tönnies described the universal stuff of this new social world in terms of Will—familistic as against contractual Will, Gemeinschaft und Gesellschaft. For Durkheim its nature lay in the shift in human sentiments, in the loss of ethnic (or in his words "mechanical") solidarity in favor of transinstitutional (or "organic") solidarity. Many social theorists, historically minded, seeking a magnificent romantic vista of continuity of peoples through time and in spite of crisis, found it in the Volksgeist, or in the traditions, or in the Kultur. Heralded by the pre-Hegelian romanticists, institutions became the substantial focus of organization theory. The new society developed its rationale in terms of its institutional system. Ironically, institutional theory, so central to the concerns of social science theory today, was an achievement not of the social scientists but of the nineteenth-century poets, folklorists, and Kultur theorists.

The institutional characterization of the substance of the new society of the nineteenth-century world understandably became a powerful conceptual tool for introducing a sense of order in the new historical age. There is ample reason for this fact. For the concept of institution embraces ideas of tradition, association, symbol, slogan, philosophy, and intellectual system. When one starts thinking institutionally, he is organizing a whole world of ideas and action. This is, for example, what Marx found in the concept and he obviously felt that if the concept was good for organizing a theory about history, it would be good for organizing a theory in history. Unlike Marx, who proposed to organize both in his time, most social scientists have been content with developing an institutional theory with some historical relevance, or at least some kind of historical proximity.

15 Compare, on this point, E. L. Tuveson, Millennium and Utopia: A Study in the Background of the Idea of Progress (Berkeley, 1949); and Ernst Cassirer, The Philosophy of the Enlightenment (Princeton, 1951).

16 Cf. the excellent anthology of these and later definitions edited by Irving L. Horowitz, The Anarchists (New York, 1964).

However, identifying the substance of the new society as institutional does not identify the matrix of that substance. The institutional theorists themselves came up with many different suggestions. One group—among which we include Ward, Sumner, Keller—traced their institutional answer to the biopsychological traits of members of the society. Thus, they found the substratic character of the new society of the nineteenth century in the biopsychological motivation pattern of human beings. "Need" is the passion that spins the plot. With perhaps less biological orientation, the need-motivational approach is still the chief intellectual interest of the culture-and-personality school of anthropologists as well as the value-orientation school of Parsonian sociologists. Another group of theorists have found the matrix of organization in the interactional system which members of a society establish. Thus, Simmel, Park, Burgess, Mead found the stuff of society in the fact that people have "impact value" for one another. Society is a giant manifold of fairly orderly, uniform, predictable patterns of interaction, some primary, some derivative. Some theorists, such as Gumplowicz, stress conflict and its resolution. Some—for example, Eric Fromm, Harry Stack Sullivan, A. H. Maslow, David McClelland—are interested in a hierarchy of interactional behaviors. The pessimistic school of Smithian economics, linking love of self and thrift, placing love of tomorrow against love of today, pain against pleasure, future against present pleasure, developed a hieratic theory of economic interactions. Some later economists had trouble with such hieratic notions; Keynes, for example, having fallen in love with ballet, evidently felt that just as man creates an infinite choreography of dance, why can he not create an infinite choreography of economic and political organization?

The preference for some kind of verticalized social organization theory pervades the interactional approach to institutional theory as it has other forms of social organization theory. Thus the Chicago sociologists selected competition as the basic interaction, thus explaining all forms of interaction as derivative from it. Marx, institutional theorist that he was, looked beyond the conflictive interaction of interest-bound groups, and found his morphogenic principle in the hierarchy and historical rotation of interest-bound groups in competition with one another for space and goods.

ORGANIZATION THEORY
AND THE ATOMISTIC MODELS

The dominant theories of social organization are still the global theories; the morphogenic principles are still formulated in terms of some variant of universal process, universal substance, universal dynamic. However, another strategy of interpretation of social organization is possible, one which rejects explanation in terms of variables operating outside the system (the *transcendental* model) as well as explanation in terms of all the variables operating within the system (the *immanent* model). The *atomistic* model seeks to interpret social organization in terms of some part or parts of the system selected as representative of the total system. This model characterizes both the theories of the middle range and those of limited empirical range.

What are the basic themes of the atomistic model? First, there is the theme that structure is a residuum, that the structuralization of function is a residual process. The structure that emerges with action is a situation emergent; it is a product of human action, whether joint or collective, similar or coincident action. This theme has many respectable and some venerable labels. Thus, in Smithian economics collective structures are minimal as well as residual: "private vices, public good." The residuum theme underlay the great communitarian movements of the nineteenth century, the Owenite, the Fourierist, the Icarian, and so forth. It is the primary theme of utilitarianism, which was as close to a general model of social organization theory as liberal political action has ever or is probably ever likely to come.

A second major theme characterizing the atomistic model views the human group as a collectivity of coacting individuals possessing certain biopsychological traits. It is a theme that may be summarized by such general terms as rationalism or voluntarism; it accents human beings as judgmental, decision-making, choice-declaring creatures. This theme finds its most graphic expression in the research design models of decision-making behavior, so popular in market and communication studies. A third characteristic theme in the social atomistic approach to organization theory appears in the attention currently paid to empirical bounded and bonded systems of action—factories, firms, offices, community councils, schools, houses of prostitution, military establishments, and so forth. The unit of study is no longer the "person" but systems of action. In this sense act theory has come to dominate the whole atomistic approach to social organization. Just as we have an act theory of personality (regarded as a system of behavior), as in the instance of George Herbert Mead and the symbolic interactionists, so we have an act theory of social organization, as in the case of Talcott Parsons (or the less prominent Florian Znaniecki or P. A. Sorokin or L. L. Bernard). Today our focus is on systems of action bounded and bonded by actors. These are studied as systems, in terms of the relationship of the whole to the parts (as in the case of Parsons), or the relationship of the part to the whole (as with Chester Barnard or Elton Mayo).

Conceptual frameworks of social atomistic theory

It is quite possible that the bulk of organization literature today falls within the general pattern of social atomistic theory. What conceptual frameworks have been provided by these ventures in organization theory? At least three may be noted.

First, there is what may be called the *teleological organic* framework, the oldest and most venerable of the group. The point here is simple: Once one starts talking about a system the functional relationship of parts to one another and to the whole, then one has invoked the imagery of the organism—the organismic metaphor of philosophical idealism with its major doctrine of internality of relations. The prevailing metaphysical position of contemporary organization theory can well be seen as some variant of this metaphor. When the organism serves as the master model, then, as Aristotelian logic long ago demonstrated, teleology becomes an essential dimension of theory. Comte initiated among social scientists the longtime immunity from teleological metaphysics; but today whether research centers on personality, or community, or decision-making, or information system science, social theory is unabashedly teleological. For example, integration of a system is generally considered a function of the overarching goals or purposes of the system. Purpose is either there initially, or develops interactionally, or, as in information science, it is built into the system. Occasionally there is awkward hesitancy over "goal" or "purpose"; instead, the term dominant or latent "function" is used.

Unquestionably, there are many teleological answers to the problem of the integration of systems, and there will probably be more. Concern with integration—whether conceptual or social, political or cultural—reflects the contemporary sense of crisis in culture, a sense of crisis stemming in part from a mood which equates specialization with fragmentation. The teleological shorthand or "condensation devices" of integration will continue to fascinate us, just as fresh and reputedly faithful maps of uncharted oceans and frontiers fascinated our ancestors. Teleological integration by consensus and consent-building—through consensus and consent-building—through conferences, labor-management negotiation, arbitration boards—held social scientists in its spell during the 1920s and 1930s. More recently, perhaps disillusioned by the slowness as well as by the limitedness of consensus, social scientists have turned to the possibilities of integration by coordination. One wonders about the rhetoric of motives which underlies this shift. Mary Follett argued decades ago that people who like power over people are also afraid of people, are magnetically drawn to increasingly verticalized hieratic structures of coordination. There is surely some merit in the thought. When we coordinate, the accent is on efficiency; when we build consensus, the emphasis is on effectiveness. How, then, can we achieve the best of all possible worlds with both effectiveness and efficiency? This is surely a major administrative problem of contemporary developed societies.

The second conceptual framework which we find among contemporary social atomistic approaches to organization theory is equilibrium theory. Though long known in economics and though biologists, physiologists, and psychiatrists have made giant strides with it, sociologists have only begun systematically to exploit it. Enormously descriptive and explanatory, equilibrium analysis does tend toward a built-in bias—the value judgment that equilibrium is better than disequilibrium, limited better than unlimited disequilibrium, controlled or managed better than uncontrolled equilibrium. It should be noted also parenthetically that the great global theories of organization, certainly the great revolutionary theories, were *disequilibrium* theories, and so are many current theories of deliberate development or managed change today.

The third major conceptual framework of social atomistic theorizing about organization is motivation theory. Ordinarily, motivation models represent attempts to explain the whole in terms of the traits or variables of the part. Motivation theory is probably one of the most bewildering wastelands of conceptual confusion in social science literature today. Yet, despite its inadequacy as a system of theory, the motivational approach, second only to equilibrium analysis, is possibly the most popular contemporary conceptualization of organization.

We may identify four motivational models of organization theory. The *technological* model, patterned after the machine, stipulates that the human being is rational, that his compliance with social values and norms occurs through rational behavior; conformity is rational. This is a familiar theme; its spokesmen form a line which starts, in modern literature, with Adam Smith and ends, temporarily, with the current president of the National Association of Manufacturers. The *consensual* model stresses that all human beings are endowed with sentiments. This sentimental model, a Rousseauan model, so to speak, underlines the human capacity for sensitivity, empathy, rapport; we live in a world of imagery which merges wish with fact, a world of sensitized concepts and emotionalized relationships. The dendrones of words are linked to the viscera of response; we are sentimental creatures. Compliance springs less from rationality than from sentiment, because feeling is more powerful for action than thinking. The *rhetorical* model explains order, uniformity, and compliance in a system as a product of persuasion. Man is a verbal creature, subject to verbal influences which play on both his reason and emotions. The problem of motivation, therefore, and thus the problem of organization, is fundamentally a communication problem.

The *learning* model, very popular among anthropologists, sociologists, and educators, holds that we learn our motives, that is, our wishes, values, needs, goals. Therefore, the dynamics of learning explains both the uniformities and the variations in organization behavior. A complication, however, lies in the fact that there are so many models of the learning process itself; until the dialogue or controversy among learning theorists is finished a reliable learning model of organization theory is not very likely.

ORGANIZATION THEORY
AND THE ESCHATONS OF CHANGE

It is common to hear the comment that any theory of organization is also a theory of change. But the converse is no less true! The concluding part of this discussion will review three great "eschatons" of change which, as metatheories, are part of our contemporary theories of social organization, just as they form a part of contemporary social behavior. An eschaton of change is a teleological portrayal of man and reality in terms of inherent "destiny" (*eschatos*). We may distinguish three cosmological eschatons, all derived from the great Greek intellectual legacies, the eschatons of primitivism, perfectionism, and evolutionism.

Primitivism: notes on the lineage and typology of an idea

In marked contrast with the Jews, there was among the Greeks before Hesiod only a vague sense of destiny; history was understood as a function of divine wills. With Hesiod there is a new perception, that of a general will. With Hesiod there is a new perception, that of a general trend or tendency: a degeneration from a golden age in the past. With Heraclitus there emerges another image of a universe, as "a rubbish heap scattered at random," an image which reflects the social revolution occurring in his own Ephesus. All things are in flux, in process; but it is process with pattern: "All events," he says, "proceed with the necessity of fate. . . . The sun will not outstep the measure of his path . . ."

Also growing up in a long period of turbulence—the 28-year-old Peloponnesian war ended when he was 24, and the end of war was followed by a reign of terror, "the rule of the thirty tyrants"—Plato discovered in his own disorganized world the clue to the inexorable pattern in the flux of things. Exclaimed Plato: "Seeing that everything swayed and shifted aimlessly, I felt giddy and desperate." His persuasive definition of history becomes a law of historical change: "All change is corruption or decay or regeneration." The latter phrase, "regeneration," is significant; the apparently inevitable decay can be broken by the moral will of man, an act of political will arresting all political change. The underlying and unchanging law of change is fully expressed in the Platonic theory of Forms: "all things are generated by participating in the Form, and they decay by losing the Form." "Any change whatever, except the change of an evil thing, is the greatest of all the treacherous dangers that can befall a thing. . . ."

Aristotle, who shared the Platonic conception of Form, thought of it as at the end of change, not at its beginning. Form is *in* the thing. Change, by revealing what is hidden in the undeveloped essence, can only make apparent the essence; the essence must unfold itself in change; potentiality through activity becomes existence. If one adds to this concept of finalism, the concept of immutability of species and the concept of continuity in reality—*plenum formarum*: there is no gap in creation—as well as the concept of gradation of increasing reality, one has the integrants of the Great Chain of Being.[17]

At what point, then, does excellence appear? Primitivism held that it occurred in the past. However, the primitivist answer is variable.

Following Lovejoy, we may distinguish two major types of primitivism: chronological and cultural.[18] The first phrases a philosophy of change which holds, regarding the time at which the most excellent condition of human life or of the world must be supposed to occur, that it may be either past, present or future. The key issue has to do with the nature of the time process: is it finite or infinite? 1. *Finitist* primitivism holds that history is a succession of events having a beginning at some more or less determinable time in the past. Some finitist primitivisms stipulate a beginning and end; others, beginning but no end. *Bilateral* finitist primitivisms include the concept of undulation (history is drama without plot; the thing which has been is the thing that shall be), the theories of decline (the notion of fall without subsequent decline, of progressive degeneration, of decline and future restoration); and lastly, theories of ascent through change (e.g., theories of continuous progress, of successive progress and decline). *Unilateral* finitist primitivisms, as we have seen, do not assume a future term of the process: beginning but no end. 2. *Infinitist* primitivisms, Lovejoy points out, are implausible in pure form, and usually appear in some compromise form, such as theories of world cycles, or theories of endless undulation. Chronological primitivism, in all of its forms, is homuncular, the essence unfolding itself, in a manner as depicted in the finitist of infinitist theories.

Cultural primitivism, in Lovejoy's language, "is the discontent of the civilized with civilization, or with some conspicuous and characteristic

17 A. O. Lovejoy, *The Great Chain of Being* (Baltimore, 1931).
18 Cf. *A Documentary History of Primitivism and Related Ideas* (Baltimore, 1935), vol. 1.

feature of it."[19] Often combined with some variety of chronological primitivism, it appears either in a pattern of "soft" primitivism, as portrayed in Golden Ages literature, or in a pattern of "hard" primitivism, as imaged in simple life literature, such as that concerning the American frontier.

Clearly, primitivism is not tied to the historical past. But it is oriented to a theory of unfolding essence, the primitive essence, whether past, present, or future. This primitive essence is the *eidos* of all golden ages, whether of Paradise Lost or of Utopian varieties. "Both types of thinking," observed J. O. Hertzler,[20] "register a protest against social conditions which are admittedly bad. The ideal states which they offer, even though they are reactionary or fantastic, criticize the existing, call attention pointedly to a host of shortcomings which cry for correction, and serve as criteria by which some defectiveness, abnormality, and perversion of existing institutions may be judged. Plato long since had grasped the thought that man is controlled not only by what he sees, but by what he imagines as desirable, when he expressed the opinion that if a man has once formed the image of an ideal state in which justice and happiness prevail, the ideal has not been conceived in vain."

Perfectionism: Aristotelian, Augustinian, Gnostic

Chronological primitivism asserted that there has been no progress in the past. However, as a theory of change it is compatible with both hopeful and despondent views about the future. Certainly it was antithetic to the idea of a *law* of progress. The idea of perfection in and through lawful change, which achieves a finalistic end, derives initially from Aristotelian essentialism, but in its own expression historically has taken several forms, which may be briefly classified as immanent and as transcendental: the *eidos* that progress is inherent in history versus the *eidos* that history is illusion, that progress (e.g., eschatalogical fulfillment) transcends history.

"If," said Aristotle, "a thing undergoes continuous change and there is a stage which is last, this stage is the end. . . ." "Last" is equated with "best." Change, then, is the realization of potentiality; it is fulfillment. "Nature," said Aristotle, "belongs to the same class as potentiality; for it is a principle of movement inherent in the thing itself." The essence of anything developing is identical with the purpose or end or final state toward what it develops.

Aristotle's essentialism involves several important implications for change theory. First: change, by disclosing what is hidden in the essence,

[19] *Ibid.*, p. 7.
[20] J. O. Hertzler, "On Golden Ages: Then and Now," *South Atlantic Quarterly*, *XXXIX* (July, 1940), 327.

can only make apparent the essence, the potentialities. Second: only if a state or person changes, and only by way of history, can we come to know anything about the essence of the person or state. Third: in order to become real or actual, the essence must unfold itself in change. Fourth: his essentialism assumes a closed system.[21] If perfection is conformity to essence, then the approximation of purpose, which is the meaning of perfection, is the key to the process. Approximation of purpose, the process of becoming, is the realization of an end which was also beginning. Destiny, which often suggests the presence of something outside the system, is the undeveloped essence, the unrealized *telos* of the system.

Pre-Socratic conceptions of nature moved successively through hylozoism, theisms, pantheism, to process.[22] Process in Aristotelian thinking is defined as unfolding of essence, of internal principle, of realization of *telos*. Since the subsequent use of Aristotelian essentialism was for many centuries identified with the Church, we may denote two kinds of perfectionisms in terms of Church leaders: Augustinian and Joachimitic perfectionism.

As Bock observes, much of the orientation of the seventeenth- and eighteenth-century versions of perfectionism derives from the preparation for them by way of the Augustinian rationalization of history. The Augustinian problem vis-à-vis history was a twofold ideological problem: (1) the contemporary view that the neglect of pagan worship and the adoption of Christianity were responsible for the disasters suffered by Rome; and (2) Aristotle's assertion of the eternal nature of the world. Augustine's resolution of this problem lay in his adaptation of Hebraic materials in a general discussion of process in history. Falling back on the concept of theocentric orderliness, on the concept of process as prior to the event (i.e., process = f(Plan), and utilizing Aristotelian Chain of Being doctrine, Augustinian perfectionism merged teleological process with fulfillment outside of history. It has since then been a favorite theme of numerous religious utopias—e.g., the chiliasm of the Anabaptists, the millenialisms of the nineteenth century[23]—and of all philosophies of a universal and transcendent sort.[24] The Augustinian eschaton temporalized the Great Chain of Being: the chain is a ladder up which higher forms ascended through time (which is conceived of in epochs), out of conditions represented by present lower forms. Theologically, "progress" is redemptive process.

Writing in the late twelfth century and echoing the then current

21 On this point, cf. Martin Foss, *The Idea of Perfection in the Western World* (Princeton, 1946).
22 Cf. K. E. Bock, *The Acceptance of Histories: Toward a Perspective for Social Science* (Berkeley, 1956).
23 Cf. Karl Mannheim, *Ideology and Utopia* (London, 1935), chap. 5.
24 Cf. Howard Becker, "Fields and Problems of Historical Sociology," in L. L. Bernard (ed.), *Fields and Methods of Sociology* (New York, 1934), pp. 18–34.

reversal of the passive mood about the world as well as responding to the pressure for a formula that would put together man's hope for salvation and his hope for a better earth, Joachim of Flora—Dante called him "the Calabrian abbot filled with the spirit of high prophecy"—formulated a trinitarian eschatology which, as Eric Voegelin has said, "created the aggregate of symbols which govern the self-interpretation of modern political society to this day."[25] These symbols, according to Voegelin, include the conception of history as a sequence of three ages, of which the third is the final Third Realm; the symbol of the leader—the paracletic figures of the *homines novi*, the Machiavellian *principles*; the symbol of the prophet of the new age to whom the course of history is an intelligible, meaningful whole; and the symbol of the brotherhood of autonomous persons. Paracletic immanentism becomes, in time, a wide spectrum which embraces humanism, enlightenment, progressivism, liberalism, positivism, Marxism. A counter-existential dream, it can be an instrument of reform, of revolution, or of utopian escape. Thus, as Voegelin observes: "The dynamics of gnostic immanentism moves along two lines. In the dimension of historical depth, gnosticism moves from the partial immanentization of the high Middle Ages to the radical immanentization of the present. And with every wave and revolutionary outburst it moves in the amplitude of the right and left."[26]

An eighteenth-century *philosophe*, Chastellux, put the matter in a generational setting and summarized it thus: "We have admired our ancestors less, but we have loved our contemporaries better, and have expected more of our descendants."[27]

Evolutionism: some continuities and varieties of an idea

In primitivism change is viewed as degeneration; in perfectionism it is seen as improvement; in both there is movement with direction. In what respects, then, does evolutionism differ?

Initially, evolution was also represented as change with direction. Thus, Aristotle regarded reality as the informing of otherwise formless matter, which, because of the stubborness of matter, took time.[28] Matter was thought of as continuous ("the serial universe") and as undergoing continuous change. A living organism, in the Aristotelian

[25] Eric Voegelin, *The New Science of Politics* (Chicago, 1952), p. 111.
[26] *Ibid.*, p. 176.
[27] Quoted by C. L. Becker, *The Heavenly City of 18th Century Philosophers* (New Haven, 1932), p. 129.
[28] F. S. C. Northrop, "Evolution in Its Relation to the Philosophy of Nature and the Philosophy of Culture," in S. Persons (ed.), *Evolutionary Thought in America* (New Haven, 1950), p. 44.

view, is a life history. Potentiality, through form-by-privation,[29] becomes actualized: herewith, thus, is understood the process of novelty, of emergence. In the Aristotelian view evolution is "the teleological process in time directed toward one and only one absolutely predetermined goal."[30]

It should be noted that in Aristotelian evolutionism "time is of the essence," literally: the Great Chain of Being is temporalized. But the temporal process is seen as the embodiment of the hierarchical order; time is the actualization of the formal order in otherwise unformed matter. The nineteenth-century concept of time as actualization, not as *given* and substantialized in a serial universe but as *ongoing*, created a revolutionary concept of evolution, but one without the single goal-directedness of the Aristotelian view.

The change can be seen in Darwin's "new view" of the classification of living forms. The appearance of novelty represented for him the introduction of time within the relatedness of the biological forms themselves.[31] Said Darwin: "A natural arrangement must be genealogical." Thus both actualization and origin of form are seen as temporal. Here, then, lies the source of Darwin's concept of the role of "descent"; specifically it lies in his doctrine of "the common parentage of allied forms." Novel species existed first as varieties, in time selected out gradually by natural processes. Concludes Northrop: "Upon the basis of biological data of the natural history type alone, Darwin is led to the same rejection of irreducible formal and final causes and to the same conception of natural design and adaptation having its basis in purely mechanical causes to which . . . Galilei and Newton were guided in their studies of the inorganic world."[32] Stated in different terms, with Darwin the Aristotelian preformation or encasement theory is replaced by an epigenetic theory which conceives of novelties and individualities as the products of an ongoing creative synthesis.[33]

---

[29] In the Aristotelian view, the quality which is sensed in a material substance is its positive form. The presence of a given positive form implies the potentiality of its opposite—"cold": "hot"; "wet": "dry." This is the basis of the doctrine of form-by-privation, which was Aristotle's answer to Parmenides' difficulty: "novelty" out of "nothing." Potentiality, through form-by-privation, can replace its opposite.

[30] Northrop, "Evolution in its Relation to the Philosophy of Nature," p. 52.

[31] The repudiation of Aristotelian evolutionism did not begin with Darwin. One finds it in Galilei and Newton, for example, for whom qualities are mere appearance. For general discussions, cf. Lovejoy, *Great Chain of Being, op. cit.*; Northrop, *ibid.*; also Collingwood, *op. cit.*

[32] Northrop, *ibid.*, p. 58.

[33] In a rather different vein the epigenetic thesis is developed by Henri Bergson in his *Creative Evolution* (New York, 1911). Embracing a vitalistic thesis, Bergson is concerned primarily with the theme that at the heart of things is the vital impulse (*l'élan vital*), life or consciousness, which expresses itself in an upward tendency or striving to increase individuality. Life is both dynamic and creative; the direction which it takes in its creation of the new is not predetermined; an element of chance is involved, the process essentially unpredictable. What was originally a single tendency, life, when it breaks up or divides, tries to preserve in the diversified and specialized forms everything which was present in the primitive tendency.

The repudiation of Aristotelian evolutionism involved a return to the Democritean and Platonic philosophy of science, to the distinction between nature as sensed and nature as scientized, to the doctrine of Universal Matrix which underlies all appearance and from which everything in existence is derived, to the doctrine of Natural Law as immanent in the very nature of things. The form which this view of evolution takes depends upon the kind of fundamental universal matrix which is assumed to be the basis of all reality. If it is thought to be of a mental or spiritual nature, the result is spiritual monism or Idealism; if it is matter, then Materialism. The former postulates distinct levels of reality arranged in descending steps from the most spiritual and dynamic to the least spiritual. The process productive of these distinct levels is explained in different ways. According to Neo-Platonism, each level of existence is creative of the one below; the process proceeds from the most perfect to the least perfect. The lower level depends upon the next higher level, and can only be explained in terms of the next higher level. The whole determines the part, not only its properties but its very being. To this category of downward emergence theory belong Bergson and the modern vitalists. Another mode of explaining the origin of different levels of reality is by the process of logical or dialectic deduction of the various levels from some all-inclusive idea or universal, such as the idea of Being. According to Leibnitz, who rejects inert substance entirely, there is no substance except the soul; matter is a sleeping soul. There are descending levels of reality, down to inorganic matter; there is no lower limit. In any group of lower and higher, the higher furnishes the control or soul of the whole. This concept has a close resemblance to the modern gradient theory in biology.

Contemporary evolutionism is largely the ancient concept of emergence. In Idealism, emergence proceeds downward, from spirit to matter; in Materialism, it proceeds upward from matter to mind. In its Aristotelian form, emergence stipulated a purposive principle, *entelechy*, *nisus*. In its non-Aristotelian form, emergence is understood in terms of temporal process without formal guidance. The process from Chaos to Cosmos is a matter of chance aggregation and novelty. In its classic mechanistic form, the concept of emergence gets along without the teleological principle; in its place is substituted the concept of Force. Classically, matter and force were conceived as distinct entities; matter was inert, force active; there was a corresponding dualism of mind and body as distinct entities. The second stage in the development of modern physical theory is represented by the concept of matter-in-motion (hylo-kinetics): force is a prime factor underlying all physical reality. The third stage expresses a doctrine of energetics: substance is reduced to energy, the primary principle of the universe.

The distinction which was made in the discussion of perfectionism between immanent and transcendent perfectionism finds a mild parallel in evolutionary theory. In the Comtean view, the evolution of culture is independent of nature, is transcendent; in the Spencerian view, culture and nature have the same evolutionary pattern. The difference between them lies in the dominant analogy. In the first, man's own self-consciousness, historical consciousness of his own corporate action, provides the model "The historical conception of scientifically knowable change or process," writes Collingwood,[34] "was applied, under the name of evolution, to the natural world." Structure is resolvable into function: actualization is the structuralization of function. There is development but without formal guidance.

Among the social sciences the Comtean concept of an evolutionary cultural process transcending nature has rather vigorously rejected identity with the concept of an evolutionary biological process. (Table 2 may be a helpful mode of comparison between these two concepts.)

TABLE 2.   BIOLOGICAL AND CULTURAL EVOLUTION: A TABLE OF CONTRASTS

Category	Biological	Cultural
I. Relation between forms	All forms genetically related; their development divergent; parallels superficial, uncommon	Forms genetically related; but parallels and historically independent sequences exist; divergences secondary
II. Complexity	Substitutive	Accumulative
III. Divergence	Change, convergent at times, occasionally parallel, ordinarily divergent	Change follows parallel trends
IV. Organizational levels and types	Developmental levels characterized by qualitatively distinctive patterns of organization. Types=f (particular genetic processes)	Concept of integrational levels. Types=f (successive stages, regardless of particular traditional structures)

At first enamoured with Spencerian unilinear conception of evolution, social theorists placed particular cultures in stages of a universal sequence: here belong Morgan, Tylor, Maine. The second variety of cultural evolutionism, influenced by biological evolutionism, sought to establish

[34] Collingwood, *op. cit.*, p. 12.

universal sequences in culture per se: here belong the writings of Childe and White.[35] The third, representing a kind of dialectical synthesis, may be called multilinear evolutionism. It seeks to find, not stages of a universal sequence, but parallel developments in different cultures, parallels having a limited occurrence. The thesis that significant regularities in culture change do occur; the search is for "if-then" associations.

There are many ways to epitomize the terrain covered in this discussion of these eschatons of change. One way, by no means exhaustive, simplifies the shift in change theory thus: from *telos* to chance; the contemporary task is to find in probability the sense of direction which formerly was found in purpose and essence. Bronowski's language illuminates this point.[36] "This is the revolutionary thought in modern science. It replaces the concept of the inevitable effect by that of the probable trend. Its technique is to separate so far as possible the steady trend from local fluctuations. The less the trend has been overlaid by fluctuations in the past, the greater is the confidence with which we look along the trend into the future. We are not isolating a cause. We are tracing a pattern of nature in its whole setting. We are aware of the uncertainties which that large, flexible setting induces in our pattern. But the world cannot be isolated from itself: the uncertainty is the world."

---

[35] The methodology here involved averaging all environments together in order to establish a constant factor; in this manner the peculiarities of habitat and contact were eliminated. Darwinian concepts were directly adapted: invention for variation; learning for heredity; cultural adjustment and choice for adaptation and selection. In place of the Darwinian "common parentage of allied forms" there is the basic similarity of universal, immanent, abstract social processes, e.g., urbanization, industrialization, bureaucratization, etc.

[36] J. Bronowski, *The Common Sense of Science* (Cambridge, 1953), pp. 86–87.

BILL HARRELL # Symbols, perception, and meaning

It matters little therefore to the pertinent knowledge of nature that the substance of things should remain recondite or unintelligible, if their movement and operation can be rightly determined on the plane of human perception. It matters little if their very existence is vouched for only by animal faith and presumption, so long as this faith posits existence where existence is, and this presumption expresses a prophetic preadaptation of animal instincts to the forces of the environment. The function of perception and natural science is, not to flatter the sense of omniscience in an absolute mind, but to dignify animal life by harmonizing it, in action and in thought, with its conditions.

GEO. SANTAYANA,
Skepticism and Animal Faith, p. 104.

The history of Western thought is characterized by a persistent and nagging dichotomy variously expressed as the ideal and the real, mind and matter, subjective and objective, the "inside" and the "outside." Even the conceptualization of the individual and society tends to take on the characteristics of this elemental distinction. Certainly a large part of the intellectual dialogue that has taken place since the pre-Socratic philosophers has concerned itself with this issue, hoping to resolve the problem either in favor of one of the conceptual poles or within a larger synthetic framework.

I

Kant is usually credited with the development and definition of the modern form of this controversy. For example, Plato and Aristotle both understood that perception was refractive and illusory and were, therefore, cautious in their assertions about the external world, but they still assumed that "things-in-themselves" could be known. Plato's recognition of this condition of inquiry led to his rejection of the empirical method but not the assumption of an external and knowable reality. From that time to the time of Kant, Western thinkers tended to work from the premise that the problem of knowledge was essentially the problem of integrating concepts and percepts or clearly describing and categorizing "things-in-themselves." Kant, of course, denied this assumption while also denying the skepticism of David Hume which promised to destroy all confidence in the possibility of scientific knowledge. While Hume undermined our confidence in the assumption of order, Kant attempted to return that confidence, though he was to place the locus of order in a different realm.

Hume culminates the skeptical trend, originated by Descarte's advocacy of systematic doubt, destroying the notion that the perceiver was a simple recording device of an orderly and real universe outside. Kant returned the concept of order, and the possibility of knowledge, by making it a characteristic of the recording device itself, of mind. Kant is also the author of the modern social science legacy which insists upon a distinction between what is scientifically knowable and what is not subject to scientific verification. The former involves the empirical, and its mode of inquiry is pure reason, while the latter refers to the world of morality which cannot entertain questions of fact and its mode of inquiry Kant calls practical reason.

Hegel denied Kant's distinction and insisted on the factual nature of the ideal, thus objectifying the ideal. History then, as ideas or culture and custom along a time dimension, becomes the proper object of scientific inquiry. While ideas are the engines of history, the independent variable, they are subject to limitation by the realm of external facts or external conditions. Therefore, "we have to take history as it is. We must proceed historically-empirically."[1] However, these external facts are not

---

[1] Quoted by Herbert Marcuse, *Reason and Revolution*, Beacon Press, 1960, p. 225. See also G. W. F. Hegel, *Philosophy of History*, H. G. Bohn, 1861, pp. 8–12.

meaningful in themselves; in Hegel's terms they have no self-evident potentiality or telic direction. This discovery is made possible only by the creative application of mind.

Marx adopted the dynamic framework of Hegel's historical philosophy but chose to reverse the priority of the dichotomous factors under consideration here: making the external conditions or material forces the independent variable and ideas the dependent variable. While this does not return thought to pre-Cartesian naive realism it does reassert the fundamental importance of external facts and relationships to scientific inquiry. Obviously, ideas are still relevant to the Marxian scheme of things since he saw "class consciousness" as a necessary condition of historical process. But unlike Hegel, who saw external realities as simply delimiting the number of historically successful ideations, Marx argued that these objective conditions played a fundamental role in the determination of the specific form and content of ideas or consciousness.

The ideas briefly outlined here are an important part of the historical background of modern sociological thought. They not only are key substantive intellectual contributions but also illustrate the general dialetical exchange which is characteristic of this controversy as it was developed in literally hundreds of theoretical works. The principal contribution of the modern theorist has been to replace the a priori categories of mind as formulated by Kant with historical or cultural content. This tendency suggests that we have followed the lead of Hegel, though as the teleological assumptions of his philosophy were abandoned in favor of less dynamic structural descriptions, the notion of a conditioning reality has also dropped away. It is interesting and appropriate that contemporary action theory is considered to be neo-Kantian rather than neo-Hegelian.

The mind as cultural and historical content moved toward its logical conclusion in German historical relativism with Max Weber's work being one of the better expressions of this theoretical disposition. Its most recent and influential form emerged from the anthropological literature as cultural relativism. Cultural relativism is a more diffuse current of thought but has undoubtedly had a fundamental impact on Western civilization comparable to the Copernican, Newtonian, or Darwinian revolutions. Whether the idea was recognized and expounded in formal social science treatises or intuitively grasped and expressed in artistic works, there is the almost immediate awareness that the assumption of order has been compromised. As the commitment to an external order is forsaken and the postulation of a priori categories of mind is relinquished the question of order becomes a subject of considerable concern. Quite obviously, if there is to be either a science of human behavior or human morality there must be an assumption of human order. The solution to this problem was, again, to raise the ideal to the level of a fact and thereby make culture and a datum subject, as such, to scientific analysis. As a factual order culture was conceived of as having patternment, but patternment created and defined by the culture itself and in the tradition of German historical sociology, it was assumed that each culture would define, order, and respond to its own peculiar laws. The systematic description of these events was the chosen task of post-Malinowskian functionalism.

American action theory is best understood in this context. Talcott Parsons, for example, begins with the assumption that internalized cultural content, values, attitudes, and modes of evaluation are the substance of mind and the source of human behavior. While he formally postulates other sources of behavior outside of mind such as biological need dispositions and social systems, they are theoretically stillborn since they are always dependent factors that take on meaning only in light of culturally derived orientations.

Another action theorist, George Herbert Mead, was impatient with theoretical frames of reference which made antecedent assumptions about the content of mind, and his principal work was devoted to the problem of just how mind came to have content. His rejection, however, of any notion of a determinant reality leaves one in doubt as to just how a mind comes to have the particular content that it does. The dichotomy of the "inside" and the "outside" is denied and the notion of experience becomes not only the data of social science but its theoretical content as well. As ingenious and important as his symbolic interactionism is, it would in the last analysis only satisfy a behaviorist.

When the action of sociology's subject matter is seen as emanating from the "inside" it, of course, calls into question the action and orientation of the scientific observer. The subjective bias of the observer becomes highly problematic and threatens Humeian disillusionment unless some objectifying criteria are found. The method of comparing cultures has hoped to overcome this epistemological burden but the question of contradiction between a methodology of comparison and a relativistic frame of reference is yet to be adequately explored. Whorf felt that his analysis of language and perception offered us a well-curbed path that would lead away from a very latent, and therefore difficult to perceive, source of ethnocentrism. His recommendation that all social scientists should learn a non-Indo-European language is well taken, but will this truly diminish ethnocentrism and, as the suggestion implies, increase objectivity; or will it simply multiply the number of ways in which the observer can be ethnocentric?

Let these problems rest for the moment, however, and let it be understood that a large segment of sociological analysis, from W. I. Thomas' "definition of the situation" to Parson's pattern variables, has sought the locus of human behavior "inside" or in mind. The development of this line of inquiry as a convincing frame of reference ultimately depended upon either the isolation or formulation of a mechanism by which the internalization of social values can be explained. Clearly this mechanism was found in language as principally developed in the work of G. H. Mead, with important contributions being made by Ernst Cassirer, Benjamin Whorf, Edward Sapir and others.

In sociology at least, both functionalist and non-functionalist seemed fairly well satisfied that many old and annoying problems had been laid to rest. Through the mechanism of symbolization the principle of emergence became a more plausible justification for sociology as a direct frame of reference, indirectly fulfilling the dreams of Durkheim and hopefully establishing the discipline as a science with its own "laws." The distressing issues generated by the controversy over "human nature" were shunted aside as complicating irrelevancies. Sociological issues are assumed to be resolvable by value identification, value categories and historical or contemporary descriptions of values in conflict.

This paper intends to approach the question of the relationship of values to behavior by examining the assumed mechanism of value internalization—language or symbol—and its role in perception and evaluation. In turn, this effort necessarily involves a critical analysis of the meaning of meaning.[2] We will turn first to a consideration of the Whorf-Sapir hypothesis.

II

Whorf

The Whorf-Sapir hypothesis indirectly complements both action and value theory. The proposition that the categories of experience and the relationship between these categories are determined by the categorical and relational properties of language include among these "properties,"

---

[2] The reader may feel some discomfort over the rather loose identification of the terms language, symbol, norm, value, culture, ideas, etc. However, in a very general sense these terms are synonymous. Clearly, symbol can have a larger meaning than value; their meanings are not necessarily coterminous. Though whether or not their meanings are coterminous is one of the major issues of this paper. What all of these concepts have in common is that they all customarily reside "inside" in the context of the traditional epistemological and behavioral issues concerned with the dichotomy of "inside" and "outside," subject and object, psyche and society, the ideal and the real, etc. Contemporary theories of action are centrally committed to the "inside" and depend either directly or indirectly upon the symbolic interpretation of human consciousness and meaning. The principle issue and argument developed in this paper requires no finer terminological distinction.

The definition of meaning used here is also unfortunately general, but is the best possible for this writer at this time. By meaning I mean, that which is in some sense determinant of human behavior. These "forces" may reside "inside," in the mind or symbol system of ego, or "outside," in the physical environment, thou (the plural, you, when organized being social structure), or in the biology of ego.

values. It helps account for and explain the stability of human behavior by providing the raw material for building normative systems as well as a mechanism which will account for the general and consistent definition of behavioral situations.

The nominalistic or extreme interpretation of the Whorf-Sapir hypothesis is usually associated with Whorf. Though undoubtedly his work was not intentionally or avowedly nominalistic, the nature of Whorf's methodological commitments tended to force the hypothesis into this frame of reference. When he says, "The *Why* of understanding may remain for a long time mysterious; but the *how* or logic of under-standing—its backgrounds of laws or regularities is discoverable,"[3] he clearly means that these laws are discoverable by linguistic analysis. However, there is some confusion as to just what linguistic analysis involves. When Whorf demonstrates the "patternment" aspect of language his analysis delimits possible sound combinations, but when he is concerned with the significance of "patternment" to thought, cognition, or mind he talks about grammar.[4] That is, Whorf's analysis is of sound patterns but his conclusions refer to meaning patterns, e.g., logic.

This is an understandable confusion commonly made by the advocates of language as meaning, but it involves a rather bothersome tautology. The fact that sound patterns and meaning patterns do exist and are both essential aspects of language does not mean that there is any necessary causal connection. The causal connection cannot be made without the previous assumption of connectedness. In somewhat more contemporary terms this suggests that the "patternment" discovered by descriptive linguistic analysis parallels and is determinant of the "patternment" discovered by logical and psycholinguistic analysis. This type of con-nection is at best highly problematical and as yet has never been empir-ically demonstrated. This confusion is compounded by the focus on grammar's role in language when considering language as a determinant of meaning. Grammar is not a determinant of meaning; it is meaning, it is logic in and of itself and cannot be explained in terms of sound patterns.

Furthermore, there is the tendency to shift from the argument that language *permits* logic to the position that language *is* logic or determines it. This, however, does not explain the logic or meaning itself and has the unfortunate consequence of tending to exclude the consideration of the dynamics of meaning derivation—clearly, an unnecessary chore if language is equated with meaning.

However, further discussion of these issues must wait until after the exploration of some of the problems of language and perception that are

[3] Benjamin Lee Whorf, *Language, Thought and Reality*, Wiley, 1956, p. 239.
[4] *Ibid.*, "Language, Mind and Reality," pp. 246–270. See also "Science and Linguistics," pp. 207–219.

ordinarily associated with Whorf. At this point it will appear that Whorf's position is stated too extremely and therefore a "straw man" is under construction. The intention, of course, is not to struggle with straw men but to state the problem as clearly as possible, a job which is sometimes facilitated in the beginning by the oversimplification of the issues. I am convinced that the principle difficulties of the Whorf hypothesis which can be clearly outlined against an extreme or over-simplified version, are applicable to the more sophisticated manifestations of these ideas in Whorf and other symbolic analysts such as Mead and Cassirer. These criticisms also have implications for action theory, whether of Parsonian or Meadian derivation.

Let us examine the Whorf hypothesis in the simplest context. The colors red and green are not given categories but must be learned as aspects of a language system, in this case English. As we know, other languages utilize not only different words for color but break up the spectrum in a different way. In the case of the red and green categories, we may assume that a father who already makes these categorical distinctions may play a game with his child, teaching him the distinction through the use of red and green blocks.

The question, of course, is whether the father teaches the distinction or merely the labels for the distinctive colors. What if the father was rather sinister and experimentally minded and taught the child that both the red and green blocks (as we label them) were "red." No doubt the child would refer to the block whether red or green as "red" but the crucial point here is, could he make a color distinction? He probably could and, in fact, doesn't the ability to make empirical distinctions presuppose the possibility of socialization? That is, we often remark that language permits generalization but rarely observe that the phenomena generalized must be generalizeable.

If the father teaches the child "red block" and "green block" and then shuffles them, the child obviously can sort them by color.[5] It also means that he can make the distinction without benefit of language, otherwise one has to assume that the word "red" was associated with each block (not with the sensation "red"). A reverse instance of this would be a situation in which our hypothetical father presents his, by now, confused child with 100 blocks, pure white and with the same dimensions—say 1″ x 1″ cubes. Now the father divides the blocks into piles of 50 each and labels one pile "red blocks" and the other "green blocks"—providing the child with categories to order his perception of these blocks. Again, he mixes the blocks and instructs the child to divide them into "red" and "green" piles. Can the child do it? Of course not, unless by some extra-

---

[5] For an interesting experiment which supports this point, see Z. M. Istomina, "Perception and Naming of Color in Early Childhood," *Soviet Psychology and Psychiatry*, Winter, 1963, pp. 37–45.

ordinary feat of visual dexterity and memorization he could associate the color label with *each* block in their original piles, and thereby re-sort them properly. This is a shell trick too complex for us to expect much success. Obviously, then, language categories *alone* do not make distinctions—they exist in reality, on the "outside."

The socialization of the child with respect to color depends upon his ability to make the real optic distinction between red and green and a socialization process which attempted to impose distinguishing categories by the introduction of different word labels for identical objects would clearly fail. Different names for identical twins does not mitigate the perceptual confusion.

The same logic holds as we move from one language system to another or one culture to another. We can come to make meaningful color statements in this new language, not only because we have learned the new words or sounds but because we share an optic ability and an external reality. The fact that the color spectrum may be sliced up differently in the two languages is very important, but it should not be emphasized to the point of denying the ability of most men to actually make the same kinds of empirical distinctions. Again, such an assumption makes the process of acculturation as well as socialization totally inexplicable.

Cassirer

Generally, the extreme commitment to linguistic relativism has given way to the position that languages vary in their efficiency in describing various aspects of reality, and in their focus; but that they actually screen out whole areas of perceptual possibilities in the empirical world is usually denied. However, it is quite common to reject the nominalist position with respect to phenomena which are unambiguously empirical

> Languages differ not so much as to what *can* be said in them, but rather as to what it is relatively easy to say. In this connection it is worthy of note that the history of Western logic and science, from Aristotle down, constitutes not so much the story of scholars hemmed in and misled by the nature of their specific languages as the story of a long and successful struggle against inherited linguistic limitations. From the time when science became observational and experimental this is easy to see: speech habits were revised to fit observed facts.

> The impact of inherited linguistic pattern on activities is, in general, least important in the most practical contexts, and *most important in such goings on as story telling, religion, and philosophizing which consists largely or exclusively of talking anyway*. Scientific discourse can be carried on in any language the speakers of which have become participants in the world of science, and other languages can become properly modified with little trouble; *some types of literature, on the other hand, are largely impervious* to translation.[6]

[6] Charles F. Hockett, "Chinese Versus English: An Exploration of the Whorfian Theses," in M. H. Fried, *Readings in Anthropology*, Crowell, vol. 1, p. 248, emphasis added.

while continuing to apply it to the non-empirical. For example, Hockett does this in the following statement:

While Hockett makes the distinction between "practical" activities and by implication non-practical or impractical activity, the meaning seems to be that the Whorfian principle is not generally valid when applied to empirical phenomena but quite plausible when applied to the non-empirical which is just "talking anyway," i.e., noise. Though somewhat cruder, this is a similar position to that of Cassirer and other advocates of the symbolic basis of meaning. For example:

> . . . what science *seeks* in phenomena is much more than similarity; it is order. . . . But all systems of classification are artificial. Nature as such only contains *individual* and *diversified* phenomena. If we subsume these phenomena under class concepts and general laws, we do not describe facts of nature. Every system is a work of art— a result of conscious creative activity.[7]

> . . . It (the word) is not simply a *flatus vocis*, a mere breath of air. Yet the decisive feature is not its physical but its logical character. Physically the work may be declared to be impotent, but logically it is elevated to a higher, indeed to the highest rank. The *Logos* becomes the principle of the universe and the first principle of human knowledge.[8]

These statements are rather importantly ambiguous. If Cassirer truly feels every system is a work of art, does science "seek" order or does it create order? Does it, in other words, create order, any order, or is science finitely limited to orderly alternatives? The same questions might be asked of Cassirer's discussion of form.

The source of this ambiguity is the failure to make the distinction between the symbol's importance to our ability to conceptualize order and its role in the actual determination of that condition. Obviously symbolization is a key factor in the conceptualization of order, at least at the very complex level achieved by man, but to say it permits the conceptualization of order is quite a different proposition from saying that it either determines order or is order itself. In the latter case meaning becomes associated entirely with the symbolic function and creates a similar problem to that discussed previously involving the socialization of the child regarding color distinctions. It assumes that the relationships or connections are completely supplied by the symbol system and are in no way a part of a perceivable reality. Again, we fail to ask the question is the phenomenon generalizeable or, in this instance, can we convincingly describe relationships between any unit and any other unit?

If we assume there are relatable and unrelatable units in reality we, of course, immediately undercut the premise of symbolic theory. However, this is the beauty of the symbolic premise and the source of its

---

[7] Ernst Cassirer, *An Essay on Man*, Yale University Press, 1944, p. 209, emphasis added. See also Cassirer, *Language and Myth*, Dover Publishers, 1946, pp. 7 ff.
[8] *Ibid.*, p. 111.

insight because on these terms it cannot be undercut. Man can and has related almost everything to almost everything else. This, unfortunately, is also what is wrong with this frame of reference. Since it permits any conception of unit among a cluster of items, it makes all meaning possible and consequently no meaning possible. If everything can be true, nothing can be false.

The major road out of this murky swamp is not a logical one but an empirical one. Assuming any meaning is possible, that any unity can be conceptualized, the question is, "While everything is symbolically possible, does everything actually occur?"

Symbolic unity will not satisfy the demands of a meaningful meaning. For example, Cassirer criticized Bergson's and Nietzsche's responsive theory of art which describes great art as emerging from the polar forces of orgiastic emotions and dream states or the Dionysian and Appolonian contrast. Cassirer says: ". . . Artistic inspiration is not intoxication, artistic imagination is not dream or hallucination. Every great work of art is characterized by a deep structural unity. We cannot account for this unity by reducing it to two different states which, like the dream state, and the state of intoxication, are entirely diffused and disorganized. We cannot integrate a structural whole out of *amorphous elements*."[9] Now, we may be able to account for the unity with symbolization but we cannot account for the meaning.[10]

Cassirer ignores the total context of Nietzsche's work, his fundamental concern and insight which is to a considerable degree the legacy of modern throught. Nietzsche would certainly agree that traditionally or historically form, unity, etc. were connected with what was understood to be meaning but these notions were made meaningful not because they described a unity but because the persons who described this unity *believed* in the suppositions underlying the construction of conceptual unity. Nietzsche, of course, says this belief is gone, and therefore, meaning died, along with God. But, again, language or symbolization does not solve the problem of meaning, in that it suggests to us *how* we construct form, but it tells us nothing of meaningful or meaningless form. That is, generally it provides no finite parameters for choices of form and therefore the choices are theoretically arbitrary. Arbitrary form is just as meaningless as "arbitrary sense data."

Of course, in one sense form may be considered to have meaning per se. There are a number of more or less systematic bodies of data and

9 *Ibid.*, pp. 162–163, emphasis added.

10 Cassirer seems to recognize this aspect of meaning in his discussion of "mythical thinking" but fails to reconcile it with his notion that meaning is essentially a symbolically derived unity. This problem seems to me to be consequence of his failure to adequately consider, or at least handle, the relation of the part to the whole, and what might be paradoxically called reductionistic element in the concept of emergence, both of which are discussed below. See Cassirer, *Language and Myth*, pp. 23–43 and *Substance and Function*, Dover Publications, 1953, chap. VI.

related hypotheses in the literature of sociology and psychology which suggest that conceptual frameworks which are open-ended may be generally unsatisfactory to man and there is, as a consequence, a pressure to find closure or unity. The suicidal response to normlessness as described by Durkheim is motivated by an anxiety born of an inability to tolerate non-closure and, therefore, doubt in the moral order. Riesman's "other-directed" personality type suggests a similar inclination and the "strain toward consistency" described by Sumner postulates a principle of closure as a factor in culture change. Festinger's notion of "cognitive dissonance" and Osgood's development of the "principle of congruity" are based on parallel assumptions and are supported by convincing evidence.

Each hypothesis in this handful of examples requires the act of symbolization as a necessary condition to the described phenomena but the behavior itself is not symbolically or culturally ascribed. To say that man moves toward closure, or desires closure, or "needs" closure characterizes a human trait and not internalized culture content. That is, if there is anything to this proposition, it is the fact that man gains satisfaction from the direct unmediated experience of the integration of symbolically mediated meanings. But even if we insist on the "need" for unity or closure we do not at the same time require that closure itself be the only requirement of satisfaction and meaningful response. There may well be other needs and other conditions of a biological, psychological, sociological or cultural nature which obviate certain types of closure and, thereby, delimit the possible number of social forms.

Finally, Cassirer's position involves one other major problem relevant to our discussion, namely the assumption of "amorphous elements" which suggests the Gestalt argument that the whole (in this case the symbolically derived unity) gives meaning to the parts, the parts having no meaning or character in and of themselves. While the Gestalt argument has been invaluable in pointing out the importance of the addition of meaning by the process of organization, the assumption that each element derives its meaning only from the whole leaves us with the logically unsatisfying alternative that the meaningful whole is made up of meaningless parts.[11] We can creditably accept the proposition that the whole is greater than the sum of the parts but not that the sum of an aggregate of zeroes is one. In fact, the contemporary use of the concept of emergence, when it is consciously used at all, is closer to the latter proposition than the former. The implications of this tendency are discussed below.

In this context a critical analysis of the following statement by Cassirer should help illuminate the position being argued here: "Each

---

[11] Floyd H. Allport, *Theories of Perception and the Concept of Structure*, Wiley, 1955, chap. 19, especially pp. 551–566.

partial experience is accordingly examined as to what it means for the total system; and this meaning determines its degree of objectivity. In the last analysis, we are not concerned with what a definite experience 'is,' but what it 'is worth'; i.e., with what function it has as a particular building stone in the structure of the whole."[12] The extension of this analogy would suggest that a building stone assumes objectivity only after the building is finished. As a *building* stone this is, of course, true but does not the stone *qua* stone delimit the possible manifestations of the structure? If it does, it does not simply receive meaning or definition from the building but it also *gives* definition to the building; a determinant quality that it had previous to the actual building or the conception of the building.

In making unity meaning and also the source of meaning of the part, Cassirer asserts that the source of meaning is meaning. There is some truth in this tautology in the sense that an event outside of a frame of reference may go unnoticed or seem irrelevant. But how can we argue that the event or thing is characterless while we must determine at the same time whether or not the event is relevant or irrelevant to the frame of reference? The frame of reference provides the criteria but only the event or thing can meet or fail to meet the criteria unless we admit the concept of criteria itself is totally absurd.

We can also find in the realm of animal experience meaningful responses to the environment without reference to a symbolically mediated unity. If we are willing to consider fear to be a meaningful response, we have evidence that birds,[13] chimpanzees,[14] and human children[15] give meaning to objects never previously seen and unrelated to any symbolic form. In more explicit social science terms they fear objects which are not culturally defined. And in turn, these objects and the direct experiencing of them, by humans at least, may well be the functional (in the Malinowskian sense) correlates of a culture trait embedded in a complex of interrelated cultural meanings.

The drift of this argument is that the whole, the unity, is not itself entirely the source of meaning whether or not the unity is supposed to be symbolically derived or otherwise. Each part has a shape, a character, even an organization which delimits the possibilities of relatedness to other parts. Furthermore, these parts not only have symbolic meaning

---

12 Cassirer, *Substance and Function*, p. 277.
13 A. Portmann, *Animals as Social Beings*, Viking, 1961, pp. 138–139.
14 H. F. Harlow, "Mice, Monkeys, Men and Motives," *Psychological Review*, Jan., 1953, pp. 23–32; D. O. Hebb, "On the Nature of Fear," *Psychological Review*, Sept., 1946, pp. 259–276.
15 C. W. Valentine, "The Innate Basis of Fear," *Journal of Genetic Psychology*, Sept., 1930, pp. 394–419. See also D. O. Hebb, "Drives and the Conceptual Nervous System," *Psychological Review*, July, 1955, pp. 243–254, N. E. Miller, "Learnable Drives and Rewards," in S. S. Stevens (ed.), *Handbook of Experimental Psychology*, Wiley, 1951, pp. 442–448.

but a *real* meaning. This meaning amounts to the fact that each part is empirically distinguishable from some other part. This suggests meaning as a *minimum* has three fundamentally different forms: (1) the meaning of the part as it is related to the whole; (2) the meaning of similarity or sameness; and (3) the meaning of difference or contrast. All of these formal elements of meaning can be considered to be understandable only in terms of symbolization and tend to be so considered by writers like Whorf and Cassirer. However, as I have suggested earlier, we have some difficulty in explaining socialization if we assume all meaning flows from language. We must not forget that the meaning of *symbol* is that it stands for something. While the cultural evidence suggests that man can give things and the relationship between things, almost any symbolic meaning, we are making the "standing for" aspect of symbols pointless—locating not only meaning but reality entirely "in" language. Once we reach this point we are at a loss to distinguish between language and noise.

III

Again let me illustrate, this time with the elephant-blind man parable so often used in arguing these matters.[16] To be sure, each blind man has a different perceptual experience but if we assume that language is in this parable represented by the blindness, and delimitation of experience by each blind man's one feel, we can readily see that his conception of elephant is incomplete. At the same time we can see that even this conception is clearly related to "elephantness" and would not have been possible if the referent had been some other animal, say a rabbit. Of course, the experience of the elephant leg may lead to a category which includes both elephants and tree trunks but it will not very likely lead to a category which includes rabbit legs and tree trunks.

To carry the analogy further, suppose our several blind men were not asked to describe the nature of an elephant but were each given a billiard ball to hold and describe. Certainly the response variation would be much narrower than the response to the elephant experiment and language would surely reflect this lack of variation. Whatever the languages of these races of blind men, the word for elephant would have meanings that are widely variable, but at the same time practically finite, while the world for billiard ball would have virtually the same meaning.

Perhaps the more difficult issue and also the more crucial one is the presence of relational characteristics "outside" which force our symbols, not only into terms of broad distinction but form as well. Indeed, Levy-

---

[16] S. S. Sargent and R. C. Williamson, *Social Psychology*, Ronald. 1958. The entire text of the John G. Saxe poem-parable is reproduced on pp. 5–6.

Strauss suggests that language itself is a tooling response to the fundamental problems of human *relationships*:

> We may now ask whether, in extending the concept of communication so as to
> make it include exogany and the rules flowing from the prohibition of incest, we may
> not, reciprocally, achieve insight into a problem that is still very obscure, that of the
> origin of language. For marriage regulation, in relation to language, represents a
> complex much more rough and archaic than the latter.
> But it is for this very reason that the position of women, as actually found in this
> system of communication between men that is made up of marriage regulations and
> kinship nomenclature, may afford us a workable image of the type of relationships
> that could have existed at a very early period in the development of language
> between human beings and their words. As in the case of women, the original
> impulse which compelled men to exchange words must be sought for in that split-
> representation which pertains to the symbolic function. For, since certain terms are
> simultaneously perceived as having a value both for the speaker and the listener, the
> only way to resolve this contradiction is in the exchange of complementary values,
> to which all social existence reduces itself.[17]

Thorpe in his discussion of Diamond's work on the origin of language
makes a similar point: "These studies indicate that language emerged out
of requests for assistance addressed by one person to another in those
small, local, seminomadic groups of primates out of which human society
seems to have developed. From this the author (Diamond) hazards a guess
as to the earliest meanings of these requests. He suggests that they were
requests for actions requiring the maximum of bodily effort, requests to
break, cut, smash, kill and destroy."[18]

These statements suggest that the very use and development of
language indicates an antecedent perception and evaluation of a relational
event or condition. While these antecedent events cannot be considered
to cause language, they can nevertheless be seen as a pressure toward its
development and that this development must be seen as a reflection of a
real condition which narrowed the range of probable occurrence of the
invention of language and, therefore, culture. When sociologists and
other social scientists make statements to the effect that "while nature
(human nature and physical environment) clearly circumscribes and
defines limits to the possibilities of human meanings, these limits are so
broad and flexible that for practical purposes they might just as well be
considered non-existent," they are dodging an important task to discern
in exactly what instances it is one or the other.

The generalized nature of human needs, drives, and conditions may
certainly be culturally expressed in numerous ways but it is a question
of real importance as to just what the latitude of variability is among these
expressions. Not to mention the possibility that specific and necessary

[17] Claude Levi-Strauss, "Language and the Analysis of Social Laws," *American Anthropologist*,
April–June, 1951, p. 160.
[18] William H. Thorpe, *Biology and the Nature of Man*, Oxford University Press, 1962, pp. 72–73.

social conditions (without cultural content) and characteristics of the physical environment may create problems which further delimit the range of variance.

An example of a possible "specific and necessary social condition" is the symbiotic relationship between the male, female, and offspring which in turn gives rise to important conflicts which must be resolved—the Oedipal situation for example. As Weston LaBarre has suggested, this condition may well be the reality which created the necessity for the invention of the incest taboo. This cultural event, the creation of the incest taboo, clearly depends upon the possibility of the symbol but in this instance the symbol did not create relationships per se but was responsible for the alteration of conflict-laden relationships without symbolic content to a symbolically qualified relationship with less or no conflict. The motivation to change must be considered as derivative of an immediate perception of a relationship between elements if we are to explain the change at all because the problem was between the component parts of the structure and not a characteristic of the isolated parts. Still the problem is not understandable without the recognition of the peculiar characteristics of each part.

The gibbon family has a similar problem but it is more directly handled. When the male child becomes competitive with the father for the sexual favors of his mother, the father simply banishes him from the nest. However, this encounter in no way threatens the life of the child or the survival of the species since the child is already biologically capable of an unprotected existence. This solution to the problem among homo sapiens would not have such a fortunate consequence because of the well-known dependency of the human child until quite late in life.

I am not prepared at this time to argue for the substantive validity of LaBarre's thesis but it does appear that it provides a useful illustration, along with the general philosophical framework developed by Freud, as to possible factors involved in the non-cultural delimitation of the expression of generalized biological drives. It also provides a general model of the processes and conditions characteristic of emergent phenomena. Obviously, the biological description of each of the relevant actors in this Oedipal drama is necessary, involving not only biological needs but biological conditions as well. There is a necessary symbiotic connection between these variables but this very exigency also creates a survival problem—sociality is necessary but it is also a threat. Clearly, there is no biological solution but there is a cultural one and apparently in this particular case the cultural solution reflects a response to pressures which are quite specifically and narrowly interpreted. Consequently, we find a cultural trait inexplicable without recognition of biological interdependence, and biological interdependence inexplicable without reference to the biological characteristics of the three participants. At the same time each of these three distinguishable conditions is not adequate to the explanation of the other two.

One might easily and usefully expand LeBarre's frame of reference by the assumption that man is basically self-centered. This may be considered a general condition of conflict capable of giving rise to culture under which the Oedipal conflict may be subsumed. That is, it seems likely that among the protohumans there were other areas of conflict within the protofamily which were necessary to resolve, morally, if the species were to survive and immediate human needs and pleasures were to be indulged. This would help explain strong family moral edits which do not seem to fit the Oedipal pattern as well as expand the theoretical necessity of strong moral controls beyond the family into a larger human group, society itself.

Social stratification is another universal cultural form which is of great interest to the sociologist and the exact meaning of this universal presence has been the focal point of a long and heated controversy. I have in mind, of course, the controversy surrounding Davis and Moore's functional theory of stratification.[19]

The principal error of the Davis-Moore formulation is its one-dimensionality. That is, their most important consideration is what is functional for society without due consideration of the functional needs of man. Individuals are relevant only in the sense that their survival and status needs are seen as energy sources for a social system which delimits their expression and attainment for its own purposes. However, it may well be that what is considered functional for the society is simply a reification of what is functional for the dominant class in society. In fact, Marx's concept of alienation goes even further, suggesting that institutions which promote the integration of capitalist society may fail in their satisfaction of the functional needs of men whether bourgeois or proletarian.

Clearly, the needs of a social system may not be those of man. Likewise, neither the social system as such, nor the dominant class within the social system, are the only source of need expressions or definitions. While the universality of social stratification may imply that there exists univeral need dispositions, it does not on the other hand necessarily follow that whatever need dispositions are involved in human behavior are universally met. Davis and Moore, of course, do not suggest this but they

[19] Kingsley Davis and Wilbert E. Moore, "Some Principles of Stratification," *American Sociological Review*, April, 1945, pp. 242–249.

do ignore the biological and psychological dimension of this problem because of their focus on the social system.[20]

Not only biological and psychological questions, but other sociological questions are raised if we recognize that along with the universality of social stratification is another, almost equally universal phenomenon, rebellion against the given system which yields few rewards or promise of rewards for those in the lower strata.[21] This rebellion is important to the consideration of social stratification regardless of its particular manifestation. It may take the form of migration or abandonment of the traditional social order as was the case in late medieval Europe where the serfs departed from the feudal lands to reside in the emerging towns and centers of commerce; or spontaneous and unorganized slave revolts in the antebellum South; as well as highly class-conscious political action which we associate with nineteenth-century labor revolts or the French Revolution. In fact, Moore suggests that in the developing world the prospect of industrialization may in many cases have "a greater appeal to women, young men, unprivileged and disaffected casts . . ."[22] The choices and actions which flow from this type of appreciation of the industrial process is surrounded by traditional social and cultural conditions but the *choices*, the actual decision to make the leap, cannot be considered determined by those conditions. Their explanation requires the consideration of variables located elsewhere, in psychology or biology —perhaps in human nature, because if we continue to define "mind," action orientations, and need dispositions, solely in terms of internalized culture content, there is absolutely no way of accounting for this type of statement of preference. In this case, a statement of preference is frequently in direct conflict with the values of the established society and assumed by some to be thoroughly internalized.

Again, this is not to insist upon the substantive validity of the above propositions with respect to the nature and origin of specific human

[20] To this point the principal underlying assumption of this essay has been hidden. Since it is now emerging, it should be made explicit. That is, I am not commited to an objective science for its own sake but an objective science informed by a critical philosophy which is in turn informed by the finding of objective science. In the last analysis, who gives a hang whether an institution is functional for society or not if it is not functional for all the men involved. Man is a social animal not for society's sake but for the animal's sake. I believe this is the sentiment which underlies the suggestion that we ask not only, "how and what do we know?" but also, "knowledge for what?"

[21] This tendency toward rebellion may not only flow from the absence of need-satisfying conditions but may reflect as well the experience of relatively greater amounts of social pressure and more or less arbitrary impositions. Simmel is instructive on this point: "In every hierarchy, a new pressure or imposition moves along the line of least resistance which, though not in its first stage, usually and eventually, runs in a descending direction. This is the tradegy of whoever is lowest in any social order. He not only has to suffer from the deprivations, efforts, and discriminations which, taken together, characterize his position: in addition, every new pressure on any point whatever in the superordinate layers is, if technically possible at all, transmitted downward and stops only at him." Kurt H. Wolff, ed., *The Sociology of Georg Simmel*, Free Press, 1950, pp. 236–237.

[22] Wilbert E. Moore, *Industrialization and Labor: Social Aspects of Economic Development*, Cornel University Press, 1951, p. 41.

institutions, but to recommend a particular type of approach to the study of society and human behavior—an approach which does not fall into a trap set by totally idealistic formulations. The following remarks by Herbert Marcuse, in reference to the neo-Freudians, are pertinent to this issue:

> Freud recognized the work of repression in the highest values of Western civilization which presuppose and perpetuate unfreedom and suffering. The Neo-Freudian schools promote the very same values as cure against unfreedom and suffering—as the triumph over repression. The intellectual feat is accomplished by expurgating the instinctual dynamic and reducing its part in the mental life. Thus purified, the psyche can again be redeemed by idealistic ethics and religion; and the pyschoanalytic theory of the mental apparatus can be written as a *philosophy of the soul*. In doing so, the revisionists have discarded those of Freud's psychological tools that are incompatible with the anachronistic revival of philosophical idealism—the very tools with which Freud uncovered the explosive instinctual *and* social roots of the personality.[23]

Certainly, ideas should be given their place in the scheme of things but not to the exclusion of objective societal, biological and environmental conditions. These objective variables are excluded when they are assumed to be almost infinitely malleable with a meaning totally derived from their definition as opposed to their being. These conditions may be directly expressed in or greatly limited by culture. At the same time, it should also be made clear that such an assertion does *not* make it necessary to assume culture is entirely the primary or secondary expression of drive states.

These problems parallel the problem encountered in the case of the perception of a billiard ball and the elephant. At one level of analysis all cultural and social universals must be considered to be perceptually analogous to the *reality* of the billiard ball. At another, and perhaps more meaningful level, the universality of the incest taboo is virtually invariant throughout all known culture. To otherwise account for this fact requires the assumption of either (1) historical "invention" in the original culture of man and subsequent cultural transmission, or (2) historical "invention" and transmission through culture contact. In the first case we have no way of explaining the persistence through time of this defined cultural trait in contrast to other relationships that have been "invented" and subsequently abandoned. And in the second case we have no way of explaining why this particular trait would have been universally accepted while others have not.[24]

[23] Herbert Marcuse, *Eros and Civilization*, Vintage Books, 1962, p. 219.

[24] Many aspects of this argument are similar to the argument developed by Goldenweiser in his very insightful discussion of the "limitation of possibilities and convergence" which is summarized as follows: "A limitation of possibilities checks variety. In relation to historical series of linked objects or features this means that wherever a wider range of variability in origins and developments coexists with a limitation of end results, there will be reduction in variability, decrease in dissimilarity, and increase in similarity or convergence." Alexander Goldenweiser, *History, Psychology, and Culture*, Knopf, 1933, pp. 45–46.

On the other hand, we can clearly see that culturally defined relationships are more analogous to the perceptual reality of the elephant—social stratification systems, for example. Here there is a more diffuse perceptual pressure and the possibilities of variance are immense. But even then, if we are to assume the possibility of meaningful moral systems, cosmologies and art, we cannot describe them as consisting "largely and exclusively of talking."

I V

This essay is written in the tradition of the concept of emergence, or at least in one aspect of that tradition, but contends that the concept has been misunderstood and consequently misused. Emergence has been applied more as an intellectual or professional strategy than a conceptual tool in that it has functioned to rationalize a more or less discrete realm of inquiry (society and culture) in terms of its own principles, laws and facts but has ignored the crucial implications of this concept. Sociologists have by and large ignored a central question implicit to the idea of emergence—the question of the determinant relation of one level of reality to another. This is not reductionism, but a central issue in emergent theory. Quite rightly, we have emphasized that one analytical level is not sufficient to the explanation of another, but at the same time we have forgotten that it is necessary.

The line of reasoning presented here admits, and in fact advocates, that symbols are necessary to the explanation of meaning but, on the other hand, they are not a sufficient condition of a meaningful meaning. Of equal importance is the recognition that immediate sensations are necessary but not a sufficient condition of meaning. A brief discussion of Mead's contribution to this line of inquiry may help clarify this matter.

Mead

Mead cogently argues that symbols permit meaning, but this is not enough.[25] "Perspective" without an assumed reality, without some "animal faith" in the more or less veridical relationship between the thing or the relationship between things and their meanings makes "taking the role of the other" a hollow, meaningless, memorization of noise. Symbolic interactionism means nothing if the symbol is confused with the word or the sound. The analysis of the interaction of value perspectives is only a concern with conceptual smoke and disembodied soul unless there is

---

[25] George Herbert Mead, *Philosophy of the Act*, University of Chicago Press, 1938, pt. II, especially chaps. VII, X, XI, XII. See also the "Fragments of Whitehead," sec. E, pp. 538–548.

something real. Why do people change their minds? What makes them admit they were in error? What makes them refuse to admit they were in error? What makes them right? How can we possibly explain or predict the synthesis of values in contradistinction to facile analysis of this synthesis after the fact?

Mead obviously postulates an external and relevant reality but, much like Cassirer, makes it conceptually irrelevant in the formulation of his epistemology. In the context of a discussion of the spacial interaction of the observer with a contact and visual field Mead makes the following observation: "It is in this situation that the individual as a physical object appears, and it is here that projection, so far as it takes place, has any reality in spatial experience. It implies a spatio-temporal world that is there and *cannot be used* to account for the world that is there."[26] The question, however, is not can we know this world, that is, the really real, but mustn't we assume we can know it and in more detail, if there is to be a viable activity known as the search for truth and knowledge.

Mead makes this assumption only at the broadest philosophical level— that is, the possibility of projection requires the assumption of a spatio-temporal world but denies the possibility of knowing any of its specific characteristics. Thus denying the possibility of knowing or *assuming* any determinant qualities in reality. This position parallels and complements the usual social science assumption about man's biological nature, assuming its general existence, but denying its inclusion in behavioral theory either on agnostic grounds or by assuming man's nature is almost infinitely malleable.

The denial of this and Mead's position may appear to be undignified intellectual grasping for straws to rationalize the continued pursuit of one's life goals but it is a dilemma not unlike that of Kant's vis-à-vis the impressive logic of Humeian skepticism. It is also what Santayana meant by "animal faith."

The plausibility of Mead's notion of perspective is undeniable—it rightfully holds the position of an epistemogical axiom. The idea of perspective is crucial to any theoretical approach to a reality of more than two dimensions—a reality which includes the third dimension of space, the fourth of time, and the fifth of social-psychological being. Obviously, we must walk around an object, so to speak, before we can know it and no doubt symbolization makes this possible. However, the conclusion that these symbolically rendered interactions must finally constitute knowledge leads to a familiar quandary; is knowledge *only* what we think it is, or socially speaking, is knowlege *only* a consensus derived from a synthesis of interacting experiences? Mead clearly thinks so, and

[26] *Ibid.*, p. 243, emphasis added.

this is most apparent in his discussion of universals as a universe of discourse: "A universe of discourse is simply a system of common or social meanings. The very universality and impersonality of thought and reason is from the behavioristic standpoint the result of the given individual taking the attitudes of others toward himself, and of his finally crystallizing all these particular attitudes into a single attitude or standpoint which may be called that of the 'generalized other.'"[27]

This orientation presents a number of problems. In the first place it assumes the necessity of "taking the role of the other" without really questioning whether the role will be assumed. That is, knowledge and understanding of a perspective does not mean it will be integrated into one's universe of discourse. Oddly enough, the tendency to see the inevitability of the integration of a perspective into a universe of discourse suggests that Mead makes an assumption closely akin to naive realism. The implication is that if we see an external event through the eyes of the other we will be conceptually and behaviorally determined by that event or condition.[28] Apparently, Mead's behaviorism is not as distinct a departure from positivism as is usually assumed. While the exposure to another perspective certainly alters the condition of consciousness in that we become aware of another's experience, it does not necessarily alter our own conceptual scheme with which we order the content of our own experience. Symbolic interactionism explains how the integration of various perspectives is possible; it does not account for the actual act of integration or non-integration of a perspective into one's own frame of reference.

Mead's schema also will not illuminate those instances where two or more isolated groups come to very similar cultural conclusions. There are certain areas of cultural consensus or universals which could not have possibly arisen from the interaction of all who share a frame of reference. Such a condition suggests the presence of universal problems and justifies going beyond Mead's behaviorism to speculation about the nature of nature—human and otherwise.

This form of speculation will very likely bear a certain resemblance to Hegel's dialectic which assumes a synthesis may be in error, thereby keeping alive the concept of reality. This reality-oriented frame of reference will hopefully lead beyond Hegel to the development of a set of

---

[27] George Herbert Mead, *Mind Self and Society*, University of Chicago Press, 1934, p. 90.

[28] This assumption parallels a similar oversight by Weber in his development of the concept of verstehen. The following remarks by Carl J. Friedrich are to the point: "This comprehending of other human beings from inside, as it were, undoubtedly constitutes an advantage of the studies concerned with man. But to this advantage corresponds a disadvantage not properly analyzed by Weber which results from the 'Missverstehen' or misunderstanding other human beings." "Some Observations on Weber's Analysis of Bureaucracy," in Robert K. Merton *et al.* (eds.), *Reader in Bureaucracy*, Free Press, 1952, p. 32.

human requirements which must be more or less met by cultural synthesis, forming the basis of a theory which promises to predict rather than merely describe. That is, we are led beyond Mead's "reality" as existential experience to the use of this experience to formulate specific underlying "laws and conditions." It may well be that we will not come to know the "things in themselves" but we will be led beyond common sense facts (Mead's experience and behavior) to educated guesses about things in themselves as the basis of a predictive science. Epistemologically this orientation will be close to that of Marx and Freud in the sense that it postulates an external and determinant reality which is at the same time the possible subject of misconception, error, false consciousness, or illusion *as well as* constructive cultural interpretation.

The difference is suggested by a comparison between Mead's and Freud's concept of self. Mead postulates, as the fundamental elements of self, the "I" and the "me"; the "me" being the "organized set of attitudes of others which one himself assumes" while "the 'I' is the response of the organism to the attitudes of the others."[29] But what is important here is that the "I" is always uncertain, "what that response will be he (the I) does not know and nobody else knows."[30] That is to say, the "I" can only be known after the fact.

It is a common practice to equate Mead's concept of "I" and "me" with Freud's id and superego but there is a fundamental and quite significant difference. The superego—"me" parallel will generally hold but the very essence of the concept of id (and libido) is its specific and real content. Its theoretical usefulness requires that it have this content, it is an independent variable which sets the human animal in motion in a particular way, with a specific teleology and the other structural variables (superego and ego) are understandable only as they relate to this force. Again, the question is not whether Freud's theoretical content was right or not, but whether his theoretical framework contained predictive potential. This is another way of saying was Freud's theory of personality development capable of being proven correct or incorrect? While recognizing the validity of many of the criticisms of Freud's theory, especially by the experimental psychologists, it is apparent that the scientific potential is still there. True enough, there are operational problems and, likewise, there is no doubt that Freud and psychoanalysts in general, are inclined to force the categories of the Freudian framework upon their data after the fact, but these are substantive and methodological imperfections rather than fundamental and insurmountable methodological errors. In the theory's favor, is the fact that its three major analytical

---

[29] Mead, *Mind, Self and Society*, p. 175.
[30] *Ibid.*, p. 175.

dimensions have an empirical content[31] and are related by a dynamic logic. The system is closed and the state of one analytical element is deductable from the state of the other two.

Mead's self concept on the other hand, boils down to internalized culture content with no way of knowing how it comes to reside there except through exposure. The use of this content, the "me," as the basis of prediction is inescapably tautological. The "I" by definition has no knowable determinant and becomes conceived as determinant only as a new experience which inevitably combines and becomes at one with the "me." This is not to deny the great legacy which Mead has left us but simply to recognize that Freud leaves us a legacy which provides the ultimate luxury of the possibility of proving him wrong while Mead does not.[32]

The meaning of "house" may require symbols to account for the integration of the sense perceptions of the four sides, but the perceptions cannot be indiscriminately related. The demonstration of error is not entirely a question of social pressure or persuasion but of lining up real things, events and relationships with symbolic renderings. The knowledge of relationships requires symbols but the fact that some relations are persistently described by man in time and space suggest that relations are not only symbolic events but real events as well.

Of course, the persistence of certain described relationships throughout human society may be accounted for by reference to limitations or categories of mind in the Kantian sense. This approach *can* provide intuitive confidence for universally perceived relationships but it presents serious problems in accounting for the various ranges of perceptual variance which has been illustrated with the elephant and billiard-ball events. Clearly an adequate theory of human behavior requires not only an explanation of universal traits, but variance and change as well— neither Kant's philosophically derived categories of mind nor Weber's cultural-psychological categories of orientation (i.e., values) are adequate to these theoretical needs.

V

We have suspected the dichotomies of the past enough, and while this suspicion has borne fruit, it is time that we return to a conceptual posture cognizant of problems of order and change; issues of non-rational behavior as well as issues of error. This involves a notion of interaction,

[31] The id is empirical in the strictly material sense, the superego in the normative sense, and the ego in the behavioral sense.

[32] Ironically, the neo-Freudians are probably closer to Mead than Freud in this matter. See Marcuse, *op. cit.*, "Epilogue," pp. 217–251.

which is, after all, only another term for experience, but an interaction not only between ideas or values but a determinate analysis of the interaction between discretely conceived elements and complexes of the ideal and the real.

This analysis requires that we go beyond experience, that is, go beyond our data, using experience to formulate the nature of the interacting variables. This certainly must be seen as an ideational process, but an ideational process which is not the end of learning but the beginning. When ideas are assumed to be general description of experienced realities and not merely another way of relating amorphous elements, the motivation is necessarily created to predict the consquences of these conditions, thereby testing the ideas. Conceived as such, the ideas can be wrong or right, a necessary precondition for scientific inquiry. Likewise, the ideational process that we call culture may or may not complement the conditions of reality and much of the dynamics of culture may well reflect the effort of man to accurately confront the conditions of his existence. Action theory simply leaves us holding the phenomenolistic bag, a bag which may on one occasion be full of variance and on another occasion, invariance; but in neither instance are we equipped to explain why it happens to be manifested in one way rather than another. Within the action frame of reference, the value theorist has attempted to use data in a manner which promises to yield scientific dividends but this promise is rarely realized. For example, a dynamic concept like value conflict is useful but it is still unable to handle the forces at work in situations where highly integrated value systems produce human misery and guilt while other human aggregates seem to live quite comfortably, oblivious to the contradictory values they hold, yielding little if any conflict or guilt.

The issue is not between the choice of a frame of reference which assumes that symbol systems determine the way in which we perceive reality or that perceived reality is the causal force behind the employment of symbols—both of these assumptions seem to be partially true. The question is when and under what conditions do percepts structure concepts and concepts structure percepts. This to be sure is a paraphrasing of an old philosophical saw but an old saw that contains an issue which social scientists have unfortunately tried to avoid rather than surmount.

Social Causation

Florence, philosophical thought... principal pillar and only of scientific thought...

The use

GEORGE A. THEODORSON *of causation*

in sociology

From the time of the emergence of modern science in the seventeenth century until the twentieth century the concept of causation seemed firmly established in scientific thought. The cause-effect schema provided a framework for ordering the vast array of facts uncovered in scientific investigations. Indeed a great deal of scientific investigation was concerned with a search for causes. Causation was conceived of as an invariable, temporal, and asymmetrical relationship between phenomena, in which the existence of one phenomenon in a given form inevitably leads to the existence of a second phenomenon.

However, even during this period the concept of causation was not unchallenged. David Hume declared that the events of nature are separate events with no necessary and inherent connection between them. He maintained that the causal link is imposed on nature by man's expectations.[1]

---

[1] David Hume, "An Enquiry Concerning Human Understanding," in *Enquires Concerning the Human Understanding and Concerning the Principles of Morals*, 2nd ed., Oxford: Clarendon Press, 1951, pp. 73–79.

However, philosophers such as Hume did not succeed in modifying the position of causation in scientific thought. It remained ". . . the great central pillar not only of scientific thought but of all thought."[2]

CAUSATION CHALLENGED

The crucial challenge to the concept of causation in scientific thought occurred with the advent of quantum physics early in this century. In quantum physics the principle of indeterminacy has replaced laws of deterministic causation. In his classic discussion of the revolutionary changes which have occurred in the theoretical structure of modern physics, Arthur Eddington has written: ". . . in primary physics, which knows nothing of time's arrow, there is no discrimination of cause and effect . . . Secondary physics can distinguish cause and effect but . . . it is indifferent as to whether or not strict causality prevails."[3] Putting the matter more strongly, Bertrand Russell has declared that causation is "a relic of a bygone age."[4]

The undermining of the principle of causation in the physical sciences was soon followed by an attack on the use of the concept of causation in the social sciences. An increasing number of social scientists sought to avoid the use of the term "cause" in their writings. What are the alternatives to the conception of causation in sociology? If the cause-effect schema is to be abandoned, it must be replaced by some other conceptual framework.

ALTERNATIVES TO CAUSATION

The two major theoretical orientations which emerged in sociology as alternatives to the conceptual framework of causation are strict empiricism and functionalism. Neither of these has proved to be a satisfactory substitute for causation. We shall examine the problems of each in turn.

Strict empiricism seeks to avoid the problem of causation by emphasizing statistical relationships between variables, and by speaking of these relationships as correlations or associations rather than as causes and effects. The term contingency is substituted for the term causation.[5] Moreover, the strict empiricist denies the need for or scientific value of "theoretical abstractions" such as causation. He claims no need, therefore,

---

[2] W. Macneile Dixon, *The Human Situation*, London: Penguin Books, 1958, p. 349.
[3] Sir Arthur Eddington, *The Nature of the Physical World*, London: Collins, 1928, p. 241.
[4] Bertrand Russell, "On the Notion of Cause," in *Mysticism and Logic and Other Essays*, London: Longmans, Green, 1918, p. 180.
[5] George A. Lundberg, *Social Research*, New York: Longmans, Green, 1942, p. 73.

for any other conceptual model to replace that of causation. Instead he concentrates on describing the observable facts of social life. With increasingly refined measurement devices and careful sampling techniques he seeks objectively to uncover the interrelationships of the real world. It might seem that the empiricist has with one blow cut through the entanglements of the Gordian knot of causation. Unfortunately, the solution to the problem is not that simple, and strict empiricism raises more questions than it answers.

First of all, it is impossible for the empiricist to eliminate a theoretical orientation from his investigations. All scientific investigation involves theoretical assumptions, and when these assumptions are not explicit they are always implicit.[6] The conclusions of the scientist never simply mirror the empirical world. The investigator's theoretical orientation enters into his research at every point, influencing the selection of the problem he will investigate, his formulation of the problem, his choice of methodology, and the interpretation of his findings. Strict empiricism, therefore, has not eliminated abstract theoretical conceptualizations, but rather has made these conceptualizations implicit rather than explicit, assumed rather than stated.

We may ask then, what is the implicit theoretical framework of most current empiricism? The answer is that while ambiguous, it is basically causative. The terms independent variable and dependent variable in most usage certainly imply a cause and effect relationship. As Blalock has noted, "Mathematically we may mean by dependent variable whatever variable appears on the left-hand side of the equation. But, in terms of the real world, we usually mean by dependent variable a factor which we take to be caused by some combination of other variables, which we refer to as 'independent.'"[7] The use of such terms as "contingent upon," "dependent upon," and "asymmetrical relationship between" has obscured but has not eliminated the assumption of causation.

An implicit causative theoretical framework is far less satisfactory than an explicit causative model. For one thing, implicit assumptions do not provide systematic guidelines for the selection of theoretically significant problems for empirical investigation. Considerable dissatisfaction has been expressed with the manner in which problems are selected for investigation in much of current sociological research. Blumer speaks of the chaotic way in which variables are selected for analysis.[8]

[6] For a discussion of this see Theodore Abel, "The Present Status of Social Theory," *American Sociological Review*, April, 1952, pp. 159–160; and Bernard Barber, "Structural-Functional Analysis: Some Problems and Misunderstandings," *American Sociological Review*, April, 1956, p. 131.

[7] Hubert M. Blalock, Jr., "Further Observations on Asymmetric Causal Models," *American Sociological Review*, August, 1962, p. 543.

[8] Herbert Blumer, "Sociological Analysis and the 'Variable,'" *American Sociological Review*, December, 1956, pp. 683–684.

Becker wrote of "measurement faddism" in American sociology, in which problems are selected for study not because of their importance but because they readily lend themselves to analysis with currently popular tools of measurement.[9] Znaniecki has complained of the narrowness of most current investigations, and the ignoring of the multiplicity and complexity of social phenomena.[10] Bierstedt has asked, "Is sociology to be a niggling business, doing the easy thing because it is accurate, and avoiding the difficult thing because it is imprecise ?"[11] These and many other critics have expressed dissatisfaction with the manner in which problems are selected for investigation in much of current sociology. Without an explicit theoretical framework there is no consistent basis on which to select important problems for investigation, and the basis for selection then tends to become what readily lends itself to a particular method of investigation. The attempt, then, to replace the conceptual framework of causation with pure empiricism has led to the mushrooming of numerous studies which attempt to be methodologically rigorous but are of questionable significance.

Moreover, the extent to which these studies are even methodologically rigorous is open to question. It is very questionable whether methodological rigor is really possible without an explicit theoretical framework. When, for example, a particular measurement technique is selected for use simply because it is most likely to yield "statistically significant" results, the degree of rigor involved is dubious. Furthermore, simple observation of the "real" world does not automatically distinguish the independent from the dependent variable. Neither do most statistical devices make this distinction. Nearly all common statistical tests of correlation or association measure symmetrical relationships.[12] In the end the researcher must rely on "theory, knowledge, or even intuition" to distinguish between the independent and dependent variable.[13] When the causative assumptions upon which the decision is based are implicit rather than explicit, they are not readily susceptible to logical, systematic analysis.

Finally, it should be noted that a great many of the researchers involved in investigations that might be classified as empiricist in orientation are not ideological empiricists, but simply practicing empiricists. They

[9] Howard Becker, "Vitalizing Sociological Theory," *American Sociological Review*, August, 1954, pp. 377–388.

[10] Florian Znaniecki, "Basic Problems of Contemporary Sociology," *American Sociological Review*, October, 1954, p. 519.

[11] Robert Bierstedt, "Sociology and Humane Learning," *American Sociological Review*, February, 1960, p. 5.

[12] Even those measures of association which are considered asymmetric do not relieve the investigator of the necessity of deciding which is the independent and which is the dependent variable.

[13] Kenneth Polk, "A Note on Asymmetric Causal Models," *American Sociological Review*, August, 1962, p. 541.

tend to be non-theoretical rather than anti-theoretical. If anything, this increases their tendency to accept implicit theoretical assumptions, which are for the most part primarily causative in nature.

It is apparent, then, that strict empiricism has not provided a real alternative to causation.

Functionalism

The second major alternative to the conceptual model of causation in sociology is functionalism or its equivalent structural-functionalism. Not all functionalists are opposed to causation,[14] but on the whole functionalism has represented another attempt to avoid causation, substituting instead such concepts as function and dysfunction, system equilibrium, balance, etc. Recently functionalism has come under considerable criticism.

One major criticism is that functionalists commonly confuse function and cause.[15] Functionalism has experienced somewhat the same problem as strict empiricism in its attempt to avoid the question of causation. Many functionalists, while presumably not involved in the search for causes, tend in fact to treat functions as causes. This they do by identifying the consequences of a behavior pattern with its cause.[16] Recognizing this confusion, there has been a growing emphasis among the functionalists themselves on explicitly differentiating functional and causal analysis.[17]

A second criticism of functionalism is that a great deal of functional analysis hinges upon the false assumption of system integration.[18] The assumption of the necessary integration of a social system is in fact an attempt to give functional explanations a causal quality. If a social system necessarily tends toward integration and equilibrium, then a change in one part of the system necessarily leads to a balancing change in another part of the system. The result is a modified type of causation which is an automatic balancing of pressures and forces. In fact, however, social systems do not necessarily constantly tend toward integration and equilibrium. Social systems may exist for long periods of time with

[14] See Kingsley Davis, "The Myth of Functional Analysis as a Special Method in Sociology and Anthropology," *American Sociological Review*, December, 1959, pp. 767–768.

[15] See Harry C. Bredemeier, "The Methodology of Functionalism," *American Sociological Review*, April, 1955, pp. 173–180; and Ronald Philip Dore, "Function and Cause," *American Sociological Review*, December, 1961, pp. 843–853.

[16] Bredemeier, *op. cit.*, p. 173.

[17] Charles P. Loomis and Zona K. Loomis, *Modern Social Theories*, Princeton: Van Nostrand, 1963, p. 614.

[18] For a statement of the principle of system integration see Talcott Parsons, Robert F. Bales, and Edward A. Shils, *Working Papers in the Theory of Action*, New York: Free Press, 1953, p. 103. For a discussion of this view of social systems see Barber, *op. cit.*, p. 130. For criticisms of the assumption of system integration see Dore, *op. cit.*, pp. 845–846; and Francesca M. Cancian, "Reply to Stinchcombe," *American Sociological Review*, December, 1961, p. 931.

considerable disintegration and disequilibrium. Here can be seen the inadequacy of the mechanical or even the organic model when applied to social phenomena. Human reactions involve a conscious element not found on the mechanical or organic level. Individuals and groups may choose to suffer in order to preserve certain valued patterns of behavior rather than make an integrative and "functional" adjustment. Individuals may maintain conflicting and contradictory roles, perhaps thereby reducing their level of efficiency, without ever becoming either psychotic or personally integrated. Apparently it is the causal logic of the functionalists which leads them to see a constant tendency toward the integration of society and to emphasize the elements of cooperation, organization, and adjustment. Karl Marx, with a different causal logic, in viewing the society of his day, saw a constant tendency toward disintegration, and emphasized the elements of conflict, disorganization, and maladjustment. Of course it is possible to make the functional assumption of integration relatively valid by removing all time limits. Given *enough* time, perhaps several hundred years, a malintegrated aspect of a system would probably tend to become integrated. However, by that time another aspect of the system might be in disequilibrium. The significant point is that at any given period of time there is no necessary tendency toward the integration of a social system.

The fallacies in the functional assumption of necessary integration including the tendency to confuse function with cause may be illustrated by the functional view of social stratification. In the usual functional analysis of social stratification the system of differential rewards is explained by the scarcity of talent, the differential degress of contribution to society of different roles, and the necessity of motivating individuals to strive for roles requiring greater skill and training.[19] Often the logic becomes causal. Because society must motivate individuals to fill more socially valuable roles requiring greater talent and training, a system of differential rewards develops. The implication follows that those in-

---

[19] See Kingsley Davis and Wilbert E. Moore, "Some Principles of Stratification," *American Sociological Review*, April, 1945, pp. 242–249; Kingsley Davis, *Human Society*, New York: Macmillan, 1949, pp. 364–389; Kingsley Davis, "Reply," and Wilbert E. Moore, "Comment," *American Sociological Review*, August, 1953, pp. 394–397; Bernard Barber, *Social Stratification*, New York: Harcourt, Brace & World, 1957; Wilbert E. Moore, "But Some Are More Equal than Others," *American Sociological Review*, February, 1963, pp. 13–18. For criticisms of the functional analysis of social stratification, see Melvin M. Tumin, "Some Principles of Stratification: A Critical Analysis," *American Sociological Review*, August, 1953, pp. 387–394; Melvin Tumin, "Reply to Kingsley Davis," *American Sociological Review*, December, 1953, pp. 672–673; Melvin M. Tumin, "Rewards and Task-Orientations," *American Sociological Review*, August, 1955, pp. 419–423; Richard L. Simpson, "A modification of the Functional Theory of Social Stratification," *Social Forces*, December, 1956, pp. 132–137; Walter Buckley, "Social Stratification and the Functional Theory of Social Differentiation," *American Sociological Review*, August, 1958, pp. 369–375; Melvin Tumin, "On Inequality," *American Sociological Review*, February, 1963, pp. 19–26; Walter Buckley, "On Equitable Inequality," *American Sociological Review*, October, 1963, pp. 799–801; George A. Huaco, "A Logical Analysis of the Davis-Moore Theory of Stratification," *American Sociological Review*, October, 1963, pp. 801–804.

dividuals[20] receiving the greatest rewards are, for the most part, those making the greatest contribution to society. The weaknesses of this analysis are readily apparent. First of all, it is in some respects tautological. How can sociologists determine a hierarchy of roles based on degree of contribution to society? It is the cultural values (and the power structure) which determine which roles make the greatest contribution to society. In the United States entertainers are among the most highly rewarded, presumably because their talents are scarce and their social contribution extremely valuable. However, in the Soviet Union their rewards are far less and they are not considered as valuable as in the United States, even though their talents are as scarce there as here. Medical doctors are more highly rewarded and regarded in the United States than in the Soviet Union, but in the Soviet Union university professors receive far higher status and (relative) rewards than in the United States. In some societies priests have been considered the most valuable contributors to societal welfare. Who contributes the most to society—entertainers, medical doctors (or medicine men), scholars, priests, military men, or businessmen? The answer of course depends on the values of the particular society. Rare talent and a long and arduous training to become an excellent actor in a society where actors have low status will not bring high rewards. We must then, as a minimum, rephrase the functionalist statement to say that the roles valued highly in a society receive higher rewards to motivate individuals to strive for them.

However, even this statement has limited validity. Any role involves a complex of functions, duties, privileges, and rewards. The particular content of a given role complex is neither inevitable nor necessarily a functional unity. Often only a few of the elements comprising its rights and duties are directly tied to its major function. Other functions may be assumed by the role occupant, or assigned to him by others because of his position in the power structure even though he may not be the best qualified to carry them out. Thus a role complex may become greatly enhanced in power and rewards. Additional functions, not inherently related to the original function of the role, may be used or indeed even acquired to justify additional rewards. Thus the differential distribution of rewards in a society tends to become elaborated far beyond what is needed to motivate the performance of culturally valued roles.[21]

---

[20] While Davis and Moore claim that their analysis relates to the system of positions in society and not to the individuals who occupy these positions, in fact their analysis is not so limited. "When Davis and Moore go on, however, to speculate about processes motivating actors to fill these positions, and the relation between the superior capacities or training of actors and the highly rewarded positions they must fill, then Davis and Moore must relinquish their claim since they are clearly concerning themselves with characteristics of individuals and how these aid such persons in attaining certain positions." Buckley, "Social Stratification and the Functional Theory of Social Differentiation," *op. cit.*, pp. 371–372.

[21] This tendency is noted by Dennis H. Wrong, "The Functional Theory of Stratification: Some Neglected Considerations," *American Sociological Review*, December, 1959, p. 782.

Other factors also limit the validity of the structural-functional explanation of social stratification. For example there are always many more individuals able to perform a culturally valued role than are given a chance to achieve it.[22] Often many (who are potentially able) would be willing to perform these roles with lower rewards than their present occupants receive (a situation neither functional nor efficient for society). The raising of rewards by the deliberate creation of shortages in certain occupations has been a widely recognized practice over the centuries. Functionalists recognize that "other factors" modify the functional explanation of the differential distribution of rewards. The factors discussed here, however, would "modify" the functional explanation to such an extent as to challenge its basic validity, except within very strict limits. Basically, false assumptions of integration and causation have led to a seductive but largely invalid analysis of social stratification.

Finally, one other criticism of functionalism may be mentioned. Borgatta has accused the functionalists of a tendency toward a value bias. Often a functionalist judges what the goal of a "dynamically moving system" should be. He speaks as though the goal were inherent in the system itself, but in reality it is based on the values of the functionalist himself. Patterns of behavior are then evaluated as functional or dysfunctional according to whether they contribute to the achievement of this goal.[23] Given an appropriate frame of reference, it is possible to view anything as functional or dysfunctional.

These criticisms do not deny all value to the functional approach. For certain purposes a functional analysis may be both useful and valid. However, it would have to be recognized as analysis from a given, limited perspective, providing a supplement to and not a substitute for causal analysis. Functionalism does not provide an all-embracing model, a complete theoretical framework for all sociological analysis. Probably most of the problems the functionalists face today are due to an attempt to do too much with this schema. Like strict empiricism, functionalism has not provided a satisfactory alternative to causation.

PERSISTENCE OF CAUSATION

The failure of a satisfactory alternative to develop in social theory has led to a persistence of the use of causation. Isolated facts do not constitute a science. The object of science is to find order among facts.[24] A conceptual framework is needed for the ordering of facts, and causation

22 See Tumin, "Some Principles of Stratification: A Critical Analysis," *op. cit.*, p. 389.

23 Edgar F. Borgatta, "Reply to Ogles," *American Sociological Review*, August, 1960, p. 561.

24 Morris R. Cohen and Ernest Nagel, *An Introduction to Logic and Scientific Method*, New York: Harcourt, Brace & World, 1934, p. 245.

provides such a framework. Despite the severe attacks to which causation has been subjected, the concept of cause is still widely used by sociologists today.

Causation combined with strict empiricism

In a recent article Dore suggests that causation is still useful for sociology because it is a young science.[25] He proposes, in effect, a combining of causation with strict empiricism. According to Dore, sociologists should seek to build a body of causal laws based on the observation of concrete "events." (By "events" Dore means behavior and expressed attitudes.) Supporting reductionism, Dore maintains that sociological concepts are merely *summaries* of specific actions and beliefs of individuals—nothing more.[26]

By making his causative model explicit, Dore avoids the problems of implicit causation characteristic of most strict empiricism, as discussed above. However, the combination of causation with strict empiricism still involves a major fallacy. It is the implicit assumption that the observation and summary of concrete events automatically lead to causal laws. The sociologist then becomes a totally neutral and detached observer, who needs only to feed objective data into electronic computers and out will come summaries of the patterns of social interrelations and societal institutions, and finally analytical causal laws of social behavior. But in practice there is no justification for such an assumption. Although all sociological generalizations are, in the last analysis, based on the actions and beliefs of individuals, the latter do not automatically add up to generalizations. The vast number of individual acts and beliefs are incomprehensible without ordering. They are ordered into a logical framework by the sociologist, who selects and emphasizes some, and ignores others. Moreover, as mentioned above, correlational devices are symmetrical and the investigator must determine which variable is the cause and which is the effect. It is the sociologist's logical system which determines the way he orders the events he observes, the interrelationships he induces, the generalizations and conclusions he reaches. Basically the weakness of combining causation with strict empiricism is that it involves the supposition of and a search for absolute causes. The futility of this supposition will be discussed in greater detail below.

Multiple causation

It has been suggested that multiple causation provides a solution to the problem of causation. The development of multiple causation indicates

[25] Dore, *op. cit.*, p. 848.
[26] *Ibid.*, pp. 843–853.

a recognition of the futility of searching for single absolute causes. Attempts to explain social behavior in terms of one basic determining cause, e.g., geographic determinism, are rejected, and it is recognized that a given phenomenon may have several contributing causes.

An illustration of the development of multiple causation may be found in criminology. Early criminological theories ascribing crime to a single cause such as biological structure, or poverty, or psychological abnormality have been replaced by a multicausal theory of crime. "Its essence is that crime is a consequence of many causes, of which the most often cited include mental deficiency, economic distress, broken homes, association with criminals, and personality defects. The principal polemics of these theorists are against anyone whom, they charge, over-emphasizes a single factor."[27]

Although multiple causation provides a definite advance over uni-causality, it does not solve the basic problem of causation. The usual investigation of multiple causes still tends to involve a search for absolute causes. However, combining several possible causes does not provide *the* cause. In addition to any given number of causes, many other possible "causes" could be uncovered by using other theoretical frames of reference. All logical possibilities are never exhausted.

Multiple causation may be useful in uncovering a new frame of reference. A new "analytical" variable may be seen as underlying previously recognized causes. Sutherland's differential association theory of crime provides an example of this. In developing his theory of differential association Sutherland was seeking to uncover a basic and analytical causal principle underlying the multitude of generally accepted specific causes of crime. Sutherland wrote: "I reached the general conclusion that a concrete condition cannot be a cause of crime, and that the only way to get a causal explanation of criminal behavior is by abstracting from the varying concrete conditions things which are universally associated with crime."[28] Moreover, ". . . Sutherland endeavored to phrase and rephrase his theory so that it would account for the genesis of every case of crime which he encountered."[29] The controversy[30] which followed the publication of Sutherland's theory has for the most part been concerned with whether or not it is true—that is, whether the principle of differential association does in fact provide the basic cause of crime. Thus there is again a search for one absolute cause. Seeking an analytical variable underlying numerous recognized causes can be of significant theoretical

---

[27] Daniel Glaser, "The Differential-Association Theory of Crime," in Arnold M. Rose (ed.), *Human Behavior and Social Processes*, Boston: Houghton Mifflin, 1962, p. 427.

[28] Albert Cohen, Alfred Lindesmith, and Karl Schuessler (eds.), *The Sutherland Papers*, Bloomington, Ind.: Indiana University Press, 1956, p. 19.

[29] Glaser, *op. cit.*, p. 429.

[30] *Ibid.*, pp. 430–432.

value. However, the investigator must beware of the fallacy of regarding this new underlying cause as *the* final cause.

Multiple causation is a useful approach insofar as it is tentative and flexible. It becomes misleading when it is assumed that absolute and final causes have been discovered just because the investigator has four or five causes rather than one.

Causation and the model of classical physics

A third modern conceptualization of causation in sociological theory has been in the form of the model of classical physics. Parsons and Bales have attempted to formulate sociological laws which are directly analogous to principles of classical mechanics, even taking their terminology from classical mechanics.[31] Another attempt to use the model of classical physics in sociology is found in the work of Stuart Dodd, who has paraphrased Newton's laws of motion in sociological terms.[32] Lundberg regards this as a convergence of the thinking of Parsons, Bales, and Dodd, and as evidence of the acceptance of the theory and method of natural science in sociology.[33]

It is strange that there should be an attempt to fit sociology into the model of classical physics at the very time when the underlying assumptions of classical physics, in fact its very foundations, have been challenged and irrevocably shaken. While some physicists maintain there is still a limited realm of validity for classical physics—the realm of the macroscopic world (excluding phenomena at high velocities), others question the long-range tenability of any dividing line between a microscopic and a macroscopic world. D'Abro maintains that "the two worlds exhibit no clearcut separation; and so we must suppose that the strange characteristics of the new world are present also in the world of our common experience. If this be the case classical physics, even in the macroscopic world, must be superseded by quantum physics."[34] Bridgman also maintains that "any altered meanings which are thus forced on us (in the microscopic realm) are ultimately altered meanings in the domain of everyday life. Strictly speaking, there is no such thing as a 'microscopic world,' for example; there is merely an altered macroscopic world. . . ."[35] Waismann, too, feels: "It is hardly to be expected that the revolutionary change in our concepts thus inaugurated will remain confined to the study of

---

[31] Parsons, Bales, and Shils, *op. cit.*, pp. 102–103.

[32] Stuart Carter Dodd, *Dimensions of Society*, New York: Macmillan, 1942, pp. 743–746.

[33] George A. Lundberg, "Some Convergences in Sociological Theory," *The Americal Journal of Sociology*, July, 1956, pp. 21–27.

[34] A. D'Abro, *The Decline of Mechanism in Modern Physics*, Princeton: Van Nostrand, 1939, p. v.

[35] P. W. Bridgman, "Science and Broad Points of View," *Proceedings of the National Academy of Science*, June, 1956, p. 315.

quantum phenomena. For one thing, the notions of space and time will probably have to go into the melting pot."[36] In any case "the emergence of new ranges of facts have shaken the presuppositions on which classical physics was built . . ."[37] The very substance of which the physical universe is composed is not of the nature assumed by classical physics. "The conviction that physical reality may be regarded as a constant substantial quantity persisting through time was the *leitmotiv* of classical thought . . . (However) the ideas of *quantity* and *constancy* fail at the microphysical scale. The fact that these ideas preserve their usefulness within the realm of middle dimensions does not diminish in any way the philosophical significance of their basic inadequacy . . . The inapplicability of the concept of constant quantity to the basic elements *or rather events* of the physical world makes much of nineteenth-century thought as well as its twentieth-century prolongations obsolete."[38]

In physics the principles of classical physics are maintained within a limited realm, despite the fact that many of the assumptions on which they are based are now regarded as invalid, because they are useful in dealing with macroscopic physical phenomena. If sociological data readily fell into the mechanical model, a heuristic argument might be advanced for using these principles in sociology too. Obviously this is not the case. In fact in many ways social data are much closer to the data of quantum physics, and the problems of theory in quantum physics are quite similar to the problems of sociological theory. It would seem that while the newer physics is moving closer to sociology, some sociologists are attempting to move sociology closer to the older physics. The argument might be advanced that the stage of classical mechanics is a necessary first stage for a young and developing science. There is no logical basis for this assumption. It is no more necessary for sociology to go through the stage of classical mechanics than it is for a newly industrializing nation to go through the stage of stream power.

A LIMITED CONCEPTION OF CAUSATION

Fallacy of absolute causes

The major weakness of most attempts to maintain the causative framework in sociology is that they involve a persistence of the assumption that science can find absolute and final causes. In fact this can never be.

---

[36] F. Waismann, "The Decline and Fall of Causality," in R. J. Blin-Stoyle *et al.*, *Turning Points in Physics*, Amsterdam: North-Holland Publishing Company, 1959, pp. 147–148.
[37] *Ibid.*, p. 114.
[38] Milic Capek, *The Philosophical Impact of Contemporary Physics*, Princeton: Van Nostrand, 1961, pp. 325–327.

The scientist seeks to analyze and understand reality, but his generalizations never mirror reality. Scientific generalizations are conceptions of reality, constantly being refined, perhaps coming closer and closer to what may finally be accepted as "reality," but always remaining approximations.[39] The real world is vastly complex, and beyond the grasp of human comprehension in its totality. Therefore any generalization is inherently a simplification. Moreover, we can never obtain a completely objective view of the world. Eddington has said, speaking of physics, ". . . the world of physics is a world contemplated from within, surveyed by appliances which are part of it and subject to its laws. What the world might be deemed like if probed in some supernatural manner by appliances not furnished by itself we do not profess to know."[40] Certainly this is also true of the social world.

There has been some recognition in sociology of the fallacy of absolute causation. The conceptualization of multiple causation, discussed above, involves a certain degree of awareness of this problem. Merton warns against "the fallacy of misplaced concreteness," in which abstract conclusions based on a few elements are thought to apply directly to complex concrete situations.[41] It is well recognized that different scientific disciplines, by utilizing differing theoretical frames of reference, may provide differing, yet equally valid, causative statements in analyzing the same phenomenon. Thus if human behavior were studied by a human biologist, a psychologist, a psychiatrist, and a sociologist we would expect and accept as valid at least four different causal systems.

It is suggested here that this limited awareness of the fallacy of absolute causation be broadened, so that the entire notion of absolute causation is replaced by a limited conception of causation, causation dependent upon a theoretical orientation. This means, essentially, that all statements of causal relationships are regarded as valid only within the limitations of an explicitly stated frame of reference representing a particular theoretical model. All scientific generalizations, then, are regarded as simplifications of reality, and Merton's fallacy of misplaced concreteness would be extended to any generalization that is conceived of as a true law of nature. The principle of differing theoretical frames of reference now readily acknowledged between disciplines would be applied within a discipline.

[39] As Cantril puts it: "Scientific procedure thus becomes a never-ending process of guessing, a constant attempt to create an hypothesis which will be more adequate, more inclusive, than the last one." Hadley Cantril, *The "Why" of Man's Experience*, New York: Macmillan, 1957, p. 3.

[40] Eddington, *op. cit.*, p. 188. See also Louis De Broglie, *Physics and Microphysics*, London: Hutchinson's Scientific and Technical Publications, 1955, pp. 129–131; Waismann, *op. cit.*, p. 114; Bridgman, *op. cit.*, p. 317.

[41] Paul F. Lazarsfeld and Robert K. Merton, "Friendship as a Social Process: A Substantive and Methodological Analysis," in M. Berger, T. Abel, and C. H. Page (eds.), *Freedom and Control in Modern Society*, Princeton: Van Nostrand, 1954, pp. 61–62.

In discussing the relativity of the concept of causation in modern physics, Bridgman points out that the statement of a causal relationship implies the whole system within which the relationship occurs.[42] Lins, recognizing the impossibility of comprehending the totality of phenomena all at once, speaks of the necessity of breaking it up "by systems of reference, which are relatively closed areas of causation."[43] According to Lins causal factors are "logico-functionally interrelated in the situational field."[44] However, we need to go even further in recognizing the relativity of causation. It is not simply a question of changing conditions from one time or place to another. In viewing a given situation, varying causative relationships may be recognized by applying different frames of reference. For, as Cantril has pointed out, "the variables scientists use do not exist in their own right. They are only aspects abstracted out of a total situation by scientists as inquiring human beings endowed with the capacity to manipulate ideas."[45] Thus, it is not only by studying new phenomena that we may see new causal relationships, but also by shifting our perspectives on the same phenomena.

It should be emphasized that we are not proposing a type of relativism which would threaten to undermine the foundation of science. Limited causation, that is, causation dependent upon a theoretical orientation, does not imply that the assertions of any individuals or groups as a reflection of their "point of view" have scientific validity. A causal relationship stated in terms of an explicit theoretical orientation requires verification in the traditional scientific manner. The conceptualization of limited causation does not to any extent limit the applicability of the canons of science. Any scientific principle must be based on empirical observations and on research which is subject to replication. It is essentially the consensus of the scientific community, using the criteria of the scientific method, which in the long run must determine whether a given causal principle has scientific utility and validity.

Some advantages of limited causation

A few examples of the utility of a limited conception of causation will be presented here.

The conception of limited causation in terms of limited theoretical models, first of all enables us to better understand the contributions of thinkers in different periods of history. Becker spoke of the need to relate the work of a theorist to the setting in which he operates, urging

---

42 P. W. Bridgman, *The Logic of Modern Physics*, New York: Macmillan, 1927, p. 83.

43 Mario Lins, *Foundations of Social Determinism*, Rio de Janeiro: Mario Lins, 1959, pp. 83–84.

44 *Ibid.*, p. 87. The situational context of causation is also emphasized by MacIver. See R. M. MacIver, *Social Causation*, Boston: Ginn, 1942.

45 Cantril, *op. cit.*, p. 4.

that the core theorems of the classical theorists be related to their respective settings which in some ways were radically different from the setting of contemporary sociologists.[46] In the same vein, Shibutani supports Goethe's contention that ". . . history is continually rewritten, not so much because of the discovery of new documentary evidence, but because the changing perspectives of historians lead to new selections from the data."[47] More specifically, Meadows tells us that each period of Western history has conceptualized reality in terms of "its dominant metaphysical analogy."[48] He goes on to say, ". . . there is in each period of scientific conceptualization a dominant metaphor, . . . this metaphor determines the patterns of model analysis in the period, and . . . the metaphor itself is in part a reflection of the social structure of the period."[49] An analysis of a writer's work in terms of his setting, his perspective, or his dominant metaphor is in fact an attempt to understand the more subtle aspects of his frame of reference. The conception of causation within limited theoretical models enables us to discover presently unrecognized validity in the works of an earlier period by clarifying the theoretical framework within which certain principles have validity. While these principles originally may have been stated as universal and absolute, and later rejected as not universal, we may now delineate a limited theoretical framework within which they have validity.

Second, a limited conception of causation provides a check on the tendency to overextend a theoretical model. Often there is a compulsion to encompass and explain more and more within the framework of a given model.[50] Thus a useful point of view may come to be regarded as the only valid point of view by a particular "school." When a limited conception of causation is acknowledged, all models are recognized as limited abstractions from and simplifications of reality. No one then can be viewed as all-encompassing or embracing the final truth.

Third, a limited conception of causation provides an understanding of the role of systems of logic in the formulation of principles of causation. Furfey has pointed out that a logical system makes a particular "proof" acceptable.[51] In terms of the conceptualization presented here, the

[46] Becker, *op. cit.*, p. 379.

[47] Tamotsu Shibutani, "Reference Groups as Perspectives," *The American Journal of Sociology*, May, 1955, p. 564.

[48] Paul Meadows, "Models, Systems and Science," *American Sociological Review*, February, 1957, p. 3.

[49] *Ibid.*, p. 4.

[50] *Ibid.*, p. 7. See also Llewellyn Gross, "Preface to a Metatheoretical Framework for Sociology," *The American Journal of Sociology*, September, 1961, pp. 125–136. In discussing the closely related problem of different language schemes in sociology Gross writes, ". . . the major effort of professionals is devoted to extending the jurisdiction of their own scheme at the expense of others." In Llewellyn Gross, "An Epistemological View of Sociological Theory," *The American Journal of Sociology*, March, 1960, p. 445.

[51] Paul Hanly Furfey, "The Formalization of Sociology," *American Sociological Review*, October, 1954, p. 525.

logical system is part of the theoretical framework within which causal laws are formulated. Not only may systems of logic vary from one culture to another and from one period of history to another, but each theoretical model to some extent also involves its own logical system.[52] Each system of logic in turn provides a somewhat different causal logic. Since each is an abstraction from, rather than direct reflection of, reality it is quite possible for more than one causal logic to be valid at the same time, each within its particular logical and conceptual framework.

Causation as a heuristic device

A limited conception of causation would not prevent the practical application of scientific principles to real life problems. On the contrary, causal principles stated with a recognition of theoretical limitations would be more applicable than principles stated in absolute terms. By recognizing that causal laws are limited to frames of reference, we do not thereby make them more relative or less accurate portrayals of reality. Causal principles thus stated must still rest upon empirical verification and the consensus of the scientific community. With the theoretical boundaries recognized, our principles may be regarded as the closest approximations to reality thus far attained, and may be applied to real life situations with a recognition of their imperfection. The imperfection, of course, reflects the limits of any theoretical model.

Some psychological adjustment may be required on the part of the applied social scientist—a greater degree of acceptance of uncertainty. This type of adjustment has also been required in physics. Meyer tells us, "In classical physics scientists actually believed that their models represent more or less accurately what is going on in nature."[53] Today in physical science models are no longer regarded as direct reflections of reality, but rather are conceived of as composed of ideal elements— abstractions and simplifications of reality. Moreover, Meyer contends ". . . scientific prediction does not refer directly to the so-called course of nature but to our models."[54] This changed conception of the nature of the principles of physics has not reduced their application to practical

---

[52] Kaplan writes: "That the world of ideas has no barriers, within or without, does not call for one true 'Logic' to govern it. The conviction that there is such a logic—as it happens, ours—is a parochialism like those of which comparative ethnology made us painfully aware in the course of the last century. . . . Not only language and culture affect the logic-in-use, but also the state of knowledge, the state of inquiry, and the special conditions of the particular problem." Abraham Kaplan, *The Conduct of Inquiry*, San Francisco: Chandler, 1964, pp. 8–9. See Kaplan's full discussion of logics-in-use, pages 8–11.

[53] Herman Meyer, "On the Heuristic Value of Scientific Models," *Philosophy of Science*, April, 1951, p. 114.

[54] *Ibid.*, p. 113.

problems. Although no longer conceived of as absolutes, they are still heuristically useful.

This heuristic conception avoids the entire problem of the "real" existence of causation. We cannot in fact know whether real and ultimate causes exist in the universe. We only know of reality what we perceive of it, and we never can perceive it all, in all its complexity, within one integrated theoretical model. We do know that within given theoretical models causal principles can be stated, and we know further that these causal principles are heuristically useful.

It is interesting to note that all societies use the notion of causation in everyday life.[55] It provides a needed ordering for social life. The logic of causation permits prediction without which cooperation and social organization would not be possible. It is also interesting to note that while causation involving time sequence is accepted in everyday life in the East as in the West, Eastern philosophy rejects this conception of causation as essentially an illusion. Instead, all is seen as interdependence, correlation, and coordination. The failure of the East to develop science probably is related to its intellectuals' rejection of causation, illustrating the heuristic value of the concept of causation in science.

CAUSATION AND
CROSS-CULTURAL RESEARCH

A major problem of any attempt to arrive at scientifically valid causal principles of human behavior is that in every society there are culturally defined principles of causation accepted by the members of that society as objectively and universally true. We have maintained that causal principles are limited to a theoretical model, and we have stressed the possibility of obtaining various valid causal interpretations of the same phenomenon by shifting theoretical orientations. However, it has been pointed out that the distinction between scientifically valid and scientifically invalid generalizations remains. Science requires the critical analysis of culturally defined principles of causation and their rejection if they do not meet the criteria of scientific verification. A problem arises, however, because every social scientist as a member of a particular society uncritically maintains at least some of the causal assumptions of his culture. These assumptions are not based on the logic of any scientific model. The scientist himself usually is unaware of these assumptions. Insofar as his research is limited to his own society he is likely to remain unaware of them.

[55] Emile Durkheim, *The Elementary Forms of Religious Life*, New York: Free Press, 1947, p. 363.

It is important to distinguish between theoretically limited causation and culturally limited causation. In this paper we have been advocating theoretically limited causation, that is causal principles stated in terms of explicit, limited theoretical models. Causation limited by unrecognized, uncritically accepted cultural assumptions is the antithesis of this scheme. In the attempt to bring to light hidden cultural assumptions, cross-cultural research plays a crucial part.

It is not difficult to recognize the culture-bound nature of much of current sociological research. Correlations found in American society often are assumed to reflect natural laws and mechanistic causes. Cultural effects and limitations are not known. Testing a relationship in different situations within the same culture to some extent provides a more universal basis for generalization, but does not provide a substitute for cross-cultural research. Within even a complex culture various sub-structures reflect certain cultural "themes" or culture-wide patterns.

When certain attitudes are found to be intercorrelated in the United States, it cannot validly be assumed that these attitudes are inherently related to each other. It may be that certain attitude clusters exist in American society because of the distribution of groups within this society, and thus the interrelationship of these attitudes may be due simply to historical factors. Thus for example, an attribute such as religiosity, which may be measured by indices such as church attendance, conceivably may be either positively or negatively correlated with attitudes defined as prejudiced. If in the United States a high correlation between these two variables is found, we have learned something about the nature of American culture, largely a result of historical factors, but we have not established that there is any necessary or inherent connection between these two variables. If it is then found that these two variables are highly correlated with certain other attitude variables, we may have uncovered certain attitude patterns found in American society. However, we cannot assume that these same attitudes would be correlated in India or China.[56] Therefore there is no basis for referring to such attitude clusters as universal personality types. Much of the research centered on the concept of the "authoritarian personality" suffers from this error. Based on studies of the United States, and to some extent Germany, many writers have given the impression that they have discovered a universal personality type.

Classical ecology provides a well-known example of the erroneous statement of universal causal principles on the basis of studies limited to the United States, and primarily to Chicago.[57] Social ecology today has a broad cross-cultural base, but many other areas of American sociology remain as culture-bound as was classical ecology. For example, many of

[56] See the discussion of relationship of correlation and causation above.
[57] See George A. Theodorson, *Studies in Human Ecology*, New York: Harper & Row, 1961.

the non-ecological generalizations of American urban sociologists are based overwhelmingly on studies of cities in the United States, but are nevertheless stated as universal principles.

In addition to the objective analysis of human behavior in various cultural contexts, there is another useful, but less often considered form which cross-cultural research may take. At times it may be valuable for the scientist to take the point of view of another culture and attempt to understand the causal logic of that culture. Every society has a system of causation, for a system of causation makes prediction possible. As Durkheim has said, ". . . the co-operation of many persons with the same end in view is possible only when they are in agreement as to the relation between this end and the means of attaining it, that is to say, when the same causal relation is admitted by all the co-operators in the enterprise."[58] The same conception of causal relationships is accepted by the members of a group, according to Durkheim, because the conception of causality is given to the individual, ready-made by the group. Durkheim goes on to say: "The principle of causality has been understood differently in different times and places; in a single society it varies with the social environment and the kingdoms of nature to which it is applied."[59]

The system of causation of a given society is, to a certain extent, a series of self-fulfilling prophecies. One dilemma of social science is that it attempts to predict the behavior of men who themselves in every society have always established a predictive system (that is, a system of causation). Ignoring this fact has lead to the basic fallacy, discussed by Blumer, of most variable analysis in sociology. This fallacy is the assumption that the independent variable automatically exercises its influence on the dependent variable. Between the action of the independent on the dependent variable is an intervening process of definition and interpretation.[60] In this process of definition the causative system of a society plays a significant part. The beliefs of the members of a society about the nature of the relationship between two variables in part helps to determine that relationship.

The distinction between an objective and a cultural approach to cross-cultural studies may have a parallel in the distinction between latent and manifest functions. Latent functions may be conceived as the conceptualization of functions in terms of the logical and causative system of the scientist. The latter may vary from an attempt at the greatest possible objectivity and theoretical sophistication to a simple reflection of the investigator's culture. Manifest functions, then, may be

58 Durkheim, *op. cit.*, pp. 443–444.
59 *Ibid.*, p. 369.
60 Blumer, *op. cit.*, pp. 685–687.

conceived of as functions from the point of view of the logical and causative system of the society itself. It has been observed that sometimes through the activities of social scientists latent functions become manifest.[61] This in fact means that the causal logic of the theorist (regardless of its validity) has been incorporated into the logical system of the culture.

The search for basic uniformities in human behavior (e.g., the functional requisites of all societies) reflects the objective approach to cross-cultural research. The question arises, are there patterns of behavior unique to the predictive system of particular societies?[62] Are these often ignored by scientists, or forced into their logical system? Perhaps there is a need for a greater emphasis on the study of the manifest system of various societies, the manifest system in its own terms as a system of logic and causation with self-fulfilling prophecies.

CONCLUSION

Causation, once the firm foundation of science, came under severe and effective attack with the development of quantum physics. The undermining of causation in the physical sciences soon was followed by a challenge to the use of causation in the social sciences. The two major attempts to replace the causative model which developed in sociology were strict empiricism and functionalism. Neither has provided a satisfactory alternative to causation. Because of the lack of a satisfactory alternative, causation has continued to figure prominently in sociological analysis. Attempts have been made to make the causative model more acceptable by combining causation with strict empiricism, by introducing the concept of multiple causation, and by using causation in the framework of the model of classical physics. The basic weakness of these attempts is that each implicitly assumes the possibility of discovering absolute and final causes.

In this paper it has been suggested that causation be maintained in the social sciences, since no satisfactory alternative has been found, but that it be modified so that we conceive of limited rather than absolute causes. A limited conception of causation meets many of the theoretical objections which have been raised against causation. In fact most of the

---

[61] Dore refers to this as the "self-falsifying assertion," *op. cit.*, p. 845. Louis Schneider and Sanford M. Dornbusch discuss this in relation to religion in "Inspirational Religious Literature: From Latent to Manifest Functions of Religion," *The American Journal of Sociology*, March, 1957, pp. 476–481.

[62] This question to some extent is related to Bell's conception of the use of the "operational code" of a society as a mode of prediction. See Daniel Bell, "Twelve Modes of Prediction —A Preliminary Sorting of Approaches in the Social Sciences," *Daedalus*, summer, 1964, pp. 855–856.

criticisms of causation are criticisms of an absolute conception of causation.

In research and analysis a limited conception of causation means that the theoretical frame of reference from which a causal relationship is stated is made explicit and recognized as limited. A theoretical orientation is always present, whether recognized or not, in all scientific endeavor. The two key elements suggested here are the explicit statement of the theoretical model and a recognition of its limitations. The usual scientific explication of "conditions" in research tends to ignore the conditions imposed by one's conceptual structure. The sociologist more than the physicist is in a position to contribute to the advancement of science by pointing out and studying the role of social, logical and ideological factors in the creation of universal causal systems, and the role of theoretical structure in the formation of causal structure. Causal systems are dependent upon the system of concepts being employed. Thus, just as conceptual systems necessarily select only certain analytical aspects of total reality, so causal structures necessarily refer to certain analytical aspects of total reality. Hence changes in theoretical perspective involve changes in the causal system related to that theoretical structure.

Occasionally a certain theoretical orientation may be deliberately extended beyond its usual limits in order to use, as Bierstedt has suggested, a theoretic bias as a heuristic device. Bierstedt has written: "The theoretic bias would enable us to push a particular interpretation of social phenomena just as far as it is reasonable to go in our effort to shed illumination upon it."[63] The theoretic bias could be used heuristically to counterbalance an opposite existing (and possibly previously unrecognized) theoretic bias. In the past there has been a tendency for a theoretic orientation to be followed by its opposite, but this has been done in the name of truth, not as a heurstic device. Several examples come to mind. Most early studies of preliterate societies were made by missionaries who usually emphasized the dysfunctional aspects of these cultures. The missionaries were followed by the functional anthropologists who emphasized the positive function of all aspects of these cultures, and their functional integration. Now we hear of psychiatrists studying the neuroses found in these same cultures. The early sociologists, including Park and his associates, emphasized competition as the basic process in human life. The rejection of this orientation was followed by an emphasis in sociology on the importance of cooperation in social life. Even today a great deal of sociological writing implies the assumption of the basically cooperative nature of man.[64] Other examples could be found. An

[63] Bierstedt, *op. cit.*, p. 8.

[64] Ralf Dahrendorf speaks of this as the "utopian image of society" and urges the adoption of a conflict model for the explanation of sociological problems. "Out of Utopia: Toward a Reorientation of Sociological Analysis," *The American Journal of Sociology*, September, 1958, pp. 115–127.

emphasis on the individual in psychology was followed by an extreme emphasis on the group in early sociology. An early period in which theory was dominant in sociology was followed by a dominant emphasis on empirical research. Yet from each orientation, even after it is rejected, a residue of useful findings and insights remains and helps to build up the accumulated data of the discipline. Thus this process involves the progress of science, and is not merely a meaningless series of reactions and counter-reactions.

In conclusion, we may emphasize the importance of maintaining a broadminded and flexible attitude. Since we never can have more than approximations of the truth, each new perspective, each challenge to established doctrines should be given full consideration.[65] With this point of view there is no room in a science for irreconcilable and hostile schools of thought, each claiming a monopoly on final and ultimate truth.[66]

Limited causation necessarily involves limited theoretical models. No one model can encompass all of the vast complexities of social life. A series of limited models, each with a somewhat different theoretical focus, will bring us closer to an accurate understanding of reality than we can possibly have with one comprehensive theoretical system which is unaware of its limitations and ignores all alternatives.

Limited causation within limited theoretical models permits us to maintain the useful causative schema in sociology. We need not cease to talk about causes simply because quantum physics and scientific philosophers have found that earlier universal causes no longer apply to their new theoretical models.

[65] Or going further, as Gross has proposed, the deliberate challenging of established principles and assumptions may be made an integral part of sociology through the use of neodialecticism. Gross, "Preface to a Metatheoretical Framework for Sociology," *op. cit.*

[66] This is in accordance with Gross' analysis of the need for tolerance of differing language schemes within sociology. Gross writes: "It is the responsibility of the protagonists of each scheme to see that the others are properly assessed, and thus they must work on the principle that each and every scheme may possess a measure of ascendency over the others, warranting some claim for jurisdiction within the total set of languages." Gross, "An Epistemological View of Sociological Theory," *op. cit.*, p. 445.

Theory in anthropology: developmental or causal?

LEON J. GOLDSTEIN

INTRODUCTION

The question which is the title of the present paper may be given at least two interpretations. It may seem to suggest that in the end the choice we confront in determining the nature of theory in anthropology is limited to the two characterizations mentioned. Perhaps this will prove to be the case, but one cannot very well say that it is until all of the various kinds of theoretical orientation that have been proposed for anthropology—functionalism in its multiplicity of forms, structural analysis, various concerns with configurations, themes or patterns, and what have you—have been subject to review and either shown to be special cases of one of these two or dismissed as having no theoretical worth. To undertake such a task would require nothing less than an anthropological companion to J. H. Woodger's classic of a generation ago, *Biological Principles*,[1] and is clearly beyond the scope of this paper.

[1] J. H. Woodger, *Biological Principles*, Routledge & Kegan Paul, 1929.

But the title may be given a more modest interpretation which accords with my intentions here: to consider the relative merits of developmental and causal theory formation in anthropology. More particularly, I wish to examine some claims which have been made on behalf of developmental theories and, by means of consideration of several recently proposed examples of developmentalism, determine whether or not they are more suitable in the explanation of sociocultural phenomena than their causal counterparts.

By "causal theory" or "causal theories of the usual sort," I mean theories which claim that some aspect or other of the sociocultural system, the so-called dependent variable, is in some way affected by certain other aspects of the sociolcultural system, the independent variables of the theory. One might say that the form taken by the dependent variable is *causally* determined by the independent variables. In such theories temporal *sequence* is not a factor, a point which is sometimes obscured when writers emphasize that the change they study takes place in time. All change, to be sure, is temporal in character, and every instance of change is a determinate sequence, but until the social sciences develop theories which require them to treat time as a measurable variable, emphasis on the point seems of little moment. The point of a causal theory then, is that when the conditions sufficient for the realization of a determinate form in the dependent variable are themselves realized, then that form may be expected. The sequence of development is of no theoretical consequence. I take it that the theory of kinship contained in G. P. Murdock's *Social Structure*[2] is a causal theory of the usual sort, but I shall defer showing that it is until somewhat later in my discussion.

In contrast to causal theories, developmental theories take the order or sequence of development very seriously indeed. Here, too, we must not permit the temporal character of all change to intrude itself and so obscure the point. All change takes time, and each particular sequence of change has a determinate order of development. But if from the standpoint of causal theories the order of development of a given sequence is contingent and is to be understood only through discovery of the actual historical order of the emergence of those conditions sufficient for the realization of each of the stages which constitute the sequence in turn, the standpoint of developmental theories requires that the very order of development is significant and if properly understood will reflect the working of developmental principles or evolutionary laws. Leslie White, a leading proponent of developmentalism, says: "Evolution may be defined as a temporal sequence of forms: one form grows out of another; culture advances from one stage to another. In this process time is as integral a factor as change of form. The evolutionist process is irreversible

2 G. P. Murdock, *Social Structure*, Macmillan, 1949.

and nonrepetitive." And he adds that "it is the sequence of forms, the one growing out of another, irrespective of particular time and place, that is significant."[3] Some developmentalists say that the very nature of socio-cultural development or change necessitates that the succession of stages reveals a growing increase of complexity of one sort or another. From the standpoint of the more usual casual theorizing, one would say that *if* it has been established that there has in fact been a growing increase of complexity, *it is because* at each stage the sufficient conditions for such an increase were present, a matter to be demonstrated by whatever historical or anthropological methods are suitable to the task. Later in my discussion, when I recur to this difference between developmental and causal approaches, I shall characterize them as having, respectively, categorical and hypothetical conceptions of the nature of laws in science.[4]

Before turning to the first main task of the paper, the presentation of several instances of developmental theorizing in anthropology, I want to distinguish between developmental theorizing and certain other conceptions with which students of present-day anthropology may think to bind it. As is well known, the leading advocates of developmental theory formation are Leslie White and the people who tend to subscribe to his views. Over the years, White has been an articulate proponent of a number of positions—culturology, i.e., that cultural phenomena are to be studied as if they were independent of all else and never explained in biopsychological terms, though not infrequently the culturological standpoint is given an ontological formulation according to which culture is a reality *sui generis*; a materialism, not unlike Marx's, according to which technological change is essentially the motive force of cultural development; a "thermodynamic" conception of culture which conceives of culture as an instrument for the capture and use of energy as a means of human adaptation to environment, and, concomitantly, takes progress in culture to be defined in terms of increasing efficiency in such capture and use; a view of men as essentially uncreative and totally molded by culture together with a seeming refusal to take seriously the possibility of human freedom,[5] and, of course, a certain conception of the

---

[3] L. A. White, *The Evolution of Culture*, McGraw-Hill, 1959, pp. 29 f.

[4] But I might say at once, that by "hypothetical" I refer to the well-known view of explanation in science as hypothetico-deductive. On that view laws by themselves do not necessitate that anything in particular happen, but rather, that laws taken with particular conditions account for other conditions. Given the law, then if the antecedent then the consequent; not given the law hence the consequent. Adherents to developmental theories, on the other hand, seem to think that the nomological character of the phenomena studied necessitates the happening of whatever happens.

[5] Though this may appear to be a consequence of White's culturological commitment, that it is more likely rooted in his materialism is suggested by the fact that those who disagree with him are charged not with taking seriously the possibility of human freedom, but with believing in something called "freedom of the *will*," hence, presumably, subscribing to some form of mind-body dualism; see the index to his *The Science of Culture* (Farrar, Strauss, 1949), under "Free Will." But even without raising metaphysical questions, one could arrive at similar conclusions about individuals and their freedom given a categorical conception of scientific laws. As I have already indicated in the text, we shall see that this view is implicit in developmental theorizing.

evolution and progress of culture[6]—but it is certainly not the case that if one subscribes to any one of them, or particularly to his developmental or evolutionary conception of theory in anthropology, one is logically required to take them all. There is nothing inconsistent about adopting the culturological standpoint, which has long been a common one among anthropologists, without being an evolutionist or defining culture in terms of energy. As it happens, however, those who are best known among the anthropologists who follow White's evolutionism, say, the authors of *Evolution and Culture*[7] or Betty J. Meggers,[8] tend to agree with him on the other matters as well, and this may lead some to suspect that there really is an intimate logical connection which binds all of the elements of his system in an all-or-nothing package. In what immediately follows and for the most part, though not entirely, in this paper, I shall be concerned only with their conception of anthropological theory as developmental.

DEVELOPMENTAL THEORIZING

In what follows, I shall present accounts of four attempts to do theoretical work in developmental ways. In recent years, evolutionists have been distinguishing between "general evolution," which they take to concern the progressive development of human culture "in general" or taken as a whole, and "specific evolution," which deals with the adaptation of particular human groups to particular environments.[9] All of the examples to follow represent the latter perspective, and are attempts to make intelligible certain cultural sequences from the developmental perspective of specific evolution. It is widely held that the goal of theory formation in science is the construction of systems of propositions which when taken together with specific statements of fact enable the deduction of still other statements of fact, the situations described by these latter statements hence being explained or predicted.[10] But I think it best in the present context to make not these formal expectations of reasonably mature sciences our test of theoretical work, but rather the extent to which the particular inquiry seeks to make intelligible whatever its subject matter may be. In none of the instances to be presented can

---

[6] See his works cited in notes 3 and 5.

[7] M. D. Sahlins and E. R. Service (eds.), *Evolution and Culture*, University of Michigan Press, 1960.

[8] See, for instance, B. J. Meggers, "The Law of Cultural Evolution as a Practical Research Tool," in G. E. Dole and R. L. Carneiro (eds.), *Essays in the Science of Culture in Honor of Leslie A. White*, Crowell, 1960, pp. 302–316.

[9] See, for instance, Sahlins and Service (eds.), *op. cit.*, chap. 2.

[10] C. G. Hempel and P. Oppenheim, "The Logic of Explanation," in H. Feigl and M. Brodbeck (eds.), *Readings in the Philosophy of Science*, Appleton-Century, 1953, pp. 319–352; for a more recent review of the issues involved, see Israel Scheffler, *The Anatomy of Inquiry*, Knopf, 1963, part I.

it be said that the theorist presents us with a set of purely formal theoretical propositions, but in each the particular writer tries to make intelligible —explain in some sense—the course of a given development, and in each this is done from an evolutionary or developmental perspective.

Social stratification in Polynesia

The first and most extensive attempt to offer the sort of explanation we are now considering is Sahlins' account of social stratification in Polynesia.[11] The problem is to explain the differences in the social structures of peoples whom there are reasons—linguistic and other—to believe share a common historical and cultural origin. Sahlins makes clear what he intends to do in the very first words of his Introduction:

> This is a study of adaptive variation in culture. It attempts to relate differences in an aspect of the social systems of aboriginal Polynesia—stratification—to differences in the adaptation of the cultures to their environments. Technology is the subsystem of culture which articulates with environment; hence, the methodology of this study consists of relating variations in social stratification to variations in technological and environmental conditions. Stratification is viewed as an aspect of social structure functionally adjusted to the technological exploitation of the environment.[12]

One may wonder why a study devoted to what Sahlins intends to do is treated as an instance of developmental anthropology. An attempt to show how an antecedently given condition of culture varies as its bearers seek to adapt to new and various environments and, in consequence, develop new and various technologies would seem to point to casual explanations of the usual sort. And there are other statements in Sahlins' book which seem to suggest the same thing; one example will show what I mean: "Other factors being constant, the degree of social stratification varies directly with productivity."[13] There does not seem to be anything particularly developmental or directional in such statements of "functional" variation. But Sahlins intends that his book reflect the developmental perspective of evolutionism, and I think that some effort ought to be made to read it so as to make this come out. But before this can be done, some attention must be paid to the two perspectives of evolutionism as these are delineated in the aforementioned collaborative volume, *Evolution and Culture*.

The reason we must turn to the two perspectives is that it is not clear in what sense Sahlins' book is evolutionist. Happily for our present concern, the very chapter of the collaborative volume which is relevant

[11] M. D. Sahlins, *Social Stratification in Polynesia*, University of Washington Press, 1958.
[12] *Ibid.*, p. ix.
[13] *Ibid.*, p. 5.

here, the one called "Evolution: Specific and General," was the one written by Sahlins himself, and if it should provide the means whereby to decide the way in which his own book is evolutionist, we may well have some confidence in our solution. The problem arises because it is not immediately clear just where the developmental character of the book on Polynesia is to be located. The starting point of the study is the ethnographic data on fourteen societies, related to be sure, yet different in important ways. In particular, Sahlins holds that these societies differ among themselves with respect to degree of social stratification, though amid the differences there emerge clearly two kinds of systems—ramage systems and descent-line systems, both of which I shall characterize briefly a bit further on—and he attempts to show that the particular extent to which either one is present in a given Polynesian community is, given the character of its technology, an outcome of its adaptation to its environment.

On the face of it, all this would lead us to suppose that we have here to do with what, in the collaborative volume, Sahlins calls "specific evolution," for this is concerned with the course of cultural development attendant upon the adaptation of a people to its environment. The point is that the various stages of such a development represent different adaptations of the same people—the authors of the volume speak of the phylogenetic continuity of specific evolution as distinct from the discontinuity of general evolution, to which they say a number of different peoples have contributed—to what is usually the same environment, each adaptation a consequence of new technological developments. " *Viewed specifically*," Sahlins writes, "the adaptive modifications occurring in different historical circumstances are comparable; each is adequate in its own way, given the adaptive problems confronted and the available means of meeting them."[14] But in the work on Polynesia, we are really not presented with the sequence of development for each of the societies studied. Rather, for the most part we are given an account of it in the so-called "ethnographic present," though upon occasion, when his sources permit, Sahlins will report on what he takes to have been the historical development in this or that respect. And while I have just quoted him as saying that from the vantage point of specific evolution "the adaptive modifications occurring in different historical circumstances are incomparable," the Polynesia book is clearly a comparative study of Polynesian societies. I should think that it is only from a comparative perspective that he is able to see each of the studied societies as adaptive variations of what was presumably, originally, one cultural theme.

The second perspective is that of general evolution, and as that is presented in the collaborative volume it is clearly not applicable here. To begin with, the course of general evolution is said to encompass human culture taken as a whole—as distinct from the specific cultures of

---

[14] Sahlins and Service (eds.), *op. cit.*, p. 26; his italics.

individual groups or societies—and while it cannot be said that the proponents of the general evolutionary perspective have made clear how one can define that whole so as to make it a manageable subject for scientific inquiry, the culture area which is Polynesia is hardly to be taken for it. Sahlins and his colleagues of the collaborative volume argue, however, that from the standpoint of interest in the whole of human culture one may discern over the centuries the emergence of ever more efficient ways of capturing and utilizing thermal energy, and that this provides a criterion for making non-relativistic judgments about progress in culture.[15] It is not claimed that any one culture will pass through all of the stages of this progress. On the contrary, they maintain that a people that has carried progress to a point which has never before been reached, has exhausted its potentiality for progress and cannot be expected to do more than concern itself with the adaptation of its culture to the environment in which it finds itself.[16] The standpoint of general evolution is not itself, we are told, concerned about the adaptation of a specific culture to a specific environment. Taking culture as a whole is supposed to enable us to ignore such environments, which are said to balance or cancel each other, and our judgments with respect to progress are made simply in terms of the efficiency with which energy is trapped and used. But while in one sense the standpoint of general evolution is concerned with only a small number of the individual cultures which have existed during the course of man's career on earth, namely, those comparatively few cultures which actually contributed to the course of cultural progress, in another all may be taken within its purview since presumably it should be possible to say which of any two given cultures is the more progressive, i.e., which comes nearer to the highest point yet achieved, or which of them is the more efficient. (Of course, all this presupposes that it proves possible to make such determinations as well as to define culture in the energy terms required by the theory, a possibility which is by no means obvious.)[17] It would appear, then, that the

---

[15] The proclivity of writers of this school to think of progress solely in technological and thermodynamic terms may serve to reinforce their tendency to belittle individuality and be unconcerned with human freedom. One expression of this is Sahlins' justification of despotic polities in the name of industrial modernization (*American Anthropologist*, 1962, *64*: 1071–1073), though it is likely that he would claim to be explaining, not justifying. We shall see later on that what is involved in such a claim is the categorical conception of scientific laws to which I have already referred.

[16] In the final chapter of *Evolution and Culture*, "The Law of Evolutionary Potential," Service speaks of the possible *facts* of the "phylogenetic discontinuity of progress" and the "local discontinuity of progress" as if they were *laws* of culture—in the categorical sense of law common to members of the evolutionary school—and proposes to the United States certain policies on the assumption that its being surpassed by the present-day underdeveloped areas is inevitable given the workings of these laws. How one may square having policies at all with such a conception of inevitable development is something we may wonder about.

[17] Albert C. Cafagna's claim—in Dole and Carneiro (eds.), *op. cit.*, p. 118—that "When Leslie A. White asserts that the degree of evolution of culture can be measured by the amount of energy harnessed per capita per year, he is offering, in essence, an operational definition of 'evolution,'" is entirely mistaken since neither White nor anyone else has specified the operations in terms of which the required measurements can be made; cf. *Evolution and Culture*, p. 76.

perspective of the book is not that of either of the two described in the collaborative volume. The only way to make it compatible with the standpoint of specific evolution would be—or so it seems to me—to treat the different Polynesian cultures, and particularly their social structures and degrees of social stratification upon which so much of Sahlins' attention is focused, as different steps or stages in the same course of adaptation acted out in a number of different places. We assume that a number of different societies have all passed through or are passing through the same course of development, but at different speeds. Consequently, different societies reach a given stage of development at different times. If we could catch them all at approximately the same time, we would not only have an ethnographic description of the entire culture area as it is at that time, but we would also be able to order the individual social descriptions in an evolutionary-sequential way. It need not, of course, be that all fourteen cultures represent stages in the *same* course of development; there could be more than one. But if I understand the point of specific evolution, one cannot talk about it unless one shows how a given people and its culture adapted to their environment in the course of some period of time, each step seemingly representing a readaption the moving force of which is new technological or thermodynamic developments. Clearly, no comparative study of different cultures described in the ethnographic present could illustrate the course of this kind of specific adaptational evolution except on the kind of assumption I have just mentioned. I do not think, however, that this assumption is one that Sahlins wishes to make,[18] and I rather suspect that his assumption is of a somewhat different kind. And that is, that each of the ethnographic presents catches each of the fourteen Polynesian cultures studied in some one stage of its own particular course of specific evolution. That each of them had developed to that stage in accordance with the evolutionist perspective is simply assumed and not defended.

We may now turn to a brief characterization of what the book actually purports to do. "It has been postulated," its author says, "that the degree of stratification in these societies is an adaptive feature related to increasing productivity."[19] Sahlins claims that the societies he studies may be divided into four groups, the criterion of the division being the degree and complexity of its system of social stratification. And the degree of

---

[18] Although, when he says, in summing up his discussion of ramages on p. 180, "These variations of ramage systems illustrate a developmental sequence of a certain sort," and that "It is not accidental that this developmental sequence closely follows the gradient of stratification described earlier in this work," he certainly makes it seem plausible that his evolutionism takes this "unilineal" form. But it would be impossible to square this with his continued emphasis upon adaptation to a *particular* environment, and it is this latter, after all, that is a major theme of the book.

[19] Sahlins, *op. cit.*, p. 107.

stratification of a society is itself taken to be a consequence of that society's degree of productivity. The more productive a society is, the more likely it is to produce a surplus, and the more highly stratified it is likely to be. Sahlins notes that while it has been claimed that eastern and western Polynesia give evidence of being separate "historical currents," the degrees of social stratification in these societies cut across these currents, and thus he concludes that "the historical difference between western and eastern Polynesia . . . does not account for the degree of stratification in the various cultures. On the contrary, the degree of stratification is seen to be entirely an adaptive variation when the cultures are classified on this (eastern and western) historical basis."[20]

In addition to his concern with stratification per se, Sahlins considers two different kinds of social organization, ramages and descent lines.[21] These, too, are treated as adaptive in nature, emerging in consequence of the ecological problems the society must deal with. A ramage is taken to be "a nonexogamous, internally stratified, unilineal—in Polynesia, patrilineal—descent group. Distance from the senior line of descent from the common ancestor is the criterion of stratification."[22] Since no two persons in a ramage stand precisely in the same relation—when both degree of kinship *and* time are taken into account—to the common ancestor, each one of a "group of descendants from a common ancestor holds a different status, one precisely in proportion to his distance from the senior line of descent in the group."[23] Sometimes an entire society may be a single large ramage, but this need not be and one may find societies with an hierarchical ordering of ramages. Ramified societies are centrally controlled.

In contrast to ramified societies, Sahlins describes a number in which "the political system was one of localized, discrete, patrilineal descent lines. The descent lines held titles, and titles bestowed office in local territorial entities, villages and districts. Status did not depend—at least not in the same way as in the ramified systems—on distance from the main line of descent, but rather on the traditional position of one's title in the territorial hierarchy of titles."[24] Sahlins calls these "descent-line systems of social organization." Unlike the ramified systems, they are "local groupings of relatively small, unrelated, patrilineal units."[25] In both ramified and descent-line systems, there is no one always-realized norm, but, rather, the instances of each kind differ from one another in various ways.

20 *Ibid.*, p. 137.
21 There is, in addition, the social organization of the coral atolls, but they are more variable and do not have the clear character of the other two.
22 Sahlins, *op. cit.*, p. 140.
23 *Ibid.*, p. 141.
24 *Ibid.*, p. 181.
25 *Ibid.*, p. 194.

Sahlins contends that the maintenance of kinship ties, as well as their character, "seems to be an adaptation to economic necessities of co-operation." Since the two kinds of systems are different, it is presumed that they are adapted to different economic ends. "The ramified system is adapted to the exploitation of different, widely spread resource areas, which adaptation on an economic level is manifest in sporadic, seasonal, or total specialization of familial production." Thus, a diverse, complex and spread out environment would require diversity of occupation for its proper exploitation, and the centralizing tendencies of a ramified system would provide precisely the sort of political control needed to keep such an economy functioning in an orderly way. "On the other hand, if in the process of fission, the household or family which buds off tends to move into an area identical to that of the parent group as regards the type of strategic goods producible, the kinship between the two groups might weaken and dissolve. Descent-line systems are those adapted to exploitation of similar resources by the different lines." Since under the circumstances described neither group could contribute significantly to the diversification of the consumption of the other, there is no economic need for them to remain joined and, hence, no pressure to institute political forms to that end.[26]

In summary, in *Social Stratification in Polynesia*, Sahlins reviews a good deal of ethnographic writing to the end of arguing that both the degree of social stratification and the forms of the social system are adaptational in character and serve to make it possible for a people of determinate culture to utilize the environment in which they find them-selves as best they can, given the level of that culture. And if we are to put his account of the matter in the context of his well-known views, we must presume that each instance presented is to be understood as a stage in that culture's particular sequence of adaptation as understood from the perspective of specific evolution.

Evolution of the state

Few subjects have been of such perennial and pervasive interest to students of the development of institutions as the origin of the state, the emergence of political institutions where previously they were absent. It would seem, therefore, to be appropriate that this interest be reflected in our sample of developmental studies, and we are fortunate that a suitable and well-presented essay on the subject was recently published by Morton Fried.[27] The problem Fried is concerned with is the "pristine"

---

[26] *Ibid.*, pp. 202 f.
[27] M. H. Fried, "On the Evolution of Social Stratification and the State," in S. Diamond (ed.), *Culture in History, Essays in Honor of Paul Radin*, Columbia University Press, 1960, pp. 713–731.

emergence of the state as distinct from its development in this or that place as a consequence of contact with already existing states. Modern observers can only describe instances of the latter, and, as it happens, we have no description of societies going through all of the stages of Fried's account. Nonetheless, it is Fried's "intention to discuss in detail the things which it seems to [him] must have occurred in order to make the previous transitions possible." The goals of his paper are summed up as follows:

> ... (1) to suggest some specific institutional developments, the occurrences of which are normal and predictable in viable societies under certain conditions, and in the course of which the whole society perforce comes into a new level of socio-cultural organization; (2) to suggest some of the conditions under which these institutional developments occurred and came to florescence; (3) to indicate as a by-product, that the movement occurs without conscious human intervention, the alterations taking place slowly enough and with such inevitability that the society is revolutionized before the carriers of the culture are aware of major change.[28]

Immediately thereafter, Fried denies that he has the "intention of supplying a single master key to a lock that has defied the efforts of great talents from the time of the Classical civilizations to the present" and allows that other sequences might have similar results. One may presume that he wishes to avoid the charge that evolutionists in anthropology seem so easily attracted, that he is offering us but another unilinear schema. But one may wonder how seriously to take the disclaimer. After all, it is not the case that Fried offers his account as one which makes best sense of evidence we have about the development of social stratification and political institutions in some given society, or a group of related ones. Rather, he suggests that this is the way this sort of development is likely to have happened—whenever it happened. Proposed alternatives, which he invites, would presumably be alternatives to the general schema he offers, not ways in which it happened in some places just as Fried's might have happened elsewhere.

Let us now turn briefly to the course of the development as Fried presents it. In his view, we have to deal with a sequence of four stages— the non-rank, the rank, the stratified, and the state societies—and in his essay he presents summary characterizations of them as well as explanations of the transition from one stage to the next. The non-rank society is essentially an egalitarian one, "in which there are as many positions of prestige in any given age-sex grade as there are persons capable of filling them." These societies are said to be essentially hunting and gathering ones, lacking notable harvest periods and large stores of food. There is no particular specialization or division of labor, and such exchange as

[28] *Ibid.*, p. 714.

there is tends to be casual. But "In all egalitarian economies . . . there is also a germ of redistribution.[29] . . . In such an embryonic redistributive system the key role is frequently played by the oldest female in the active generation, since it is she who commonly coordinates the household and runs the kitchen."[30]

About the rank society, Fried says that it "is characterized by having fewer positions of valued status than individuals capable of handling them" and that "most rank societies have a fixed number of such positions." The easiest way to limit status is to have succession to a status position depend upon order of birth, but there are varieties of ways and variations upon them. The higher ranks of the system have important economic functions, and "Depending on the extent and maturity of the redistributive system, there will be greater or lesser development of the hierarchy." The hierarchy, however, is not to be thought of as exploitive: "The kingpin of a redistributive network in an advanced hunting and gathering society or a simple agricultural one is as much the victim of his role as its manipulator. His special function is to collect, not to expropriate; to distribute, not to consume."[31]

In contrasting the sort of society we have just been talking about with that of the next stage of his developmental sequence, Fried says that "the rank society operates on the principle of differential status for members with similar abilities, but these statuses are devoid of privileged economic or political power," whereas "the stratified society is distinguished by the differential relationships between the members of the society and its subsistence means—some of the members of the society have unimpeded access to its strategic resources[32] while others have various impediments to their access to the same fundamental resources." It is the passage to this form of society which, in Fried's view, lays the basis for a complex division of labor and the emergence of socioeconomic classes.[33]

With the emergence of the last stage of the sequence, the state, we find the organization of social power on a "supra-kin basis" and the development of new institutions for the control of the people, the settlement of disputes, and the expression of sovereignty. In Fried's view, the course of the development of stratified societies leads to the point where kinship-based social systems are no longer capable of holding up under the burdens imposed upon them. As long as the stratified society is simple, it is possible to develop means for the extension of the network of kinship to aspects of life not covered by genuine kinship relations.

[29] I.e., of food.
[30] Fried, *op. cit.*, pp. 715 f.
[31] *Ibid.*, pp. 716 ff.
[32] In a note at this point, Fried says: "Strategic resources are those things which, given the technological base and environmental setting of the culture, maintain subsistence."
[33] Fried, *op. cit.*, pp. 721 f.

But in time this leads to a state of affairs in which non-kin agencies are developed and the political state comes into being.[34]

This sequence of stages is not something that is said simply to happen, as if no attempt to make it intelligible is possible. In Fried's view the factors which bear upon the development are matters of ecological adaptation and subsistence. Growth of population leads to social fission, the beginnings of specialization, and the first steps in transforming an egalitarian society into a rank one.[35] Technological developments that make it advantageous to make access to certain strategic resources the prerogative of certain groups, lead to the emergence of stratified societies.[36] And still further technological developments, particularly those having to do with large-scale irrigation, are said to lead to the pristine emergence of the state.[37] Fried speaks of these transitions as "inexorable" as well he might, given the categorical nature of laws of development. And yet we may wonder about the character of this inexorability. If the stages of the sequence follow one another because of the technological and ecological reasons given, then one must suppose that were those absent, the development described would not be realized. Thus it would seem that despite his developmental intentions, the mode of explanation actually employed when Fried deals with specific problems is hypothetical and causal. We shall discover this to be true of the remaining examples as well and shall consider the implications of it later on in the paper.

Religion and culture in Japan

We turn next to an attempt by Richard Beardsley to apply the developmental or evolutionary perspective to an account of the development of Shinto religion in the context of Japanese culture change.[38] In his view, the various phases of the history of Shinto are responses to or reflections of "evolutionary developments in Japanese culture." And this is said to result in the formulation of "an evolutionary hypothesis for comprehending Shinto." It seems from this that religion is treated as an epiphenomenon, and that it is actually " Japanese culture as a whole" which is subject to evolutionary development. Beardsley holds that Shinto is a response to a development the main motive force of which is economic, though sociopolitical matters are recognized as having some relevance.

In an early summary statement of what he proposes to demonstrate, Beardsley says the following.

[34] *Ibid.*, pp. 727 f.
[35] *Ibid.*, pp. 719 f.
[36] *Ibid.*, p. 724.
[37] *Ibid.*, pp. 729 f.
[38] R. K. Beardsley, "Shinto Religion and Japanese Cultural Evolution," in Dole and Carneiro (eds.), *op. cit.*, pp. 63–78.

... Three main phases are recognized: (1) a cult of local powers and local spirits, associated with early phases of prehistoric culture; (2) a cult of personalized spirits and gods associated with the emergence of aristocracy in protohistoric and early historic centuries; (3) a phase marked by two developments, (a) appearance of evangelistic sects, corresponding to the rise of an entreprenurial class and dissolution of the feudal regime, and (b) invention of a nationalist supercult, corresponding to the emergence of a modern nation-state in the nineteenth century.[39]

For our purposes, the above is quite adequate and I shall not bother to add summary statements of the character of culture and religion during each of the three phases. Since Beardsley is not reporting mere temporal coincidence, one may wish to have some analysis of the logic of his phrases "associated with" and "corresponding to," particularly since when he writes that the deified heroes and high gods stage of Shinto religion "is considered here to be functionally a response to the rise of autocracy,"[40] he seems to open the way to a causal, non-developmental interpretation. But presumably his developmentalism is to be seen not in the relation of the epiphenomonal religion and that which it reflects, but rather in the succession of the stages of Japanese history and culture. Since the paper does not really deal with that, his claim that he offers "an evolutionary hypothesis for the comprehending of Shinto," must rest upon the assumption that such a developmental account of Japanese history could be had. But even that does not alter the oddity of the claim that a series of epiphenomena, the stages of Shinto, are developmentally related.

Evolution and Yankee kinship terminology

Early in her contribution[41] to the volume honoring Leslie White, Gertrude Dole says the following:

In a comparative study of kinship by Murdock, the nomenclature of the "Yankees" has been classed with those of the Eskimos and Andaman Islanders as "lineal" or "Eskimo." This is an apparent anomaly, since these three peoples represent different levels of cultural development. The Yankees have one of the most complex cultures known, while the Andamanese have one of the simplest, a fact which led Murdock to conclude that there was no necessary association between particular patterns of kinship terminology and levels of culture.[42]

She does recognize that Murdock showed that there is a relationship between kinship nomenclature and other aspects of the social structure, but since she holds that the "form which a social structure will take is fundamentally dependent on the type of subsistence technology with which it is associated," she thinks that "we might expect that kinship

[39] *Ibid.*, p. 66.
[40] *Ibid.*, p. 69.
[41] G. E. Dole, "The Classification of Yankee Nomenclature in the Light of the Evolution of Kinship," in Dole and Carneiro (eds.), *op. cit.*, pp. 162–178.
[42] *Ibid.*, pp. 162 f.

nomenclatures would show some relation to level of technological development. Convinced that, given their disparity in level of cultural development, the kinship systems of the three mentioned peoples must certainly have differences, she proposes to examine them in detail in order to see what they are.

Though there is no particular recognition of it, it is worth noting that what Miss Dole's theoretical standpoint requires is not that there be a developmental relationship between kinds of kinship nomenclature, but, rather, that each system of nomenclature suited be to the sort of technologically determined social structure with which it is associated. The increasing complexity which is taken to be the mark of a course of development need not, presumably, be found in those elements of the sociocultural system which *reflect* but do not *effect*, i.e., epiphenomena or what Marxists call "the superstructure." If this is denied, there are two difficulties to be faced. The first is that it is not only assumed that kinship systems are dependent on technology, but that in its various stages even the dependent or epiphenomenal factor must exhibit certain characteristics, viz., increasing complexity. But surely this is an empirical matter which can be determined only be research, not settled by assumption. The other is that to insist that the sequence of kinship systems must in fact display the increasing complexity expected of developing phenomena, may lead one to think of its development as independent at the cost of its presumed dependence upon technology. As in the case of Beardsley on Shinto, Miss Dole would like to claim that kinship systems are epiphenomenal yet have the characteristics of developmental phenomena.

To return to the paper itself, the three kinship systems are described and the claim made that with all their similarities they have noteworthy differences. After noting some similarities between the three patterns of nomenclature she points to what she takes to be a "fundamental" difference.[43] "All Primitive and Secondary Isolating[44] nomenclatures are classificatory, grouping some collateral relatives with lineal; while the Modern Isolating[45] is descriptive, distinguishing all collateral relatives from lineal." She goes on to say that "all the peoples who have Primitive or Secondary Isolating nomenclatures also have relatively primitive cultures, with very simple social structures. All those which have the Modern Isolating pattern have much more advanced cultures with relatively complex social structures."

The developmental character of her thinking is quite apparent in the presentation of her discoveries, and it is her clear intention to conclude that as societies become increasingly complex they take on systems of

---

[43] Dole, *op. cit.*, pp. 172 ff.
[44] The Andaman and Eskimo patterns, respectively.
[45] The Yankee pattern. All three set off, or isolate, the nuclear family from other kin, hence the term "isolating."

kinship nomenclature which accord with that complexity and which could not be anticipated in societies of different character. But then, in order to make the relation between kinship pattern and sociocultural character and complexity seem intelligible, she provides some illustrations of just how the pattern in question is suited to the degree of cultural complexity with which it is associated. I should like to present just one example of this, her contrast of modern isolating nomenclature with the others, after which I shall offer some comments on it.

> . . . (1) Instead of classing together lineal and collateral relatives in the grandparent and grandchild generations as do the Primitive and Secondary Isolating, Modern Isolating nomenclature differentiates *all* lineal from collateral relatives. This is because property is inherited primarily in a lineal pattern, and because an individual is not responsible for the support and protection of his collateral relatives. (2) In its more precise form, the Modern Isolating pattern expresses differences in degrees of consanguinity among collateral relatives in each generation, which is not true of the Primitive or Secondary Isolating. The function of this feature is to differentiate between relatives according to inheritance rights, especially to subsistence property. (3) Finally, the Modern Isolating pattern groups together relatives of different generations, whereas each generation is terminologically distinct in both the Primitive and Secondary Isolating patterns. In industrial society many people have almost no contact with offspring of their parents' siblings. When this is true, it is not likely that they will be concerned enough with more distant relatives to differentiate them with special nomenclature . . .[46]

I shall not stop to wonder about the significance of the "mentalistic" character of the last sentence quoted, though members of Miss Dole's school may take rather a dim view of it. I am much more interested in the hypothetical "when" with which the sentence opens. It is presumably Miss Dole's intention to say that as a culture in the course of its development becomes modern, particularly in the areas of technology, economy and property, certain determinate conditions arise which make previous kinship patterns no longer suitable and necessitate the emergence of new ones. But she does this in such a way as to undercut the developmental character of her explanation. For in effect, she shows that whenever conditions result in the separation of some kinds of relatives from others, this will come to be reflected in the nomenclature of kinship. Even if in fact culture *A* has been transformed from premodern to modern, and it is demonstrable that it once had a secondary isolating one, Miss Dole's way of explaining that transition of nomenclature pattern is not developmental but causal. She *implicitly* refers to causal laws which connect factors which isolate kin of varying sorts to kinship terminologies in which these isolatings are reflected. The pattern of the culture's development—whatever *in fact* it has been—seems not to the theoretical point. The new pattern emerged, Miss Dole says implicitly, not because the

---

[46] Dole, *op. cit.*, p. 175; her italics.

premodern *A* has been transformed into a modern *A*, but because isolatings of determinate character emerged, and whenever such isolatings emerge such patterns may be reasonably expected regardless of the complexity of the culture.

ARE THERE LAWS OF DEVELOPMENT?

Those who maintain that the main thrust of American anthropology since the pioneer days of Franz Boas has made evolutionary anthropology untenable because the evidence amassed has failed to support the expectations of the evolutionists, would seem to be agreement with my view that there are no laws of development, but it could be shown that they are addressing themselves to a different kind of question than the one that concerns us here. They take the question to be factual, and conclude that the evidence fails to support the claim that there are such laws. But they do not argue that there is anything inherently implausible about the possibility of such laws. In view of that conception of the issue, the response of present-day evolutionists makes perfectly good sense. They seek to present the accumulated data in such a way as to support their developmental conceptions. The question that I wish to raise, however, is logical, not factual. Can there be laws of development? Or, could laws of development do what we expect theoretical science to do? But though my question is logical, I cannot expect to emerge with a conclusion certified as indubitable by the rules of deductive logic. Such a conclusion would easily prove to be circular, and no one who was antecedently committed to views other than mine would feel compelled to accept the premises of my argument. But I do hope that in the course of what follows I can make my negative answer seem plausible.

Certainly, the general question we are dealing with has come up before. Thus Karl Popper, addressing himself to the question of whether or not there can be a law of evolution or any scientific law having the characteristics required for the realization of T. H. Huxley's expectation that "Science will sooner or later . . . become possessed of the law of evolution of organic forms—of the unvarying order of that great chain of causes and effects of which all organic forms, ancient and modern, are the link," answers, "No."

> . . . The evolution of life on earth, or of human society, is a unique historical process. Such a process, we may assume, proceeds in accordance with all kinds of causal laws, for example, the laws of mechanics, of chemistry, of heredity and segregation, of natural selection, etc. Its description, however, is not a law, but only a singular historical statement. Universal laws make assertions concerning some unvarying order . . ., i.e., concerning all processes of a certain kind; and although there is no reason why the observation of one single instance should not incite us to formulate a universal law, nor why, if we are lucky, we should not even hit upon the

truth, it is clear that any law . . . must be *tested* by new instances before it can be taken seriously by science. But we cannot hope to test a universal hypothesis or find a natural law acceptable to science if we are forever confined to the observation of one unique process. Nor can the observation of one unique process help us to foresee its future development. . . .[47]

Popper then goes on to deal with possible counter arguments—denial of the contention that the evolutionary process is unique, and assertion that even in unique processes we may discern trends upon the basis of which we may be able to formulate testable hypotheses—but I do not wish to repeat his discussion here. The main point of the quotation above is that a set of sentences in which an observed sequence is characterized cannot be taken as a law in which the events making up that sequence are explained, and I am certain that readers familiar with recent evolutionary writings in anthropology will see its relevance to our discussion. One example will have to suffice, what Elman Service, in the final chapter of *Evolution and Culture*, calls "the law of evolutionary potential." It may be historically demonstrable that any culture that has contributed to a general evolutionary advance, defined in the energy terms Service and others prefer, has never in fact contributed still another advance. In Service's view, this is to be explained by the law just cited, which he formulates as follows: "The more specialized and adapted a form in a given evolutionary stage, the smaller is its potential for passing to the next stage."[48] At first blush this may seem actually to do the job—on the assumption that the "law" can be confirmed—but reflection on its key terms leads to some doubt in the matter. And that is because the ideas of more or less specialized and adapted and of greater or lesser potentiality for evolutionary advance do not having meanings which would make it possible to apply them. We have simply no way of determining for any given cultural form the degree of its adaptation and the measure of its potentiality for advance. Thus it appears that Service's "law" is not a law after all, and what it does is to sum up in a phrase the claim that things in fact have happened in a certain way. But as Popper says above, in order to explain these happenings we would still have to have recourse to causal theories relevant to the phenomena in question.

It would appear, then, that the kind of discussion we find in Popper's book is certainly relevant to dealing with the question of this point of the paper and to analysis of present-day evolutionism in anthropology. Indeed, there is quite a voluminous literature in which ideas which bear on these matters are discussed,[49] but in what follows I do not intend to make use of

[47] K. R. Popper, *The Poverty of Historicism*, Beacon Press, 1957, pp. 108 f.; his italics. The quotation from Huxley is given by Popper on p. 108.

[48] Sahlins and Service (eds.), *op. cit.*, p. 97.

[49] One could, for example, discover in the evolutionist literature elements of all three of the notions which constitute the title of G. Bergmann's "Holism, Historicism, and Emergence," *Philosophy of Science*, 1944, *11*: 209–221.

it. It is evident enough that the existence of this literature has not really had any effect on the development and discussion of the ideas which we are here concerned with in anthropology. It seems to me more useful to endeavor to answer the question which is the title of the present section through examination of the four sample instances of developmental anthropology discussed in the previous section. That they are developmental in intent and orientation is patently clear, and I think they will serve our purpose even if I am not able to determine in a statistical sense just how representative they are of the work of the evolutionists. I might add that while I have used the collaborative volume on *Evolution and Culture* as a source for the views and theories of the school around Leslie White, I do not consider an analysis of that book as a whole, even if I wanted to produce one, a substitute for the job of seeing just what there is in the actual doing of developmental anthropology.[50] Only by studying what developmentalists do when they *do* anthropology—*not talk about it*—can we find out what it is.

The question to which we might turn our attention here is: How do present-day developmental anthropologists actually explain the socio-cultural material with which they deal? Presumably, if there are laws of development at all, the attempt to answer such a question might give us some clue to their nature.[51] Let me begin by noting two tendencies within our sample of four; one, a totalistic or holistic tendency to think that particular aspects of a culture must be understood only in terms of the totality of which it is a part, and the other a tendency not to. I think that a survey of the writings of evolutionist anthropologists would show a general inclination among them, possibly among them all, to subscribe to some totalistic view, but in my opinion it is the papers of Beardsley and Dole in which this tendency is most clearly expressed in our sample. I do not wish to suggest that the other two writers do not incline to totalistic views, but only that such views are not as central—if even relevant—to their studies discussed above. It may well be that present-day evolutionism is always holistic given its concern with the adaptation of a culture as a whole or with comparing the extent to which one total culture is more or less efficient in its capture and use of energy than another. Neither of these interests of evolutionism as a perspective is immediately pertinent to the Beardsley and Dole papers, yet the totalistic conception of explanation of cultural phenomena is still to be found in both. Beardsley wants to show that the whole of the given stage of Japanese culture is relevant to any understanding of the character of that

---

[50] Think of all the philosophical writers who have discussed "Malinowskian Functionalism" on the basis of his *A Scientific Theory of Culture*, University of North Carolina Press, 1944, or his *Encyclopedia Britannica* article on "Anthropology," without troubling to work through the actual functionalist analyses of Trobriand culture that Malinowski produced in the course of much writing.

[51] There is nothing necessary about this, but it is certainly reasonable.

stage's religion. And Miss Dole argues that a totalistic view is needed to make sense of kinship nomenclatures. Thus, she says that the level of cultural development is relevant to an understanding of the phenomenon in question, certainly a totalistic notion, and she deems it an "anomaly"[52] that Murdock's contrary opinion could be right, though his treatment of kinship systems as casually affected by certain determinate elements of social structure is a far cry from treating them as anomalous.

The totalistic conception of these writers suggests certain logical problems. One has to do with the construction of the whole. It is one thing to say that a culture *is* a unified whole in some significant sense, but it is quite another to discover that whole and learn about its character. Ethnographers do not, after all, have intuitions of the whole, but rather put together their accounts on the basis of piecemeal observation. From a strictly holistic point of view, there ought to be no recognition of proper parts short of the total culture itself, yet given the way that total cultures come to be known it is hard to see how such a claim could be justified. In addition, there seems nothing a priori unreasonable about focusing attention upon proper parts which seem to have some degree of intelligibility in themselves. The totalistic viewpoint maintains that a sociocultural system has no proper parts, and what seem to be such parts are only aspects or facets of a whole. The problem of making sense of the temporal development of any such whole seems to be of insuperable difficulty. The anthropologists who hold such views frequently say that the nature of the whole is a reflection of—or determined by—its technology, but it is one thing to say this and quite another to formulate testable theories which enable us to explain an actually given culture in terms of its technology. And thus we end up confronting unmanageable wholes, not able to say how determinate parts are causally affected by other determinate parts, but rather, forced to talk about change as such which just happens. One may presume that such theoretical commitments were back of earlier tendencies of evolutionist writers to concern themselves about processes of change to which specific—or historical—events were beside the point.[53]

When we actually examine the papers of Beardsley and Dole, however, we do not find them beset by these difficulties of their totalistic commitment. They are certainly not given to insisting upon the simple reasonableness or naturalness of change. Rather, they want to show that the particular forms taken by the cultural phenomena about which their

---

[52] Dole, *op. cit.*, p. 162.

[53] A subject to which F. J. Teggart devoted part II of his still very much worth reading *Theory of History*; see his *Theory and Processes of History*, University of California Press, 1941; paperback edition 1960, pp. 77–151. The relevance of Teggart's views to present-day developmentalism will be apparent to anyone who examines, for example, White, *The Evolution of Culture*, pp. 29 f.

papers are concerned are intelligible, not because the form of the whole requires it, but because of the forms or characters of *specific other parts* of the sociocultural systems. When Beardsley wants us to understand why it is that Shinto takes the form it does at any given time, he tells us about social classes coming to dominate or rising in importance, or of national political developments. When Miss Dole wants us to understand why one sort of nomenclature prevails here and some other kind there, she tells us about specific economic arrangements which organize kin in varying ways and fix any individual's social relationships to the people he is related to, bringing him into close contact with some and separating him from others. If these are to be taken seriously, as there is every reason they should, we must suppose these authors to be implying that if the factors to which they refer were different, then the cultural phenomena being explained would have been different. If they do not mean this, if the claims one sometimes finds in evolutionist writings to the effect that the given developments are inevitable or necessary are to be understood as precluding the possibility of alternatives to what actually happened, it is hard to know how we are to take the explanations they give.

When we turn to the studies of Sahlins and Fried, which are not totalistic in the clear way that the other two are, we find the same kind of explanation. Fried tells us what precisely has to happen before certain degrees of stratification emerge or before the state comes into being. He uses the evolutionist's categorical terminology—"inevitability" and "inexorable"—yet his mode of dealing with particular questions does not seem to be of that sort.[54] Similar remarks may be made about Sahlins' book, much of which is taken up with detailed accounts of the factors he deems relevant to explanation of the forms and degrees of social stratification. Here, too, one must presume that if these are intended seriously we must take them as implying that had the factors in question been other than they were, the sociocultural phenomena being explained would have been different. We shall want, then, to say that in all four of our sample studies the particular explanations offered presuppose causal theories of the usual kind according to which factors of the sort cited

---

[54] It may be noted, however, that Fried's totalistic and categorical theoretical inclinations come out much more explicitly in his earlier and well-known paper: "The Classification of Corporate Unilineal Descent Groups," *Journal of the Royal Anthropological Institute*, 1957, *87*: 1–29. His totalist or holist view is clearly expressed in his refusal to allow that "the content and function of the institutions studied are comparable in societies of differential cultural complexity" (p. 2). His categorical developmentalism appears when he says: ". . . I prefer the hypothesis that the same form of the equalitarian clan preceded all forms of the conical clan and that the conical clan was dependent on the prior existence of and emerged from some form of the equalitarian clan . . ." (p. 6). (I omit quoting a qualification which simply recognizes that some societies may acquire advanced forms, without passing through all of them, through diffusion.)

result in phenomena of the sort explained.[55] And so it would seem to turn out that in those very places where we reasonably sought to find instances of developmental laws we find instead examples of explanation which implicitly presuppose the opposite.

At this point, there may be some who will strongly suspect that the issue between causal and developmental theorizing in anthropology must surely be merely verbal. I think, however, that such a view would be incorrect. That developmentalists seem unable to explain sociocultural phenomena except in causal-theoretical terms is certainly a significant discovery, yet this in no way alters the fact that they are trying to defend a conception of anthropological theorizing which is not causal and hypothetical. In addition to the expressions of this we have already encountered in the course of previous discussion, it may be worth citing another. According to Robert Carneiro, "One of the principle objectives in studying ongoing process in a system is to formulate the laws that are operative in it. Scientific understanding of a process is achieved when it can be shown to be the *necessary consequence* of known laws."[56] This view of the necessitarian character of scientific laws may be compared with the following remarks of Edgar Zilsel: "Astronomers cannot predict from Newton's law what the position of the planet Mars will be on next New Year's Eve. In addition to the law they need the knowledge of the positions, velocities, and the masses of a few celestial bodies at some given time: they need knowledge of 'initial conditions' as the physicist puts it. Knowledge of a law, therefore, is not a sufficient but only a necessary condition of prediction."[57] Neither the fact that Carneiro talks about "process" and Zilsel about a specific event, nor that Zilsel's example deals with prediction while Carneiro seems to be talking about the explanation of a process, affects the point of the present comparison: For Carneiro the working of a law is inexorable and it has necessary consequences; for Zilsel it is hypothetical, and what happens in accordance with it depends upon the initial conditions to which it is applied. Whatever one may wish to say about these views of Carneiro, it is clear that they are not exemplified in the actual attempts at explanation that we have just considered. For far from showing that each phenomenon dealt with is the "necessary consequence of known laws," our four authors seek out the particular causal factors without which what emerged would not have.

---

[55] Cf. C. G. Hempel, "The Function of General Laws in History," *Journal of Philosophy*, 1942, *39* : 35–48; reprinted in H. Feigl and W. Sellars (eds.), *Readings in Philosophical Analysis*, Appleton-Century, 1949, pp. 459–471, and in P. Gardiner (ed.), *Theories of History*, Free Press, 1959, pp. 344–356.

[56] R. L. Carneiro, "The Culture Process," Dole and Carneiro (eds.), *op. cit.*, p. 147; italics are added.

[57] E. Zilsel, "Physics and the Problem of Historico-sociological Laws," in Feigl and Brodbeck (eds.), *op. cit.*, p. 714.

Causal theories

It cannot be said that the question of the previous section, "Are there laws of development?", has actually been given a conclusive answer in the negative. But it is certainly of some significance to find that precisely in those writings in which we might expect to find such laws if we are to find them at all, we find, rather, at least by implication, the opposite. In every instance considered, the writers of our sample offered accounts of sociolcultural phenomena which seemed implicitly to presuppose causal laws of the usual kind. In the present section, I want briefly to characterize such laws. It is not that I expect to offer a full logical account of them, but I do want to show that such laws do not exhibit the feature of temporal sequence that developmentalists seem to think is essential to theories in anthropology. From this, it will be possible to show that certain other consequences of the developmental approach to theorizing—that such theories are categorical and necessitarian and that their application is incompatible with human freedom or the existence of real alternatives— are mistaken. As in the case of developmental theorizing, I shall begin my account of causal theorizing in anthropology with an account of an actual attempt to formulate a causal theory, that developed in Murdock's *Social Structure*.

As is well known by now, the problem to which Murdock's book is for the most part addressed is that of making sense of the development and change of systems of kinship nomenclature. On the basis of an examination of what he takes to be the relevant data, he concludes that the form taken by any such system will be consequent upon the forms taken by four other variables of the social system: the rules of residence, descent and marriage, and the form of the family. After formulating his theory in a general way,[58] he then proceeds to derive from it certain consequences, which following general usage he calls "theorems," and to test these theorems against data culled from ethnographies. While he takes it that the evidence tends to confirm his theory, there are a good number of disconfirming cases, and, thus, it cannot be said that the theory is complete. I do not, however, intend to discuss this problem. From the standpoint of our interest here, it would not have mattered if the theory were entirely disconfirmed.

What this theory in effect affirms is that when the conditions sufficient to the realization of any particular system of kinship nomenclature are realized, we may reasonably expect that the system will itself be realized. To be sure, one may understand developmental theorists to be making the same claim, but they would want to say that these conditions are the total

[58] Murdock, *op. cit.*, p. 138.

system of culture—presumably in consequence of its technological development—having reached a stage in its evolution which necessitates the emergence of the kind of kinship system in question. Murdock's theory, on the other hand, seeks to specify just what precisely those aspects of the sociocultural system are which are causally related to the development and change of kinship systems. From the vantage point of this kind of theorizing, one may say that both the totalistic emphasis of developmental anthropology and the position of the particular culture from the perspective of general evolution are irrelevant to the explanation of a kinship system. Whatever may be the causes for this given culture having the rule of residence it has, the rule of descent it has, and likewise for the rule of marriage and the form of the family, since in fact it does have them, we can understand why it has the particular form of kinship system it has.

We have already seen that Gertrude Dole deems it anomalous that kinship systems should be independent of evolutionary sequence,[59] and Morton Fried has sought to overcome this by arguing that even if the forms of the kinship systems of cultures markedly differing in the extent of their developments are comparable, "the content and functions" of these institutions are not.[60] Yet the kind of theory they oppose has the logical advantage of being more general than their own. In addition, it makes it possible to consider certain *possible* developments without the use of such terms as "retrogression" or "retrogressive." Both of these advantages come simply from freeing the theory from the ties of temporal sequence which developmental theories must insist upon. I hope that this will not be misconstrued so that I am understood to be suggesting that sociocultural change is not temporal or that it cannot be *described* as a sequence of stages. On the contrary, I would not know what it would mean to deny that any particular course of change was both temporal and sequential. What I want to say, however, is that to construct a theory with determinate temporal sequences built into it is to limit the generality of the theory. A theory which seems to explain the sequence a–b–c–d but *could not* explain a–b–c–b or a–b–c–a is clearly less general than one which can.

What I have been trying to say might become clearer after a quick examination of an attempt to treat Murdock's views as developmental. Focusing attention on the eighth chapter of *Social Structure*, James B. Watson argues that the views it contains are developmental because "if and when it changes, a given type of kinship system can only become one of a relatively limited number of other types." Paying scant attention to the significance of his observation that Murdock's "conclusion is arrived at through consideration of inherent limitations, or limited possibilities,"

[59] Dole, *op. cit.*, p. 162.
[60] Fried, "The Classification of Corporate Unilineal Descent Groups," pp. 1 f.

Watson concludes that "the formulation is of the Developmental type in which a linear regularity, here kinship forms, is laid down."[61] Now it is, indeed, the case that Murdock has a table in which the possibilities of the change from determinate forms of kinship system are presented,[62] but this represents a summary of conclusions based upon a theory which is not developmental at all. He does not claim that given the inherent nature of this or that form of kinship system change must inexorably follow in such a way and no other. Rather the successor state of the kinship system will depend upon the forms or states of the independent variables of the theory. Though logically there is no contradiction in supposing that any form of kinship system may succeed any other, in fact this seems not to be the case. Kinship systems do not succeed one another at random, but the existing system and the forms of its determining variables limit the alternatives for change. Certain possible forms that a given variable may take may well be ruled out of a given situation on the grounds that its presence is not compatible with the existence of the present forms of others of the variables. The successor states of the kinship system will be determined by the way in which the variables determinant of its state change, and since the possibilities for this are not unrestricted, neither are the possible successor states. In sum, Watson took certain consequences of the theory—the realization of which would always be a determinate temporal sequence—for the actual theory itself, failing to see that these are consequences of a causal theory of the usual sort.

All this points to the following: To be concerned with determinate temporal sequences—whether they be actually realized sequences, which may have been described by ethnographers or historians, or theoretically possible ones, instance of which may have but need not actually have been realized—is to be concerned with something that is comparatively specific or concrete. But to be concerned with theories which explain temporal sequences is not to be restricted to such sequences. Our theories explain sequences by relating them to the conditions sufficient for their development, but they are not themselves developmental or sequential. A nondevelopmental causal theory of the usual kind would clearly be more general than any account of a sequence of development. Even if we could have laws of development, we would still want to have explanations for them, and this would lead us to consideration of causal theories. It is, I think, significant that in all of the examples of developmental anthropology we have considered in this paper, explanations of the studied sequences or developments or evolutions are always such as to presuppose causal laws. And this is precisely what one expects: the particular course of

[61] J. B. Watson, "Four Approaches to Cultural Change: A Systematic Assessment," *Social Forces*, 1953, *32*:137–145, 140 f.
[62] Murdock, *op. cit.*, pp. 252–257.

development is explained by appeal to laws of greater generality. Even if the claims of the developmental anthropologists could be realized, and laws of development more general than particular developmental sequences are formulated, it is a commonplace in the history of science that laws of lower generality need to be explained by laws of greater generality. Since reference to determinate temporal sequence is clearly a restriction upon the generality of sociocultural laws or theories, we would expect that the laws of development could be explained by laws more general still, not restricted in this way. One might, perhaps, make the same point in a somewhat different way. We need not deny that the course of culture history or the history of some particular culture could be characterized in evolutionary or developmental language, but any correct account of such development would be a correct description of a long and complex historical event. It would be particular and not general. Even if one could accept the standpoint of general evolution and agree that some proposed claims concerning the order of general evolutionary development was well founded and in accord with the best available evidence, this account would still be particular and historical and would certainly not be self-explanatory.

FREEDOM, MORALITY, AND SCIENCE:
A CLOSING DIGRESSION

It is not possible in comparatively few words to do justice to the subject indicated by the title of this closing section, but it does seem to me worth taking just a bit of space in order to indicate how certain conceptions of science *implicit* in the developmentalist ideal of theory formation in anthropology may be related logically to views *actually held* by present-day developmentalists with respect to such matters as freedom and morality. As readers familiar with their writings know, they tend to see the use of such terms as obfuscating rather than clarifying the actuality of human existence, and they take interest in individuals to be incompatible with the requirements of a science of culture. Thus, invention is always taken to be the putting together of pre-existing cultural elements in new ways, the possibility of human creativity being denied. The individual is taken to be only a passive recipient of what his culture offers, thus making the experience of freedom and obligation merely apparent or chimerical, corresponding to nothing in the reality of human life. There are, to be sure, any number of factors which enter into this view being arrived at by given individual developmentalists. Some may believe that science must reflect the actual nature of reality,[63] and given their

---

[63] For a recent discussion of the anisomorphy of science and reality, see M. Bunge, *Metascientific Queries*, Thomas, 1959, chap. 5.

espousal of culturalogical methods and evolutionist doctrine feel impelled to reach such conclusions. There may be, too, a failure to distinguish between the methodological requirements of a given discipline and the treatment of them as metaphysical doctrines which clearly transcend those requirements.[64] And, in addition, there may be ideological[65] and metaphysical[66] elements involved in such conclusions as well. But as interesting as the tracing and analysis of such matters might be, they are irrelevant to the present paper. I want here only to make some brief remarks on the possible contribution of the logic of developmentalism to the conclusions in question.

One central way in which developmental theories differ from causal theories of the usual kind is that the former are categorical in application while the latter are hypothetico-deductive.[67] In their application to actual phenomena, causal theories do not maintain that the realized phenomena were in any way necessary, but only that given the theoretically sufficient conditions for the appearance of some phenomenon we have reason to expect that it will appear. There is a widely held view that the applicability of scientific procedures to the study of any sphere is compatible only with that sphere's being a causally determined system in the sense that there are no real alternatives even if the limitations of our knowledge prevent our actually knowing what is in fact necessitated. Yet this point of view, though certainly compatible with the findings of science, is not logically derived from those findings and represents only some kind of metaphysical determinism which is held by those who hold it quite independently of science. To build a bridge requires the *application* to the task of certain branches of theoretical science, and the successful completion of such a structure and its continued existence may certainly be cited as additional evidence in confirmation of the theories involved. Yet the law-dependent character of all this in no way entails that some La Placean "intelligence,"[68] knowing the laws which govern the physical universe and having a complete state description of the universe, say, some ten thousand years ago could have predicted

[64] Cf. My "The Phenomenological and Naturalistic Approaches to the Social," in M. Natanson (ed.), *Philosophy of the Social Sciences: A Reader*, Random House, 1963, pp. 288–301, particularly part I.

[65] Cf. the reference to Sahlins cited in note 15; and, despite his disclaimers, Service, in Sahlins and Service (eds.), *op. cit.*, pp. 110–122.

[66] This is implicit in the claim that their opponents believe in something called freedom of the *will*, i.e., are metaphysical dualists rather than materialists, as well as in the free use of terms such as "supernatural," "human soul," and the like in polemics. One recent example is J. A. Ford's note "A Whimper from a Pink Granite Tower," *American Anthropologist*, 1964, 66:399–401, though others might be cited.

[67] An account of the hypothetico-deductive method may be found in virtually any textbook on philosophy of science; in addition, the well-known essay of Hempel and Oppenheim, *op. cit.*, particulary Part I.

[68] P. S., Marquis de La Place, *A Philosophical Essay on Probabilities*, Dover, 1951, p. 4.

the building of the bridge. I should want to say, then, that so far as the *logic* of the usual sort of causal explanation is concerned, there is nothing about it that is incompatible with the human freedom of our experience, for it in no way requires that the initial conditions to which we apply it be necessary.[69]

The matter is otherwise when we consider developmental theories. It is perhaps odd to speak of their logic when there really do not seem to be any and when, as we have seen, their most serious advocates presuppose the usual kind of causal theories when they are actually engaged in trying to explain cultural phenomena. Yet we have seen that the tendency of those who advocate developmental theory formation in anthropology is to see theories of science as necessitarian in character. They are said to tell us how things *must* develop, any alternative view being dismissed as the introduction of an irrational element incompatible with scientific analysis. It is surely such a conception as this which leads Service, in his contribution to *Evolution and Culture*, to the conclusion that the "law of evolutionary potential" absolutely entails that the next major evolutionary advances, i.e., advances in the capture and use of energy, will come from the presently underdeveloped countries, and so the United States (and, I should presume, the Soviet Union as well) must look ahead to a time when its position will be subordinate to those countries. Likewise, Sahlins' justification-in-the-guide-of-explanation[70] of authoritarian or totalitarian regimes on the ground that the historical circumstances brook no alternative and that moral considerations ought not to be intruded into our treatment of such matters, must, likewise, rest upon a necessitarian conception. In sum, quite apart from whatever other intellectual commitments may be at work in leading these writers to their views of human freedom and responsibility, it does seem to be the case that belief in categorical laws of development, presumably reflecting the necessitarian nature of the phenomena to which they are to be applied, lends some support to these views. But once we see that the theories actually developed through scientific investigation are in all instances hypothetical in their applications, we can see that the possibility of such theories is in no way incompatible with human freedom and the reality of alternatives.[71,72]

---

[69] This is but one small point in a vastly complex subject, but the only one of concern to me here. For a small sample of the range of the problems of science and freedom, one might mention but two recent discussions: S. Körner, "Science and Moral Responsibility," *Mind*, 1964, 73:161–172; and the discussion of "Free Will and Causal Prediction" in F. S. C. Northrop and H. Livingston (eds.), *Cross-Cultural Understanding*, Harper & Row, 1964, pp. 356–364.

[70] In the reference cited in note 15.

[71] Cf. the remarks of C. I. Lewis, *An Analysis of Knowledge and Valuation*, Open Court, 1946, pp. 3 f; and C. S. Peirce, *Collected Papers*, Harvard University Press, 1931–1935, 1.403 (i.e., vol. 1, par. 403) and 6.35–65.

[72] I am grateful to my colleague, Professor Louise E. Sweet, for her kindness in calling my attention to publications I might otherwise have missed.

WILLIAM H. DRAY

Singular hypotheticals
and historical explanation

I

No problem about the nature of historical inquiry has received more attention from philosophers in recent years than the problem of historical explanation; and none, perhaps, bears more directly on the question of history's relation to the social sciences. As is well known, the stimulus for much of what is currently being written comes from C. G. Hempel's classic paper, "The Function of General Laws in History," which offered historians a choice only between giving "scientific" and giving "pseudo" explanations.[1] This paper looms so large, indeed, that most contributors to the literature have quickly found themselves classified as either pro-

[1] *The Journal of Philosophy*, 1942, pp. 35–48; reprinted in P. Gardiner (ed.), *Theories of History*, Free Press, 1959, pp. 344–356. Hempel has restated and developed his position in "Explanation in Science and in History," in R. G. Colodny (ed.), *Frontiers of Science and Philosophy*, The University of Pittsburgh Press, 1962, pp. 9–33.

Hempelian or anti-Hempelian—as if only two views about the logical structure of explanation in history could seriously be entertained.[2]

The theory of historical explanation propounded by Alan Donagan, parts of which I propose to examine, is of special interest because it is not so easily pigeonholed in this way. Like the extreme Hempelians, Donagan insists that historical explanation, as much as scientific explanation, has to be strictly deductive if it is to escape the charge of being incomplete or defective. But like many of those who oppose the extension of the Hempelian model to history, he allows that general laws of human action are neither known by historians nor needed to explain what historical agents did. In claiming thus to escape between the horns of an embarrassing dilemma—the conclusion either that historical explanations (since they rest on laws which are formally without exception) are logically tight but empircally bogus, or (since they make do with statistical generalizations) are empirically genuine but logically loose— Donagan argues, furthermore, that his position represents a detailed working through of the views of the idealist philosopher, R. G. Collingwood in *The Idea of History* and some of his other works.[3] There are points on which he develops Collingwood, and others on which he thinks him mistaken. But on the whole, what he offers is Collingwood's answer to Hempel in Hempel's own language.

With much of what Donagan has to say I find myself in substantial agreement; and one of my purposes in writing this paper is to draw readers' attention to it. I want also, however, to express some reservations about certain features of his account—less with reference to whether it offers a faithful interpretation of Collingwood (for which he generally presents impressive evidence), than to whether it presents us with a faithful reconstruction of the historian's concept of explanation. I shall first give a brief exposition of what I take to be Donagan's general position, especially the more important claims he makes about the logical shape of the explanation of human actions in history by contrast with the explanation of physical occurrences. In the body of the paper, I shall then discuss some difficulties which certain of his doctrines seem to me to raise: in particular, his contentions that knowing "what" and knowing "why" in history come to the same thing; that historical explanations, when completely stated, in fact represent past actions as deducible from what their agents "thought"; and that non-Hempelian explanations of human actions in terms of the choices, if not the reasons, of historical agents are always in principle possible. I shall express doubts

---

[2] For a division into *three* camps see M. Mandelbaum, "Historical Explanation: The Problem of Covering Laws," *History and Theory*, 1961, pp. 229–242.

[3] Oxford University Press, 1945. The most important other works are Collingwood's *An Essay on Metaphysics*, Oxford University Press, 1940, part III, C; *An Autobiography*, Oxford University Press, 1939; and *The New Leviathan*, Oxford University Press, 1942, part I.

whether, as it stands, Donagan's account can be accepted in all its details as an elucidation of the concept of explanation historians actually operate with. This is a claim, it should perhaps be added, to be distinguished from the mere observation that not all historical explanations fully display its structure as they are ordinarily presented or accepted.

In outlining and discussing Donagan's views, I shall draw chiefly on two sources: a recent article, "Historical Explanation: the Popper-Hempel Theory Reconsidered,"[4] and the relevant portions of his book, *The Later Philosophy of R. G. Collingwood*.[5] Occasional reference will also be made to what he has said in earlier pieces on the same subject, since there appears to be an essential continuity of doctrine.[6]

II

The view that Donagan conceives himself as attacking could be put summarily as follows. To explain an event is to deduce the statement that it occurred (or show that this could be deduced) from statements asserting the occurrence of certain antecedent or simultaneous events (call them "initial conditions"), with the help of a certain empirically verified general law or conjunction of such laws. The explanandum consists of a statement reporting the occurrence of what is to be explained. The explanans consists of statements of initial conditions and general (i.e., universal) laws. The logical relation between explanans and explanandum must be deductive. According to Hempel, these requirements hold for the explanation of human actions in history as much as for the explanation of any other kind of event.

In opposing this position, Donagan follows Collingwood in holding that the historical explanation of a human action involves, not relating it in some such way to another event, but "discerning" the thought of the agent who performed it (VHT, 205). The explanandum consists of a statement reporting the performance of the action. The explanans attributes certain "thoughts" to the historical agent. Examples would be the explanation of Brutus' joining Cassius' conspiracy by reference to his resolve to protect the Republic at all costs (PHR, 20–21); or of the invasion of Britain by Julius Caesar by reference to his intention to occupy the country (LPC, 183–185); or of the failure of the early Danish invaders of Britain to settle the lands they conquered by reference to their being plunderers first and settlers by afterthought (EH, 436). In all these cases, what the agent *did* is explained in terms of what he

[4] *History and Theory*, 1954, pp. 3–26 (designated in the text hereafter as PHR).
[5] Oxford University Press, 1962 (designated hereafter as LPC).
[6] Relevant writings include: "Explanation in History," in P. Gardiner (ed.), *Theories of History*, Free Press, 1959, pp. 428–443 (designated hereafter as EH); "The Verification of Historical Theses," *The Philosophical Quarterly*, 1956, pp. 193–208 (designated hereafter as VHT).

thought—at any rate, in a broad Collingwoodian sense of the term "thought" (EH, 437; LPC, 220). Donagan agrees with the Hempelians, however, that such explanations are formally sound only if there is a relation of logical deduction between explanans and explanandum.

Besides accepting this formal requirement of the Hempelians, Donagan accepts also the demand that what is asserted in the historian's explanans be empirically verified. This comes out in his account of the historian's procedure in arriving at his explanations, which might be characterized as "hypothetico-deductive" (LPC, 182 ff.). Given that Brutus joined Cassius, the historian's problem is, in the first instance, to elaborate various hypotheses as to the beliefs, intentions, motives, etc., which constituted what Collingwood calls the "inside" of his action.[7] He can claim to have explained what Brutus did if he can show that one and only one such "thought" hypothesis, of the many which may logically entail the explanandum, survives empirical testing. The testing of a thought hypothesis consists of the deduction from it of other actions which Brutus would have performed if that hypothesis were true, and then looking for evidence of his having or not having done them. The empirical legitimacy of the historian's explanatory hypothesis depends upon these deductions being falsifiable in principle. Its final acceptance depends upon its being the sole survivor of actual attempts at falsification.

The immediate problem raised by this account of the historian's explanatory procedure is how the deduction of actions from hypotheses concerning the agent's thought can be effected without assuming the truth of some general laws. After all, Hempel had not denied the possibility of "thought" (he prefers the term, "motive") explanations; he had simply insisted that they were incomplete unless the historian could call upon some psychological law which, by providing a hypothetical premiss, would license deduction of the action from the agent's thought.[8] Now Donagan readily allows that no deduction is possible without a hypothetical premiss; but he claims that the statement of the agent's thought itself yields such premisses. Thus from the statement, "Brutus was resolved to protect the Republic at all costs," he says, can be derived by logical analysis the hypothetical statement, "If Brutus believed that to protect the Republic it was necessary to perform a certain act, he would perform it"; and this, together with the further "thought" statement, "Brutus believed it necessary to join Cassius' conspiracy in order to protect the Republic," logically entails the explanandum, "Brutus joined Cassius" (PHR, 20). The deduction-licensing hypothetical here is not, of course, a *general* hypothetical; it is *singular*, since it refers only to Brutus,

---

[7] For Collingwood the "outside" of a historical action is "everything belonging to it which can be described in terms of bodies and their movements." The "inside" is "that in it which can only be described in terms of thought." *The Idea of History*, p. 213.

[8] "The Function of General Laws in History," *op. cit.*, pp. 352–353.

rather than to all men of a certain kind; and it is consequently not a "law" in the sense required by Hempelian theory. Its logical efficacy, however, with respect to the particular explanatory deduction required, is no less than that of a corresponding general law.

The gist of Donagan's account is thus that thoughts can explain actions because the attribution of thoughts to an agent, since it entails singular hypotheticals which set forth what the agent would do under various circumstances envisaged by him, can logically entail the action to be explained. And empirical verification of the historian's explanans is achieved by further exploiting these deductive possibilities. It was in recognizing the need for such deduction, according to Donagan, that the original Hempelians (by contrast with their faint-hearted successors)[9] were strong; for unless an explanation rules out the possibility of the non-occurrence of what is to be explained, we cannot claim to know why *it*, rather than something else, occurred on the particular occasion we have in view (EH, 430; PHR, 7—9). The weakness of the Hempelians was their failure to realize the logical relevance and potency of singular hypotheticals.

In order to round off this brief account of Donagan's thesis, I should perhaps make it clear that he allows that few "thought" explanations satisfy his deductive criterion as they are actually stated—a concession of the sort that almost everyone who elaborates a model of historical explanation, deductive or otherwise, finds it necessary to make. Historical explanations are almost always stated *incompletely*. Donagan's thesis is thus more precisely put as the claim that the completion of a "thought" explanation, although it renders it deductive, does not transmute it into a Hempelian subsumption. A complete explanation of anything—this follows directly from the deductive thesis—requires reference to a *sufficient condition* of that thing (LPC, 202). In historical explanation, this means specifying the thought of the agent to the point where it becomes a sufficient condition of the action. But this sufficiency, it is claimed, can be certified without reference to general laws.

What would an historian's explanans have to contain in order to set forth the sufficient condition of an action? Following Collingwood, Donagan holds that it would have to include reference both to the agent's beliefs about his situation (what Collingwood calls his *causa quod*) and to what he intended to bring about (his *causa ut*) (LPC, 192 ff.). In the more complicated cases, Donagan adds, it would require reference also to inferences drawn from them (LPC, 193; PHR, 20). The *causa ut* is itself divisible into the agent's *plan*, if he had one, and what might

[9] Donagan has in mind all those who argue that "defective" general laws of various kinds may afford satisfactory explanation. See, for example, Patrick Gardiner, *The Nature of Historical Explanation*, Oxford University Press, 1952, pp. 93 ff.; or M. Scriven, "Truisms as the Grounds for Historical Explanations," in Gardiner, *Theories of History*, pp. 464 ff.

be called his *policy*, which would include not only the *purpose* he had in mind but also the *conditions* under which it was to be pursued. Although Donagan does not explicitly say so, it would seem that the *causa quod* would also be divisible into the agent's beliefs about the *facts* of his situation, and his estimate of the likely consequences of the various courses of action open to him (i.e., his *causal beliefs* in the more usual sense of "cause"). According to Donagan, both *causa ut* and *causa quod* entail singular hypotheticals referring to action by the agent (LPC, 195). It seems to be his view, however, as the example concerning Brutus and Cassius will have indicated, that the singular hypothetical which plays a role analogous to that of the general law in a Hempelian explanation would normally be derived from the *cuasa ut*: for example, Brutus' resolve to protect the Republic at all costs. What corresponds to Hempel's statement of initial conditions in an historical explanation would normally come from the *causa quod*: for example, his belief that it was necessary to join Cassius in order to achieve this end.

III

Now the first difficulty I should like to raise about Donagan's account concerns his claim that it is a peculiarity of "thought" explanations in history that a proper account of them breaks down the distinction that we should ordinarily try to draw between establishing or stating historical facts and explaining them. Certainly Collingwood himself, in a much noted passage of *The Idea of History*, seems to have entertained the paradoxical conclusion that it does so. Donagan quotes him thus: "When (an historian) knows what happened, he already knows why it happened" (p. 214). And Donagan's own elaboration of what this means is plausible enough: "an historian," he says, "explains a fact in the very process of establishing it, and the mere statement of an historical fact is also its explanation" (LPC, 201).

What we are offered here is actually a pair of arguments. The first is that the historian cannot *establish* an historical fact without discovering its explanation. In Donagan's view, many theorists of history have been led to wrestle with unreal problems through ignoring this fact. Patrick Gardiner, for example, in *The Nature of Historical Explanation*, discusses at length how an historian would set about answering a question like, "Why did Louis XIV die unpopular?" (p. 96). "An historian," Donagan contends, "could not be faced with this question unless he could prove the fact; and it is hard to see how he could prove *this* fact unless he also knew its explanation" (EH, 432). The second argument is that we do not really know *what an action is* until we know *all* the thought of the agent which will eventually enter into its explanation. Thus to know merely that Caesar invaded Britian in 54 B.C., Donagan insists, is not yet to know what "the historical fact" really was. To employ Collingwoodian terminology, it is to know "little more than the outside of that event" (LPC, 201). Until the historian goes further, "what happened" remains unknown. Neither of these arguments appear to me well conceived. Both, I shall suggest, rest on a failure to ask, when historical explanation is given, precisely *what* is being explained by reference to *what*, and in answer to *what kind of question*.

It is interesting to note, in appraising Donagan's defence of Collingwood here, that, according to him, it has been a feature of a number of attacks on Hempelian theory that Hempel's opponents have missed the point. They have done so because they have failed to notice that all Hempel claims to elucidate is the form of explanations of *why something in fact occurred*. For this reason, arguments which purport to show that Hempel's theory distorts the structure of explanations of how something could have occurred, or of how something was done, or of what something amounted to—three types which have sometimes been represented as raising difficulties for Hempel's analysis—really do not come to grips with Hempel's claims (PHR, 3). Donagan's thesis, by contrast, *does* allegedly come directly to grips with these claims; what it elaborates is an alternative account of the structure of at least some explanations of why something in fact occurred. The things in question, it is natural to assume, are human actions. For, like Collingwood, Donagan regards it as the historian's business to study, not mere "events," but "conscious actions." "Every historical fact," he says, "is about an action" (LPC, 201).

Now it does not seem to me that Donagan can defend Collingwood's paradox, while at the same time claiming both that historical explanations explain why something in fact occurred and that what they explain is human actions, in the perfectly acceptable sense of "action" which he derives from Collingwood. The historian's explanandum, according to Donagan, will report the fact that a certain action was performed. But an action, on the Collingwoodian theory, is "the unity of the outside and inside of an event" (LPC, 192); and the thought-side of the event, which enters into this unity, thus belongs to the historian's explanandum : it is part of what is to be explained. It can hardly therefore, without triviality, provide the historian with an explanans if we go on to raise the question why what is specified in the explanandum occurred.

There is a commonsense way out of the difficulty. But it appears to be barred by Donagan's denial—essential to his defence of the paradox— that anything less than knowledge of the action which includes *full* knowledge of its thought-side is knowledge of what an historian has to explain. For otherwise it could plausibly have been argued that an action such as Caesar's invasion of Britain, which already, in being described as an invasion, is represented as having a thought-side (his intention to get there, for example), is to be explained by reference to *further* "thoughts" of the agent (his plan to occupy the country). The suggestion that we can in this way know a fact (that Caesar invaded) without knowing its explanation (in order to occupy the country) is, however, explicitly rejected by Donagan as an "obvious" but invalid objection to Collingwood's paradox (LPC, 201). To know only a part of the agent's thought, he claims, is not yet to know the historical *fact*; and to go on to discover the fact, since it leaves nothing further to discover, is at the same time to discover the historical explanation. We are left then with the consequence that full specification of the agent's thought must appear in *both* explanans and explanandum. This leaves the explanation itself open to a charge of circularity.

To this conclusion the objection might perhaps be raised that the explanation is not *just* circular. For the explanandum includes more than the agent's thought: it includes the whole action which expresses it. And it might be argued that the thought which is specified in the explanans is thus not intended to explain the *thought*, identically specified in the explanandum, but rather to explain *the action as a whole*. If this is to rebut the charge of circularity, however, it must surely be taken as tantamount to admitting that what is explained is really the action's own *outside*—the part of the explanandum not identical with a part of the explanans. And to make this clear, all mention of the agent's thought should really be transferred from the historian's explanandum to his explanans. Unfortunately, to defend Donagan's claims in such a way would involve denying a major Collingwoodian doctrine: that historical explanation is of actions rather than of "mere" events.[10] There are hints, nevertheless, that Donagan seriously considers accepting this way out of the difficulty. Thus, in an early attack on what he takes to be W. H. Walsh's intuitionist interpretation of Collingwood (VHT, 193, n. 3), he offers the following elucidation of the second part of the puzzle passage previously quoted from Collingwood. In the claim, "When (the historian) knows what happened, he already knows why it happened," he says, the word "it" has a vague antecedent. Mistakenly, Walsh took it to refer to the agent's thought, and concluded that Collingwood regarded thoughts as self-explanatory. Donagan argues that it refers only to the *event*. The inside, in other words, explains, not itself, but the outside.[11]

10 Although Collingwood himself sometimes uses "event" to *include* expressed thought—as when he distinguishes (p. 213) between the outside and inside of an "event" in the past—he also refers to "mere" events where he wishes to *contrast* outside with inside (p. 214).

11 A similar construction might be put upon Donagan's claim that, like Popper, he is concerned "solely with causal explanations of events" (PHR, 3), and again, that both history and neurophysiology investigate "the bodily movement which Brutus made when he stabbed Caesar" (LPC, 293).

As an account of what historians actually do when they give explanations, this conclusion seems to me odd enough to warrant resistance. And there are suggestions that Donagan himself prefers another way of rendering Collingwood's doctrine coherent. The historian, he tells us at one point, when he learns of Caesar's invasions of Britian and subsequent withdrawals, asks himself, "What was the nature of these acts?" (LPC, 182). Again, "the most elementary historical explanations are of acts of individuals," he says "and consist in a full statement of what those acts are, both outside and inside" (LPC, 206). If we can take these statements at face value, we get a very different account of the nature of historical explanation. The historian's explanandum, we seem to be told, consists of a report of the occurrence of a certain action, incompletely specified. The explanans consists of a complete specification of the *same* action. Our previous suggestion as to how Donagan's account might avoid circularity involved relegating all mention of the agent's thought to the explanans, the physical side of his action being referred to the explanandum. The present one requires specification of the whole action in *both* explanans and explanandum, the two specifications, however, being different. We might move, for example, from characterizing Caesar's action as an invasion to characterizing it as an attempt to conquer the country. In doing so we would explain in the sense of making it clear *what it was* that Caesar did: in Donagan's own words, we would make clear "the nature of the act."

Now I do not want to deny that historians ever explain in the sense of showing us *what things really are*.[12] Indeed, I should want to claim rather that this is a very important kind of historical explanation, and one from which the Hempelian theory unfortunately diverts attention. But there are at least two difficulties involved in any attempt to defend Collingwood's paradox by interpreting the historian's question as a "What is it really?" question. The first is that if explanations-why are thus to be reduced to explanations-what, it is difficult to see how Donagan's shaft against Hempel can be said to find its mark any more successfully than those of the critics he began by setting aside. For it could be claimed that he, too, ignores Hempel's claim to analyze only explanations of why something in fact occurred. The second difficulty is that such reduction of why-questions to what-questions, if made the basis of a general theory of historical explanation, goes clean against what historians constantly represent themselves as doing: among other things, raising and answering why-questions. The latter consideration, although not final, warrants at least a further attempt to elicit an independent logical structure for explaining why in the case of human actions. But

[12] For a discussion of this sort of explanation see my "'Explaining What' in History," in Gardiner, *Theories of History*, pp. 403–408.

we can scarcely go back to analyses which represent historical explanations as circular, or as having sheer physical occurrences as their subjects. To escape from the difficulty, I suggest, we need to take seriously the commonsense objection which Donagan dismissed as fallacious: that the historian begins with knowledge of an action performed, including a thought-side, and gives an explanation of it by relating the whole of it to thought of the agent which, in some important sense, is *not* a part or "side" of the action to be explained. With this possibility in mind, let us look briefly again at the example Donagan considered: Caesar's invasion of Britain.

What raises the *demand* for explanation here? Toward what is the historian's why-question directed? Not his knowledge that certain human bodies moved across a certain stretch of water; rather his knowledge that Caesar *invaded*. Now, so long as we are content to refer vaguely to "Caesar's action," or to "what Caesar did," his plan to occupy the country may certainly be regarded as, in some sense of interest to Collingwood, a "part" of it. But this sense is not relevant to the analysis of the explanation he gives in answer to the question, "Why did Caesar invade?" To get the structure of *that* explanation straight, we need to ask what belongs to the explanandum and what to the explanans. The explanandum reports the invasion; the explanans attributes to Caesar a plan of conquest. What we explain, in such a case, it should be noted, is Caesar's action *as specified in the explanandum*; we do not explain "the action" in some sense which leaves its final specification open. As Hempel originally put it, the subject matter of explanation is the occurrence of an event of a certain kind.[13] And Donagan elsewhere appears to accept this principle. Thus, in discussing the explanation of a letter of Dr. Johnson as an expression of his righteous indignation, what can be explained, Donagan says, is only its having "certain general features"; we cannot explain its being written "just as it was" (EH, 435). It should be clear that no historian would claim to answer why-questions about "what happened" in the sense of explaining its happening just as it did. Yet it is such a sense which appears to be required by Donagan's elucidation and defence of Collingwood's paradox. It is only this which would seem to justify our leaving indeterminate the specification of the action to be explained until we see what will count as its explanation—then incorporating the latter into the final specification of what we claim to have explained.

To escape from such difficulties, I should want to argue that in the analysis of "thought" explanations of action, we must be prepared to distinguish, as Donagan does not always seem to, between two different logical roles which knowledge of the agent's thought must play. The first (if I may put it this way) is that of raising the status of a mere physical

---

[13] "The Function of General Laws in History," *op. cit.*, p. 346.

event to that of an object of historical interest: a human action in the Collingwoodian sense. The place of such reference to thought is exclusively in the historian's explanandum. The second is that of providing an answer to the historian's question why what is specified in the explanandum occurred. Thus reference to Caesar's plan to occupy the country is in no way required to specify his action as an invasion, whereas reference to his intention to land regardless of opposition may be. Of course, if we had wished, we could have asked a why-question about Caesar's action specified as an attempted conquest rather than as an invasion; *what* is to be explained is up to us. In that case, however, reference to his plan of conquest would belong in the historian's explanandum as the thought which helps to *constitute* the action to be explained; and by changing our question we should have ruled out this thought as a possible explanatory factor. A satisfactory explanans would now have to make reference to some further thought of caesar's.

Considerations of this kind dispose of the second of the two arguments Donagan employs in defence of Collingwood's paradox; that we do not know what the action really *is* without knowing its thought-side. But the first argument is no more tenable than the other. The historian can have *established* his explanandum before he discovers his explanans. Indeed, Donagan virtually admits this himself when, in complaining that to know that Caesar invaded is to know "little more than the outside of that event," he conceded, in effect, that it is to know at least *a little* more; and again, when he sets the stage for the *discovery* of an historical explanation with the declaration: "It is well known that Julius Caesar twice invaded, and, after short campaigns, withdrew" (LPC, 182). In any case, it should be clear that hypothetico-deductive reasoning, if it is legitimate to use it at all in history, is quite capable of establishing the historian's explanandum without also establishing his explanans. In the present instance, it would be enough for the historian, in seeking to establish the hypothesis that Caesar invaded, to eliminate such contenders as that he was taking his troops for a pleasure cruise, or a practice maneuver, or a friendly call. It is quite unnecessary to attempt the falsification of the further hypothesis that Caesar planned to occupy the country. This would become necessary only if we went on to seek an explanation for what we have already established. I conclude, therefore, that Collingwood's paradox does not survive examination.

IV

I should like to turn, now, to the second of the three problems in Donagan's account which have been selected for discussion: the contention that the internal structure of historical explanation is deductive.

Two preliminary remarks may perhaps help to bring the problem into focus. First, it should be noted that the point at issue is entirely one about the *internal structure* of the explanation. It is to be distinguished, therefore, from questions about the degree of evidential support historians may achieve for their "thought" hypotheses[14]—Donagan's own claim that this amounts to "scientific corroboration" suggesting a whole further dimension of difficulty for the acceptance of his theory as a whole (LPC, 190; PHR, 20–21). Second, there is, of course, no question that explananda reporting actions can be logically deduced from appropriate singular hypotheticals, together with other singular statements about the agent's thought: Donagan's example about Brutus, already cited, is straightforward enough. Where the deductive claim begins to raise questions is the point at which the hypotheticals are themselves said to be deducible from the "thought" hypotheses of the historian (PHR, 23; LPC, 190).[15] There are grounds, I think, for doubting that Donagan's thesis here can be defended as he states it; and in addition to certain cautions which he expresses himself, I shall suggest some further modifications of it which would seem to be required. In the final section of the paper, I shall test my understanding of the account I have attributed to him by trying to connect it with what he has to say about the way decisions, choices, and reasons may enter into historical explanation.

Can the action of an historical agent be strictly deduced from what Donagan, following Collingwood, calls its thought-side? Or, more strictly, in view of what was said earlier in rejection of Collingwood's paradox: Can the assertion that an action was actually performed at a certain time be deduced from any attribution to the agent of thoughts which are other than those required to constitute it an action of the kind specified in the historian's explanandum? On the face of it, this is not easy to believe. And some of the sample deductions Donagan offers are not very plausible. The statement that the Danes were "plunderers first and settlers by afterthought," he declares, "immediately implies the law-like statement that if those Danes had opportunity of sufficient plunder in a territory, they would not settle in it"—from which the deduction of their behavior in England is said to follow with the aid

---

[14] Difficulties raised in this section and the next about the deductive thesis generally would nevertheless be relevant to a critique of the claim that the historian's verification procedure is hypothetico-deductive. For a non-deductive alternative see W. B. Gallie, "Explanations in History and the Genetic Sciences," in Gardiner, *Theories of History*, pp. 397–398.

[15] Donagan points out that it is thus the thought hypothesis, strictly speaking, rather than the singular hypothetical itself, which plays a logical role in historical explanation analogous to that of a general law or theory in scientific explanation. Explanations of physical occurrences do not usually employ singular hypotheticals; but this is because we are usually interested in explaining them not only as exemplifying certain kinds of reaction or behaviour, but also as exemplifying behaviour of certain kinds of things. In cases where we do employ singular hypotheticals, asserted of a named physical object (e.g., "my car," "John's throat"), we assume these are deducible from general hypotheticals. As will appear below, Donagan denies that we make the same assumption in history.

of a further premiss (EH, 436, 439).[16] Again, from the hypothesis that Caesar's invasion had been a successful punitive expedition, rather than an attempted conquest, and that he wrote his *Commentaries* with a view to self-advertisement, it is said that we can deduce that he would have written of this intention in his *Commentaries* (LPC, 184). It is hard to imagine the historians who made the original assertions resting comfortable with such "deductions".[17]

For this sort of objection, Donagan at times suggests an answer which itself makes the deductive thesis rather difficult to maintain, as stated. For he appears to agree that concepts like "being resolved" or "being plunderers first," which are commonly applied to human beings in respect of their rational activities, are logically *porous* (EH, 436). To attribute thoughts to an agent by means of such concepts, as we (and historians) actually use the language, is thus consistent with the agent's not always acting in the way that concept may lead us to expect. It is not a part of the ordinary logic of "holding a principle," for example, that a man should apply it on every appropriate occasion. To say, as Donagan's deductive thesis seems to require, that the only sense in which a man can act against his principles is to *change* them involves a considerable "tightening up" of an existing conceptual network, and cannot be represented simply as a refusal to base a theory of explanation on careless or improper usage. Indeed, under "the presupposition of individual choice" —which Donagan contends historians make, at least "methodologically"[18] —it might be argued that such conceptual looseness has a certain positive utility; for a man's character will presumably be thought of as consisting, at least partly, in mere trends observable in his past decisions. I mention this difficulty, however, only to let it pass in favor of theoretically more interesting ones which lie behind it. For the same reason I shall only mention the further difficulty that the concepts under consideration are also usually vague. *What* counts as falling under them at all, quite apart from whether it must *invariably* fall under them, is often indeterminate.

A more interesting problem for the deductive thesis is the fact that the exercise of "mental" dispositions—if I may use Rylian language for a moment[19]—can be private as well as public. And I should want to

[16] Donagan himself later repudiated a further "deduction" originally asserted in discussing this example: "that their literature and religion (if any) would glorify war" (PHR, 21). It is difficult to see, however, *why* some such deduction should not be possible on Donagan's theory.

[17] For another example, see LPC, 186.

[18] Donagan states it thus: "in a situation of a given kind, a man's intentions must not be assumed to be the same as those of any other man, whatever their psychological or sociological similarities; or the same as his own intentions in other situations of the same kind" (PHR, 19). Further citations relevant to the meaning of this principle will be found on p. 19.

[19] See G. Ryle, *The Concept of Mind*, 1949, especially chap. IV. In EH Donagan acknowledged indebtedness to Ryle (p. 433). For other examples of a Rylian approach to the problem, see P. Gardiner, *The Nature of Historical Explanation*, Part IV; and P. H. Nowell-Smith, "Are Historical Events Unique?" *Proceedings of the Aristotelian Society*, 1956, pp. 107–160.

point out, in this connection, that although Donagan declares that every part of the historian's thought hypothesis—*causa quod* as well as *causa ut*— entails singular hypotheticals about the agent's *behavior* (LPC, 195), he does not seem to be a logical behaviorist. What he does deny—to return now to Collingwoodian language—is that an agent can properly be said to have a thought which does not find *expression* in an occurrence. The expression, however (unless I have completely misunderstood him), although it would usually assume the form of a physical movement, does not *have* to be physical: it could be what Donagan calls an "internal utterance" (LPC, 194). It would follow, therefore, that one could not *deduce* from the attribution of a thought to an agent at a given time that he would *act* in an appropriate way at that time, if by this is meant that he would give his thought physical expression (i.e., "external utterance") at that time. I think Donagan is probably correct to represent Collingwood as having committed himself, in one or two passages of *The Idea of History*, to the contrary view. Yet in the previously unpublished parts of the Epilogomena to that work, where such a lot is made of the fundamental contrast between thought of all "levels" and the *immediate experience* (or "feeling") which Collingwood appears to regard as its vehicle, a less restricted view of what can "express" a thought may be discerned (LPC, 219–220). This suggests a modification of the sense in which we are to take the "inside-outside" terminology itself—one of the points on which Donagan might, I think, have reformulated and corrected Collingwood's own claims.[20]

It might be added, in this connection, that the plausibility of inferring overt activity—human actions which can be objects of historical concern—in fact varies considerably from concept to concept within the indicated range. Thus the claim that the Danes were "plunderers first" attributes to these agents a thought or mental disposition whose exercises are almost entirely overt and physical, so that if we could take the concept as non-porous and precise, we might say that it is part of what is meant by applying it to the Danes that they should *actually* plunder when given an opportunity, just as it might be said to be part of the meaning of calling a piece of glass brittle that it should actually shatter when stoned. It is less obvious that a man's "being resolved" must show itself on all appropriate occasions in relevant, resolute activity; and less obvious still—if I may hark back to the case of Dr. Johnson's letter—that anything overt is logically required in the case of "being indignant." It seems to me that it would be quite consistent with our conception of explanation by means of such concepts that we should

---

[20] For a development of this point, see my "R. G. Collingwood and the Acquaintance Theory of Knowledge," *Revue internationale de philosophie*, 1957, pp. 425–432. The outside would be what expresses the thought, whether physical or not; the inside would be what is expressed.

accept it, as a satisfactory explanation of his writing the letter, that Dr. Johnson was indignant, while refusing to hold that we could *deduce* that, in the circumstances, he would necessarily express his indignation in the way specified in the historian's explanandum. In other words, not only could we not deduce, given his indignation, that Dr. Johnson would write the exact letter that he did (see §III), but we could not deduce either that he would write one with "certain general features." It is true that from the statement that the letter was an expression of Johnson's indignation we may be able to deduce that it has "certain general features"—but that is another matter and does not establish Donagan's thesis.

At this point I think it is both legitimate and helpful to turn upon Donagan a criticism of Collingwood's own account which he *did* very properly make (LPC, 202–204). Donagan finds important, and generally correct, the Collingwoodian contention that the explanation of actions is to be given *entirely* by reference to the thought of the agent: it is the agent's *conception* of his situation, not his *actual* situation, that explains his doing what he did. But there is *lacuna* in this account, we are told, which makes it unacceptable as a comprehensive theory of historical explanation. For historians are interested not only in what historical agents tried to do, but also in whether they succeeded. The notions of achievement and failure, furthermore, are often built right into the very specification of what the agents did, and thus enter the historian's explanandum. But the explanation of, say, a general's victory, by contrast with the explanation of his setting about winning it in the ,way he did, obviously requires reference to the *actual* situation: the situation—and this includes the activities of the enemy—must cooperate. And that means that explanation in such cases cannot be achieved by deduction from hypotheses about the agent's thought alone.

By Donagan, however, such cases are regarded as no more than a class of exceptions to a Collingwoodian analysis which is generally satisfactory. What he seems not to notice is that *every* thought explanation, if it is to yield strict deduction of an overt action, requires a premiss about the actual situation. Donagan concedes that *exactly the same* thought explanation could be given of "Brutus killed Caesar (by stabbing him)" and of "Brutus stabbed Caesar (where Caesar does not die)," the latter dropping reference to the success of the action (LPC, 203). But reference to exactly the same thought would also explain "Brutus *attempted* to stab Caesar"—in fact, it would do so where no "action" above the threshhold of historical interest ensued at all. If the agent's control over his own body, at least, is a generally necessary condition of action in the historically interesting sense, then clearly we can *never* (as a matter of mere logic) deduce individual actions from statements about the agent's thought alone; we can never, as Collingwood has generally been thought to use the term, deduce the "outside" from the "inside." We shall always need an "efficacy" premiss, asserting something about the agent's powers and opportunities.

Even if we waive the problem of the admissibility of private expressions of thought, and even if we assume we could in every case supply an "efficacy" premiss, there are further difficulties in the deductive thesis as often presented, as Donagan himself points out. I think particularly of the criticism he levels at Collingwood for assuming that the agent's *causa ut* and *causa quod* together constitute a sufficient condition of his action (LPC, 193). What Collingwood did not see, according to Donagan, was the additional requirement that the agent should (at any rate in all but the simplest cases—see PHR, 20) put his *causa ut* and *causa quod* together and recognize, by an "act of practical reasoning," that the particular action he performed was rationally required by them. I take this to mean that, in spite of his own claim that each part of the historian's thought hypothesis directly entails singular hypotheticals about behavior, Donagan sees it as possible that the agent should fail even to *attempt* to act in accordance with his resolution and beliefs on a particular occasion. This brings out clearly one of the several ways in which the attribution of thoughts is logically porous with respect to appropriate actions. And admitting it considerably complicates the historian's alleged deduction. For it now becomes crucial that the latter be able to assert, whenevei he explains an action, that the agent did on that particular occasion perform such an act of practical reasoning.

The difficulty of obtaining independent verification of this crucial premiss is significant in view of Donagan's assurance that "complete" explanations, in the sense he explicates, are quite often given by historians. The problem this raises for the deductive thesis must not be overstated, however. For it would surely be generally agreed, by non-deductivists as well as deductivists, that a "thought" explanation *would* be undermined by any evidence that the agent whose action is to be explained did *not* realize that his *causa ut* and his *causa quod* together gave him reason for doing what he did—that he simply failed to see the "connection." And it appears that by "practical reasoning" Donagan means no more than such realization: he does not make it a general requirement of historical explanation that the historian "tune in" to the agent's actual flow of consciousness (LPC, 194).

A defender of the deductive thesis might thus well insist that what the present argument brings to light is not a defect of principle in the deductive theory of explanation, but only a way in which a crude statement of it may need modifying and refining. And the same might be claimed of the arguments which preceded it. Such arguments, indeed, might be welcomed by deductivists; their force, they might argue, is simply to make more explicit what is really involved in any claim deductively to have explained an action by reference to an agent's "thoughts." By noting the kinds of challenges which might have to be met by anyone claiming to have given such an historical explanation, it is progressively made clear that a fully satisfactory one must not employ concepts that are vague or porous (although it seems that the ones historians use generally are so); that its concepts must not leave open, in the case under examination, the possibility of purely private expressions (although perhaps most of the concepts falling into the range we are concerned with are the kind that do so in some degree); that "thought" premisses must be supplemented by "efficacy" premisses whenever the explananda specify more than the agent's attempt to act (which is almost always the case in history); and that the agent actually drew the practical conclusion which the considerations attributed to him as his "thoughts" really justified (although historians would probably be reduced in most cases to the mere assumption that this was so).

Such requirements, it seems fair to remark, have not always been clearly recognized when illustrative deductions of actions from thoughts have been offered by deductivists. And some of them—especially the need to exclude, or have warrant for ignoring, purely private expressions—make it difficult to claim that even the modified deductive thesis formulates a criterion which could often be satisfied by historians. In one of the earlier papers (EH, 434), Donagan himself confessed to "diffidence" about applying the deductive thesis to history, even as an ideal. In view of the difficulties noted, perhaps this was not unwarranted.

V

But the problems just considered are not the only ones which the deductive thesis, as Donagan states and amends it, appears to raise. For when we turn to look at what he has to say about the way reference to an agent's decision or choice may function in an historical explanation we discover that, on Donagan's considered view, even the satisfaction of the conditions already laid down may be insufficient to ensure deducibility of the action to be explained. An important issue in this connection is how Donagan's conceptual claims interlock with his indeterminism about human actions—a feature of his account which is initially surprising. For it is commonly assumed that a deductive theory of explanation is incompatible with metaphysical libertarianism.[21]

---

[21] More strictly, this is assumed on the further assumption that all actions are explicable. The latter, however, appears to be an assumption Donagan makes.

About the role of decision or choice in thought explanations, Donagan has this to say: "A rational being is one who has the power of deciding which action he will perform of the various ones he recognizes as possible for him on a given occasion" (LPC, 230). He adds that when a man acts for reasons, "an irreducible component of the explanation of his act is that he chose to act upon those reasons" (LPC, 231). Now the concepts of decision, choice and reason do not enter at all into most of Donagan's statements of his deductive model: these are in terms of *causa ut, causa quod* and practical reasoning. It seems proper to assume, however, that an agent's reasons (ignoring the "objective" sense in which a situation may be said to provide reasons without the agent's knowing it) are to be identified with his *causa ut* and *causa quod*, since it is upon these that his practical reasoning must be brought to bear. If so, what we are now apparently being told is that, even if an agent recognizes that his *causae* jointly require him to act in a certain way (i.e., he performs a relevant act of practical reasoning), and this way is possible for him (i.e., we have an "efficacy" premiss), we still cannot legitimately deduce that he *will* act this way. For deduction, we need the additional premiss that the agent decides or chooses to act in the way he recognizes his reasons require.

It may perhaps be thought that acceptance of the latter claim raises no special problem for Donagan's deductive thesis, apart from the difficulty of verifying assertions about the agent's decision or choice. All that it may appear to entail is still further modification of what was said to be required if an historical explanans is to set forth a sufficient condition of its explanandum, namely, the addition of the agent's decision or choice. It is important, however, to ask what *sort* of decision or choice on the part of the agent can plausibly be held to be an "irreducible component" of every historical explanation. For neither of two possibilities which immediately suggest themselves would be very satisfactory to a deductivist who was also a libertarian.

One of these is the forming of a resolution by the agent to act in the way described in the historian's explanandum, at some time antecedent to the action itself. Brutus' resolve to protect the Republic at all costs could be construed in this way. But decision or choice in the sense of antecedent resolution is clearly not a *generally* necessary condition of the sorts of action historians claim to explain: history is not limited to a study of what is deliberately anticipated. Such decision or choice would not, in any case, consitute "thought" *additional* to the agent's reasons, as Donagan's theory appears to require. On the contrary, it would itself provide the agent with a possible reason for acting, leaving it open, under libertarian assumptions, whether, at the appropriate time, he would in fact act in accordance with it. Thus Brutus' resolve would have provided him with such a reason if he had placed great value upon consistency; but he might still have decided, in the event, to act contrary to it. Donagan makes it clear that the "principle of individual choice," as he accepts it, does not imply that human beings are necessarily fickle (PHR, 19). It does, however, imply that up to the moment of acting, they can always change their minds. Antecedent resolution therefore offers no basis for explanatory deduction.

Is the indispensable decision or choice, then, one which the agent makes at the time of acting? There is, indeed, a quite familiar (if somewhat elusive) sense in which every action must have thus been "chosen" by its agent—a sense in which it follows *logically* from "He did it" that he "chose" to do it. Without the agent's "choosing" to act, it might be said, there is no action at all in the Collingwoodian sense. *What* the action is, furthermore—how it should be characterized—depends on what the agent "chooses" it to be. Caesar's landing in Britain, for example, would no more qualify as an invasion if Caesar had "chosen" it only as a punitive raid than it would if his ships had accidentally drifted ashore. Not that it is essential to our concept of human action that what was done should in every case have been "chosen" *as described in the explanandum.* For (to press further a point raised in §IV) we sometimes incorporate unintended consequences into what an agent is said to have done: generals "lose" battles as well as "win" them. The point is that, even in such cases, a relevant "choice" is still required (as was argued in a different context in §III) to help *constitute* the action what it is said to be: battles cannot be lost, for example, without "choosing" to fight them. This point, however, provides no support to Donagan's thesis. For the logical role of the "choices" envisaged makes them essential, not to every historical explanans, but to every historical explanandum. To deny deducibility without reference to such "choices" would thus actually undermine the deductive thesis. It would concede, in effect, that the historian's explanans can *never* set forth a sufficient condition without adding to it something which is part of what is to be explained.

That Donagan's thesis is nevertheless involved in this difficulty may most easily be concluded from what he has to say about the explanation of actions which are believed to have been done *without* reasons: cases which Donagan considers in order to show how very far a deductivist can go in attributing an "unconditional power of choice" to an agent. It is a metaphysical presupposition of historiography, he tells us, that when a man decides to act, "[f]or such decisions he may have reasons or he may not" (LPC, 230). A man may decide to play golf, for example, "for no particular reason." Indeed, "even when a man has a reason for a decision, a similar point holds. Why act on that reason rather than on another." When a man acts "for no reason at all," Donagan continues,

"it is sufficient explanation of his act to say 'That is what he chose to do.'"
But unless we are prepared (as Donagan sometimes seems to be)[22] to
accept the paradoxical notion that a thing can explain itself, the whole
theory of historical explanation surely becomes incoherent at this point.
For (to revert again to the terms and issues of §III) choosing to do the
particular thing the agent does is just the "inside"—in this case, the whole
"inside"—of what is to be explained. And answering the question,
"Why did he do it?" with "He just chose to do it" adds nothing to what
has already been asserted.

No doubt, "He just chose to do it" is informative in what it denies:
it denies that the agent did what he did for any particular reason. But this
scarcely justifies our calling it an *explanation* of his doing it. If it seems odd
to say, without qualification, that "He chose to do it" is no explanation at
all, this may be because in certain circumstances it might count as the
explanation of what Collingwood called the "mere event": it might
explain a physical occurrence as an action. It might also count as a partial
explanation of "the nature of the act," since it emphasizes its arbitrariness.
What it can never be is an explanation of why the action occurred: this
could surely be questioned only under pressure of an assumption that
every action must have a Collingwoodian explanation. Donagan himself
seems occasionally to waver a little on the point: he seems to imply that
what is simply chosen, although it may be in some sense "intelligible,"
may not be strictly explicable. Thus he observes, of a man's choice of
ultimate principles, that the "only explanation" possible is" that is how
he chose" (PHR, 19)—as if he recognized how close this is to allowing
that for such there can really be no explanation (unless we can accept
explanation of a different, perhaps Hempelian, kind). Again, in discussing
"man's power to survey different reasons for acting, and to choose to act
in accordance with one reason rather than another," he declares that the
choice neither requires nor admits of "further explanation" (LPC, 231)—
as if he was aware that demands for explanation would scarcely be
satisfied by assurances that what was done was no accident.

Where an action *is* done for reasons, however, much of what Donagan
says suggests still a third interpretation of the claim that reference to
decision or choice is indispensable for historical explanation. This is that
the historian needs to discover, not that the agent chose to do the action
as specified in the explanandum (something already known), but that
he chose to do it for reasons set forth in the explanans. As various
quotations have shown, Donagan's libertarianism leads him to claim that
an agent, after "surveying" his reasons, can act "upon" one reason rather
than another. The choice that is indispensable to the explanans is thus a

[22] For example, he quotes with approval an early statement of Collingwood's: "An act of the
will is its own cause and its own explanation" (LPC, 231).

choice of *reasons to act upon*. In the case of Caesar's invasion of Britain, for example, what would go into the historian's explanans is not the action-constituting decision to invade—this belongs to the explanandum—but the reason-selecting decision to occupy the country.[23] Donagan argues that the latter decision, if the explanation completely accounts for the action, must logically entail the former, or must do so taken together with other "thought" premises. Hence his representation of historical explanation, where reasons are involved, as showing the deducibility of choices from "prior" choices: the "priority" of explanatory choices, unlike antecedent resolves, is a matter of logic. Hence also the claim that explanatory deduction is compatible with the presupposition of free choice: the choices of action and of reasons upon which to act may be simultaneous.

Perhaps few would wish to quarrel with one major concern of Donagan's doctrine here: that an agent's merely *having* a certain reason does not account fully for his acting in accordance with the practical conclusion that follows from it. It is not even enough that the agent thought his reason "adequate" (LPC, 231). We need to know also that he decided to act for its sake. Evidence that he did not do so would, at any rate, destroy the explanatory force of the reason.[24] The notion that an agent should *choose* the reasons upon which he is to act is nevertheless a puzzling one. For it seems to be implied by Donagan's claims in this connection that we could accept it as an explanation of what an agent did that he acted for a certain "chosen" reason, even though we knew that he recognized better reasons for doing something else. As Donagan himself puts it: "History explains a man's action by referring to the reasons upon which he actually chose to act, not to the reasons he thought most adequate." To assert that an agent can *act* contrary to reason—contrary to his own reason, and not just contrary to some objective standard of rational behavior—is, of course, a straightforward expression of rational indeterminism. It makes an important addition to Donagan's metaphysical claim that "[n]either a man's situation as a whole nor any element in it determines his acts" (LPC, 205). But to assert that what a man does in such cases can still be *explained* in terms of his beliefs, plans, purposes, and policies regarded as reasons for acting, is a further claim, and one which a rational indeterminist could consistently question. What is at issue, it might be objected, is not the truth of libertarianism, but the meaning of explanation.

The difficulty would be felt most strongly by those who would

[23] The latter, of course, is a decision constitutive of Caesar's action as conquest; but this is irrelevant since such action is not in this case what is to be explained.

[24] This is a point which was not taken into account in my *Laws and Explanation in History*, Oxford University Press, 1957, chap. 5, which presents a theory in many ways resembling Donagan's.

make it a necessary condition of explanation that it provide "understanding".[25] Representing an agent as acting in a way which is incompatible
with the practical conclusions he himself drew from *all* he thought
relevant at the time of acting (i.e., from "adequate" reasons), and not
just from some arbitrarily "chosen" part of it (i.e., from "inadequate"
reasons), would not normally be regarded as a basis for claiming to
understand the agent's acting as he did. It would be strange, for example,
to insist that we understood Brutus' stabbing Caesar, in the light of his
adoption of the policy of protecting the Republic at all costs (which he
recognized to require Caesar's elimination), if we were prepared at the
same time to assert that Brutus considered the obligations of friendship
to take precedence over those of the state (and realized that it followed
from this that he ought not to join Cassius' conspiracy). A historian who
made such a claim might well expect to be told that he has failed to
explain why Brutus acted as he did. On libertarian assumptions, all the
assertions made about Brutus' reasons and choices could be true. But a
libertarian might still hold, either that the historian has not yet truly
discerned all the thought of the agent which was relevant to his decision,
or that like action done for no reason at all, the action was inexplicable
because it represented, although to a lesser degree, an arbitrary expression
of will. Pushing the first of these alternatives too far, of course, can
easily cost a libertarian his libertarianism. This appears to be Collingwood's fate when he applauds Hegel for allegedly maintaining that "every
historical character in every historical situation thinks and acts as
rationally as that person in that situation *can* think and act."[26] This "fertile
and valuable principle" later leads him to the conclusion that when
historical actions remain rationally unintelligible, it is "the historian
himself who stands at the bar of judgment."[27]

It is true, at least, that what historians are *looking for*, when they set
out to explain what certain agents did in terms of their thoughts, is how
what they did could have appeared to those agents the appropriate or
rational thing to do in the circumstances as they envisaged them. And this
requires reconciling what was done with *whatever* reasons are known to
have been "surveyed" (or otherwise recognized) by the agent. Donagan's
theory finds no place for this requirement. Yet the question whether
we should refuse the *word* "explanation" to what does not provide
rational understanding in the sense indicated is perhaps a matter of minor
importance. What is of interest is that Donaganian "explanations" in
terms of arbitrarily chosen goals or estimates of the situation, even if

---

[25] For discussions making this assumption see W. B. Gallie, *Philosophy and the Historical Understanding*, Schocken Books, 1964; or my "The Historical Explanation of Actions Reconsidered," in
S. Hook (ed.), *Philosophy and History*, New York University Press, 1963, pp. 108 ff.
[26] *The Idea of History*, p. 116.
[27] *Op. cit.*, p. 219.

inconsistent with others acknowledged by the agent, have a describable logical structure. They are not "vacuous," like supposed explanations of actions done for no reason at all. And, on libertarian assumptions, they may often be all we can hope to get.

Theory Formation

IV   Theory Formation

ARNOLD M. ROSE

The relation
of theory and method

BELIEF IN THE UNIVERSALITY OF METHOD

It is generally believed among scientists that, while theory varies with the investigator and is mutable, method is universal and immutable. That is, it is recognized that, in the realm of the unknown and the uncertain, alternative hypotheses and systems of explanation may legitimately be held; but the canons of proof and the techniques of verifying hypotheses must be agreed to by every scientist. Of course, it will be recognized that circumstances and the problem itself may make the use of the best techniques of research unfeasible, and second-rate substitutes then have to be tentatively employed. And, with regard to specific techniques, as distinguished from general methods, discoveries are constantly being made that sharpen, render more widely applicable, and otherwise improve the tools of research. But most scientists could probably agree that methodology changes only by accretion, while theory often changes by complete substitution, and that changes in method are slow, while changes in theory in most sciences today are rapid and dramatic. A. D. Ritchie, the outstanding British biochemist, stated the classic consensus:

> Is there anything really permanent about science which does not change from time to time and the study of which will give us an insight into the nature of science? I think there is, and it is the method. Theory may supersede theory and more accurate analysis may demolish our apparent facts, but there is a unity and continuity about the method that the mind should be able to grasp and that is the very essence of science.[1]

This consensus would have to be modified if one compares the different sciences. While physics and chemistry have relied mostly on the experimental method, astronomy—an older and even more exact science —seldom uses the experiment and relies primarily on a combination of the mathematico-deductive method and the method of precise direct observation with the aid of instruments. While most biological sciences also depend on the experimental method, anatomy relies almost exclusively on direct observation and classification. These variations in use of methods among the sciences are well known to scientists, even though they disconfirm the above-mentioned consensus, for they mean at least that the different problems of the various sciences call for different methods.

Perhaps the reason for the consensus in that, *within* any one of the established physical or biological sciences, one method or one combination of methods has proved to be most appropriate to the subject matter, and even centuries of changes in theory and in the advancement of knowledge have not shaken the supremacy of this method. Thus, while the natural scientist can recognize the need to adjust the method of research to the varied problems of the different sciences, he retains his belief in the universality and even practical immutability of method for any given discipline's problems.

Social scientists have absorbed these beliefs of the natural scientists. While the psychologist and sociologist remain slightly skeptical of the economist's use of the mathematico-deductive method, and the economist usually disdains the "crude empiricism" of the sociologist, each is somewhat charitable toward the vagaries of the other, on the ground that their subject matter is different and does not permit the use of the "one best method." The economist and the psychologist seldom confront one another, but the former's advocacy of the mathematico-deductive method and the latter's contemporary advocacy of the laboratory experiment show the sharpest contrast within the realm of the social sciences. The scientists have not understood the lesson of what they are even willing to recognize as a matter of fact: the necessity of varying the method with the subject matter. The lesson is that method is not universal, but must vary with the

---

[1] A. D. Ritchie, *Scientific Method: An Inquiry Into the Character and Validity of Natural Laws* (London: Routledge & Kegan Paul, 1923; paperback edition, 1960), p. 14.

"image of reality" which the scientist projects. This varying "image of reality" is most readily understandable in the case of different subject matter of the different sciences—astronomy *vs.* physics, anatomy *vs.* physiology, economics *vs.* psychology. But now we must add that it also applies to alternative theoretical framework within a science, since different theoretical interpretations of the same subject matter project different images of that subject matter.

We shall attempt to exemplify this last statement for the science of social psychology. Granted that it is an immature science; but it still has produced a tremendous volume of research. The methods behind this research, however, vary with the image of human behavior which the different researchers, operating from different theoretical standpoints, project. For contemporary theories alone, the most varied research methods must be called upon to aid in verification. The *Behaviorist theory* requires the use of the *experimental method*, because its image of human behavior is that it is a response to a stimulus: The behavior in question must be measured before the application of the stimulus, then the stimulus applied, and the behavior measured again (with a control group used to make sure that no extraneous factor other than the stimulus is the source of the change in the behavior). This before-after image of behavior *is* a description of the experimental method if the proper controls and measures be added, so that the theoretical framework demands the use of the experimental method and is satisfied with no other.

Those who follow the *Instinct theory*, however, cannot use the experimental method, since their image of behavior reflects, not a response to a changed situation, but a manifestation of internal, inherited *tendencies to act*. The problems are those of ascertaining in what different concrete behaviors these tendencies are to be found and how they are manifested. The method of research which best fits this image of behavior (again with the proper controls and measures added) is factor analysis. Thus the leading contemporary exponent of instinct theory, Raymond Cattell,[2] realistically finds it expedient to conduct all his research with the technique of factor analysis, just as his predecessors in Instinct theory used simpler techniques of correlation. An Instinctivist cannot properly use the experimental method, just as the true Behaviorist—if he adheres strictly to his theory—cannot use factor analysis.

Those who follow one or another *Development theory* of behavior, including the psychoanalysts, find both the experimental and factor analysis methods useless. Instead, they use *descriptions of change* in behavior over time, sometimes measured precisely and sometime not. Those who adhere to the *Psychoanalytic image* of behavior, with its emphasis

[2] *Personality and Motivation: Structure and Measurement* (New York: Harcourt, Brace & World, 1957).

on the forces of repression and resistance, and the overt manifestation of unconscious urges in camouflaged and symbolic form, must also rely heavily on the research techniques of *deep analysis* (i.e., intensive, unguided interview), projective tests, dream analysis, and so on. If those who follow some developmental theory of behavior use statistical techniques on their data, they must limit themselves to *time-series analysis or correlation*. They cannot use either the experimental method or factor analysis. So we see that different images of behavior inherent in different psychological theories logically and necessarily require different research techniques and—indeed—different methodologies of scientific verification.

The analysis presented here has assumed that theory comes first, and selects and molds method, rather than the other way around. This may be true historically for the different sciences and broad theoretical frameworks considered thus far, but it will not hold up as a universal generalization. Quite frequently, the scientist starts with an image, not of the reality of his subject matter, but of the proper scientific method, and allows his theory to be built out of the kinds of findings which that method can produce. This has been perhaps particularly true of certain psychologists and sociologists who identify the experimental method—or some presumptive equivalent of it such as partial correlation, successive breakdowns, or whatever—with science itself, and have limited their theory to a range which includes only theories compatible with the experiment. This range includes much more than behaviorism: The vigorous rejection of developmental theory by Kurt Lewin[3]—a Gestaltist rather than a behaviorist—seems to have been based on an image of science as limited to the experimental method.

Similarly, there was a long resistance to the acceptance of the Darwin-Wallace theory of evolution among certain leading scientists because they could not possibly have used the experimental method to prove their theory, but had to rely on the "historical-philosophical" method. The great biologist, R. Virchow, even argued against the mere teaching of the theory of evolution in the university classroom on this ground. He was contradicted by his equally great student, E. Haeckel, in what is perhaps the major nineteenth-century defense of academic freedom: Haeckel defended at least the students' access to the theories

---

[3] Kurt Lewin, "The Conflict between Aristotelian and Galileian Modes of Thought in Contemporary Psychology," in *A Dynamic Theory of Personality: Selected Papers* (New York: McGraw-Hill, 1935). While Lewin here aligned his image of human behavior to the requirements of the experimental method—thus eliminating both developmental and instinctivist theory—he also rejected the narrow molecularism of the Behaviorists. Thus, as one who included complex (molar) behavior and subjective variables into his image of reality, he—like other Gestaltists—was obliged to expand the experimental method. Characteristic innovations of the Lewinians include some kind of ingenuous "fraudulent" *induction* of a mental state, a randomization of the sample so as to "eliminate" the numerous extraneous variables or vectors, and the measurement of a complex response (sometimes even delayed).

of evolution and recapitulation, "since organisms could only be understood through a study of their evolutionary history."[4]

That there are varied influences on theory—including those from method[5]—is a fact quite generally recognized in other studies. Our purpose in this paper is to concentrate on the less-accepted notion that theory influences method.

The distinction between developmental and antidevelopmental theories in psychology is paralleled by the distinction between holistic and atomistic theories in biology. The atomistic theorists will use only the methods of the chemist and the physicist since their image of biological reality is that the organism is simply a sum of physical particles and the chemical processes. The holistic theorists believe that the organism has distinctive emergent characteristics which can only be understood by studying the living organism as a "*gestalt*." The holists[6] even adduce support for the *gestalt* idea from physical science: Max Born says, in his *Theory and Experiment in Physics*, "Maxwell's addition of the missing term is just such a smoothing out of the roughness of shape. . . . A synthetic prediction is based on the hypothetical statement that the real shape of a partly known phenomenon differs from what it appears to be."[7] Professor P. Dirac goes even further in explaining the acceptance of the theory of relativity: The theory of relativity was accepted for two reasons, its agreement with experiment and the fact that "there is a beautiful mathematical theory underlying it, which gives it a strong emotional appeal," and of these the latter reason, in his opinion, is the more important. Dirac goes on to say, about this aspect of theory, "With all the violent changes to which physical theory is subjected in modern times, there is just one rock which weathers every storm, to which one can always hold fast—the assumption that the fundamental laws of nature correspond to a beautiful mathematical theory. This means a theory based on simple mathematical concepts that fit together in an elegant way, so that one has pleasure in working with it."[8]

A TEST FOR THE INFLUENCE
OF THEORY ON METHOD

Thus far, we have considered only how theory in the broad sense selected a method of research which is appropriate to its image of reality.

---

[4] John R. Baker, "The Controversy on Freedom in Science in the Nineteenth Century," in *The Logic of Personal Knowledge, Essays presented to Michael Polanyi* (London: Routledge & Kegan Paul, 1961), p. 90.

[5] Abraham Maslow, "Problem-Centering *vs.* Means-Centering in Science," *Philosophy of Science, 13* (October, 1946), 326–331.

[6] For example: Marjorie Grene, "The Logic of Biology," in *The Logic of Personal Knowledge: Essays Presented to Michael Polanyi* (London: Routledge & Kegan Paul, 1961), pp. 191–205.

[7] Max Born, *Theory and Experiment in Physics* (Cambridge, England: Cambridge University Press, 1943; Dover reprint, 1956), pp. 12–13.

[8] P. Dirac, "Quantum Mechanics and the Aether," *Scientific Monthly, 58* (1954), 142.

A logical next step—which we shall not take here—would be to turn to a variety of more specific and limited ways in which theory selects and molds method. The procedure would not be a usual one; hence it is necessary to make it very explicit. It would involve a search through all aspects of method in sociology to find procedures which are not specifically demanded by the requirements of logic and science—which call for an arbitrary decision on the part of the investigator—and seek to relate these to some aspect of theory. Because we would thus be dealing with extra-scientific aspects of method, we would logically be able to claim that their choice is traceable to either psychological or sociological characteristics of the investigator. This is an interpretation which many sociologists resist, especially when we refer to the selection of these extra-scientific aspects of method as a "bias." It is to be understood that "bias" in this sense is not necessarily conscious or deliberate, that it may serve no private purpose of the investigator, that it may be unavoidable because of *lacunae* among the requirements of scientific method. Yet it seems to be an appropriate term to use to describe decisions made by researchers which neither arise from the requirements of scientific method (or are contrary to such requirements) nor are fully accounted for rationally by the investigator.

If it be granted that such decisions are the result of biases on the part of the investigator, it may still be questioned how the biases can be traced to theories held by the investigator. We do not claim that all such biases can be traced to theories; additional criteria must be applied before that can be done. In the first place, the bias, or arbitrary decision, must be logically consistent with a theory; it must "fit into" a theory held by the investigator. Secondly, it must not be idiosyncratic, not a bias of a single *investigator*; it must rather be a bias manifested by a whole school or category of investigators who adhere to a certain theory. It will not be easy to take all the steps required in the proposed investigation, and make the attribution of the bias to a whole school of investigators by showing how it crops up only among a certain school of investigators at a certain time period when the theory is prevalent among them, and not to other investigators or at other times.

In conducting such an investigation, it would not be wise to limit the definition of "theory" only to highly structured systems of thought. The term might also be used to refer to vague, scarcely formulated assumptions and ill-defined concepts concerning the subject matter. It will thus include any kind of "image of reality" concerning the *subject matter* of the discipline. Some may say that this is not a proper definition of "theory," and with such a criticism we might agree. Nevertheless, sociologists often in fact operate with crude, half-formulated theories, and our purpose is to ascertain how all in a "school" or group of investigators' *ideas* about the *content* of their subject matter (for which there is no better word available than "theory") influence their research methods. Many of these ideas may later be found to fit into a well-structured system of thought to which no one is likely to refuse the appellation of theory.

TAUTOLOGICAL "PROOF" AND ITS CURE

If our assumptions are correct (1) that many devices and decisions are made by social science investigators in their research which are not specified by the logic of their method; (2) that when these *choices in method* are compatible with their theories about the *content* of their subject matter and are made in about the same way among those who hold the same theory, they can be said to arise out of the theory—an important conclusion can already be logically derived. This is that many social science researches do not test the theory, or the hypothesis associated with the theory, they are intended to test. Rather, the researches are self-fulfilling results of the applications of assumptions that are a part of their original ingredients. That is, there is a circular logic employed in many researches: Assumptions from a theory are unwittingly employed by a researcher, who is consciously trying to confirm or disconfirm an hypothesis associated with the theory, in the application of his method, and thereby the method *logically* produces a finding which confirms the hypothesis. In other words, the process is like the children's "magical" arithmetical game of choosing a secret number, having the possessor of the secret perform a number of mathematical operations on it and then telling the resultant of the complex process, at which point the perpetrator of the "magic" can tell what the original secret number was. Many "confirming researches" in social science are just such types of logical games, in which the method logically produces the conclusion expected from the hypothesis rather than testing it with empirical data. In a sense, the broad-scale examples we have already given of our general thesis will also provide illustrations of this conclusion: Experiments will tend to support stimulus-response theories of human behavior rather than instinct or developmental theories (or, if the experiment is complicated enough, it will support *Gestaltist*-type theories). Factor analysis will find universal factors in a wide variety of behaviors and hence will confirm instinct theories as against behavioristic or psychoanalytic theories. Deep analysis into the unconscious motives of man can serve only to confirm psychoanalytic hypotheses, never hypotheses from behavioristic or instinct theories.

A few examples of a more concrete nature can also be cited. We note the higher order of animal studied by psychologists of learning whose theories favor more complex patterns of learning than those whose theories favor less complex patterns (apes as compared to rats or pigeons). Studies conducted by sociologists of the functionalist school generally find that change of behavior or attitude does not occur and that the social system is in equilibrium, whereas sociologists operating with theories of process or theories of conflict always find change (different measures are used, of course). In the many "community power" studies conducted since the early 1950s, those using some kind of Marxist theory invariably find a partially hidden "power elite" of businessmen in American society, while those who follow a pluralist theory find the businessmen competing for power and influence with certain other segments of the community. The former tend to use the "reputational" method; the latter use the "decisional" method. Examples of this sort of thing in the psychosocial sciences are almost endless.

Of course, we do not say that the conclusions of such researches will always confirm just exactly the hypothesis their investigators want them to confirm. After all, there are many aspects of the method of research which are specified by the canons of science, there are other aspects of method which are merely faulty, and there are the empirical data which may be recalcitrant to the theory. All of these may counterbalance the assumptions from the theory embedded in the research, and thus prevent the conclusion from confirming the theoretical hypothesis. In other words, *negative* findings—as social scientists have long known—do not prove much, unless the test is very carefully conducted and is "crucial," in the sense of logically admitting no alternative interpretations other than the one made. But the usual social science research which fails to confirm the investigator's hypothesis, and yet which includes assumptions from his "image of reality" in his subject matter, will also fail to confirm hypotheses compatible with rival theories.

This suggests a solution for the researcher's dilemma—of having to make decisions during the course of his research and yet avoid having these decisions reflect some aspect of his thinking which will thereby cause his findings merely to confirm his bias. That is, he should so design his research that, if it should fail to confirm his own hypothesis, it will confirm a competing hypothesis. Further, he must specify every arbitrary decision he makes during the application of his method and give his reasons for it, so that a competitor will be able to judge whether or not he would prefer alternative decisions. If so, the competitor with an alternative theory can use the same general method, but this time with the alternative decisions, and the results or the two studies should then indicate which of the alternative theories is supported by the researches.

INFLUENCE OF THE CONCEPT, THE QUESTION,
AND THE ORGANIZATIONAL SETTING

The simplest element of a theory which influences method is, of course, the concept. The history of science is strewn with abandoned concepts, some abandoned because the "reality" to which they referred were proved to have no empirical referent, and others abandoned—not because they were disproved—but because they were displaced by seemingly more useful concepts. An example of the former type would be the concept of "ether" until the Michelson-Morley experiment of 1887 suggested its untenability; an example of the latter type is the concept of "the inheritance or acquired characteristic" until it was replaced by the concepts of "the individuality of the gene" and of "natural selection."[9] Before the earlier concepts were abandoned, they played a role in the conduct of research.

Similar examples of the influence of concepts, later abandoned, on the conduct of research can be found in the social sciences. The concept of "social evolution" which dominated anthropological research from 1860 until about 1910 led (1) to a search for sequences of change that Radcliffe-Brown[10] correctly disparaged as "conjectural history," (2) to classifications of cultural forms and social structures that had meaning solely in terms of the evolutionary theory, and (3) to grossly oversimplified descriptions of customs because they were practiced by "primitive" societies. Radcliffe-Brown's functionalism, which is one of the contemporary supplanters of evolutionary theory in anthropology, in its turn has led to ignoring historical method, even though Brown himself denied being opposed to empirical research for historical sequences.

A more subtle influence of concepts than their capacity to distort reality for the scientist, is their capacity to eliminate from consideration areas of relevant reality. That is, they act as blinders which select the portion of relevant reality which the scientist can bring within the purview of his method. This is because concepts give whatever meaning there is to what he is observing to the scientist who uses them. If his concepts do not comprehend what is available for observation in the universe, perfection of method does not necessarily improve his observations. For example, the increasing understanding of the microcosmic world by the physicist during the past three centuries has resulted not solely from improvements in the power of microscopes but also from the

[9] The concepts called "newer" here have also been considerably modified by subsequent researches and theoretical developments, and while some of the later changes have parallels in aspects of the "older" concepts, it would be wholly incorrect to say that there has been any reversion to them.

[10] A. R. Radcliffe-Brown, *Structure and Function in Primitive Society* (New York: Free Press, 1952), Chap. 3, pp. 49–50.

addition of concepts with which to grasp the nature of this world. Despite the fine devices for detection available today, many types of "material" particles are known by postulation and inference only rather than by direct observation. The specification of increasingly minute, aberrant, or fleeting aspects of the microcosmic universe *by theory* has regularly led to the invention of new devices for empirical detection and observation of such phenomena *by instrument*.

Of course, the reverse has also taken place—chance observations with existing instruments or new observations with improved instruments may lead to refinements of or additions to theory (as happened when Eve Curie discovered radioactivity), but this does not gainsay that theory often advances beyond the ability of currently available method to test it.

The way in which scientific questions are posed is a function of theory. Even when concepts have been found to have empirical referents and are useful in the production of verifiable knowledge and testable predictions, they may still be misused by being framed into erroneously stated questions. A leading example, which still occasionally rises to plague the social sciences, was the psychologist's posing the search for the causes of human behavior in terms of "heredity *versus* environment." Both concepts have continuing value; the theoretical error consists in the assumption that they are opposed, or that where one is the sufficient cause of a behavior the other does not appear. Most of the researches in the subfield of differential psychology carried out during the first three decades of this century have had to be discarded because of this erroneous assumption.[11] Very few psychologists make this crude assumption today, but it has left traces in their thinking by framing their search for sources of observable human behaviors in terms of combinations of discrete hereditary and environmental influences. That is, to use an analogy from chemistry, they unwittingly conceive of concrete human behaviors as *mixtures* of forces from hereditary and environmental sources, whereas they might often be more accurately conceived of as *compounds* of such forces. Mixtures retain the characteristics of their constituent elements, whereas compounds usually exhibit entirely new characteristics and properties. One methodological consequence of conceiving of intelligence, for example, as a compound of hereditary and environmental influences would be that *no* test, not even a "culture-free" one, of intelligent *behaviors* could single out and measure the biological component in those behaviors. Only a neurological test on newborn babies might do so.

It is thus through its concepts and assumptions—which provide the elements of an "image of reality"—that theory influences various aspects of method. Conscious theory is not the only source of extra-logical influences on method; cultural and individual values may also provide

11 Anne Anastasie, *Differential Psychology*, 3rd ed. (New York: Macmillan, 1958).

sources of bias.[12] Because theory is usually more readily capable of being specified and its possible influences on method delineated, it is important that this be done for every piece of research so that the more subtle influences of cultural values can have a chance at being detected.

The organization of research and the status system among scientists are additional influences on science which occasionally exert their influence through method.[13] Especially in the physical sciences, where much of the modern equipment is expensive, the availability of large-scale funds makes it possible to use better techniques of research. The social organization of the researchers—including the ease of communication among them, their division of labor, their organization of authority—influences the way they behave in carrying out their research, including their application of research methods. Access to channels of publication influences the use of certain methods: Many social science journals, for example, cannot afford sufficient space for publication of statistical tables or description of instruments used; hence other researchers do not have access to these implements of method. The centralization of control over research—whether formally through government or informally through a tight-knit class system—has been found to inhibit innovative research in at least the medical field.[14] In 1804, Avodagro, a graduate student, advanced the molecular hypothesis, but he was not given access to facilities for testing it because it was rejected by the distinguished physicist Dalton; not until 1850 was the dictum of Dalton overcome and the hypothesis tested and proved correct in the researches of Camizzaro.

Timing and "technical" decisions

The whole question of timing in the advancement of science suggests many puzzling relationship between ideas—including theoretical ideas—and method. Whitehead[15] points out—concerning Galileo's experiments with falling bodies, showing that regardless of weight they fall with the same speed—that "so far as experimental skill and delicacy of apparatus

[12] Cf. Arnold M. Rose, *Theory and Method in the Social Sciences* (Minneapolis: University of Minnesota Press, 1954), chapter on "Selection of Problems for Research," pp. 153–168.

[13] See: Don K. Price, *Government and Science* (New York University Press, 1954); Yale Brozen, "The Role of Government in Research and Development," *The American Behavioral Scientist* (December, 1962), 22–27; Gerald Gordon, Sue Marquis, and O. W. Anderson, "Freedom and Control in Four Types of Scientific Settings," in *ibid.*, pp. 39–43; Anne Folger and Gerald Gordon, "Scientific Accomplishment and Social Organization. A Review of the Literature," in *ibid.*, 51–58; Charles D. Orth, Joseph C. Bailey, and Francis W. Wolek, *Administering Research and Development* (Homewood, Ill: Richard D. Irwin, and the Dorsey Press, 1960).

[14] Joseph Ben-David, "Scientific Productivity and Academic Organization in Nineteenth Century Medicine," *American Sociological Review*, 25 (December, 1960), 828–843.

[15] Alfred North Whitehead, *Science and the Modern World* (Cambridge, England: Cambridge University Press, 1928), pp. 144–145.

were concerned, this experiment could have been made at any time within the preceding five thousand years." The delay was on the side of theory, not on the side of method. Helmholtz in 1850 had to battle the scientific fraternity in order to measure the speed of conduction by the nerves: Everyone was sure "that the speed of nerves must approximate the speed of light, that one does not will to wiggle his finger and then wait for the impulse to arrive and the finger to move."[16]

Then there is the matter of delayed acceptance of crucial findings: Biologists carried on researches along erroneous lines for some twenty-five years after Gregor Mendel published the findings of his experiments on the genetics of wrinkled peas (in a leading journal, incidentally), simply because their theoretical ideas would not allow them to credit, or even to retest, what he had reported.

For over sixty years, it was disreputable among scientists to ask after the origin of life. Louis Pasteur, after experiments in 1864, "definitely established that it was impossible on the earth today, under controlled conditions, to demonstrate the appearance of living matter except through the agency, or as offspring of, other living material"—that is, there could be no "spontaneous generation."

> The hiatus came to an end (in 1928) with the recognition, by Professor J. B. S. Haldane, that the dictum of Pasteur was not in conflict with the backward extrapolation of the doctrine of evolution as expanded by Darwin and Wallace, if one recognizes that at the time that spontaneous generation must have occurred, according to the evolutionary extrapolation of Darwin and Wallace, there was not, by definition, any living thing on the surface of the earth. Therefore, it was possible in the pre-biotic time, to accumulate large amounts of organic material generated by non-biological processes. This, of course, cannot take place on the surface of the earth today, since there exist everywhere on the earth's surface organisms, both micro- and macro—which would transform any such organic material immediately it was formed, even in small amounts. Since 1928, it has become popular once again to examine the question of the original life.[17]

More recently, the biologists William E. Peterson and Berry Campbell reported that they were held up for nine years in their discovery of how to use cow's milk in which antibodies against infection disease had been developed, to prevent the spread of disease. It was that long before they even sought to test the belief, universal among biologists, that protective antibodies could be absorbed through the digestive system after the first few days following birth. They devised a simple experiment to show that the antibodies were absorbed into the circulatory system of an adult through the digestion of the milk of the treated cows.[18]

---

[16] Edwin G. Boring, "Science and the Meaning of its History," *The Key Reporter*, 24 (July, 1959), 3.
[17] Melvin Calvin, "Origin of Life on Earth and Elsewhere," in *The Logic of Personal Knowledge: Essays Presented to Michael Polanyi* (London: Routledge & Kegan Paul, 1961), pp. 207–230, at 209.
[18] "Conventional Beliefs Delayed Protective Milk," *Minnesota Daily*, November 18, 1955, p. 1.

Theories, and less well-formulated ideas, influence decisions in the application of statistical techniques. It has long been noted by statisticians that the degree of statistical significance required for testing a hypothesis is a function of the nature of the hypothesis, not of the requirements of mathematical statistics. The same applies to whether a one-tailed or two-tailed test is to be used. Equally influenced by the problem, though not so frequently noted by statisticians, are: (1) The size and lines of division for categories in calculating grouped means, standard deviations, and correlations; (2) the degree of curvature—if any—introduced into "a line of best fit" through a body of tabulated data; (3) the selection from among many available measures of central tendency, deviation and correlation.

Theories—or "images of reality"—(as well as values, cultural or individual) thus exercise their influence on method in a great variety of ways. The objective scientist is not he who holds that he relies on pure method in his research, but he who points constantly to the possibly biassing influences of theory and value at each step in his research operations.

CLARENCE SCHRAG

Elements of theoretical analysis in sociology

This paper presents an elementary examination of some conventional methods of theory construction and suggests criteria for their assessment.

FUNCTIONS AND STRUCTURE OF THEORIES

Theory construction in sociology has several objectives. (1) It provides conceptual frameworks that facilitate the accurate observation and the reliable description of social events. (2) It formulates laws and theories by which social phenomena can be explained. (3) It establishes a foundation of knowledge and methodology that under certain conditions makes possible the control of social affairs.

Description and explanation

Theory construction begins with the observation of events. Observation under controlled conditions helps to identify relevant variables and their relationships with the events in question. Knowledge of relevant variables and their relationships may lead to the formulation and test of theories that have explanatory power. The test of an explanatory system is its capacity to predict, and in some cases to control, the events of concern.

Consider the following illustration. A study is made of crime rates within a city. It is observed that "Crime rates are very high near the city center" and "The rates are low in the suburbs." Eventually it may be noted that "The crime rates vary inversely with distance from the center of the city." So far the statements are purely descriptive, involving only the assertion of conjunctions and disjunctions among observed data. The statements make no claims beyond the information given. They do not tell us what to expect in the future, for instance, or in cities other than the one under investigation. Such descriptive statements, even though they may be factually accurate, cannot serve as a basis for explanatory argument.

Explanation becomes possible only after a lawlike assumption has been made concerning the relationship between variables such as "crime" and "distance." The assertion that "Crime rates vary inversely with distance from the city center," when regarded as a scientific law, is more than a description of previous observations. It makes claims that go beyond the available information and is presumed to hold true for events that have not yet been observed. This lawlike assumption about events not yet observed or examined is what distinguishes the process of explanation from descriptive statement of fact.[1]

To explain an event means to account for its occurrence on the basis of lawlike assumptions. Singular assumptions are ordinarily called *laws*, while sets of interrelated assumptions are known as *theories*. Whether asserted as laws or as component parts of theories, assumptions are "if—then" statements that usually have the form: *If A is observed, then it may be expected that B will also be observed*. The assumption, along with statements describing the conditions under which the assumption should hold true, provides the logical basis for explanation. Given the assumption and the necessary conditions, the explanation follows as a logical conclusion.

Laws and theories explain by assumption what the researcher first describes by statements of fact. Sometimes the assumptions may be expressed in everyday language, while in other cases abstract theoretical concepts may be employed. Whatever the terminology, the essence of explanation is that we can use certain assumptions in order to construct a statement which describes the phenomenon to be explained. The "inverse distance law" mentioned above will serve as an example.

[1] R. B. Braithwaite, *Scientific Explanation*, Cambridge University Press, 1953; and C. G. Hempel and P. Oppenheim, "Studies in the Logic of Explanation," *Philosophy of Science*, April, 1948, 135–175.

Lawlike assumption:	In American cities, crime rates vary inversely with distance from the city center.
Condition 1:	Chicago is an American city.
Condition 2:	Census tracts a, b, c, . . . n are located in Chicago in the order of their increasing from the city center.
Derived description;	Therefore, census tracts a, b, c, . . . n may be expected to have crime rates that decrease in the order given.

Note that the descriptive statement follows as a *logical consequence* of the assumption and the stated conditions. Whenever such descriptions are corroborated by observed evidence our confidence in the assumption is increased accordingly. Should the description fail to be confirmed, the assumption would need reformulation. Empirical corroboration never serves as final proof, however. It is always possible that further inquiry will deny the previous findings or that other assumptions will provide better explanations.

An *empirical explanation*, such as the one above, occurs when an assumption enables us to fit the given event into a known pattern of empirical events. Our confidence in the assumption may be justified by the frequency with which the pattern of events is observed. By the use of analogy, we can treat the unexplained event as part of the known pattern and thereby prove an explanation. If the implications of the analogy are confirmed by observation, we have a successful explanation. Thus, the assumptions employed in empirical explanation are usually stated as generalizations from previous observations of similar, although perhaps not identical, phenomena.

Sometimes the descriptive statements involved in explanation are derived from two or more of the assumptions of a given theory. Such *theoretical explanations* have a clearer and more precise logical structure than those derived from empirical generalizations. They provide far more information because of their greater deductive potential. Their implications can be tested more systematically. To illustrate let us examine part of Durkheim's theory of disorganization.[2] Durkheim noted that social norms tend to lose their effectiveness when the characteristics of communities are rapidly changing, and that the resulting anomie is associated with the amount of deviant behavior. Accordingly, he formulated a theory of deviance and disorganization including assumptions such as those below.

Assumption 1: The greater the similarity among the members of a community, the greater their social cohesion.
Assumption 2: The greater the social cohesion among the members of a community, the greater their resistance to deviant behavior.

[2] E. Durkheim, *Division of Labor in Society*, Free Press, 1947. The distinction between empirical and theoretical explanation is similar to that proposed by A. Kaplan, *The Conduct of Inquiry*, Chandler, chap. 9.

Either of these assumptions may be used in the same way as the "inverse distance law" in explaining various kinds of social activity. To serve as an adequate basis for explanation, an assumption must (1) assert a particular kind of relationship, a universal conjunction, between two or more classes of events, (2) its empirical claims must be testable or have testable implications, and (3) the concepts employed must be independently defined. Thus, the use of Durkheim's assumptions requires that relevant conditions be indicated and that the concepts "deviant behavior," "similarity," and "social cohesion" be connected with observed data by operational definitions or rules of correspondence.

Social cohesion, for example, may be defined by the amount of agreement people exhibit in identifying their social objectives and in selecting means for achieving these objectives. Criminality may be specified as one of the indicators of deviant behavior. When the concepts are defined in this manner, the second of Durkheim's assumptions asserts that "Crime rates will be high where there is lack of consensus regarding objectives and means of achievement, whereas crime rates will be low where there is agreement on objectives and means." This facet of Durkheim's theory has received some corroboration and has become one of the cornerstones of contemporary criminology.

However, the versatility and generality of Durkheim's theory are better revealed by some of the statements that can be deduced from the assumptions mentioned. To deduce statements from the assumptions, we may employ the *transitive rule* of relationships. Under the transitive rule, if A implies B and B implies C, then A implies C.[3] Application of the rule to the two initial assumptions results in the statement that "The greater the similarity among the members of a community, the greater their resistance to deviant behavior." Heterogeneous populations, in other words, are likely to have high crime rates and other evidences of deviant behavior, while homogeneous populations are likely to have low indexes of deviance.

The above derived assumption probably has greater utility and significance than the original ones. It encompasses many of the findings of research on the relationship between deviant behavior and population characteristics.[4] It also shows how the scope and power of a theory may be considerably enhanced by the logical implications of its basic assumptions.

[3] Appropriateness of the rule depends upon the kind of relationship in question. Variables such as size, weight, etc., ordinarily come under the rule since if A is heavier than B and B is heavier than C then A is heavier than C. The "hardness" of substances as measured by the "scratch" test does not come under the rule, however. A may scratch B, B may scratch C, and yet A may not scratch C. Many relationships considered in sociology fail to meet the requirements of the rule. Thus, if A is the father of B, and B is the father of C, then A is not the father of C. Legitimate use of the rule always requires empirical justification.

[4] For a recent illustration see J. P. Gibbs and W. T. Martin, *Status Integration and Suicide: A Sociological Study*, University of Oregon Books, 1964.

It is clear from the discussion that the process of explanation involves procedures of inference and corroboration as well as those of definition and description. The interrelations among these procedures may be illustrated in the following paradigm:

$$\frac{A_1, A_2, \ldots A_n}{E}$$
$$C_1, C_2, \ldots C_k$$

Here E represents a statement describing the phenomenon to be explained; $A_1, A_2, \ldots A_n$ represent assumptions expressing regularities in the class of events of which E is a member; and $C_1, C_2, \ldots C_k$ represent statements specifying the conditions under which the assumptions in A may be expected to hold true.

We have an acceptable explanation of the phenomenon under investigation if (1) the descriptions in E are supported by observed evidence, (2) the descriptions in E are derived logically from A and C, (3) the conditions stipulated in C are observed in the cases under study, and (4) the assumptions in A are warranted by relevant evidence and experience. Explanation consequently requires the combination of postulated regularities and observed conditions in the derivation of descriptive statements that can be independently confirmed. Successful explanation cannot be achieved by logical inference or empirical inquiry alone, but only by the judicious blending of observed fact and lawlike supposition.

The coordination of assumptions and observations is essential to all forms of inquiry that have explanation as an objective. It occurs in *predictive* sciences, such as physics and astronomy, where the observation of specified conditions and the application of appropriate theories make possible the anticipation of future events. It is found likewise in paleontology and other *postdictive* sciences that are primarily concerned with the systematic organization of historical materials. Finally, the *pragmatic* sciences of engineering and management use explanation as a basis for altering the course of events by the manipulation of variables that have known consequences.

There are, to be sure, vast differences in the above fields with respect to their state of knowledge, their technique of inquiry, and the skill and perspective of their research workers. Sometimes there are also significant differences in the complexity of the tasks attempted. But the procedures of inquiry are being refined and systematized so as to justify the expectation that theoretical inference will be utilized with increasing frequency in fields of knowledge now largely removed from the domain of science.

Sociology employs in its different branches all forms of explanation.

Some of its problems are similar to those of the predictive sciences, while others involve the explanation of historical data. Again, much of sociology is concerned with matters of management and social control. For those reasons the attempt to force sociological inquiry into any single mode of theory construction would be a serious error in strategy.[5]

Analysis of structure

Any given theory is comprised largely of two sets of statements. One set defines the *concepts* of the theory. The other expresses *relationships* among the concepts defined.

Concepts are words or other symbols that provide the *vocabulary* of the theory and identify its subject matter, the phenomena with which the theory is concerned. A definition, in the language of theory, is simply the statement of an intention to use a concept in a designated way. Some concepts are defined so as to identify the *units of observation* about which the theory has something to say. These units may be things such as persons, groups, organizations, events, or activities, for example. Other concepts delineate the *classification schemes* that are used in portraying the salient characteristics of the units observed. Durkheim's theory of disorganization, for instance, calls for the classification of human populations (units of observation) according to their similarity, cohesiveness, and resistance to deviance. For each of these characteristics there is implied an appropriate classification scheme. The content of the theory— the claims made by its assumptions—deals with relationships among these characteristics and employs the relationships in an explanation of deviant behavior.

Concepts employed in classifying units of observation according to their characteristics are called *variables*. A variable in some cases may assume only two values, in this way indicating the presence or absence of a given characteristic such as criminality. Or it may classify the characteristic according to a set of qualitative categories. Thus, criminality may be classified as homicide, assault, robbery, and so on. Again, a variable may consist of a series of classes ordered according to the relative magnitude of the characteristic in question. Populations, for instance, may be classified as having high, moderate, or low amounts of criminality. Perhaps the most powerful theories, however, are those that use quantified variables, such as the number of criminal acts of a certain kind that are comitted per 100,000 persons in a given population. Such quantification, which is based on the arbitrary decision that one act of a kind is equal to another, should not be confused with fundamental measurement.

[5] C. Schrag, "Some Demerits of Contemporary Sociology," *Pacific Sociological Review*, Fall, 1961, pp. 43–51; and G. A. Lundberg, C. Schrag, and O. N. Larsen, *Sociology*, 3rd ed., Harper & Row, 1963, chap. 3.

Measurement, in the strict sense of the term, is not yet common in sociology.

Once a certain variable has been classified, it may be important to establish its possible logical combinations with other variables that are included within the vocabulary of the theory. This is ordinarily done by the cross-classification of two or more variables. For example, if the dichotomous variable, sex, is cross-classified against a trichotomous concept of criminality, there are six possible combinations of sex and crime. Combinations can be constructed, of course, for qualitative variables, quantitative variables, or mixtures of these. Each of the schemes of classification, whether for single variables or combinations, has advantages and disadvantages which depend upon the purposes for which the theory is constructed.

Whatever the mode of classification, it is important that it meet the requirements of *exhaustiveness* and *exclusiveness*. A classification scheme is exhaustive if all of the observed units fall within one or another of the classes of any given characteristic. It is exclusive if none of the units can fall into more than one of the classes. When these conditions are met, the phenomena with which the theory is concerned can be systematically observed, and the observations can be organized in terms of the characteristics that are regarded as essential to the theory.

The definition and classification of the variables with which a theory is concerned are only a first step in the task of theory construction, however. Equally important is the statement of assumptions concerning the relationships that are expected to occur among the defined variables. Ordinarily, theories assert relationships between a class of *resultant* events and a class of *determinants* which may be used in explaining the events. The events to be explained and the variables involved in their explanation are a consequence of the kinds of relationships asserted.

It is therefore essential in some theories that the distinction between results and determinants be maintained. The germ theory of disease is an example: Germs may produce symptoms of illness, but the symptoms do not produce germs. Such relationships, in which *A* has a certain kind of association with *B* but *B* does not have the same kind of association with *A*, are called *nonsymmetrical*. The nonsymmetrical relationship, "produces," may provide an explanation of disease, but it does not offer an explanation of germs.

Theories, again, may be based on *symmetrical* relationships. Symmetry means that if *A* is related in a certain manner with *B*, then *B* is related in the same manner with *A*. Symmetrical relationships have great versatility in theoretical inference, although they may be difficult to corroborate empiricially. Durkheim's theory, for instance, asserts that increased similarity among the members of a human population results in increased social cohesion, while increased cohesion likewise results in increased similarity. In such theories the direction of "cause" and "effect" is reversible, and the distinction between results and determinants is purely arbitrary. Given either variable, the other can be explained or predicted.

Numerous additional kinds of relationships are employed, of course, in theory construction. The empirical claims of a theory are always reducible to statements of relationship among variables. Fundamental statements of relationship, which cannot be derived from the remainder of the theory, are called *postulates*. Together the postulates provide rules of *grammar* that govern the process of logical inference and determine the validity of the various statements that can be derived from the theory. Statements directly or indirectly derived from postulates are called *theorems*. A theorem, such as that deduced previously from Durkheim's two postulates, is logically valid only if it follows from the postulates by appropriate procedures of logical inference. To determine the validity of theoretical statements, it is necessary to take into account the inter-relations of the theory's postulates and the rules of inference that are permitted under the relationships expressed.

Clarification of the structure and content of a theory by the logical analysis of its stated relationships and their implications is called *formalization*. Formalization is expedited by the elimination of the meanings of concepts so that the theory is reduced to a system of relationships among a set of uninterpreted symbols. Such a formal theory is comprised of logical or mathematical statements that are completely devoid of empirical meaning. They make no assertions whatever about events in the world of observation and experience.

Formalization of the inverse distance law provides a simple illustration. In place of the concepts "crime rate" and "distance from city center" are substituted the symbols A and B, respectively, and a mathematical constant, C, may be added to the vocabulary of the theory. The relationships claimed by the inverse distance law may then be expressed in equations such as:

$$A = \frac{C}{B}.$$

Some of the implications of the above equation are that for any given level of A there is an "appropriate" level of B, that if B increases in amount A will decrease accordingly, and so on. The only restrictions placed on the transformation of such equations are those inherent in the rules of logic and mathematics. Hence, the validity of formal statements is determined by rules of inference in which the structure and form of a statement are examined independently of its empirical meaning.

More complex theories, when formalized, consist of a *minimum set* of postulates from which can be derived a number of theorems that are *logically consistent*. A minimum set of postulates is one that meets the criterion of independence, or parsimony, in that none of the postulates can be deduced from the remainder of the set. Each postulate, in other words, makes a unique contribution to the theory and is essential to its argument. The theorems derived from a set of postulates are logically consistent if no pair of them is contradictory. Theories that meet the requirements of consistency and independence, in general, are logically valid. Logical validity, of course, does not insure the empirical adequacy of a theory or its competence in prediction and explanation.

Corroboration

Theories are established on the basis of current information. It usually remains for the future to provide the evidence that corroborates them or demands their reformulation. Corroboration, in any case, is a relative matter calling for judgment on the part of a researcher. Strict confirmation by crucial experimentation is largely an illusion.[6] The aim of research, therefore, is not to establish the absolute truth of certain statements but to indicate the degree of confidence that is warranted by the best empirical evidence. Fortunately, experimental and statistical designs can be used in such a way that the degree of empirical adequacy can be established for most practical purposes.

Empirical adequacy depends upon the extent to which the claims of a theory can be corroborated by competent evidence. But the claims cannot be determined until the concepts and relationships are interpreted in terms of observation and experience. The connections between concepts and evidence are ordinarily established by a *dictionary* of descriptions, correspondence rules, and operational definitions.

When concepts have been interpreted in terms of concrete data, the statements of a theory can be tested by reference to observable phenomena. If the tests tend to falsify the claims, it is always possible to revise the theory by redefining the concepts, modifying the assumptions, or changing the rules of interpretation which relate the theory to the data of experience. The process of revision and reconstruction is interminable.

It follows that theories are tested on a piecemeal basis and are accepted only tentatively until "something better comes along." To illustrate, the inverse distance law implies that there are gradients of crime rates originating at the city center and moving outward in all directions. Obviously, these claims cannot be tested in any rigorous

---

[6] P. Duhem, *Aim and Structure of Physical Theory*, trans. P. Wiener, Princeton University Press, 1953.

manner. What the researcher does is to give the law an approximate interpretation by (1) defining the city center arbitrarily in terms of land values, traffic flow, population density, etc., (2) selecting a set of census tracts, city blocks, geographic areas, etc., (3) arranging these areas roughly along a given line or direction, and (4) computing the crime rates in the different areas. If the rates, in general, decrease as the distance from the city center increases, the researcher concludes that the evidence tends to support the theoretical formulation. Otherwise, he may attempt to revise either the formula or the empirical interpretation of it so as to produce a greater compatibility between the law and the evidence.

Theories facilitate the test of assumptions and generalizations. Statements drawn from a deductive system are interdependent in a way that makes evidence which is relevant to the evaluation of one statement relevant also to the evaluation of others within the system. Because each postulate is logically connected with all of the others, the discovery that one is defective casts doubt on the entire theoretical structure. Conversely, if evidence is found that supports one of the claims of the theory, it tends to give presumptive support to the entire structure. This is why deductive theories, when they can be established, contribute more to the development of knowledge than do isolated laws and generalizations based on the observation of disparate events.

Uses of theories

The main task of any theory is to construct a calculus of relationships among classes of events such that the derived statements are (1) logically valid, (2) accurate in their claims regarding observable data, and (3) useful in describing, explaining, and controlling the course of the events with which they are concerned. In their early stages of development, theories focus primarily on the accuracy of descriptions. Later, they tend to shift their emphasis toward explanation and control.

Sociology today may employ theories chiefly for heuristic purposes. Few of its theories have been formalized, and the capacity for successful prediction and control is limited.[7] Even immature theories, however, may serve as useful guides to research and discovery. They tend in the long run to focus attention on the more promising concepts and relationships. It is not the concept, as such, that is "sensitizing,"[8] but the way it is used in conjunction with others in the processes of observation and explanation. This point is nicely indicated in the following comment:

[7] For some of the exceptions see H. Simon, *Models of Man*, Wiley, 1957; and J. Berger, B. Cohen, J. Snell, and M. Zelditch, *Types of Formalization in Small-Group Research*, Houghton Mifflin, 1962.

[8] H. Blumer, "What is Wrong with Social Theory?" *American Sociological Review*, February, 1945, pp. 3–10.

I remember how a professor of genetics many years ago showed me published drawings of cell nuclei before and after the discovery and description of chromosomes. Chromosomes kept showing up in the later drawings, not the earlier. In other words, microscopes do not reveal concepts until the concepts have been invented.[9]

The researcher perceives and reports those phenomena that he believes have relevance to the problem under investigation. Theories ought to provide guidelines that assist him in distinguishing the relevant phenomena from the irrelevant.

Theories also help to identify conditions that interfere with the process of explanation and those that make for success. The inverse distance law, for example, fails to take into account variations in the composition of the population, in policies of law enforcement and surveillance, or in social factors such as mobility and anonymity. To take these variables into consideration would complicate the application of the theory, of course, but it would also greatly increase the capacity for explanation.

Again, theories suggest further applications of explanatory systems. The inverse distance law suggests that other phenomena in addition to criminality may share the same frequency pattern. Similar patterns have been found for divorce, unemployment, welfare payments, suicide, and may other activities. By contrast, certain phenomena have a low incidence in the center of the city and higher frequencies in the outlying areas. For example, people with college educations, high incomes, who own their homes, and who are employed in the professions or in skilled occupations are found more frequently in the suburbs than in the city center. By comparing the spatial distributions of all these variables, the researcher gets a clearer picture of the social factors involved in the causation of crime and other modes of behavior.

Many of the embryo theories of sociology, however, have certain defects that restrict their usefulness as models for research and discovery. As an illustration, consider Merton's well-known paradigm of deviant behavior.[10] Merton's argument is that certain modes of behavior are produced by disjunctions which may occur between culturally defined goals and the institutionalized means that are prescribed for their achievement. Relevant modes of behavior are labelled conformity, innovation, ritualism, retreatism, and rebellion. The variables that determine which of these modes of behavior will occur in any given case are endorsements $(-)$, rejections $(-)$, or substitutions $(\pm)$ of cultural goals and social means. The patterns of determinants and results are listed as follows:

[9] E. G. Boring, "The Role of Theory in Experimental Psychology," *American Journal of Psychology*, 66, April 1953, 176.
[10] R. K. Merton, *Social Theory and Social Structure*, Free Press, 1957, chaps. 4–5.

DETERMINANTS

Goals	Means	Resulting Behavior
+	+	Conformity
+	−	Innovation
−	+	Ritualism
−	−	Retreatism
±	±	Rebellion

Thus, there are five basic assumptions in the theory, each one specifying the particular pattern of determinants under which a certain mode of behavior may be expected to occur. But there is no way in which the assumptions are logically connected. For this reason the theory is barren of deductive implications and has a limited explanatory potential.

However, there is an additional problem which is related to the incompleteness of the theory's classification scheme. Both goals and means have three qualitative subclasses, namely, endorsement, rejection, and substitution. There are consequently nine possible combinations of these subclasses taken two at a time. Only five were listed by Merton. The four missing ones are:

Goals	Means
±	+
±	−
−	±
+	±

No reason is given for the missing combinations. If their omission is deliberate, it indicates that in Merton's view the substitution of goals or means, whenever it occurs, must occur simultaneously for both variables. Such a view, of course, should be clearly stated in the theory's assumptions. But the omission may have been unintentional. If so, recognition of the oversight may instigate a search for distinctive modes of behavior that are possibly associated with the omitted combinations. Should such modes of behavior be found, the theory would be considerably enriched thereby.[11]

A classification scheme, properly employed, identifies and labels the various possible combinations among given sets of variables. Its content, however, is essentially descriptive. It makes no assumptions concerning the empirical relationships among the defined combinations, the relative frequencies of the combinations, or the conditions under which they may be expected to occur. Therefore, classification schemes, unless they

[11] For such an extension of Merton's theory see R. Dubin, "Deviant Behavior and Social Structure: Continuities in Social Theory," *American Sociological Review*, April, 1959, pp. 147–164.

are supplemented by assumptions concerning the relationships among the variables involved, do not explain anything.

Some of the alleged theories of contemporary sociology are little more than elaborate classification schemes. Thus, Dodd's TILP, Parsons' theory of action, and the functionalist doctrine, for example, may provide for the systematic description of any conceivable social event, but they do not enable the researcher to reason from assumptions and observations to an explanation of these events. To illustrate, functionalism provides for the cross-classification of (1) certain "needs" that are regarded as essential for the survival of social groups, and (2) social "practices" or "institutions" which presumably satisfy these needs. The implication is that needs can be identified independently of practices and can be used to explain variations in practice.

Most functionalists, however, have worked backward from observed practices to hypothesized univeral needs. Yet, if the needs are universal, they obviously can explain only universal practices, not variations in practice. The current solution to this dilemma is to regard practices as being either functional or dysfunctional, a solution that clearly negates the initial assumption of a causal relationship between essential needs and social practices.[12]

CONCEPTS AND RELATIONS

Observation terms and theoretical concepts

Theories, at least in their early stages of development, need to use the language of everyday observation in defining their units and variables. Even sophisticated theories, in order to make possible the evaluation of their empirical adequacy, must have rules for connecting their concepts with concrete data. The purpose of theory is ultimately to systematize the data of everyday experience, and this is possible only if the assumptions and implications have bearing upon the language of observation. For this reason the explanations deduced from theories are always translated into descriptive language. Were this not done, the test of a theory would be problematic.

The language of everyday observation does permit the statement of descriptive generalizations such as "Men commit more crimes than

---

[12] For useful reviews of functionalism see K. Davis, "The Myth of Functional Analysis," *American Sociological Review*, December, 1959, pp. 757–772; C. G. Hempel, "The Logic of Functional Analysis," in L. Gross, *Symposium on Sociological Theory*, Harper & Row, 1959; E. Nagel, *Logic Without Metaphysics*, Free Press, 1956, chap. 10; D. Martindale, *et al.*, "Functionalism in the Social Sciences," *American Academy of Political and Social Science*, Monograph 5, 1965.

women," "Income is higher in the middle class than in the working class," and "Catholic citizens are more likely to vote for the Democratic ticket than Protestants are." But such generalizations have shortcomings that make it difficult to convert them into theoretical assumptions. Observation terms lack precise meaning or uniform usage. Statements that contain them are likely to have numerous exceptions, unless they are employed only under severely restricted conditions.

The term "Protestant," for example, may refer to religious affiliation, amount of church attendance, or the degree of affective attachment to certain religious doctrines. Likewise, the political behavior of Protestants depends upon their income, occupation, place of residence, and their peer group involvements, among other things. Thus, the variety of qualifications needed to justify statements about the behavior of Protestants tends to discourage the use of this term as a theoretical concept. The same thing is true of many other observation terms.

In order to construct explanations that have greater precision, scope, and confirmability, theories have evolved various kinds of technical concepts. Sometimes the concepts are defined directly by the operations involved in classifying the phenomenon to which they refer. The religion of a person, for instance, may be indicated by the type of church he attends and to which he contributes financially. Again, intelligence may be defined by the number of correct answers a person gives in a standardized test, and so on. Such definitions, in which a given concept is related directly to observed data, are called *operational* definitions. The meanings of statements are usually fairly obvious if their constituent terms are operationally defined.

But concepts of another kind are also likely to play an important role in the vocabulary of a theory. These concepts may be highly abstract and may bear little resemblance to the terms used in every day discourse. Consider, for example, "differential association," "reciprocity," "status integration," etc., as these terms are used in contemporary sociology. Such terms are not introduced into a theoretical vocabulary be definitions based explicitly on observable data. Instead, they are introduced jointly in the assumptions of the theory and acquire their meanings from the context in which they are employed. *Contextual* definitions lay down the rules that govern the use of concepts within the framework of a theory. When the theory in which they occur is given an empirical interpretation, this confers upon the concepts their significance with regard to observed events.

The principle of "cognitive balance" illustrates the importance of the contextual meaning of concepts.[13] Essentially, the argument is that

[13] A review of related theories and findings is given in J. Brehm and A. Cohen, *Explorations in Cognitive Dissonance*, Wiley, 1962.

people we like are perceived as thinking and feeling the way we do. Suppose, then, that *A* and *B* are close friends. *A*, furthermore, is a strong supporter of a graduated income tax. According to the balance principle, he will therefore be inclined to see *B* as also favoring graduated taxes. But if *A* dislikes *B*, he will then tend to see *B* as opposing them. The basic assumption is that people will strive to maintain balanced cognitive systems or to produce balance in systems that are unbalanced.

The indicated theoretical relationships are shown in the following diagrams where *A* and *B* represent two persons and *X* represents some idea, event, person, or object about which *A* has a strong opinion. The plus and minus signs represent favorable and unfavorable attitudes of *A* toward *B* and *X*. The broken line at the bottom of each figure illustrates *A*'s perception of *B*'s attitude toward *X*.

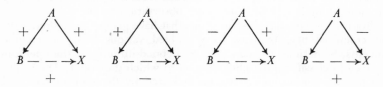

Note that *A*'s cognitive system with respect to *B* and *X* is balanced if the product of the signs attached to the arrows is positive, that is, if all of the signs are positive or if only one is positive. Conversely, the system is unbalanced if either all of the signs are negative or only one is negative. Note also that if a system of the kind illustrated is unbalanced, a change in any single sign will produce balance.

The meaning of balance in the above illustrations is contextual and depends upon the state of all of the variables in the system. There is no direct or invariant correspondence between balance and any given empirical datum.

Concepts that have contextual meanings show great versatility in theoretical discourse. While their connections with observed data are indirect and flexible, their role in the process of logical inference is precise and highly systematized. Such concepts as a consequence are of special significance in formal and deductive theories.

Induction, deduction, and retroduction

How best to generate explanatory theories is a topic of much debate. At least three distinctive points of view have been expressed on the issue. These views may be suggested in a figure according to the direction of the relationships among observed data, concepts, and theoretical assumptions.

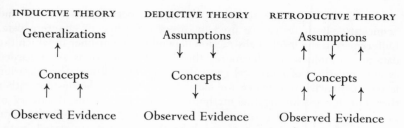

INDUCTIVE THEORY

Generalizations

↑

Concepts

↑ ↑

Observed Evidence

DEDUCTIVE THEORY

Assumptions

↓ ↓

Concepts

↓

Observed Evidence

RETRODUCTIVE THEORY

Assumptions

↑ ↓ ↑

Concepts

↑ ↓ ↑

Observed Evidence

Proponents of the inductive method tend to favor the philosophy of positivism and the operational definition of terms within the vocabulary of a theory. The extremists of this view require that all concepts be directly connected to observed evidence and that all assumptions or generalizations be testable with reference to observed data. According to their view, the theorist beings with the observation of data. Then he classifies the data into appropriate categories. Finally he measures the empirical interconnections among the defined categories.

Inductive theory is basically a statement of empirical regularities among observed variables. Its content is a variety of descriptive facts and a series of generalizations that consolidate the facts in a systematic manner. Theory construction is therefore viewed as largely a mechanical operation. "Define your terms and measure their correlations with each other" is the generic formula by which assumptions are created. For example, take any two variables from the sociologist's vocabulary, determine their correlation, and the result, if repeatedly confirmed, may be regarded as a law or a simple theory.

More complex theories, in the positivist's view, merely incorporate a larger number of variables. Regardless of the number of variables, however, mechanical methods can be employed to identify all of their possible combinations. As a consequence, the system of laws within any given domain of knowledge may be represented by a double-entry table in which each variable is cross-tabulated against all of the others. When the appropriate correlations have been observed, the cells of the table will reveal the direction and degree of the relationships among all possible pairs of variables.

The task that remains for the theorist is largely that of reducing the complexity of the table. There are several ways of doing this. Factor analysis and other statistical procedures, for example, may be used to locate families of variables that can be regrouped under more general concepts and subsumed under fewer generalizations. The objective of theory construction, in any case, is to establish a minimum set of generalizations that make possible the explanation of a maximum number of observable relationships among the variables in a given field of inquiry.

Positivists find little reason to distinguish between "variables" and "concepts." Both terms are used in direct reference to concrete data. Differences in the level of abstraction depend on the manner in which the data are combined. Furthermore, theoretical assumptions are regarded as extrapolations of empirical generalizations. In addition, formalization is seen primarily as a device for clarifying observed relationships rather than one for exploiting the methods of inference in the discovery of previously unobserved relationships. Thus, the positivist's reliance upon methods of induction tends to result in theories that are stated in the language of observation and that involve minimal use of inferential reasoning or deductive logic.

Advocates of the deductive method, by contrast, stress the virtues of formalization even in theories for which the empirical groundwork is relatively undeveloped. They point to the formalization achieved in the older mathematical and physical disciplines as a model for sociology. Much of their technique tends toward the use of analogy. Logical structures, mathematical models, and even mechanical analogues that have been established in one field of investigation are often adopted for use in another. A rather unfortunate illustration is Spencer's analogy between human societies and biological organisms. However, there are numerous instances of more advantageous use of analogy. For example, the general formula, $A = \dfrac{B}{C}$, has been employed with certain modifications in explaining the behavior of gases, the conduction of an electrical current, the movement of people seeking residences within a city, the flow of communications among scattered communities, the prices of goods in an open market, the distances travelled by people visiting national parks, and so on. Although analogy is the object of considerable distrust among sociologists, a comprehensive examination of its role in theory construction would perhaps reveal surprising evidence concerning its utility and the frequency of its use.

The main problem encountered by sociologists who use deductive methods is that of finding empirical justification for its abstract concepts. Deductive methods often assign to concepts certain logical properties which presumably explain the phenomenon under investigation. But the imputation of such properties has little explanatory value unless it can be justified by empirical evidence that is independent of the phenomenon to be explained.

Let us illustrate the above point with reference to the concept "socialization." Socialization, by conventional definition, implies that a process of learning operates so that a person acquires the social norms and behavior patterns of the groups to which he belongs. Similarities in the behavior of group members are accordingly "explained" by the statement that the process of socialization is operating. Instances in which group members fail to exhibit the expected behavior are likewise "explained" by the statement that in these cases the process is not operating. The preceding are vacuous explanations, of course, because they require that we observe the behavior to be explained before we can determine whether or not to invoke the process of socialization.

An acceptable explanation demands that we stipulate the conditions under which the process of socialization may be expected to operate and that these conditions be independent of the phenomenon to be explained. Observation of these conditions then justifies the use of the concept. When the relevant conditions are observed, we may legitimately assume that the process is operating and may attempt to predict its outcome on the basis of the theory. If the predictions are corroborated by subsequent events, our explanation is empirically as well as logically adequate. However, deductive theories often neglect the specification of conditions under which the employment of their abstract concepts is justified. As a result, the problem illustrated above with reference to "socialization" can also be noted in the use of "culture," "function," "organization," "reciprocity," and many other sociological concepts.

The defects of inductive and deductive methods are often taken into account by theorists who work simultaneously with both the data of observation and the logical abstractions inherent in theoretical concepts and assumptions. By a technique of successive approximations, the concepts and assumptions of theories may be brought into closer alignment with relevant evidence while at the same time maintaining the logical consistency required of deductive systems. This method has been called retroduction.[14] One of its major premises is that theoretical concepts are hypothetical constructions of the imagination and that their meaning and function cannot be understood unless they are examined within the context of the postulates and theorems in which they appear.

Retroductive procedures may be found in even the simplest theories. The laws of motion provide an example. Kepler, after examining the path of the planet Mars, concluded that planetary orbits follow an elliptical curve around the sun. His conception of the ellipse, while suggested by concrete observations, assigned to Mars positions that had never been observed. Newton later introduced conceptions of gravitation and acceleration in order to reduce the discrepancies between the hypothetical positions and those observed. The equations of classical mechanics continue to use concepts that for theoretical purposes may be assigned values different from those observed in concrete cases. Moreover, the explanatory power of the equations lies precisely in the fact that their claims transcend any series of previous observations.

14 N. R. Hanson, *Patterns of Discovery*, Cambridge University Press, 1958.

It is unlikely that concepts such as ellipse, gravitation, acceleration, etc., are merely abbreviated descriptions of observed facts. Rather, they are hypothetical constructs that have been assigned logical properties carefully designed to bring order into the world of experience. In the formulation of concepts and the assignment of their properties, the theorist is given license to do as he wishes. But the appropriateness of his creations is always assessed in terms of their testable consequences. Although logical consistency and deductive capacity are essential to theory, the evaluation of any empirical theory must give ultimate consideration to questions of utility related to the explanation of observable events.

Variety of Relationships

Assume that we are interested in the relationship between two dichotomous variables, A and B. We classify observed events as either possessing A or not possessing A. Allow the class "not possessing" A to be represented by $-A$. Accordingly, the events will fall into classes A or $-A$. Likewise, they will fall into either class B or $-B$. Thus, there are four possible combinations of the two variables as listed below:

	B	$-B$
A	AB	$A-B$
$-A$	$-AB$	$-A-B$

Now suppose that all of the events actually fall into only two of the four combinations, namely, AB and $-A-B$, and there are no instances of $A-B$ or $-AB$. The correlation between A and B is positive and there are no discrepant cases. This is the distribution found if the occurrence of A is both *necessary and sufficient* for the occurrence of B.

A necessary and sufficient relationship has a number of important characteristics. First is the implication, "If A, then B." Let the symbol $\rightarrow$ represent "implies." Then the preceding statement can be written $A \rightarrow B$. Now, if $A \rightarrow B$, then obviously there can be no cases of $A-B$. Furthermore, if $-B$ is observed, it must be observed in conjunction with $-A$. Thus, the statement, $(A \rightarrow B) \rightarrow (-B \rightarrow -A)$, is logically valid.

To illustrate, consider the assertion, "If an electric current flows through a wire, then a magnetic needle which is attached to the wire will be deflected." Immediately it can be seen that two statements are justified: (1) "If a current is produced, we may be sure that the needle will be deflected," and (2) "If the needle is not deflected, this signifies that there is no flow of current." In other words, the statement $A \rightarrow B$

enables us to draw conclusions about three of the four possible combinations of the two variables. That is, the combinations AB and $-A-B$ are permitted by the implication, while $A-B$ is rejected.

However, there is a second implication of necessary and sufficient relationships which allows us to draw conclusions regarding all four of the possible combinations. The point is that necessary and sufficient relationships are *symmetrical*. Symmetry means that the order of the variables can be reversed without modifying the relationship. Given A we can assert the presence of B or, conversely, given B we can assert the presence of A. More precisely, symmetry holds true if $(A{\rightarrow}B){\rightarrow}(B{\rightarrow}A)$.

The statement $B{\rightarrow}A$ denies that any cases of $-AB$ can occur. This, together with the arguments mentioned above, leaves AB and $-A-B$ as the only permissible combinations under a symmetrical relationship of the kind designated. It follows that if both $A{\rightarrow}B$ and $B{\rightarrow}A$ are true, the observation of either category of one of the variables always enables us to ascertain the appropriate category of the remaining variable.

Note that $A{\rightarrow}B$ does not necessarily indicate symmetry. Consider, for example, the relationship between court convictions, A, and law violations, B. Disregarding the possible miscarriage of justice, a court conviction implies that a law violation has occurred $(A{\rightarrow}B)$. The combination AB is therefore justified, whereas $A-B$ is disallowed. Also, if there is no violation there can be no conviction; $-A-B$ is justified by $-B{\rightarrow}-A$ which follows from $A{\rightarrow}B$. However, violations may often fail to result in convictions $(-AB)$ is permitted. Some reasons why convictions fail are that the offense may not be discovered, the offender may remain unidentified, the evidence may be inadequate, etc. Such nonsymmetrical relationships permit only limited inferences: Given A we can assert B, given $-B$ we can assert $-A$, but no inferences can be drawn from the observation of $-A$ or B. By contrast, symmetrical relationships, as already noted, allow us to draw conclusions from any of these observations. Because of their more powerful implications, symmetrical relationships may be symbolized by $A{\leftrightarrow}B$.

Many sociological theories are based on symmetrical relationships. In some cases symmetry is assumed even though it is not stated in the postulates. This is illustrated in a theory of familial structure quoted by Homans as follows:

> Societies that have avunculocal rules of residence are organized in matrilineages.
>
> Societies that have avunculocal rules of residence vest jural authority over ego in his mother's brothers.
>
> Therefore, societies that vest jural authority over ego in his mother's brothers are organized in matrilineages.[15]

[15] Quoted in R. E. L. Faris (ed.), *Handbook of Modern Sociology*, Rand McNally, 1964, pp. 961–962.

The form of the above argument is:

$$A \rightarrow B$$
$$A \rightarrow C$$
_____

Therefore, $C \rightarrow B$

Obviously, the conclusion is legitimate only if at least the second of the premises expresses a symmetrical relationship.

Much of Durkheim's theoretical effort likewise assumes symmetrical relationships.[16] Durkheim was interested in the empirical interconnections among the variables:

A. The number of members in a group.
B. The division of labor.
C. The amount of consensus on norms and values.
D. The amount of social solidarity.
E. The amount of rejection of deviants.

After examination of considerable evidence on these variables, a theory was presented which can be reconstructed from a set of four postulates.[17]

I. The greater the number of members in a group, the greater the division of labor ($A \leftrightarrow B$).
II. The greater the division of labor, the greater the consensus on norms and values ($B \leftrightarrow C$).
III. The greater the consensus on norms and values, the greater the solidarity ($C \leftrightarrow D$).
IV. The greater the solidarity, the less the rejection of deviants ($D \leftrightarrow -E$).

From these postulates six theorems can be deduced as indicated in the accompanying figure. Note that we are assuming dichotomized variables and symmetrical relationships throughout. We also retain the letters previously assigned to the variables for identification. In addition, the symbol $+$ is used to indicate a positive correlation between variables, while $-$ is used to show a negative correlation. Postulates may be identified by the roman numerals along the diagonal.

[16] Durkheim, *op. cit.*
[17] See the formalization of Durkheim attempted by H. Zetterberg, *On Theory and Verification in Sociology*, Bedminster Press, 1963, chap. 6.

	B	C	D	E
A	I	+	+	—
B		II	+	—
C			III	—
D				IV

Each of the theorems is deduced by use of the transitive rule. For example,

$$A \leftrightarrow B$$
$$B \leftrightarrow C$$

Therefore $A \leftrightarrow C$

By joining all of the postulates and theorems, it can be shown that $A \leftrightarrow B \leftrightarrow C \leftrightarrow D \leftrightarrow -E$. Consequently, only two combinations of these variables are permissible when all five are considered simultaneously. The two legitimate combinations are (1) $ABCD-E$ and (2) $-A-B-C-DE$.

The presumption that Durkheim had symmetrical relationships in mind when constructing the theory is supported by his distinction between "organic" and "mechanical" group structures. Organic groups are characterized by large size, complex division of labor, consensus on differentiated norms and values, solidarity based on mutual dependence of group members, and relative tolerance of deviants ($ABCD-E$). Mechanical groups have the opposite characteristics ($-A-B-C-DE$). Thus, the pattern of traits presented in Durkheim's typology is nearly identical to that deduced from the theory. Reconstruction of the theory clarifies the typology of group organization and identifies the assumptions that serve as its foundation.

So far we have examined deterministic relationships in which there is no tolerance for discrepant cases. Sometimes it is more realistic to employ probabilistic relationships which allow an estimated margin of error. Inferences are then based on assumptions concerning the relative frequencies with which cases may fall into the different combinations of variables. These frequencies, of course, may vary from one sample of cases to another, and the amount of variation is an important consideration in determining the degree of confidence that should be attached to inferences drawn from probabilistic relationships.

Assume that we are interested in the relationships among three dichotomous variables, A, B, and C. Assume also that we know the frequencies of the various combinations of *A* and *B* (*AB*, — *AB*, *A*—*B*, and — *A*—*B*) as well as the frequencies of the *B* and *C* combinations. Our task, then, is to estimate the frequencies of the different combinations of *A* and *C*.

Estimates may be produced by the construction of a probability model based on the known distributions. The proportion of cases that are expected to fall in the combination *AC*, for instance, may be estimated as the sum of the joint probabilities (*AB*)(*BC*) and (*A*—*B*)(—*BC*). Similar computations can be made for all other possible combinations of *A* and *C*. Confidence limits can be established for the various estimates. Such probability models, and others that are more elaborate, are useful in the practical application of complex theories, especially those that employ quantitative variables. The models are essential if we wish to differentiate between errors of estimation that result from defective postulates and those that result from faulty observation of the relevant data.[18]

Another important classification of relationships distinguishes between those that are coexistent and those that are sequential. Coexistent relationships, as indicated above, express combinations of variables that are observed simultaneously. Sequential relationships, by contrast, assert a serial order among the combinations observed over a period of time. Their essential characteristic is the orderly shifting of cases from one combination of variables to another. To prove sequence, then, we need to examine the cases over an interval of time.

What happens when a disease-producing virus is introduced into a community of healthy organisms? Some organisms encounter the virus (*A*), while others do not (— *A*). Again, some become ill (*B*), and others remain healthy (— *B*). Sequence implies that the characteristics of observed cases change over a period of time and that the changes occur in an orderly progression as follows:

Stage 1:   There is no virus. All cases are classified — *A*—*B*.

Stage 2:   Virus appears. Certain cases change from — *A*—*B* to *A*—*B*.

Stage 3:   Disease appears. Infected cases change from *A*—*B* to *AB*.

Identification of a uniform sequence in which a change in variable *A* precedes a change in variable *B* justifies the designation of *A* as the cause and *B* as the consequence. This sequential relationship is a necessary component of causal theories.

Unfortunately, sociologists devote relatively little attention to the systematic analysis of sequential relationships among social phenomena.

---

[18] Helpful discussions are found in H. Simon, *Models of Man, op. cit.*; and H. L. Costner and R. K. Leik, "Deductions from Axiomatic Theory," *American Sociological Review*, December, 1964, pp. 819–835.

More of the research effort is directed towards simultaneous observation of numerous variables and the analysis of their relationships by conventional correlation techniques. In the search for causal theories, therefore, it is often necessary to devise "artificial" methods for identifying possible time sequences in data from contemporaneous observations.

One such method is to examine the partial correlations among a set of variables to determine which of the various possible sequences best fits the data.[19] Another is to use scaling techniques to see if the variables can be ordered in terms of some conceptual dimension, such as "societal complexity," which may have implications for sequential change. This method is illustrated in a study of the relative complexity of 48 preindustrial societies.[20] Current records were investigated to discover which of the societies possess a written language, money economy, system of legal punishment, full-time specialists in government, religion, education, etc., and any given combination of these characteristics. Then the data were scaled in the usual manner. The result is a series of seven scale types which orders the societies from the least to the most complex. In the table below, x indicates the presence of the characteristic listed and — indicates its absence:

Scale Type	Money Economy	Legal Punishment	Full-Time Specialists			Written Language
			Religion	Education	Government	
I	—	—	—	—	—	—
II	x	—	—	—	—	—
III	x	x	—	—	—	—
IV	x	x	x	—	—	—
V	x	x	x	x	—	—
VI	x	x	x	x	x	—
VII	x	x	x	x	x	x

If money economy, legal punishment, etc., had their historical origins in the sequence given and if complex traits were always superimposed on simpler ones, then all societies would indeed fall into one or another of the above scale types. But the fact that the types are observed at a given time does not prove an invariant sequence. The historical trend could be towards "simplicity" instead of "complexity." Or the characteristics in question could appear and disappear in clusters that differ from one set of societies to another. There are consequently several ways of explaining

---

[19] H. M. Blalock, *Causal Inferences in Nonexperimental Research*, University of North Carolina Press, 1964.

[20] L. C. Freeman and R. F. Winch, "Societal Complexity: An Empirical Test of a Typology of Societies," *American Journal of Sociology*, March, 1957, pp. 461–466. The authors were careful not to overstate the case for sequential relationships.

the observed scale types without conceding any pattern of sequential relationships. While the methods of correlation and scale construction may be useful in formulating hypotheses about sequential relationships, the test of these hypotheses requires the kind of historical evidence that cannot be obtained from simultaneous observations.

STANDARDS OF JUDGMENT AND
STYLES OF INQUIRY

Few if any sociological theories satisfy the criteria used in evaluating the formalized research activities of some of the more mature physical sciences. Undeveloped disciplines like sociology lack the abstract and powerful vocabularies, the precise rules of grammar, and the technical dictionaries that are necessary for translating the philosophy of science into viable procedures for handling their distinctive problems. This means that there are no authenticated methods for resolving controversies over the definition of concepts, the acceptability of assumptions and theories, or even the identification of problems that are unique to sociology as a specialized field of inquiry. It may therefore be unwise for most sociologists to devote their energies to the attempted construction of abstract and comprehensive theories such as those found in the more advanced sciences. Perhaps the greater need in sociology today is for more of the modest "inference chains," "explanation sketches," and embryo theories that aim primarily at organizing selected research findings and suggesting further avenues of inquiry.[21]

The construction of embryo theories, of course, is guided by the same general objectives and procedures outlined above for more formal theories. Researchers work alternatively from an a priori base by deductive analysis and from an empirical base by inductive methods. They try as best they can to define their concepts meaningfully, to formulate their assumptions with some precision, and to trace the development of their arguments logically from assumptions to conclusions. But the absence of an established foundation of information and technology forces them to stay close to the observed data and to utilize mainly the language of everyday discourse. Technical concepts and specialized methods are introduced by minor innovations. As a result, early theories tend to focus on the development of conceptual systems that are rich in descriptive content but deficient in predictive and explanatory power. The refinements that produce empirical competence are achieved by the

[21] C. G. Hempel, "Explanations and Laws," in P. Gardiner (ed.), *Theories of History*, Free Press, 1959.

successive revisions and formalizations which result from the practical test of a theory.

Current theories of delinquency illustrate the above trends and developments. Albert Cohen, for example, rejects the notion that delinquency can be explained in terms of the characteristics of the individual offender.[22] He posits the existence of a well-organized criminal subculture which provides positive sanctions for various kinds of delinquent behavior. His argument concerning lower-class delinquency can be reconstructed in the form of an explanation sketch which leaves out much of the detailed justification:

1. The definitions of cultural objectives are approximately the same among the various social classes in American society.
2. Legitimate means for achieving the objectives are established by law and tradition. These means are also fairly uniform among the different social classes.
3. However, the accessibility of legitimate means of achievement varies among the social classes and to the disadvantage of lower class members.

The above assumptions can be used to explain observed differences in delinquency rates among the social classes. Availability of the means of achievement tends to reinforce cultural goals and norms in the middle and upper classes. By contrast, the lack of access to the means of achievement in the lower classes is associated with delinquent behavior. The mechanisms which explain the association between delinquency and restrictions on achievement are indicated below:

4. Members of the lower classes share certain problems of adjustment in all areas of institutional life.
5. The sharing of adjustment problems tends to encourage behavioral innovations, including experimentation with forms of delinquency. The experimentation is of a tentative, groping sort.
6. Experimentation with deviant activities produces a sense of interdependence among the disadvantaged persons which makes it easier for them to neutralize their feelings of guilt and to deny the legitimacy of conventional goals and norms.
7. The denial of guilt and the rejection of conventional normative standards is accompanied by a reaction-formation resulting in the inversion of cultural norms and the formation of a delinquent subculture based on nonutilitarian, malicious, and negativistic behavior.

Obviously, Cohen's attempt to substitute a sociological for a psychological explanation of delinquency is only partly successful. While individualistic notions were avoided in his early assumptions, they reappear

22 *Delinquent Boys*, Free Press, 1955.

prominently in the last two. However, a good case is made for the concept "criminal subculture," which can be interpreted to mean "socially sanctioned and systematic law violations."[23] Moreover, the explanation sketch has some of the characteristics of a formal deductive system. It appears that the stated assumptions could easily be logically inter-connected by the insertion of certain premises and inferences that were left unstated.

Explanation sketches developed subsequently by other students of delinquency reveal the impact of Cohen's work. Cloward and Ohlin, for example, begin with assumptions that are almost identical to the first three of Cohen's.[24] But they add an assumption adopted from Kobrin, dealing with the relationship between the criminal subculture and the system of legitimate norms which characterizes the broader society.[25] The assumption may be stated as follows:

> Within any given community there may or may not be a system of illegitimate opportunities (criminal subculture). If an illegitimate system exists, it may be either integrated with the legitimate system or unintegrated. When the two are integrated, the illegitimate system will have institutionalized procedures for recruiting young participants, indoctrinating them in the employment of illegitimate means of achievement, and absorbing them eventually into a set of illegitimate occupations for adults.
>
> When the legitimate and illegitimate systems are unintegrated, it may be assumed that the aforementioned devices for the social control of deviants do not occur.

Accordingly, three types of communities can be identified by con-sidering (1) the presence or absence of an illegitimate opportunity system, and (2) the degree of integration between the legitimate and illegitimate systems:

1. Legitimate Opportunity System Always Present		
2. Illegitimate Opportunity System		
Absent	Present	
	3. The Two Systems	
	Integrated	Unintegrated
4. Types of Community Social Structure		
I	II	III

[23] The essential content of the concept is not new, of course, and can be found in the works of Durkheim, Tarde, Sutherland, and others. Cohen's innovation is found in the consistent way he links the concept with others in an explanatory argument and in the demonstration of its utility.

[24] R. A. Cloward and L. E. Ohlin, *Delinquency and Opportunity: A Theory of Delinquent Gangs*, Free Press, 1960.

[25] S. Kobrin, "The Conflict of Values in Delinquency Areas," *American Sociological Review*, October, 1958, pp. 653–661.

Several commonsense implications of the above assumptions should be mentioned. Type I communities are those in which the legitimate system prevails. Because of the absence of culturally sanctioned non-conformity, deviance in such communities should be an infrequent, sporadic, unorganized activity among isolated individuals. Type II communities are those in which legitimate and illegitimate systems are integrated in a symbiotic manner so that there are two alternative avenues to the attainment of cultural objectives. Here delinquency should be highly organized, instrumentally oriented, and subject to the social controls of both systems. Delinquency, in effect, may serve as an apprenticeship for adult careers in illegitimate occupations. Type III communities are characterized by unintegrated legitimate and illegitimate systems. Here access to the illegitimate system should provide few career opportunities and only limited prospects for goal achievement. Delinquency should therefore be expressive, violent, contagious, and organized around unconventional objectives.

More specifically, the criminalistic gangs discussed by Cloward and Ohlin may be expected to occur most frequently in Type II communities, whereas the violent, conflict gangs may be expected primarily in communities of Type III. Unfortunately, the community typology does not adequately explain the distribution of retreatist gangs.

In addition, the typology of communities does not explain the fact that many youths in communities of types II and III do not participate in gang activities. Thus, the assumptions about differential access to illegitimate opportunities may tell us what kinds of gangs are likely to be found in different communities, but they do not enable us to identify the persons who are most likely to participate in gang activities.

Some further assumptions are required to identify the most likely gang participants:

Susceptibility to involvement in gang activities is greatest among persons who are alienated from the legitimate system, who blame the system rather than themselves for their adjustment problems, and who deny the pragmatic efficacy of legitimate norms.

Alienation from legitimate norms has two main sociocultural sources. First is the perception of discrepancies between official criteria of achievement (hard work, ability, initiative, etc.) and pragmatic criteria (luck, being "in the know," having the "right" contacts, etc.). Second is the perception of systematized prejudices against certain members of the community accompanied by the possession of traits (race, religion, place of residence, etc.) which serve as visible barriers against achievement.

Alienation from legitimate norms minimizes guilt feelings among nonconformists, facilitates the acceptance of illegitimate roles, and encourages the development of delinquent subcultures.[26]

[26] For a fuller examination of the theory see C. Schrag, "Delinquency and Opportunity: Analysis of a Theory," *Sociology and Sociological Research*, January, 1962, pp. 167–175.

The added assumptions enable us to state a number of informal inferences relating delinquency with racial, religious, residential, educational, occupational, and other social variables that are presumably associated with differential access to legitimate and illegitimate opportunity systems. Instead of eliminating psychological concepts, however, they imply some connections between delinquency and attitudinal variables such as the degree of potency assigned to legitimate norms, prevalence of guilt feelings, amount of extrapunitiveness, attachment to deviant subcultures, and so on. Equally significant are their suggestions concerning action programs aimed at modifying opportunity structures or revising the manner in which opportunities are perceived in some segments of society. Thus, the assumptions may afford at least a minimal theoretical foundation for projects such as Mobilization For Youth or the federal effort against poverty.

The sketches of Cohen and of Cloward and Ohlin are essentially idiographic studies, rich in descriptive detail but subject to widely varied interpretations. Before they can be tested adequately in the arena of social action, their concepts need to be related more specifically to empirical phenomena and decisions need to be made as to the logical form of their claimed relationships. The discursive arguments must be translated into nomothetic statements. Few guideposts are provided by the authors for making the translations. As a consequence, the formalizations that attend the attempted tests of these explanation sketches may or may not be consistent with the authors' conceptions.

One test, for example, reduces the assumptions to a series of statements about relationships among three abstract concepts, namely, the legitimate system, the illegitimate system, and the personal system. Although there are numerous empirical indicators for each of these concepts, those employed in the study may be illustrated as follows:[27]

A. Attachment to the legitimate normative system is defined in terms of the degree of endorsement of cultural goals, the nature of personal aspirations, and perceived opportunities.
B. Attachment to the illegitimate system is defined in terms of cognitive knowledge of delinquent practices, attitudes toward deviance, and degree of acquaintance with persons who are known law violators.
C. The personal system is defined in terms of self-conceptions, selected attitude scales, and the need for achievement as measured by Aronson's method.

[27] Only a small segment of the study is presented here for illustrative purposes. See L. C. Gould and C. Schrag, "Theory Construction and Prediction in Juvenile Delinquency," *Proceedings of the American Statistical Association*, 1962, pp. 68–73; D. S. Elliott, "Delinquency and Perceived Opportunity," *Sociological Inquiry*, Spring, 1962, pp. 216–227; L. C. Gould, *Delinquency and Community Opportunity Structure*, Unpublished MA Thesis, University of Washington, 1961; and D. S. Elliott, *Delinquency, Opportunity, and Patterns of Orientation*, Unpublished PhD Thesis, University of Washington, 1961.

The test evidence to be presented is based on perceived opportunities in the field of education, the number of personal acquaintances who are known to be law violators, and the need for achievement. Postulates derived from the explanation sketches of Cohen and of Cloward and Ohlin are:

I. The perception of legitimate opportunities has a negative relationship with the amount of delinquent contact.
II. The amount of delinquent contact has a positive relationship with need for achievement.
III. Need for achievement has a positive relationship with delinquent behavior.

Assuming transitive, symmetrical, and deterministic relationships, three theorems can be deduced from the above postulates:

IV. Perception of legitimate opportunities is negatively related with need for achievement.
V. Perception of legitimate opportunities is negatively related with delinquent behavior.
VI. Amount of delinquent contact is positively related with delinquent behavior.

Data from a sample of boys in a central city high school support each of the postulates and theorems. They also show that delinquent contact has the highest association with delinquency and need for achievement the lowest. Thus, by assigning the first priority to contact, next to perceived opportunity, and last to need for achievement, we can list the logically possible combinations of these variables in the order of their theoretical delinquency rates as follows:

Contact	Opportunity	Achievement	Delinquency rate per 100 boys	Number of delinquents
High	Low	High	55.6	25
High	Low	Low	29.0	25
High	High	High	10.9	10
Low	Low	High	7.9	21
High	High	Low	100.0	2
Low	Low	Low	6.4	18
Low	High	High	2.7	9
Low	High	Low	1.2	7

Although more accurate predictions can be obtained by the use of a greater number of variables, the data show that even a very elementary formalization of the aforementioned explanation sketches produces considerable empirical discrimination between delinquent and non-delinquent boys.

There are four sets of criteria that govern the attempted formalization of explanatory systems. First are criteria of *logical adequacy*. The principle of parsimony, for example, aims at the elimination of redundancy in the definition of concepts and at the establishment of a minimum set of postulates. Consistency requires that no pair of contradictory inferences can be drawn from the theory. Fertility depends upon how well the theory is adapted to mathematical and logical operations. The informative content of a theory is determined by the variety of claims made and the number of different ways in which they can be tested.

Again, the *operational adequacy* of a theory depends upon its testability. If the concepts employed cannot be related in some consistent manner to the data of observation, the theory must remain untested. Rules of correspondence, operational definitions, reduction sentences, etc., are devices for establishing the necessary connection between concepts and data.

Criteria of *empirical adquacy* deal with the degree of congruence between theoretical claims and empirical evidence. Thus, credibility refers to the goodness of fit between claims and existing evidence, while predictability estimates how well the claims will hold true in the future. Generality indicates the scope of the phenomena with which the theory is concerned. Comprehensiveness is determined by the number and relevance of the variables included.

Pragmatic adequacy depends upon the utility of a theory in controlling the phenomena of interest. Significance, for instance, is assessed by the capacity of a theory for solving the problems that initiate research inquiries. Feasibility refers to the costs involved in the attempt to control. Social relevance is determined by the willingness of groups and organizations to pay the price necessary for control.

Various other criteria may be employed in the evaluation of theories. Which criteria to use in any given case depends upon the intent of the researcher. This point is important because a theory may be superior in some respects and inferior in others. In order to increase the generality of a theory, for example, it may be necessary to reduce parsimony or testability. Or to increase credibility it may be necessary to limit generality. The resolution of such dilemmas is regulated by matters of personal preference and styles of inquiry. No specific method of theory construction is likely to satisfy all of the criteria mentioned.

Consider the varied styles of inquiry that are employed by reputable researchers in any given field of inquiry. Styles of inquiry are revealed in the decisions made among various possible alternatives that occur at each stage of the research process. Some important alternatives deal with the basic research objectives, the methods used in the definition and selection of variables under investigation, the designs for observing and analyzing the data, and the rules of logic that determine the structure of arguments and conclusions.

A general description of the kinds of judgments involved in all research is given in a paradigm of theory construction.

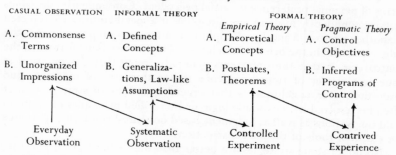

CASUAL OBSERVATION　　INFORMAL THEORY　　　　　　FORMAL THEORY

　　　　　　　　　　　　　　　　　　　　Empirical Theory　　*Pragmatic Theory*

A. Commonsense　　A. Defined　　　　A. Theoretical　　A. Control
　　Terms　　　　　　　Concepts　　　　　　Concepts　　　　　Objectives

B. Unorganized　　B. Generaliza-　　B. Postulates,　　B. Inferred
　　Impressions　　　　tions, Law-like　　Theorems　　　　Programs of
　　　　　　　　　　　　Assumptions　　　　　　　　　　　　Control

Everyday　　　　　Systematic　　　　Controlled　　　　Contrived
Observation　　　Observation　　　Experiment　　　　Experience

Thus, the objective of research may be to test the adequacy of current theories, or it may be to explore uncertain areas in order to formulate new explanatory principles and theories. Again, some studies aim at *post facto* explanations of observed events, while others strive to meet the requirements of prediction and control. There is no way at present of establishing the primacy of one of these objectives over the others.

Variables under investigation are frequently selected on the basis of current theories and previous research findings, but sometimes researchers prefer to rely more heavily on their own insight and intuition. The variables may be precisely defined, observed under rigidly controlled conditions, and recorded in terms of scalar units. Or they may be reported as they are observed in the "free state" on the assumption that generality and validity are more important than reliability for the purpose at hand. Likewise, research designs may be specified in such detail that the methods of observation, hypotheses, dummy tables, statistical operations, and confidence limits are fully established before the process of data collection beings. Other designs, however, may be so fluid and flexible that decisions at any given point in the research process are primarily determined by information gathered in the immediately preceding stages.

Possibly the most difficult decisions are those relating to the nature of the conclusions that place them in proper context with respect to prevailing opinions and theories. Some workers, assuming a Comtean hierarchy of science, try to link their findings by means of analogy with those of more mature disciplines, while others disavow analogy and attempt to develop theories unique to their own fields of inquiry. Again, research findings may be formalized in the language of logic and mathematics by means of abstract concepts only partly and indirectly connected with observed data, while in other cases theoretical concepts are avoided and findings are expressed simply as empirical relationships among observed variables.

Questions of strategy such as those mentioned are often resolved in terms of personal preference or social precedent. Consequently, decisions that are confidently made in one discipline at a specified time are rejected at another time or in another discipline. Controversy on procedures is the rule, especially in the behavioral sciences. The most striking feature of the controversy is that the opponents generally imply that the question at issue is a matter of factual evidence rather than one of judgment and discretion. Our conclusion is that crucial questions of strategy cannot often be resolved by inexorable logic or by verified principles of method. Bold innovations as well as judgment based on shared research experience are essential tools of theory construction.

No doubt some strategies are better than others for a given purpose. Our task, then, is to link strategies and purposes in a manner suggested by the best evidence and experience. The appropriate linking of strategies and objectives will inevitably entail a good deal of research on research methods and will also require that researchers include a specification of objectives as an essential part of the research process. An initial requirement, however, is that we recognize objectives as relevant factors in the selection of research methods and that the optimum connections between strategies and objectives have not yet been determined. This discussion of the elements of theory construction is intended to indicate some of the issues that are unresolved in contemporary sociology.[28]

Bibliography

Berger, Joseph, Bernard P. Cohen, J. Laurie Snell, and Morris Zelditch, *Types of Formalization in Small-Group Research*, Boston: Houghton Mifflin, 1962.

Blalock, Hubert M., Jr., *Causal Inferences in Nonexperimental Research*, Chapel Hill: University of North Carolina Press, 1964.

Braithwaite, R. B., *Scientific Explanation*, New York: Cambridge University Press, 1953.

Coleman, James S., *Models of Change and Response Uncertainty*, Englewood Cliffs, N. J.: Prentice-Hall, 1964.

Feigl, Herbert, and Michael Scriven, *Minnesota Studies in the Philosophy of Science*, Minneapolis: University of Minnesota Press, 1956, 1958.

Flament, Claude, *Applications of Graph Theory to Group Structure*. Englewood Cliffs, N. J.: Prentice-Hall, 1963.

[28] "Some Demerits of Contemporary Sociology," *op. cit.*

Frank, Phillip, *Philosophy of Science*, Englewood Cliffs, N. J.: Prentice-Hall, 1957.

Gardiner, P. (ed.), *Theories of History*, New York: Free Press, 1959.

Gross, Llewellyn (ed.), *Symposium on Sociological Theory*, New York: Harper & Row, 1959.

Hempel, Carl G., *Fundamentals of Concept Formation in Empirical Science*, Chicago: University of Chicago Press, 1952.

Lazarsfeld, Paul F., *Mathematical Thinking in the Social Sciences*, New York: Free Press, 1954.

Lazarsfeld, P. F., and M. Rosenberg, *The Language of Social Research*, New York: Free Press, 1955.

Luce, R. D., and H. Raiffa, *Games and Decisions*, New York: Wiley, 1957.

Martindale, D., *The Nature and Types of Sociological Theory*, Boston: Houghton Mifflin, 1960.

Nagel, Ernest, *The Structure of Science*, New York: Harcourt, Brace & World, 1961.

Simon, Herbert, *Models of Man*, New York: Wiley, 1957.

Solomon, H., *Mathematical Thinking in the Measurement of Behavior*, New York: Free Press, 1960.

White, Harrison C., *An Anatomy of Kinship*, Englewood Cliffs, N. J.: Prentice-Hall, 1963.

Zetterberg, Hans L., *On Theory and Verification in Sociology*, Totowa, N. J.: Bedminster Press, 1963.

LLEWELLYN GROSS

Note on selected problems in theory construction

In sociology, theory construction generally refers to those systematic procedures which promise to disclose the rational, empirical, and pragmatic principles underlying its subject matter. Such principles are designed to articulate patterns of symbolic expression which will contribute to the understanding, explanation, and prediction of social phenomena.

Theory construction may begin with the observation of individual actions and end with hypotheses and generalization about the actions of groups of individuals in a wide variety of social and cultural contexts. As an elementary illustration, assume that a roving sociologist observes a boy named "Tom" taking an apple from a stand when the seller's back is turned. Reporting this simple act in the descriptive sentence, "Tom stole an apple," goes beyond the directly seen; the report rests upon the conceptualization of Tom's act as dishonest, wrong, and secret. Tom's act may be further removed from direct observation by construing it as the manifestation of a generalized disposition to steal. Thus it may be said that "Tom is a thief," a characteristic attributed to him apart from specific "acts of stealing." The continuum of abstract inference is broadened when others along with "Tom" are viewed as members of the class, "under-priviliged youths," and the latter's acts qualify them for inclusion in the abstract class of "delinquents." The abbreviated generalization, "Under-privileged youths are delinquents," may then be proposed. However, before the generalization can be confirmed the meaning of "underprivi-leged youths" and "delinquents" must be specified in ways which permit their incorporation in a network of explanatory statements. At the most abstract level parts of this network may be expressed in the form of logical or numerical symbols having meanings independent of observation-al content. Thus, by describing the circumstances—slum living—under which the preceding generalization may be said to hold, the statement, "Under conditions, $C_1, \ldots, C_n$, (slum living) X proportion of A's (underprivileged youths) are B's (delinquents)" can be asserted as a lawlike regularity. Such a lawlike regularity becomes a universal law of nature when its conditional and probability qualifications are precisely specified.

Although sociology is now unable to specify the conditions required for sustaining universal laws it may, for exploratory reasons, simulate such laws by treating them as hypothetical generalizations. Thus, in the generalization, "All delinquents are enculturated," (All A's are B's), the term "enculturated" may serve as a theoretical reconstruction of meaning elements common to writers in criminology. Insofar as delinquents are engaged in "cultural conflict" (Sellin), or live in "subculturally structured" environments (Cohen), or become "rationalizers of deviance" (Sykes and Matza), and "utilizers of illegitimate opportunities" (Cloward and Ohlin), their acts represent specialized interpretations of the abstract term, "enculturated,"[1] By asserting that if anyone has the characteristic of being delinquent he has also the characteristic of being enculturated, the generalization refers to abstract properties considered apart from their exemplification in particular individuals. Its ordinary English equivalents include such statements as "Delinquents are enculturated" (A's are B's), "Every delinquent is enculturated" (Every A is B), "Any delinquent is enculturated" (Any A is B), "No delinquent is not enculturated" (No A is not B), "Delinquency implies enculturation" (A implies B), etc.

Statements of the preceding kind can be significant (meaningful) without being true. If "chimpanzees" are substituted for "delinquents" the resulting assertion, "All chimpanzees are enculturated," is significant, even though false. If "triangles" are substituted for "delinquents" the altered assertion, "All triangles are enculturated," is devoid of significance.

[1] For source material, see M. E. Wolfgang, L. Savitz, and N. Johnson, *The Sociology of Crime and Delinquency*, Wiley, 1962.

To formulate a true generalization, the social theorist must attend to individuals which in fact possess the properties of being both "delinquent" and "enculturated." But such a generalization cannot be taken as resting only on those individuals which fall within its range of direct observation. Unless the scope of the generalization is meant to refer to new or previously unobserved individuals it will have little scientific or practical value. To extend the scope of the generalization beyond its direct evidence reasoning must proceed from the premise, "All Observed A's have been B's," to the conclusion "All A's are B's." Since the conclusion is about all A's, some of which are unobserved, its factual truth cannot be conclusively established. Confronted with this difficulty, the theorist may interpret the conclusion, "All A's are B's," as a "contrary-to-fact conditional" expressible in the statement, "If anything were (had been) A, then it would be (would have been) B." Such an interpretation does not commit one to the truth or falsity of either the antecedent or the consequent. The antecedent becomes a possible premise for explaining phenomena only when suitable reasons obtain for subsuming some true statement under it. Indeed, some theorists hold that the generalization, "All A's are B's," must be interpreted as a contrary-to-fact conditional, else it would not be predictive of future associations between A's and B's. The generalization would express a contingent association; a regularity that is "accidental" rather than lawlike. On the contrary-to-fact assumption, sociologists will accept the alleged generalization "All delinquents are enculturated," only when they have suitable reasons for believing that if any person were delinquent he necessarily would be enculturated. Despite the apparent circularity, generalizations of this form ("All A's are B's") are used as premises in patterns of scientific explanation.

Following the lead of Hempel and Oppenheim[2] the basic pattern of scientific explanation may be divided into *explanans* and *explanandum*. *Explanandum* are the class of sentences describing the phenomena to be explained; particular fact, events or uniformities as the case may be. *Explanans* are the class of sentences brought forward to explain the described phenomena. They consist of two groups, one stating theoretical principles, general uniformities, or empirical regularities, the other stating specific antecedent conditions. To be adequate, *explanans* must have empirical content (observational test or evidential correctness) and permit of logical deduction of the *explanandum*. The pattern is exemplified in the following schema:

Explanans: All delinquents are enculturated. (Major Premise: general uniformity)
Explanans: John is a delinquent. (Minor Premise: specific condition)
Explanandum: John is enculturated. (Deduced conclusion: specific consequence)

[2] C. G. Hempel and P. Oppenheim, "The Logic of Explanation," in H. Feigl and M. Brodbeck (eds.), *Readings in the Philosophy of Science*, Appleton-Century-Crofts, 1953, pp. 319–353 (first published 1948).

When explanation is taken as an argument in which a specific consequence is deduced from the conjunction of a general uniformity and a specific condition, it offers a framework for tracing several lines of inference. No doubt, the most familiar line proceeds from specific condition and general uniformity to specific consequence. In other cases, inference may proceed from (1) specific condition and specific consequence to general uniformity or from (2) specific consequence and general uniformity to specific condition.

In *teleological explanation* the line of inference resembles (2), above. The conclusion (result) is not objectively described but desired. The interpreter does not know the general law, "All A's are B's"; he only believes that A is necessary to B and desires to have B occur. The conjunction of belief and desire then leads to the assertion of A and its occurrence as an "explanation." In short, if the interpreter believes that B is dependent upon A and desires B then he is likely to affirm A and seek its occurrence. Since the reasoning is from conclusion to premise, aided by a contingent regularity, it is a belief statement resting on extremely limited empirical grounds.[3] Granting this limitation, the problem of explaining present conditions by reference to future consequences can be partially resolved by reviewing such consequences as no more than expressions of social intentions (motives). By construing social intentions as antecedent conditions the occurrence of the desired result is "explained." In Braithwaite's words, "goal-directed behavior is explained as goal-intended behavior."[4] Although denying goal-intended behavior, the sociologist Durkheim appears to have supported goal-directed behavior when accompanied by explanations in the form of deterministic, non-purposive causes: "To show how a fact is useful is not to explain how it originated or why it is what it is. The uses which it serves presuppose the specific properties characterizing it but do not create them. The need we have of things cannot give them existence, nor can it confer their specific nature upon them. . . ." For their existence, "it is necessary again to go back along the chain of causes and effects until we find a point where the action of man may be effectually brought to bear."[5]

Sociological Functionalism is beset with teleological difficulties insofar as it has a "tendency to confuse the subjective category of motive with the objective category of function."[6] To eliminate this confusion, Merton develops the distinction between cases in which the subjective aim-in-view concides with objective consequences and cases in which they diverge. Those objective consequences contributing to the adjustment of

[3] C. J. Ducasse, "Explanation, Mechanism and Teleology," in H. Feigl and W. Sellers (eds.), *Readings in Philosophical Analysis*, Appleton-Century-Crofts, 1949, pp. 540–544 (first published 1935).

[4] R. B. Braithwaite, *Scientific Explanation*, Cambridge University Press, 1955, p. 325.

[5] E. Durkheim, *The Rules of Sociological Method*, Free Press, 1950, pp. 90–91.

[6] R. K. Merton, *Social Theory and Social Structure*, Free Press, 1957, p. 51.

a social system which are intended and recognized by its participants are called manifest functions. Those which are neither intended nor recognized are called latent functions.[7] It is said, accordingly, that the manifest function of Hopi ceremonials is to produce rain whereas its latent function is the reinforcement of group identity.[8] Translating this statement into an elliptical explanation, it may be asserted that, "Under certain ceremonial conditions group identity is reinforced." When the ceremonial is, in turn, explained by the belief (the anticipated consequence) that it produces rain, the conclusion follows that the belief reinforces group identity. In short, the explanation of the ceremony by reference to anticipated consequences becomes the antecedent for explaining group identity, an unanticipated consequence. It is apparent, then, that the manifest function can be used to account for the latent function.

In most functional explanations, reasoning proceeds from a consequence B, as a necessary condition of a system regularity S, to a cause A as antecedent. Thus, the occurrence of A is inferred from the occurrence of B and some presumed set of conditions defining S. The adequacy of this kind of explanation has been challenged on the grounds that causal alternatives to A, together with conditions for specifying S, are not usually known.[9] When there are functional alternatives (equivalents) for A, other antecedents can be inferred as causes of B, and A is not indispensable. Moreover, unless the conditions of S are specified there can be no way of knowing whether a functional alternative to A is possible within S, for such an alternative may be interpreted as an antecedent of the partially altered or entirely different system S_2. Even assuming that A were shown to be the indispensable cause of an identified system S, its effects on a different system S_2 including C, a possible necessary condition for the regularity of S_2, may remain unknown.[10] Essentially similar limitations apply to functional explanations when construed as inductive arguments.[11]

Tendency explanations presume to be indicators of general uniformities which would be manifested were their causes identified. "The peculiarity of a tendency statement is that it states that, if a thing is C, then if it is also A it is also B, when 'If a thing is A, it is also B' (i.e., every A is a B) is an ordinary scientific hypothesis; and C is an unspecified property."[12] Tendency statements differ from general uniformities of the type, "If any class of *specified* things has the property A then it has the property B," by affirming that "If any class of *unspecified* things has the property A

[7] *Ibid.*

[8] *Ibid.*, pp. 64–65.

[9] C. G. Hempel, "The Logic of Functional Analysis," in L. Gross, (ed.), *Symposium on Sociological Theory*, Harper & Row, 1959, pp. 271–307.

[10] E. Nagel, *The Structure of Science*, Harcourt, Brace & World, 1961, p. 532.

[11] Hempel, *op. cit.*, pp. 286–287.

[12] R. B. Braithwaite, *Scientific Explanation*, Cambridge University Press, 1955, p. 362.

then it has the property *B*." In the latter formulation, the properties *A* and *B* are, in principle, unspecified since they are subclasses of the class of unspecified things *C*. At best, the meaning of *C* is partially determinable by virtue of some cognitive or experiential content attributed to the association of *A* and *B*. Only when tendency statements are located within a deductive network simulating general uniformities, may the association of *A* and *B* approach some form of stable frequency (probability). When *A* and *B* are associated in more than a random number of times, useful estimates can be made about the content of the class of unspecified things *C*. Partially indeterminate contents may then be compared and properties identified.[13]

Configurational explanations endeavor to provide generalizations about properties and relations which are interactive, reciprocal and transformable, but non-random, non-linear, and non-additive. Thus, they are less likely to detail specific properties of specific events than to account for internal relations among many events in many complex forms. Patterns and qualities are assessed through a one-sided singling out of phases, modes, and styles, modulated by the changing aspects of a changing totality. Similar kinds of configurational explanations appear in much of sociology, social psychology, and history. Of direct relevance is the view that historical explanations are equivalent to sociological explanations by reason of their construction from sociological concepts. Thus, for White, the phrase, "barbarian invasion of the Roman Empire during the period 58 B.C. to A.D. 107" designates a class of events which is the logical product of at least three classes: a class of group actions, the property of invasion assigned to actions of masses of people, and the class of events occurring within the time designated. The first two classes are social, the last is physical.[14] Sociological conditions of explanation can also be found in Gottschalk's classification of historical labels as: (1) biographical entities or aggregates that answer the question, *who*, (2) group behavior or activities that answer the question, *doing what*, (3) geographical interrelations that answer the question, *where*, and (4) chronological interrelations or periodizations, that answer the question, *when*.[15]

Both sociology and history are limited by the "porous" nature of their classifications. Both disciplines often begin with the same events and trace the same or different lines of inference to the same or different conclusions. For both, the explanatory adequacy of generalizations vis-a-vis singular statements is at issue.

[13] For attempts to systematize tendency statements of the form, "If A increases then B increases," see H. Zetterberg, *On Theory and Verification in Sociology*, The Bedminister Press, 1965; and L. Gross, "System-Construction in Sociology," *Behavioral Science*, 5, October, 1960.

[14] M. White, "Historical Explanation," in P. Gardiner (ed.), *Theories of History*, Free Press, 1959, p. 369 (first published 1943).

[15] L. Gottschalk, "Categories of Historiographical Generalization," in L. Gottschalk (ed.), *Generalization in the Writing of History*, University of Chicago Press, 1963, p. 125.

In sociology, generalizations abound but the singular statements upon which they rest are seldom supplied. In history, singular statements abound but generalizations for summarizing them are rarely made explicit. The simplest form of singular statement asserts that, "Under circumstances c_1, c_2, c_3, . . . , individual a did b." To this statement, a time factor c_t, together with characteristics p_1, p_2, p_3, . . . , may be specified: "Under circumstances, c_t, c_1, c_2, c_3, . . . , individual a, characterized by p_1, p_2, p_3, . . . , did b." In some cases, the statement includes a's alleged reasons, r_1, r_2, r_3, . . . , and mentions the alternative courses of action, d, e, f, excluded by virtue of these reasons: "Under circumstances c_t, c_1, c_2, c_3, . . . , individual a acted for reasons r_1, r_2, r_3, . . . , to do b rather than d, e, f." Particularistic interpretations of this kind are inferred from tacitly held generalizations based on insightful analogies rather than from strictly inductive procedures. When articulated, such generalizations consist of sets of statements of the form: "If under conditions, C_1, C_2, . . . , C_n individuals A_1, A_2, . . . , A_n act for reasons R_1, R_2, . . . , R_n, then they will choose to do B_1, B_2, . . . , B_n." All that can be asserted is that within a limited range of conditions, a limited number of individuals will, for a limited number of reasons, act in a limited number of ways. Thus, the likelihood that "Under conditions C_i, A_j will choose B_k for reasons R_m", compared to the likelihood that "Under conditions C_i', A_j', will choose B_k' for reasons R_m',", is empirically contingent. Insofar as contingent generalizations are supported by specified types of regular association, statements of very low probability (truth frequency) can be supplanted with those of increasingly higher probability.

Assume, for illustrative purposes, that the explanation of some social process such as intergroup conflict (G) is sought in a configuration of conditions loosely designated as ethnic visibility (A), division of labor (B), mobility (C), group affiliation (D), and cultural beliefs (E). Among the types of generalizations which may be offered are the following: (1) When A, B, C, D, or E occur, either singly or in some combination, G occurs. (2) When A, B, C, D, or E occur, in certain specified combinations, G occurs. (3) Only when A occurs, together with certain specified combinations of B, C, D, or E, G occurs. (Similarly for other suitably specified sets of conditions.) (4) Only when a certain subset of A $(A_1, A_2, A_3, . . . , A_k)$ occurs, G occurs. (Similarly for other suitable specified subsets of each condition.) (5) Only when both a certain subset of A $(A_1, A_2, A_3, . . . , A_k)$ and a certain subset of B $(B_1, B_2, B_3, ... , B_k)$ occur together, G occurs. (Similarly for the joint occurrence of other suitable specified subsets of A, B, C, D, or E.) (6) Only when a certain subset of general properties $(P_1, P_2, P_3, . . . , P_k)$ of conditions A, B, C, D, or E occur, G occurs. The usefulness of such generalizations depends upon the degree to which a restricted number of conditions (or variables) is necessary for the occurrence of the others, the proportional frequency with which they actually occur together, and the extent to which their application requires relatively few supplementary premises. In most configurational explanations, the relationship between conditions and consequences is not one of precise association but of representation by means of metaphores familiar to several disciplines. It is said that A "calls for" B, A "influences" B, A "is involved with" B, A "contributes to" B, A "predominates over" B, A "supplants" B, A "is subject to" B. The translation of these expressions into symbols having the precision of such logical relations as inclusion, negation, equality, transitivity, and symmetry is a future task of theory construction in sociology.

Along with the stress on logical relations, the most significant problems of theory construction stem from diverse interpretations of the relation of (1) antecedents to consequents, and of (2) theoretical terms to observational terms. The antecedent-consequent relation poses questions of the following kind:

1. Does the relation merely describe a conjunction which has been observed because of an "accidental," "contingent," or "matter-of-fact" association? For instance, is the generalization, "In Jonesville, profits and fees as forms of income are better than salaries," of sufficient scope to be applicable to all American cities of the same type, not to mention Jonesville in 1970? If the generalization is meant to apply only to previously observed events, how can it be used to explain or predict other events of the same kind, those not yet observed or known to occur?

2. Is the antecedent-consequent relation based on something stronger than matter-of-fact association? For instance, is the statement, "No group can be coordinated without being stratified," so necessary that it cannot be denied? If it is inconceivable that any group could be coordinated without being in some sense stratified, sociologists will support the assertion, "If any human group were coordinated then it would be stratified." This use of the contrary-to-fact conditional amounts to the claim that there never has been and never will be a coordinated group that is not stratified; in short, that a necessary universal rather than an accidental universal obtains.

3. Does the consequent follow from the antecedent by virtue of a logically shared meaning, the denial of which would be self-contradictory? If so, then the consequent can be elicited from the antecedent by some kind of insightful analysis, not dependent upon previous experience. Possible instances include statements of the form, "If anyone has social status then he has social rank," and its abbreviation in the syntactical concept "status-rank." If observational evidence is not required for expressions of this kind, is logical demonstration sufficient to establish sociological truth?

4. Does the antecedent-consequent relation consist of a procedural or instrumental rule for inferring observational statements? Does it provide a basis for stating premises *from which* consequences are logically derived or is it usually employed as an empirical principle *in accordance with which* inferences are drawn?[16] For instance, rather than deriving the consequent, "The lower class is status oriented," from the antecedents, "All subcultural groups are status oriented" and "The lower class is a subcultural group," does the sociologist typically reason that, "Since the lower class is a subcultural group it will be status oriented"? If he does follow such a principle he may be propounding a rule of inference which, in the absence of finer distinctions, can be appropriately viewed as correct or incorrect rather than true or false.

5. Can the antecedent be part of a lawlike generalization when it is devoid of empirical content? If the antecedent is only "vacuously true" will its usefulness then depend upon its inclusion in a deductive system, some portion of which has empirical content? Can the consequent be a part of a lawlike generalization if it contains individual names, refers to particular groups, and designates definite locations? Most sociologists would probably hold that all antecedents and consequents should possess some degree of empirical content. With few exceptions they favor generalizations which can be directly reduced to empirical observations.

6. Is the meaning and use of the antecedent-consequent relation dependent primarily upon context? In differing contexts, the relation may appear to be logically, causally, or descriptively either contingent or necessary. Do these possibilities then reflect cultural circumstances, including the syntax and semantics of language and the psychological habits of the scientist?

Controversial issues, too numerous to detail, surround the relation of theoretical terms to observational terms. The central problem revolves around the function and utility of theoretical terms and the respects in which their interpretation renders them either dispensable or indispensable in the corpus of science. Setting aside technical difficulties, it may be said initially that theoretical terms are interpreted by reducing them, directly or indirectly, to observational conditions.[17] Let us assume that some thing T has a property P, if upon its being placed under specified kinds of observational conditions specified kinds of observational consequences appear. On this assumption a group may be said to possess the property of "discrimination" if when it is confronted by persons living

[16] H. G. Alexander, "General Statements as Rules of Inference," in H. Feigl, M. Scriven and G. Maxwell (eds.), *Minnesota Studies in Philosophy of Science*, Vol. 11, University of Minnesota Press, 1957, pp. 309–330; and Nagel, *op. cit.*, pp. 129–140.

[17] R. Carnap, "The Methodological Character of Theoretical Concepts," in H. Feigl and M. Scriven (eds.), *Minnesota Studies in Philosophy of Science*, Vol. 1, University of Minnesota Press, 1956; and C. G. Hempel, "The Theoretician"s Dilemma," in H. Feigl, M. Scriven, and G. Maxwell (eds.), *Minnesota Studies in Philosophy of Science*, Vol. II, University of Minnesota Press, 1958, pp. 39–99.

under deficient social and material conditions it reacts by attributing to them qualities of inferiority which are contrary to its own norms of justice.[18] The meaning of P is then reduced to observational tests of conditions and consequences. However, since such tests often lag behind new interpretations of P they cannot be regarded as complete specification of P's meaning. Were they taken as complete specifications of P, it would be impossible to adjust P's usage to the discovery of meaningful connections between P and other terms related to T. As previously indicated, the truth of theoretical terms depends not only upon the partial specification of their corresponding empirical sentences but upon the more complete meanings attached to them through the theoretical network to which they belong. Suppose, for example, that the meaning of the theoretical term "discrimination" is stipulated in such a way that the following sentences are used to define its observational basis. Discrimination towards others is said to apply: (1) When persons with low education are rejected as coworkers, (2) When persons with substandard homes are rejected as guests, and (3) When persons with black skins are rejected as voters. "Discrimination" becomes a theoretical term insofar as the meaning it assigns to the above sentences constitutes a basis for linking them together in some kind of "logical" or "causal" structure. One such meaning is evident in the empirical generalization, "When persons of low education are rejected as coworkers and persons with substandard homes are rejected as guests, then persons with dark skins are rejected as voters." Here the implied interdependences of (1) and (2) are expanded to include (3). Sociologists would hold, of course, that the meaning content of the term "discrimination" cannot be fully reduced to or taken as equivalent to this or any other limited set of generalizations. Therefore, the present formulation can not claim that the theoretical term "discrimination" is eliminable by substituting some set of empirical generalizations or their corresponding observational terms. On the contrary, it suggests the necessity of an antecedently understood metalanguage for translating theoretical terms into observational terms.

The claim that theoretical terms contain components of meaning which are empirical as well as logical lends credence to the possibility that middle-range theories[19] supported by partial reductions to observables, may offer the most adequate approach to scientific sociology. Attempts to explicitly define the observable equivalents of broad-range theories by specifying the necessary and sufficient conditions for their application are not likely to be successful since they contain or imply concepts (parameters) which have no tangible counterparts. No limited set of

[18] See H. E. Moore, "Discrimination," in *A Dictionary of the Social Sciences*, J. Gould and W. L. Kolb (eds.), Free Press, pp. 203–204.
[19] Merton, *op. cit.*, pp. 5–10.

operations can provide decisive tests of their presence or absence for the simple reason that such operations are bound to highly restricted spacial-temporal conditions. Indeed, the most useful theoretical terms seem to be those which cannot be conclusively refuted by observation. For example, the use of the contextually open term, "reference groups," in the statement, "All socialized persons orient to reference groups," cannot be refuted by a finite number of observations to the effect that persons x_1, $x_2, \ldots, x_k$ fail to respond to reference groups, $G_1, G_2, \ldots, G_k$. The observation that particular persons do not respond to particular reference groups is too specialized to serve as an empirical refutation of the statement in question. Observational criteria are also inadequate for interpreting such statements as, "Hostility is universal but has a wide range of variation in intensity and incidence,"[20] when full account is taken of both the complexity of social action and the deficiencies of human perception.

It is worthy of note that sociologists of an earlier era seem to have recognized the extraempirical meaning of theoretical terms. Mead, for instance, contrasted concrete social classes, such as political parties, with abstract social classes, "defined by the logical universe of discourse (or system of universally significant symbols) . . . a relation arising from the universal functioning of gestures as significant symbols in the general human social process of communication."[21] Although Weber held that meaning does not refer to anything either objectively "correct" or "true" in some metaphysical sense,[22] he stated that "The highest degree of rational understanding is attained in cases involving the meaning of logical or mathematically related propositions."[23] Despite Weber's ambiguity, the dual role of observational and theoretical terms is clearly approached in one of his concluding passages: "Statistical uniformities constitute understandable types of action in the sense of this discussion, and thus constitute 'sociological generalizations,' only when they can be regarded as manifestations of the understandable subjective meaning of a course of social action."[24] No doubt, all kinds of sociological expressions, whether "theoretical" or "observational," contain extraempirical meanings. Every scientific term rests on a continuum of meanings which is at one and the same time logical and observational. Were this not the case, scientific understanding would hardly be possible.

---

20 R. M. Williams, Jr., *The Reduction of Intergroup Tensions*, Social Science Research Council, 1947, p. 51.

21 G. H. Mead, *Mind, Self and Society*, C. W. Morris (ed.), University of Chicago Press, 1934, pp. 157–158.

22 M. Weber, *The Theory of Social and Economic Organization*, trans. A. M. Henderson and T. Parsons; edited with an Introduction by T. Parsons, Oxford University Press, 1947, p. 89.

23 *Ibid.*, p. 91.

24 *Ibid.*, p. 100.

PART
V

Theory and
Social Problems

AMITAI ETZIONI

Toward a sociological theory of peace

Introduction

Can a world without war be depicted in the technical terminology of modern sociology? Can one point to processes leading from a world in which war is institutionalized to one in which it is effectively ruled out? These are the two questions a theory of peace must answer. In undertaking this task a sociologist draws on existing theories, data, and insights, as he neither commands nor claims any special knowledge of the future. Fortunately, sociological knowledge has been increasing; thus after years of empirical research and theory construction sociology is better equipped to tackle the macroscopic problems of the age.[1]

This article was written during my association with the Institute of War and Peace Studies at Columbia University. A less theoretical and more empirical discussion of the same subject is presented in the author's *Winning Without War* (Garden City, N.Y.: Doubleday, 1964). I am indebted to Peter Brooks, Harriet Gelfan, Jonathan Shay, and Martin Wenglinsky for their comments on earlier versions of this manuscript.

[1] This point is elaborated in my "Social analysis as a sociological vocation," *American Journal of Sociology*, LXX (March, 1965), pp. 613–622.

Peace defined

The first question, often raised in this context, is whether one can specify the properties of a social system which might exist without war for long periods of time. In part this is a semantic rather than a sociological problem. Depending upon how one defines peace, it becomes a more or less demanding condition. If peace is defined as the complete absence of human violence even among neighbors and members of a family, "a state of tranquility or quiet," as Webster puts it, it becomes a very difficult quality to achieve. The construction of such a system would require extensive resocialization of the world's population and very exacting mechanisms of social control. This, in turn, would generate almost unmanageable tensions which could be contained, if at all, only by an extremely totalitarian society, of the kind well depicted in George Orwell's 1984. However, if peace is viewed as the absence of large-scale, organized violence, especially among large collectivities equipped with modern means of destruction, then part of the problem is defined away, and the part left—awesome in itself—becomes more manageable.

Besides the semantic distinction between limited and large-scale violations of the peace, there are also certain assumptions we can make about the nature of social change, the degree to which major social processes are articulated, and hence the degree to which some can be altered without others. If one assumes a high degree of articulation between large- and small-scale violence, a conceptual distinction between them can be misleading, because it implies that there are separate analytic dynamics and processes which are in reality intertwined. If, however, one assumes a lesser degree of articulation of the two processes and also assumes that they are independently caused, or at least that they can be separated and then modified independently, then the distinction becomes fruitful. Finally, if one assumes that there is an inherent interdependence that requires a change on one level of the system before one can change the other, the distinction between limited and large-scale violence becomes essential.

On several grounds we suggest that this last alternative is most useful. Obviously, unless large-scale violence is prevented, national societies might not have the time needed to create a system without limited violence. One can also see the utility of separate treatment of the two problems from the fact that many national societies have actually eliminated internal large-scale violence but not limited violence. As eliminating even one kind of violence requires social changes of a gigantic scale, it seems necessary to approach one kind first and the other later with large-scale violence being the more urgent task. Above all, efforts to overcome limited violence seek to modify the existing societal system, to effect more socialization to and reinforcement of norms; in trying to remove large-scale violence, the main focus of the effort is the creation of a societal system where none exists, a quite distinct effort.

The state of peace we will focus upon here is one that knows no thermonuclear wars and no wars that could escalate into thermonuclear wars. Interpersonal violence and limited intergroup violence, which we assume can be kept from such escalation by existing mechanisms of social control, are not discussed.

A methodological note

Much sociological analysis as well as data accumulated in other fields is relevant or can be brought to bear on the problem at hand. Our endeavor is thus largely to extrapolate existing theory to a new field rather than to construct a new theory. The effort is different from most extrapolations because theorems are not just transferred from one substantive field to another, both on the same analytical level, but also from one level of analysis to another.

The first kind of extrapolation occurs when, for instance, theorems are transferred from the study of one kind of complex organization (e.g., industrial organizations) to another (e.g., military). The process then involves only abstraction and respecification. To save space, a trivial example will suffice. We find that the more workers view their foreman as a father figure the more likely they are to justify the profit-making of the factory in which they are employed. Abstractly stated, we might say that the more low-ranking members of an organization identify with those higher in rank, the more likely they are to view the goals of the organization as legitimate. We then respecify and apply this proposition to the army, for instance, and state that we expect that the more soldiers view their officers as father-figures the more likely they are to view the war effort as a just one. The proposition, like all propositions so derived, needs to be verified. The main virtue of extrapolation is to economize in theory construction, in part because it seems easy to generate propositions in this way and, more importantly, because when properly conducted, propositions thus derived are more likely to be found valid than those constructed in other ways.

In moving theorems from one level of abstraction to another, the same processes are involved except that one or more emergent properties must be added (or subtracted). This involves a greater reformulation of the propositions, and thus provides a potentially higher theoretical bonus but also increases the likelihood of error.

In constructing a theory of peace sociologists tend to transfer theorems about mechanisms that limit conflict *within* a societal system to the relations between societal systems. This may be justified on the grounds that the international system is becoming more like a societal one ("an international *community* is evolving").[2] This delays the key analytical difficulties only one step: from depicting the system of peace to explaining the transition from a precommunity to a community stage on the international scene. Hence the search for a full theoretical model of this transition cannot be limited to extrapolation of intrasocietal processes. In the following discussion we will attempt to do both: outline the system of stable peace and explore the transition to it.

A SYSTEM OF PEACE

War as a functional alternative

A common objection to the subject under study is that "there always was war" and hence the study of peace is not sociological but utopian. Viewed as a theory of history, this argument implies that peace is not only elusive but impossible; it assumes that war is not only *likely* to reoccur, but *must* reoccur; that man is determined by history rather than setting its course. It implies that the new sociopolitical environment of the second half of the twentieth century—the result of developments in the technology of weapons, of increased communication, and of nationalism—is not different enough from earlier environments to make historical projection a very risky extrapolation. In fact, as long as peace is a possibility, however low the probability and large the effort required, its study is not utopian. Men are interacting with the forces their ancestors set into motion, partially free to alter the course of history. And, we shall attempt to show, the environment has changed to such a degree that institutions that it would have been "impossible" to create in an earlier period might be feasible in the present context.

Actually, anthropologists have already shown that war is by no means a universal institution; there are societies who know no war.[3] Social scientists have also shown that there is no "war-instinct"; there is no human need or motive that cannot be gratified by means other than violence.[4] War is a culturally patterned social institution. While socializa-

[2] Talcott Parsons, "A Functional Theory of Change," in Amitai and Eva Etzioni (eds.), *Social Change* (New York: Basic Books, 1964), pp. 83–98.

[3] Margaret Mead, "Sex and Temperament in Three Primitive Societies," in *From the South Seas* (New York: Morrow, 1939), p. 23. See also William F. Ogburn and Meyer F. Nimkoff, *Sociology*, 4th ed. (Boston: Houghton Mifflin, 1964), p. 532.

[4] Margaret Mead, *And Keep Your Powder Dry: An Anthropologist Looks at America* (New York: Morrow, 1942), pp. 209–213.

tion grafts it onto the personality, its roots are social.[5] Viewed socially, war and the preparation for it serve a large variety of societal needs, from creating employment to strengthening national solidarity. Therefore it has been occasionally concluded that, at least for some social structures, the war machinery acts as a *necessary* functional prerequisite for their maintenance. This seems to be invalid on two grounds.

Our general experience shows that institutions that provide specific answers to basic societal needs can be replaced by other institutions answering the same basic needs. For example, religion, the husband-father role-pair, and the village community seemed at one time to be "inevitable" institutions answering specific societal needs. However, Communism replaced religion and religion became a deviant subculture in postrevolutionary Russia. The sociological father of many a preliterate child is his mother's brother. The suburban tract fulfills many of the functional needs the village community did. There seems to be no reason to believe that the institution of war is an exception. As far as the "economic" need is concerned, most economists who have studied disarmament conclude that even a society with a comparatively large privately owned defense sector such as the contemporary United States can readily survive disarmament.[6] This is not to suggest that there would be no severe dislocations in the process of substitution. But the survival of the society and its basic political features would not be deeply challenged.[7] War has been abolished between the Italian cities, the German states, and the Swiss cantons, all "capitalist" societies. Of course, as long as there is no world-state, it will always be possible to argue that war has not been "really" abolished but just transferred to a different level, e.g., from cities to states or from states to regions. But what follows from this and similar statements is that the final test of the feasibility of peace has yet to be made, not that we know the outcome to be negative.

Other societal functions of war (or preparation for it) are often listed, especially its contributions as an expressive (ideological and sentimental) binding force.[8] It is rarely claimed, however, that war is a necessary basis of social solidarity since it is clear that many national societies are firmly integrated without war. Whatever contributions preparation for war or defense made to the national solidarity of some societies, the fact that these contributions are miniscule for Denmark,

[5] B. Kuppuswamy, *An Introduction to Social Psychology* (New York: Asia Publishing House, 1961), p. 537.
[6] Kenneth Boulding and Emile Benoit, *Disarmament and the Economy* (New York: Harper & Row, 1963). See also U.S. Arms Control and Disarmament Agency, *Economic Impacts of Disarmament: a report of the Panel on Economic Impacts of Disarmament* (Washington, 1962).
[7] The opposite view is represented by Fred J. Cook, *The Warfare State* (New York: Macmillan, 1962). See also C. Wright Mills, *The Causes of World War III* (New York: Simon & Schuster, 1958).
[8] Positive functions of war are listed in Arnold W. Green, *Sociology: An Analysis of Life in Modern Society* (New York: McGraw-Hill, 1960), pp. 56–57; and Lowell Julliard Carr, *Analytical Sociology: Social Situations and Social Problems* (New York: Harper & Row, 1955), pp. 251 and 685.

Italy, Japan, or Britain shows that they are not a necessary condition. If war is not a prerequisite of national solidarity, it is said to be the foundation of *inter*-national alliances, e.g., the Soviet threat for NATO. This is true only to the degree that it is tautological. To the degree that alliances are formed to wage a war (or defend a group of nations from attack), the decline in the aggressive intentions or threat might well be followed by a weakening of a military alliance. But if the alliance had a non-military basis, such as economic, cultural, or political, it would be more stable than alliances evolved around war. This was demonstrated by Karl Deutsch and his associates for historical,[9] and by Amitai Etzioni for contemporary unions.[10] NATO has never achieved the degree of solidarity of the European Economic Community. In short, war seems not to be an "inevitable" social institution any more than it is an unsubstitutable psychological outlet.

Much of the debate on the subject suffers from a confusion between functional prerequisites and functional alternatives. War makes contributions to a society, but this does not mean that it is a form of conduct or an institution that is necessary for human society; the contrary is much closer to the truth.

The prerequisites of peace

What are then the conditions under which large-scale violations of the peace do not occur? The main sociological formula seems to be for the system's bonds to be stronger than the social and normative divisions of the members, i.e., violence is negatively associated with integration. This entails (a) socialization to a common set of values which are more salient than those which are divisive; (b) social control mechanisms to reinforce these shared bonds; (c) mechanisms to arbitrate differences among the actors, to limit if not settle conflicts and to "cool out" losers so as to reduce the strain put on the normative and social bonds; (d) mechanisms to revise the substance of the normative and social bonds, to accommodate environmental and intrasocietal changes (e.g., legislation); and (e) force in support of the system superior to that of any subgroup(s), to subdue deviants not bound by the normative and social bonds, who do not accept the rulings of mechanisms of arbitration or revision, and who either resist the changes introduced in the societal consensus (e.g., states' righters) or wish to force changes more rapid than the society at large is willing to take.

Not all these prerequisites are given equal weight in sociological

[9] Karl Wolfgang Deutsch, *et al.*, *Political Community and the North Atlantic Area: International Organization in the Light of Historical Experience* (Princeton: Princeton University Press, 1957).

[10] Amitai Etzioni, *Political Unification: A Comparative Analysis of Leaders and Forces* (New York: Holt, Rinehart and Winston, 1965).

writings that deal with the integration of systems. Socialization and social control are most prominently listed in what is referred to as the "integration school." The need for "cooling off" mechanisms to reduce the load on the integrating ones, especially in complex units, has not been recognized; discussions of "cooling off" usually deal with persons, not societies. The need for institutionalized avenues for social change, of revision of consensus, have much more commonly been taken into account by constitutional lawyers and political scientists than by sociologists. The importance of this mechanism for any model to be applied to international systems, in which major accommodations are yet to be made, is obvious.

The special contribution of force to the integration of systems is rarely considered. In part this is because it is believed that socialization and social control relying on expressive and instrumental (utilitarian) rewards will, can, or ought to make force superfluous; in part, because many of the writers are "liberals" and view the exercise of force, even in the service of virtue, as unethical. Actually no human society can survive without applying force to prevent some deviants from violating the normative order (and thus opening the door to others), even if it is only an occasional stoning by the community of a deviant, under conditions specified by the social norms. Moreover, force is used not just to maintain law and order in the technical sense of the term, but also to force changes willed by the majority upon reluctant minorities. If this is not done, minorities block the accommodation of the institutional structure of the society to changes in the internal balance of power and to environmental changes and endanger the foundations of law and order as well as the legitimacy of the political structure.

Variants of this general social-system model have been applied by sociologists to the study of the limitation of conflict among a large variety of groups; including races, ethnic groups, and labor and management; all groups that come into conflict within one society. For a sociologist, the extension of this model to the "world-system" is natural, since it is widely held that self-interest can be prevented from escalating into violent conflict only if curbed by systems that have the qualities of the societal model specified above.[11]

On the other hand, many political scientists, painfully aware how far the "world-system" is from meeting these requirements of the societal model, try to define a system with peace-keeping ability by using variations of the balance-of-power model.[12] In this model war is avoided because it is contrary to the self-interest of the participants; no

[11] Ogburn and Nimkoff, *op. cit.* (pp. 554–561) sketch sociopolitical proposals for peace such as the UN (p. 555) and a one-world community (p. 556).

[12] For a review of these positions see Inis L. Claude, *Swords into Plowshares: The Problems and Progress of International Organization* (New York: Random House, 1964), especially chaps. 11, 15, and 17.

commitment to a shared set of values, sentiments, or community interests is necessarily assumed. There is no central authority, although some balance-of-power models assume a "balancer," that is a country whose self-interests are served by throwing itself on the side that is losing power, thus rebalancing the system.

The main shortcoming of the balance-of-power system as a model for peace is that it reduces the probability of war but does not eliminate it. This might have been tolerable when human society could survive an occasional war, even a world war, but the larger the damage the partici-pants can inflict on each other during a breakdown of the system, the less useful a balance-of-power system becomes. Recent developments in the technology of weapons have sharply curtailed the peace value of this system. To reformulate the same position more technically, it might be said that each system of social control has a margin of error, which expresses the *probability of malfunctioning* of the system under given environmental conditions and thus *a measure of the losses caused* if the system malfunctions.[13] Many systems of social control allow a comparatively small margin of error if the measure of loss caused by such an event is considered by the members comparatively minor. Enforcement of regulations against double parking is a case in point. The traffic control system allows a comparatively large number of violations on the implicit assumption that double parking at the level it occurs, while not desirable, is not disastrous. On the other hand, violation of the ban on driving cars into a playground is considered a much graver danger, and hence the probability of malfunctioning of this ban is almost reduced to zero by placing physical barriers at the entrance. The balance-of-power system treats war like double parking: the societal model, like driving into a playground.

Other models of peaceable systems have proven to be nearly as demanding as the societal one but have a much larger margin of error. The collective security system, the image of which affected the foundation of the UN, assumes that its members will act as a community against a violator of the peace, without satisfying the above-mentioned sociological requirements of a community. Practice has shown that this is an unrealistic expectation.[14] Psychological communication theories have suggested that improved communications between opponents would allow them to

---

13 By "margin of error" we mean the size of the safeguard against failure. To use a commonplace example, if an elevator cable must be able to support n thousand pounds it is usually engineered to hold more than the minimum requirements; the precise increase in capacity might be designated as the margin of error. This concept does not define the risk which a policy-maker takes in accepting a system. ("Risk" is a subjective evaluation, affected among other things, by subjective estimates of margin of error.) It does allow one to state the probability of various types of failure. Using this concept in propositional form, we would say that the larger the margin of error, the smaller the likelihood of failure.

14 Charles E. Osgood, *An Alternative to War and Surrender* (Urbana: University of Illinois Press, 1962).

work out their differences and avoid war.[15] To the degree that these models are taken as segmented process models, i.e., as suggesting an element in the evolution of a peace system, they do point to one important component (see below). Increased and improved communication might accelerate the development of a world community that the societal model of peace requires. But to the degree that improved communication is viewed as a way to generate and maintain peace, the way psychoanalysts see "talking treatment" as therapy for neurotic patients, major necessary components are neglected. Left out is the reallocation of assets that must take place if the normative and social bonds—which communication can help to develop—are not to be undermined. (Law and order is maintained in the long run only if the distribution of wealth among the politically conscious and organized citizens roughly approximates the distribution of the power among them. As the poorer nations become more active, maintaining law and order in the world will increasingly require reallocation of the global assets.)[16] Also neglected is the creation of the force needed to control deviants, in case communication fails or until it works. Similar criticisms can be made of other models of peace, such as those which draw on economic competition[17] and cybernetic models.[18] The societal model, demanding as its requirements may be, seems to be the only one that is both complete and has a tolerable margin of error. The question needs to be faced—under what conditions, if any, can this model be realized?

PATHWAYS TO A WORLD SOCIETY

Can a world society be created? It has often been claimed that such questions, dealing as they do with social change, cannot be answered by sociological theory; in particular, not by the functional-structural type employed here.[19] Actually, functional-structural theory can and does study change by combining two intellectual devices: (a) It asks which processes, in attempting to fill the functional needs of an existing social system, can alter its structure in a way that creates new functional needs and the mechanisms for their fulfillment;[20] (b) It also asks what the functional needs of a nonexistent (imaginary) or "futuristic" social system, e.g., of a

---

15 Kenneth Boulding, *Conflict and Defense: A General Theory* (New York: Harper & Row, 1962).

16 This point is elaborated in the author's *The Hard Way to Peace* (New York: Collier, 1962).

17 Karl Deutsch, *The Nerves of Government: Models of Political Communication and Control*, especially Part II, chaps. 5–8 (New York: Free Press, 1963).

18 Francesca Cancian, "Functional Analysis of Change," in Etzioni (ed.), *Social Change, op. cit.*, pp. 112–125.

19 We shall provide an example below.

20 Talcott Parsons and Robert F. Bales, *Family, Socialization and Interaction Process* (New York: Free Press, 1955), pp. 202–216.

peace system, would be. Extrapolating the processes under "a" and projecting them against the functional-structural model of "b" allows us to forecast if, when, and under what circumstances the changing system will answer the functional needs of the desired model, and if it can then be stabilized.

The Parsonian model of socialization, of the changing system of relationships between the agents of socialization and their subject, is a case in point. It contains both an image of the future system, when socialization is completed and the subject has gained the ability to function independently, and of the factors at each stage that upset the balance and propel the system to the next level, leading toward the future system, in particular the pressure of the instrumental leader, often the father, on the child.

If the processes of change depicted under "a" lead automatically toward state "b" or if these processes can be controlled and are directed toward state "b", transition from a present to a future world can be charted. (This does not mean such a process model can be designed for any utopia. Many utopias cannot even be outlined as models that will answer the basic functional requirements for a sociological system, as they violate basic, universal sociological laws. They also tend to presuppose changes in personal character and social structure that are beyond those which even a highly self-conscious and self-controlled society can bring about.) It should, however, be noted that the range of societal targets considered achievable through planned social change is growing because of improvements in the social sciences and social engineering and the growing acceptance of government guidance. The capacity of modern society to control itself has reached a fairly high level in matters of economic policy. Self-control in other fields including political processes might also increase, though it is unlikely to match economic control in the practical future.[21]

A detailed description of the transition from the present state to a system of peace is impossible because of both the young state of the discipline and the fact that forecasting as a rule provides broad contours and not detailed process charts. Still, several characteristics of the transition can be outlined.

Self-encapsulation and its sources

One major way in which a societal model of peace might be realized is through the encapsulation of international conflicts as a self-propelling process. *Encapsulation* refers to the process by which conflicts are modified

---

[21] Kenneth E. Boulding, *The Meaning of the Twentieth Century* (New York: Harper & Row, 1964).

so that they become limited by rules (the "capsule").[22] The rules exclude some modes of conflict that were practiced earlier while they legitimatize other modes. Conflicts that are "encapsulated" are not solved in the sense that the parties become pacified, that is, all conflicts have been eliminated. But the use of arms, or some usages of some arms, are effectively ruled out. To illustrate, most observers expect the normative views of communism and the West not to become reconciled and hence suggest that the basis for disarmament is lacking. They see two alternatives: Two or more powers that are basically either hostile or friendly. Encapsulated conflicts point to a third kind of relationship. Here differences of belief or interests and a mutually aggressive orientation might well continue, but the sides effectively rule out some means and some modes of conflict. In this sense encapsulation is less demanding than pacification, since it does not require that the conflict be resolved or extinguished but only that the range of its expression be curbed; hostile parties are more readily "encapsulated" than pacified.

At the same time encapsulation tends to provide a more lasting solution than does pacification. When pacified, the parties remain independent units and, after a period of time, their differences might again lead to conflict. Once encapsulated, the parties lose some of their independence by being tied by the capsule that has evolved. It is this capsule that limits future conflicts although the possibility of breaking a capsule, of undermining the rules and bonds formed, will remain.

Capsules differ considerably in their scope and hence in their strength. Some minimal rules govern even the most unrestrained conflicts, such as consent on the proper use of the white flag and the Geneva Convention regarding prisoners of war. In the present context these minimal capsules are of little interest since by themselves they do not provide a basis on which a world society capable of significantly curbing international conflict can grow. The following discussion is concerned with capsules strong enough to rule out war.

The transition to a system of peace has to be *self-propelling*. Once a third superior authority is assumed, once a world government or powerful UN police force is introduced, an authority is assumed that can impose rules on the contending parties and thus keep their conflicts limited to those expressions allowed by the particular capsule. But such universal authority is not available and hence the analysis must turn to *conflicts that curb themselves*, i.e., through the very process of conflict the participants work out a self-imposed limitation on the means and modes of strife.

How could a conflict curb itself? One theoretical answer was advanced by Robert Park. His exact position is difficult to determine

---

[22] For an earlier discussion of this point, see Amitai Etzioni, "On Self-Encapsulating Conflicts," *The Journal of Conflict Resolution*, VIII (1964), 234–255.

because he developed his theory in a large number of articles written at different dates.[23] Park pointed out that conflict generates interaction between the parties to the conflict. Conflict brings the parties to know each other and to communicate with each other, which in turn leads to the evolution of shared perspectives and bonds, till the conflict turns into competition (*competition* is used by Park and many other sociologists to refer to a conflict that is limited by a set of rules).[24] Homans supported this line of analysis by suggesting that communication breeds affinity.[25] Among political scientists, those who favor the evolution of an Atlantic community stress that increased communication (or consultation) between Washington and the European capitals would advance this evolution. A study by Daniel Lerner lends support to this proposition; he showed that French businessmen who come more in contact with foreigners tend to be more favorably disposed toward them than those French businessmen who have fewer such contacts.[26]

The theorem that increased communication between parties is the mechanism through which conflicts are encapsulated and that this mechanism emerges from the conflict itself seems to us valid only under certain conditions. It seems valid if the parties to a conflict have similar values and sentiments. Communication can make the parties aware of this latent consensus and draw on it to build up procedures for settlement of conflicts and for the legitimation of resolutions passed. Under these circumstances, communication might also serve to work out limited differences of interest or viewpoint within the framework of shared values and sentiments.

But when the basic values, sentiments, and interests of the parties to a conflict are not compatible, increased communication only highlights this incompatibility, dispels hopes of a settlement or an accommodation, makes the parties more conscious of the deep cleavages that separate them, and increases hostilities.

To illustrate, the more the United States and its Western European allies openly discuss their strategic differences, the more evident it becomes that the difference is unbridgeable. Aside from differences regarding the evaluation of the Communist threat, experience with conventional war, estimates of the danger of unintentional triggering of nuclear war, geopolitical differences, and differences in styles of military planning, there is the all-important fact that a nuclear war *limited* in territorial scope, which the United States does not desire but could

---

[23] Robert E. Park, *Race and Culture* (New York: Free Press, 1960); and his *Human Communities* (New York: Free Press), 1952.

[24] See Carr, *op. cit.*, p. 137. See also Green, *op. cit.*, pp. 59–60.

[25] George C. Homans, *The Human Group* (New York: Harcourt, Brace & World, 1950), pp. 110–117.

[26] Daniel Lerner, "French Business Leaders Look at EDC: A Preliminary Report," *Public Opinion Quarterly*, XX (1956), 212–221.

survive, might well spell *total* destruction for Western Europe. No amount of communication or negotiation can alter this deep difference of interest.

To reformulate this point: The greater the differences between parties to a conflict, the smaller the encapsulation attainable through increased communication. Or, to put it more sharply, the greater the need for communication, the less effective it is likely to be.

That communication cannot serve as the propelling force for self-encapsulation when conflict is pervasive limits the value of this mechanism for encapsulation of international conflicts because it is often all-encompassing, with few values shared by all parties. Compared to most intrasocietal conflicts, international conflict tends to be particularly boundless.

For encapsulation of international conflicts the distribution of power among the parties seems to be more important. Encapsulation is advanced when it serves to protect the more powerful participants against demands of the rising participants for a greater share of the power. In this sense encapsulation is analogous to the introduction of welfare legislation by the Tories in Britain or by Bismarck in Germany. In the following pages we will spell out this proposition, drawing on developments in East-West relations between 1945 and 1964. The historical material serves as more than an illustration of an analytical framework in the usual sense of the term, since there is only one international system of the kind we are dealing with here, and the transition toward peace is inevitably a transition within that system. Actually, the importance of historical trends for the analysis at hand is so great that it might be claimed that the theoretical propositions derived from intrasocietal analysis are used to gain some insights into these trends as much as they are used to highlight a model of self-encapsulation of conflict.

Pluralism and encapsulation

The number of actors participating in a system has often been related to the stability of the system. The balance-of-power system seems to require at least four participants.[27] Systems with three participants tend to lead to the coalition of two against the third.[28] Bipolar systems, i.e., with two participants, have been shown to be particularly difficult to pacify. Single actor systems are by definition pacified. The participation of a large number of actors has been considered particularly conducive to peace, following the application of a full-competition model to the

[27] On this system see Morton Kaplan, *System and Process in International Politics* (New York: Wiley, 1957), chap. 2.

[28] Georg Simmel, *Conflict*, trans. Kurt H. Wolff (New York: Free Press, 1955).

international scene.[29] Note however that these propositions assume that the actors are interchangeable in the sense that they have the same or similar power. In actuality, the most outstanding characteristic of international reality is that the participants differ drastically in their power, ranging from superior nuclear powers to underarmed, poverty-stricken tribal states.[30] Moreover, the relative power of any two nations is significantly different according to the sector of international relations under discussion and the particular matter at hand. A realistic model must hence take into account the relative power of the participants relevant to the issues at hand, rather than focus on the number of the participants. To reformulate our encapsulation proposition in this context, encapsulation seems to be enhanced by the transition from a duopolistic state of power to one in which its distribution is more pluralistic, a transition to be referred to as de-polarization.[31]

International relations approximated a state of duopoly between 1946 and 1956. It was in this period, the height of the Cold War, that the two fairly monolithic camps, one directed from Moscow and the other from Washington, both armed with nuclear armaments which no other bloc commanded, faced each other across the globe. While there were quite a few countries that were not aligned with either camp, their military and political weight was small. This duopolistic situation was not conducive to encapsulation. The sides focussed their attention on keeping their respective blocs integrated and on enjoining third countries from swelling the ranks of the opposite camp. Each bloc checked the other hoping for an opportunity to expand its own area of influence, while waiting for collapse of the other. (The symmetry was far from complete: the West would probably have returned to the anarchy of nation-states had the Eastern block disintegrated, while the East would have at least tried to impose a monopolistic state if the West had disintegrated. Similarly, the East was more actively expansionist—at least in the late forties—while the West was more defensive. The East however was first to recognize the limits of the duopolistic conception.) There was little inducement for encapsulation under these circumstances. Whether this was due to special historical circumstances or is a general characteristic of duopolistic systems is still an open question.

The shift from duopoly toward pluralism generated a constellation of power more conducive to encapsulation. Between 1956 and 1964, in each of the two major camps a secondary power rebelled. There were immense differences between de Gaulle's France and Mao's China in their relations to their respective nuclear overlords, as well as in cultural, economic,

---

[29] Boulding, *Conflict and Defense, op. cit.*, chaps. 12 and 13.
[30] William T. Fox, *The Super-powers* (New York: Harcourt, Brace & World, 1944).
[31] I am indebted to John Galtung for this term.

and military qualities. However, both formerly were weak powers and had followed a foreign policy formulated in foreign capitals; both, under reawakening nationalism, increased their power, and correspondingly followed a foreign policy of their own. This autonomy might be reduced in the post-Krushchev era in the East or in a post-de Gaulle era in the West, but the restoration of the duopoly of 1946–1956 seems most unlikely. In any event, in the period of 1956–1964 the net effect of the the rebellion of the secondary powers was to draw together the two overlords. Seeking to maintain their superior status and fearing the consequences of conflicts generated by their rebelling vassals, the overlords set out to formulate some universal rules they wanted all parties to observe. The treaty of partial cessation of nuclear tests that the U.S. and the U.S.S.R. tried to impose on France and Communist China was a case in point. Efforts to stem the availability of nuclear weapons to additional powers was another. Suggestions to inspect atomic plants, mainly aimed at insuring the exclusive use of atomic research for non-military purposes in third countries, pointed in the same direction.[32] The 1963–1964 *detente* which isolated Communist China and France and the Geneva disarmament negotiations in which the two countries did not participate were other characteristic reflections of this period.

One characteristic these measures share is the service of the more "narrow" needs of the superpowers and the simultaneous advance of the "general welfare" of the world. They can therefore be presented in terms of universal values and implemented in world institutions. Thus, the prime motivation of the 1963 nuclear test treaty might have reflected the desire of the U.S. and the U.S.S.R. to remain the only super-powers, but it also indirectly reduced the dangers of nuclear war and was presented to world public opinion as if the prime motive were the advancement of peace and disarmament. This is a familiar pattern, one under which interest groups in a body politic, whether a nation-state or a village community, work out solutions. They seek to find values held by the community in terms of which they cloak their causes. However this is not without value for encapsulation. Indirectly these values affect the selection of the course of action an interest group follows and provide a common basis on which similar interests of divergent powers can be harmonized and their ties in the shared community deepened.

How much encapsulation will be generated in the particular case under study was impossible to foretell by the end of 1964. If this process does not evolve further, it might well be in part due to the fact that the rebellion of the vassals was not complete, and thus no genuine pluralistic system of four or more participants was created, one in which the pressure to generate "rules of the game" might be larger. Also, in this

[32] *The New York Times*, November 22, 1964.

transition period, efforts to salvage the duopolistic bloc system still had a retarding effect on encapsulation, reflected particularly in pressures against appearing conciliatory, compared to the more belligerent secondary powers, in the contest over the loyalties of these and other bloc members. Such pressure curbed U.S.S.R. concessions to the West in matters concerning the outlawing of wars of national liberation, because of Russia's effort to counter China's appeal to other Communist countries and parties. Similarly, these pressures prevented the U.S. from taking more initiatives toward increasing the *detente* with the U.S.S.R., especially in the German issue, because of competition with France over European leadership and the courting of West Germany. But such a "transition" between two periods more clearly governed by one model is by no means unusual. To the degree that the preceding analysis is valid one would expect encapsulation to slow down if duopoly were again to be approximated, and to accelerate if efforts to salvage the two blocs were given up as futile. In the latter case pluralism would increase and the two superpowers would feel freer and under more pressure to advance community rules.

International floating vote

The significance of the existence of a sizeable floating vote, of votes that are not committed to any one party, for the *maintenance* of a democratic system has often been pointed out. It is less often recognized that the *emergence* of a significant floating vote supports the *development* of a peace system by accelerating encapsulation. In the same period in which depolarization occurred, in the sense that the internal solidarity of the East and the West declined, the bipolar system was further weakened by the increase in the number of nonaligned countries. The group of non-aligned countries grew to be the largest. The status of non-alignment was built up as both the East and the West increasingly recognized its legitimacy.

The growth in number and weight of the floating votes made several contributions to encapsulation. Around it evolved a major shared norm between the East and the West (and the third countries):[33] It limits the conflict between the East and the West by declaring one major sector of the international system outside the conflict as far as armed means are concerned. While the norm was violated in Vietnam, Laos, and in a few other places, it was widely observed and violations became less frequent. At the same time reliance on non-violent means such as trade, aid, and

[33] The substance of the norm is also to be taken into account. Not all shared norms are pacifying. In the late forties and early fifties, the East and West also had agreed: They both wished that all third countries would join a bloc. But as each expected the same group of countries to join its respective bloc, this shared norm was a major source of conflict. In contrast, the new shared norm requires a country not to join the other side's bloc. Under this norm a country can satisfy both the East and the West by joining neither, which is a much less conflict-prone state.

propaganda commanded an increasing proportion of the efforts of the U.S. and U.S.S.R. in third countries, roughly moving from above a quarter in the mid-fifties to close to three quarters in the mid-sixties.[34]

The norm supporting non-alignment is of special interest to the study of encapsulation as it does not bar conflicts but only rules out intervention by force. Peaceful appeals, especially those aimed at internal changes in the country, such as progress toward freedom and social justice, or socialism, are "allowed." This quality of the norm had a double effect. First, it forbade (and quite successfully) forcing countries into a bloc, which would have weakened the general movement toward regulation of the conflict and, if continued, would have reduced and potentially exhausted the floating vote. Second, the norm left room for the expression of the ambitions of both sides without violating the rules curbing the conflict.

The "open frontier" proposition applies here. The proposition states that when the parties to a conflict have an open "space" in which they can make gains more readily than by encroaching on each others' domain and in which the rewards of expansion are at least as high, conflict between the parties is reduced. This is especially true as long as the parties to the conflict do not have the same commitment to expansion and refrain from the use of force toward each other in the competition over the previously undivided space. The courting of non-aligned countries, without territorial conquest or annexation, provided an "endless," that is, inexhaustible "frontier." This is not to imply that the parties will be engaged in an endless contest over the favors of these countries. The decline in the amount of foreign aid both the U.S. and the U.S.S.R. were willing to give by the early sixties as compared to late fifties suggested that they were growing tired of the contest. (The U.S.S.R. has increased it a little following the intensification of its contest with Communist China over the same territories.) The "frontier" seems to deplete the energies devoted to conflict. There was no evidence that as the sides grew tired of this mode of conflict they became reinterested in other, especially more violent, modes.

Buffer states are especially important for prevention of limited wars that might escalate into an all-out war. Contrary to a widely held belief, the creation of buffer states, from Austria to Afghanistan, from Finland to Burma, did not create a dangerous vacuum in the period under study, but keep the superpowers apart. This was so because the buffer states were in effect protected by an implicit agreement of both superpowers, to come to their defense if they are attacked by the other. This "remote deterrence" was at least as effective as the positioning of troops in such a country in curbing a field of influence but has less retarding effects on social change

[34] For details see Amitai Etzioni, *Winning Without War* (New York: Doubleday, 1964).

in the country and, the record shows, is less prone to escalation.

In addition to defining major segments of the international system out of the zone of armed conflict between the two camps, the several non-aligned territories were so located that they provided a pacifying buffer zone between the East and the West. A comparison of the relations between the two blocs as they eye each other across non-aligned Austria, or Cambodia, or Burma, with situations in which East and West faced each other without such a buffer, as in Germany, Korea, and Vietnam, illustrates the point.[35]

Above all, the increase in the floating vote, like the decrease in bloc solidarity, largely increased the range of political activities and sharply reduced the pressures to turn to military alternatives. The more rigidly the sources of power (e.g., votes) and the rewards to be had (e.g., economic assets) are divided between two parties, and the more integrated these parties are, the less the weaker of the two can expect to gain power and improve its share in the allocation of assets by non-violent means. The more the avenues of political efforts such as campaigning (to appeal to the floating vote) and bargaining (to split away a segment of the opposing party) are (or seem to be) futile, the greater the pressure toward armed showdown. The more constitutional or otherwise legitimate avenues of expressions are closed, the higher the pressures toward change by force.

These general rules apply with special strength on the international level. Here the use of armed means is considered less illegitimate than in a national society ("war is the continuation of diplomacy by other means"); the normative bonds among the actors are much weaker, and the hostility more totalistic; there are few constitutional avenues for expression and no force controlled by the system to curb drives toward violent "solutions." The decrease in solidarity of the blocs and the increase in the number and appeal of non-aligned countries was hence of special importance in reducing the pressure toward armed advances and increasing the premium on other political efforts.[36]

The floating vote is to be viewed as a reward that shifts to the favored side; the values according to which the floating vote shifts become the values the competing sides seek to promote, or at least to appear to be promoting. In the period under study, the non-aligned countries on

[35] Other factors, such as the fact that these are divided countries, are also at work, but need not be discussed in this context. Where East and West directly "touched" in non-divided countries, the situation was also tense—e.g., Greece and Yugoslavia. The relations here became pacified because Yugoslavia served as a buffer state after leaving the Soviet bloc in 1948. But the situation on the Turkey-U.S.S.R. border remains tense.

[36] As far as the blocs were concerned; French recognition of Communist China; a "hot line" between the White House and the Kremlin on which the Macmillan government was refused a "hook up"; increasing trade between West Germany and the Communist bloc; American aid to Poland; sale of wheat by Canada to Communist China—were all harbingers of a more open, flexible, political stage.

balance rewarded moderation as they, like floating voters often are, were politically "between" the sides to the conflict. The non-aligned countries stand to lose from a U.S.–U.S.S.R. war and to gain from peaceful competition between them over the favor of third countries. Hence, it is not surprising that between 1956 and 1964 the third countries frequently used their growing influence to encourage encapsulation. Non-aligned countries tended to favor reduction of armaments and of Cold War tensions, increase in the capacities, power and status of the U.S., and cessation of hostilities and exclusion of armed interventions in international conduct.

Psychological components

The importance of psychological factors such as anxiety, hate, and paranoia in blocking encapsulation and the value of understanding, trusting, and above all communicating with the other side in accelerating encapsulation has often been questioned. According to one school, these factors are the factors that conflicts are made of and changes in these factors allow their solution ("War begins in the mind of man," and "If people define situations as real, they are real in their consequences"). On the other hand, the realistic school tends to view the psychological factor as one factor among many, including manpower, raw materials, armaments, and the like. Our position is an intermediary one. Rather than simply stating that both psychological factors and non-psychological ones are important, that where there is a motive there will be a trigger, but that where triggers are barred, hostile motives do not make a war, we will try to specify some of the points of articulation between psychological and other factors, as they are related to the problem of encapsulation.

Psychological measures seem to be necessary as part of the *preparatory* (or background) steps required if encapsulation is to be effectively initiated. Modern interstate relations are highly ideological. International conflicts involve large-scale, intrasocietal mobilizations that are prepared through education and indoctrination of the masses. Since, for reasons that have yet to be explored, it seems easier to arouse the masses than to reduce their hostility to other nations, special efforts must be undertaken if two or more nations are to move from a state of total conflict to a stage from which encapsulation can be firmly launched. One effective measure is the creation of international "semi-events," that is, events that are engineered in order to alter the psychological atmosphere.[37] Between June and October, 1963, the Kennedy administration helped to create a series of such events, and the U.S.S.R. reciprocated; these resulted in the

[37] Some encapsulation might be initiated under most circumstances, but for the process to take off, psychological preparations would seem to be needed if the initial relations among the nations involved were hostile.

"relaxation of the Cold War tensions" known as the 1963–1964 *detente*. (An earlier *detente* was created during the 1959 visit of Premier Khrushchev to the U.S. and terminated by a counterevent, the U-2 flight.)

Once started, the decline in hostile attitudes helped the achievement of domestic political support for measures such as the August 1963 test treaty (which needed the ratification of the Senate) and made moves such as the Soviet-American commitment not to orbit weapons of mass destruction less politically risky in the pre-election period.

Once those arms control measures were taken, they generated further improvements in U.S.-U.S.S.R. relations. Actually, for a while, the process gained so much momentum that the White House was concerned that the psychological factors might reverse themselves, and pressure the U.S. administration into more arms control measures than the government was ready to enter into at that point. (*This had happened* when in 1958 the Administration, expecting to negotiate a test treaty but not to agree to one, came under so much public opinion pressure that it felt compelled to match a unilateral Soviet declaration of a moratorium on testing.[38] Brakes were applied in October, 1963, with the expectation of releasing them after the election.)

In short, it seems (a) that the government has mustered some control of the psychological processes that affect international relations; and (b) that while some psychological measures might have to precede firm launching of encapsulation, assuming that initially there was a highly hostile atmosphere, once the process is rolling it generates psychological support on its own.

At least two other psychological interpretations of the initiation of encapsulation in the period under study have been advanced. According to one, the door was opened to encapsulation after the Cuban blockade discharged a large amount of frustration that Americans had accumulated over the Cold War years. The traditional American foreign policy expectation is that periods of war will be short, wars will end with an American victory, followed by the restoration of peace. In contrast, the Cold War required a continual state of mobilization, prolonged tensions without the prospect of victory. The resulting frustration was deepened by the widely held belief that the Communists were more successful than the West in Asia, Latin America, and Africa. Under the pressure of these frustrations, efforts to reach accommodation with the U.S.S.R. became associated with weakness, if not surrender, and a "tough" verbal position (but not moves that could lead to war) gained much popularity. The establishment of a Communist government in Cuba, the 1961 Bay of Pigs invasion that failed, and the positioning of Soviet missiles in Cuba in 1962 further extended the American frustration. While initially the 1962

[38] Richard J. Barnet, *Who Wants Disarmament?* (Boston: Beacon Press, 1960), p. 37.

blockade raised many fears, its ability to yield a Soviet retreat and not to lead to war gave it the status of the first American victory in a long time. The blockade's successes were widely viewed as supporting the "hard line" thesis (i.e., suggesting that power politics could be used in the nuclear age), yet the psychological effect was one of cathartic release and it generated an increased readiness to negotiate arms control measures with the U.S.S.R.

Another interpretation associates the initiation of encapsulation with the unfolding of a different psychological process: the effects of the increased visibility of the Sino-Soviet cleavage. In 1962 Communist China attacked the U.S.S.R. publicly, criticizing U.S.S.R. involvement in Cuba as "adventurism" and its retreat as "defeatism." The U.S.S.R. (like the U.S.) continued its economic and military support to India when it came under Chinese attack in 1962. About the same time, the American-French dispute forced itself on the public's attention.

Initially, the popular American press and, as far as we can tell, the public at large, tended to ignore the split in the East (or regard it as a "put-up job") and to disregard the rift in the West (or consider it as minor). But the facts finally gained recognition, and the hostile rejection by the public of Mao and of de Gaulle replaced part of that formerly saved for the U.S.S.R. The U.S.S.R. seems "reasonable" and "responsible" compared to Communist China; Russia seemed willing to share with us the concern over nuclear proliferation and the dangers of war provoked by over-eager allies. It even won some sympathy as it, "like us," was troubled by the rebellion of its junior allies.

The recognition of the splits in the alliances had two psychological effects: It undermined the prevailing simplistic black and white image of the forces of light fighting the forces of darkness. Both camps seem to have "grey guys," and the sharp differences between the camps declined. As a result, it is suggested, the ideological fever of the international atmosphere declined, tension was reduced and encapsulation enhanced.

Such "tension reduction" is of general importance for the initiation of encapsulation as long as all negotiations between the sides are blocked by ideological considerations because, for example, politicians find it hard to face their voters with the outcome of such negotiations. Any give and take, even when completely symmetrical, tends to be viewed as a weakness, a concession, if not appeasement and treason. Reduction of the ideological fervor opens the public to see that some genuine give and take is possible and that certain kinds of accommodation serve both sides to the disadvantage of neither.

At the same time bifurcation of the images of each camp and increased realization of the complexities of the world, an awareness that "our side, too, might sometimes be wrong," not only reduced the general level of international tensions and ideological nature of the conflict, but shifted the focus of the xenophobia. Within the Communist camp, Red China (with considerable disregard of its actual foreign policy) became the villain; in the West the focus of American self-righteousness became de Gaulle. These two replaced the previous almost exclusive preoccupation with Soviet Russia. Rechanneling of hate took place along with its reduction.

What the relative contribution of each of these psychological processes was to the development of the atmosphere necessary for the launching of encapsulation cannot be determined without the benefits of a major study devoted to this question alone. It seems to us that the initiation of symbolic gestures by the Kennedy administration and their reciprocation by the Khrushchev government was the most important one of the three, with the release of frustration and bifurcation of the images palying secondary roles. At least these deliberate efforts at tension reduction were closest, in time, to the period in which encapsulation was initiated.

Other factors

Given a proper psychological state, mass democracies are able to move toward the limitation of conflict. Encapsulation can then proceed as a sociopolitical process of community building and as a process of formalization of implicit rules and the strengthening of sanctioning institutions. Each of these subjects deserves a major analysis in its own right and can here be only briefly outlined. Formalization cannot advance much without community building; hence this process is charted first.

Sociopolitical processes that support encapsulation are those that reduce the differences of interest and viewpoint of the conflicting parties and build shared ties among them. The evolution of intermediary bodies for consensus formation is of special value for encapsulation. The formulation of an agreed upon policy always requires a process; even when basic values are shared, differences of interests and viewpoints among various subgroups must be worked out. A government whose policy is not backed by such a process of consensus formation will find the implementation of its policy expensive and difficult, if feasible at all. For the formation of a new community, of new authorities and rules (which a peace system requires) consensus formation is indispensable, since the number of policies to be agreed upon is much larger than in an existing community, and the normative basis to build on, much more narrow. Hence the special significance of consensus formation for encapsulation.

For a consensus formation structure in a society, corporation, or village to be effective it must take place on several levels of the institution simultaneously. Rather than attempt to reach consensus among all parties in one general assembly, the "population" (which might consist of individuals, plants, departments, or nations) is divided into subgroups that are more homogeneous than the population at large. These groups work out a consensus among their respective members and are then represented, as if they were basically a single unit, on the next level of consensus formation. Such interlevel processing might be repeated several times. In the American political system, for instance, the primaries and national conventions and, to a degree, postelection negotiations over participation in the cabinet, provide such a multilayer consensus formation structure.

Regional organizations, communities, and blocs might serve as "intermediary bodies" for the international community. We are dealing here with a developing and not with an existing structure, thus the intermediary bodies are considerably more advanced than the "top" layer, one in which global consensus is to be worked out. Several factors affect the contribution of these bodies to the evolution of the social foundations of a peace system:

    a. Transient blocs have much less such value than lasting federations;

    b. Regional organizations that have narrow scopes of function have much less value than those broad in scope;

    c. Only regional organizations that have an initial functional scope large enough to serve as a takeoff basis will continue to grow into communities broader in scope (though not necessarily into full-fledged peace systems);

    d. Regional bodies that are formed against other regional bodies, if the goals are offensive or defensive, tend to retard rather than to advance encapsulation as they repeat on a large-scale the features of nationalism including interunit conflict. This is particularly true for military alliances but economic associations also can be such "antiblocs," acting as the basis of offensive or defensive economic moves against some other bloc. On the other hand, regional bodies aimed at internal goals, such as more rapid growth or mutual assistance, as in "welfare" communities (e.g., the EEC) or development associations (e.g., in Central America), are more likely to serve as intermediary layers in the process of community building.

    e. Finally, only regional bodies that allow the process of *upward transfer* to continue are ultimately productive for encapsulation. *Upward transfer* is a process in which units that join a larger system transfer some of their power, rights, and sentiments to the center of the system of which they are a part. Studies of social structures as different as the American federal government and the Southern Baptist Association have shown that once a center of effective authority is established, it tends (under circumstances and for reasons that cannot be discussed here) to grow in power, rights, and command of loyalties.[39] The center has to be effective, for if the initial authority is weak it will not trigger the upward transfer process. The central authority of the Federation of the West Indies, disbanded in 1961, is a case in point. The federal government had next to no force at its command, a miniscule budget, and little symbolic value as the charismatic leaders of the member islands did not join the federal government. On the other hand, the history of the United States and many successful federations is one of growing control by federal government over force, economic and administrative processes, and of the attention and loyalties of the citizens, once the central government was firmly initiated. A social unit can, by the use of ideological and political mechanisms, advance or retard this process. Only those units that encourage the process, or at least are not fully successful in blocking it, provide a middle plateau for the development of the sociological foundations on which a world community might be erected.

The last phase of this upward-transfer process is particularly difficult to chart at this stage of our knowledge and history because, while some crude contours of regional communities have started to appear, failures still outnumber successes by a large margin, and there are only the most tenuous signs of what the top layer might be like. The nature of the last phase is particularly obscured at the transitional stage, as the development of intermediary bodies often uses the flame of regional and bloc chauvinism to melt away some sovereignty, especially that of nations, in favor of regional organizations or regional states. But without such chauvinism, or without the Cold War, initiatives to form the Atlantic, the East European community and many other regional bodies, would not have been undertaken. Similarly, a major driving force behind attempts to form common markets in Central America, in various parts of Africa, in the Far East, and elsewhere, is the desire to counter actual or anticipated consequences of the European Economic Community. Progress, in short, might not be unilinear but dialectic. Rather than states forming regional bodies that serve as a smooth transition to a global body, the regional bodies might first move apart, exhibiting hostility and generating interregional tension. This might seem counter to the need for global integration, but this very conflict can prepare the ground for the ultimate "synthesis" of regional blocs, initially acting like a "thesis" and an "antithesis."[40]

The existence and strengthening of *cross-cutting international organizations*, organizations with members from two or more regions, would enhance the development of a global society under certain conditions and

---

[39] Amitai Etzioni, "Atlantic Union, Southern Continents, and the U.N.", in Roger Fisher (ed.), *International Conflict and Behavioral Science* (New York: Basic Books, 1964).

[40] Amitai Etzioni, "The Dialectics of Supranational Unification," *The American Political Science Review*, *LVI*, no. 4 (December, 1962), 927–935.

have a dampening effect on interregional conflict. The conflict reduction effects of cross-cutting multiple memberships are often stressed in sociology, but it should be noted that, in this context, this effect is not automatically assured. Actually conflict might be heightened rather than reduced if the cross-cutting organizations are not universal but serve to tie two or more regions—e.g., North America and Western Europe—into a bloc. Such cross-regional organizations could, for instance, serve to sustain duopoly and retard the emergence of pluralism, to strengthen the parties to a global conflict rather than set limits to interregional conflict.

Second, these cross-cutting organizations are effective only if their functions are sociologically important in the sense that they effect the global allocation of assets and attract ideological commitments. A universal postal service or a board for allocations of radio frequencies has hence little, if any, conflict dampening effect. On the other hand, a GATT, extended to nations of all regions, might have some such effect, as a similarly extended International Multilateral Force would probably have.

But even a universal organization that serves many important functions would be more a source of tension and conflict than a basis for their limitation if it were dominated by one region, or group of regions, to the partial or complete loss of responsiveness to the others. Actually, an organization that does not allow politically effective regions to participate and to gain representation more or less proportional to their power, would provoke more conflict, the more powerful it is and the more loyalty it commands.

The second major aspect of encapsulation is the evolution of the rules and of agencies for their enforcement. Here there is much room for the application and development of the sociology of law. There are some obvious applications, such as theorems concerning change through legislation, which suggests that one need not wait until all the units involved are ripe for progress before it can be initiated, but also warns against excessive reliance on legislation when there is only a narrow foundation of political consensus. A premature world law might be treated like Prohibition, providing large profits to arms smugglers and repeal of the law rather than lasting disarmament.

Less often discussed among sociologists and rarely studied empirically are subjects that are quite widely explored by professors of law and the philosophy of law, such as the comparative effectiveness of various sanctions for the evolution and enforcement of various laws. These questions are of special relevance for the verification of disarmament treaties and alternative responses to violation. The concern here is first of all with protecting the existing international law from erosion, accelerating its growth and therefore providing mechanisms for its formulation. Here a key problem is the conversion of implicit and "understood" rules into explicit and enforced law. One of the reasons that the Soviet positioning of missiles in Cuba in 1962 created a deep furor in Washington was the fact that the U.S. saw the development of an implicit agreement with the U.S.S.R. that barred attempts at sudden changes in the strategic balance of power. The U.S.S.R., it seems, was not aware of such an agreement and quite unprepared for the tidal wave of reaction its move evoked. This is not to suggest that if the U.S.S.R. had been aware of such a consensus it necessarily would have refrained from violating it, but it surely would have been more reluctant to do so, and the danger of war by miscalculation would have been diminished.

Similarly, by the end of 1964 the U.S. and the U.S.S.R. were formally committed not to orbit weapons of mass destruction but had no explicit agreement to bar other military systems from space. Both countries talked about "the exclusive use of space for peaceful purposes" as if they had implicitly agreed to such a norm. But without a formal agreement the temptation may well prove too great and soon the peace of space will be violated by one side which will then charge the other with a violation. This is not to suggest that the formalization of a limitation on the use of arms would prevent it, if such a violation would prove vital to the security of one of the sides. But extensions of the arms race are rarely that important. When the advantages and disadvantages of extension are more closely in balance, the existence of a formal ban could tip the scales.

When rules are formalized, effective verification and response machinery must still be created. The formal 1954 agreements to neutralize Laos and limit arms supplies for Vietnam were supervised by an understaffed, underfinanced, ill-equipped, politically deadlocked commission. Since 1959, each side has accused the other of violating these agreements; the completely inadequate enforcement machinery provided neither a clear picture of who was first to violate the agreements nor what a proper response should be, short of disregarding the agreement.

Similarly, the positioning in 1956 of a UN force at the Gaza strip on the border between Israel and Egypt largely pacified this border. Other areas in which rules can be made more explicit, more encompassing, better enforced, and serve a gradual transition toward a peace system include open, non-military zones (e.g., Antarctica, Outer Space), neutral zones (e.g., Austria), non-nuclear clubs, and regional arms-control systems.

A transition course from the presocietal stage of the international system to one that answers the full list of functional requirements of a global society has been outlined here. It is not suggested that the international system necessarily will follow that course or, if it starts on this path, it will follow it all the way to its end. There are, however, some signs that it will turn this way and charting the course contributes to those who seek a better understanding of international relations and those interested in understanding how to better them.

The transition, as outlined here, involves not the elimination of conflict but rather its encapsulation. The evolution of the capsule which could keep conflict unarmed might be initiated when the configuration of power is conducive, for which the rise of pluralism and of a sizeable floating vote seem important, and when the psychological atmosphere is ripe. Once initiated via encapsulation, the full evolution of an international societal system requires the formulation and enforcement of rules and the construction of the social foundations such formulation and enforcement would necessitate. This, in turn, might take place when regional bodies provide intermediary levels for a global consensus formation structure. The top layer of this structure might emerge out of a process of upward transfer of power, rights, and loyalties to a central organ of the emerging world community.

A theory

JACK L. ROACH

# of lower-class behavior

M ost sociological inquiry is strongly influenced by a form of socio-cultural determinism which emphasizes meaning, the symbolic world, and social relations, and holds that non-social factors cannot be seen as causal of behavior. While this kind of deterministic framework may generally be of value, unnecessary strictures are placed on socio-logical investigation when there is an insistence upon a narrow interpre-tation of causation. As Max Weber observed, "In all the sciences of human action, account must be taken of phenomena which are devoid of subjective meaning. . . . It is altogether possible that future research may be able to discover non-understandable (i.e., non-meaningful) uniformities underlying what has appeared to be a specifically meaningful action."[1]

Sociological explanations of the behavior of lower-class persons illustrate the limitations which exist if non-meaningful phenomena are

[1] Max Weber, *The Theory of Social and Economic Organization*, trans. A. M. Henderson and Talcott Parsons, Oxford University Press, 1947, pp. 93–94. Parenthetical expression ours.

ignored. Although material conditions of economic deprivation pervade the lives of lower-class persons, these conditions are usually ignored in sociological explanations of lower-class behavior. Interpretations are relied upon suggesting an image of man appropriate to the conditions of life and culture of the middle class but of doubtful relevance to the lower class.

The basic characteristics of sociocultural determinism are discernible in sociological treatments of *motivation* and *causation*. Following an assessment of the general use of these concepts as well as their application to the lower class, a theory of lower-class behavior is presented in which causal primacy is given to non-social determinants.

MAN AND HIS MOTIVES

Sociological treatments of motivation range from ignoring the topic completely to the unique appraisal of Gerth and Mills who see motives as "specialized systems of utterances that are of instrumental value for self-justification and deceit."[2] For the typical sociologist, however, the study of motivation is tantamount to an inquiry into values. As Bernard puts it, "The sociologist takes it for granted that the individual has certain psychological equipment, that is, he can be motivated, he will be active. What the sociologist is interested in, however, is the organization or channeling of this motivation. . . . For understanding behavior—both rational and non-rational—the concept of value is invoked."[3]

Sociologists, then, see a motivated person as one who is acting in terms of an internalized value system which guides his selection from available means in order to attain desired ends. Value-oriented behavior differentiates human motivation and behavior from drives and behavior at the infrahuman level. *How* man is affected by values, that is, the processes through which values become "part of" the actor, is poorly understood although much has been offered in explanation. Sociologists seem to write more intelligibly on the nature of the values which become internalized by *modal* actors and on the consequences of this internalization for behavior. At first glance the number and apparent diversity of values discussed in the literature are reminiscent of the instinct school of the past, since it often appears as if a unique value has been posited for every observed act. For the most part, however, the profusion of values dealt with are slight variations of basic themes which are reducible to a relatively small number of "value orientations."[4]

[2] Hans Gerth and C. Wright Mills, *Character and Social Structure*, Harcourt, Brace & World, 1953, p. 117.
[3] Jessie Bernard, *American Community Behavior*, Holt, Rinehart and Winston, 1962, p. 14.
[4] A widely used reduction of value systems is seen in Florence Kluckhohn and Fred Strodtbeck, *Variations in Value-Orientations*, Harper & Row, 1962.

Sociologists have differed as to which of the variety of values potentially affecting the actor is to be accorded primacy. In modern sociology the focus is increasingly upon *status values* as basic to the actor's motivational system. As Dennis Wrong writes, ". . . although sociologists have criticized past efforts to single out one fundamental motive in human conduct, the desire to achieve a favorable self-image by winning approval from others frequently occupies such a position in their own thinking."[5] This interpretation of man's central motive is regarded by Zetterberg as "a strong contender for the position as the major Motivational Theorem in sociology."[6]

A number of contemporary sociologists present similar conceptions. Parsons' writing, for example, is interwoven with versions of the motivational theorem. Its significance in his theoretical system can be seen in his assumption that, ". . . approval and esteem, both external and internal, that is, ego's own self-appraisal and esteem, may be regarded as the first-line stabilizing or control mechanisms of the social system."[7]

It is not likely that the motivational theorem is a sociological fad that will soon run its course, for the status motive is fundamental to many specialties in contemporary sociology. Reissman,[8] for example, notes the extent to which social class studies are concerned with the status dimension to the near neglect of other important features of stratification. The major premise of industrial sociologists, according to Baritz,[9] is that workers are preoccupied with the quest for approval and acceptance. Still another example is the "status-frustration hypothesis." This widely used contemporary theory of deviant behavior is founded on the assumption that *the basic motive of the actor is the satisfaction of status needs*.[10]

The perspectives on man and his motives crystallized in the motivational theorem are not a recent "emergent," for many social scientists who shaped much of the thinking of modern sociologists held similar ideas on man's compelling needs. These conceptions figure prominently, for example, in Thomas' "four basic wishes,"[11] in James' "hierarchy of selves,"[12] and in Lynds' "cravings of the human personality."[13]

[5] Dennis Wrong, "The Oversocialized Conception of Man in Modern Sociology," *American Sociological Review*, April, 1961, p. 189.

[6] Hans Zetterberg, *Social Thought and Social Practice*, Bedminster Press, 1962, p. 91.

[7] Talcott Parsons, *The Social System*, Free Press, 1951, p. 264. See also Gerth and Mills, *op. cit.*, p. 112; Albert Cohen and James Short, "Juvenile Delinquency," in Robert Merton and Robert Nisbet (eds.), *Contemporary Social Problems*, Harcourt, Brace & World, 1961, pp. 102–103; Harry Bredemeier and Richard Stephenson, *The Analysis of Social Systems*, Holt, Rinehart and Winston, 1962, p. 91.

[8] Leonard Reissman, *Class in America*, Free Press, 1959.

[9] Loren Baritz, *The Servants of Power*, Wesleyan University Press, 1960.

[10] For an examination of the premises of the status-frustration hypothesis, see Jack L. Roach and Orville Gursslin, "The Lower Class, Status Frustration, and Social Disorganization," *Social Forces*, May, 1965, pp. 501–510.

[11] W. I. Thomas, *The Unadjusted Girl*, Little, Brown, 1923, p. 4.

[12] William James, *Principles of Psychology*, Holt, Rinehart and Winston, 1890, Vol. *I*, p. 195.

[13] Robert Lynd, *Knowledge for What*, Princeton University Press, 1939, pp. 193–197.

CAUSES AND CAUSALITY
IN SOCIOLOGICAL ANALYSIS

Most of the controversy in sociology on the causes of man's behavior concerns such issues as the specific *processes* of causation, the *measurement* of causal factors, and the appropriate *model* of causality. Disagreement also exists on the general nature of the causes of social behavior, but for most sociologists social causation is contingent on meaningful acts. The emphasis on meaning as the *causal* component in social behavior is largely a consequence of the work of Max Weber, the founder of social action theory. Comparable uses of the meaning concept are prominent in the contributions of leading American sociologists of the past and present. Most notable is Thomas' "definition of the situation."[14] Thomas' formulation of the definition of the situation is an early articulation of emerging lines of thought on social behavior and its causes—ideas which are now strongly embedded in American sociology. He held that human behavior occurred only under conditions represented by the concept of "situation." The situation usually includes factors that exist only for the actors; i.e., how they perceive the situation and what it means to them. To Thomas these circumstances of human behavior made it crucial that, in addition to empirical descriptions of the observable or objective aspects of the situation, adequate attention be given to the situation as it appears to the interested persons. "Facts," in Thomas' view, do not have a uniform existence apart from the persons who observe and interpret them. The significant facts are the ways in which different people come into and define situations. The similarities between Thomas' contributions and social action theory are suggested by Wolff:

> The definition of the situation quickly became in American sociology and social psychology the dominant phrase for denoting two facets of the theory of social acts; (a) it pointed to the requirement of determining the meaning of a situation to the actor, thus involving social science in the use of categories of meaning, motive, and attitude. (b) It stressed the fact that a dimension of such meaning was cultural in character: i.e., shared, symbolically formulated, and transmitted through the process of socialization; internalized in the personality of the actor and yet also confronting him as the shared attitudes and beliefs of his fellows.[15]

BIOSOCIAL MAN
AND THE NON-SOCIAL ENVIRONMENT

A further understanding of sociological conceptions of causation can be gained by noting the characteristics of man and the conditions of his

[14] These brief remarks on Thomas' views are based on *Social Behavior and Personality: Contributions of W. I. Thomas*, Edmund Volkart (ed.), Social Science Research Council, 1951, pp. 2–7.

[15] Kurt H. Wolff, "Definition of the Situation," in Julius Gould and William L. Kolb (eds.), *A Dictionary of the Social Sciences*, Free Press, 1964, p. 182.

existence which most sociologists do not consider significant for socio-logical inquiry. These factors, usually referred to as non-social, concern (1) man's biological nature, and (2) the material world.

Some writers believe that adequate attention is given in social science to man as a biosocial entity. In their view there are "no serious scientific students of man any more who dare to ignore his 'bestial' affiliations."[16] Such evaluations may be valid for certain divisions of psychology and anthropology, but it is difficult to see their applicability to sociology. To be sure, most sociology texts affirm that "the biological matrix is just as important to the understanding of human society as is the cultural matrix."[17] But once expressed, such ideas are seldom put to any further use. The few works that present a relatively extended account of man's physical nature usually suggest that biological factors function only as limiting conditions of social behavior or agree that a certain type of biological endowment is a necessary condition for the development of social behavior.[18] Virtually no attention is given to "creature needs" of *adult* members of society, for it is presumed that as the individual becomes progressively socialized, physical needs are brought under con-trol, and man's animal nature is more or less contained by his social nature.[19]

Some sociologists have vigorously opposed this limited conception of man and his needs. Dennis Wrong, for example, asserts that in accepting the profundity of the saying, "man lives not by bread alone," it is often forgotten that "in the beginning there is the body."[20] He chides soci-ologists for their overreaction to the "specter of biological determinism," suggesting that biological determinism is scarcely more dogmatic than the dogmatism that rejects any serious consideration of man's biology as a datum for sociology.[21] Wrong appears to be one of the few sociologists who is seriously interested in providing substance for the thesis of biosocial man, rather than simply voicing an objection to the prevalent orientation. In order to find studies which attempt to translate into practice the belief that a "theory of human behavior must embody important and fundamental postulates concerning the biological nature of man,[22] it is usually necessary to turn to writings of the culture-and-

---

16 John Gillin, "Grounds for a Science of Social Man," in John Gillin (ed.), *For A Science of Social Man*, Macmillan, 1954, p. 11. More generally, see Radhakamal Mukerjee, "General Theory of Human Nature and Evolution," *Sociology and Social Research*, April, 1962, pp. 317–325.

17 Kingsley Davis, *Human Society*, Macmillan, 1949, p. 33.

18 For a sophisticated treatment of the "biological factor," unusual in introductory texts, see Robert Bierstedt, *The Social Order*, McGraw-Hill, 1963, chap. 3. Essentially, however, Bierstedt concludes that biological factors should be seen as limiting conditions, not as determinants.

19 Harry Johnson, *Sociology*, Harcourt, Brace & World, 1960, pp. 135–136.

20 Wrong, *op. cit.*, p. 191.

21 *Ibid.* For similar observations, see Alvin W. Gouldner and Richard A. Peterson, *Technology and the Moral Order*, Bobbs-Merrill, 1962, p. 6.

22 Gillin, *op. cit.*, p. 11.

personality school or to specialties within social psychology.[23] In short, while most sociologists acknowledge the existence of biosocial man, little is done to use the implications of this reality in an explanatory framework.

Claims that man's physical milieu or material conditions of life play a significant role in shaping social behavior are distressing to the typical sociologist.[24] In varying degree and form such assertions are involved in the several versions of environmental and economic "determinism" to be found in sociology. Basically, these are represented by the field of ecology and the technology and social-change school. Although championed by ardent spokesmen throughout most of the history of modern sociology, these specialties have had to direct almost as much effort to defense of their claim to be bonafide sociologists as they have been able to devote to the advancement of their ideas. Adherents of "conventional ecology," for example, are accused of using a system of analysis based on biotic and physical premises which denies the relevance of social values and human volition.[25] Assertions that no type of modern ecology is founded on a simple attempt to apply rudimentary biological or physical concepts to social phenomena have made little impression on critics. The majority of sociologists remain ambivalent, at best, toward most ecological versions of environmentalism. Only the voluntaristic branch of ecology, which assumes that values are the significant determinants of man's location over space, seems to have gained much approval.[26] In general, sociologists are unreceptive to theories which appear to rest on premises of "environmentalism" in any form. Steward summarizes the standard position as follows: "Environment is relegated to a purely secondary and passive role. It is considered prohibitive or permissive, but not creative. It allows man to carry on some kinds of activities, and it prevents others."[27]

For most sociologists the relevant environment is the *social* environment and above all the social environment as *perceived* and *interpreted* by the actor.[28] In this view people do not respond directly to an outer reality but to the "meaning of objects which are defined within a cultural system

[23] See, for example, Anthony F. C. Wallace, *Culture and Personality*, Random House, 1961. An instructive analysis of the various uses of biological determinants in social science is given in Raymond D. Gastil, "The Determinants of Human Behavior," *American Anthropologist*, December, 1961, pp. 1281–1291.

[24] For a sample of some older types of environmentalism to which sociologists objected strenuously, see the essays in Jerome Davis and Harry E. Barnes (eds.), *Readings in Sociology*, Heath, 1927, Book II, Part I, "Society in its Physical Environment."

[25] Sidney M. Willhelm, *Urban Zoning and Land-Use Theory*, Free Press, 1962, p. 20.

[26] *Ibid.*

[27] Julian Steward, *Theory of Culture Change*, University of Illinois Press, 1955, p. 35.

[28] As Linton puts it, "between the natural environment and the individual there is always interposed a human environment which is vastly more significant." Ralph Linton, *The Cultural Background of Personality*, Appleton-Century, 1945, p. 19.

and social organization."[29] The connections of these concepts of environment to Weber's use of "meaning" and Thomas' "definition of the situation" are clear.

More difficult to assess is the status of the several types of technological and economic materialism which have been in and out of favor over the years. Under the leadership of Ogburn a high point of influence of the technology and social change school occurred during the 1920s and 1930s. For the next several decades a reaction set in against seeing technology as a major determinant or in any sense "causal" of the phenomena of interest to sociologists. In the past few years, prompted largely by the advent of automation and the surge of interest in underdeveloped lands, the technology and social change thesis is again becoming prominent in the literature. At the same time the old controversies concerning the role of technology in social causation are being renovated; viz., the separation of material from non-material culture, the ascription of causal primacy to technology, and the role of material (i.e., inanimate) objects in causation.

The technological theory of social change is one version of the general framework of economic materialism. Some refer to this thesis as a form of Vulgar Marxism. No doubt this evaluation is partly responsible for the ambiguous position of the technology and social-change school in American sociology. As a *general* explanation, the economic interpretation of social causation and change, receives considerable attention in sociology, but largely for purposes of refutation or as a backdrop for a discussion of *ideology*, the force which most sociologists believe to be the "prime mover."

Sociocultural determinism
and the behavior of the poor

It has been proposed that sociological inquiry is unduly restricted by an emphasis on a limited range of social behavior and a selective interpretation of social causation. In this framework man's basic motives are linked to status needs; biological factors and physical conditions of life receive only perfunctory treatment and are not believed to be causally involved in social behavior. Since most American sociologists study the "middle-range" motives of a middle-range population, it could be argued that they need not ordinarily be conerned with the effects of

---

[29] Wynona S. Garretson, "The Consensual Definition of Social Objects," *The Sociological Quarterly*, Winter, 1962, p. 107.

material conditions, nor with man as a physical animal.[30] Thus a rationale exists for adhering to the orthodox stance that non-social elements can be treated as "constants" devoid of causal implications, and for focusing on what sociologists see as the central problem of middle-class America— the threat to, or actual deprivation of, status. Can sociologists safely assume, then, that (1) the environment never impinges directly upon man but only through the cultural milieu? or that (2) deprivation of physical needs is not as significant to man as the meaning of the deprivation?

Most sociologists would probably agree that these assumptions should be seen as approximations of "what usually holds." But when might these assumptions not be applicable? For instance, what degree of physical press must be present before social functioning is significantly affected? Are there instances when the *objective* situation is at least as determinative of behavior as the *definition* of the situation? Such instances are conceivable; among them, human behavior in an aboriginal, subsistence economy. However, one need not go so far afield, nor need the example be so markedly anomolous with respect to that which is typically studied in sociology. A "test case" is present in the conditions of poverty and the behavior of the poor in contemporary America. Here, it would seem, is a range of phenomena not adequately explainable in terms of the "causes" emphasized in sociocultural determinism.

It seems evident that at least two assumptions of this framework— e.g., that physical needs and material conditions are of little consequence in sociological analysis—are inappropriate in studies of the poor. In spite of this, the recent return of sociological interest in poverty is shaped by the same orientation that prevails in investigations of the status striving of junior executives.[31] Now, as during the Great Depression and before, sociological research is directed to the *meaning* of joblessness, the *subjective* experience of being poor, and the impact on *self-esteem*. Insofar as attention is paid to material conditions of deprivation it is largely for descriptive purposes. Such characteristics of the poor as low income and slum housing are typically used as indices for classification and rarely figure in causal analysis.[32] The only noticeable difference in the

---

[30] Indeed, there seems to be a focus on a select segment of the middle class. Talcott Parsons' "actor," for example, is usually a professional or businessman, and the head of a nuclear type, four-member family. Gouldner's claim that Parsons excludes, ". . . elements in the biological constitution and physiological functioning of man, as well as features of the physical and ecological environment," is applicable to most sociologists. Alvin Gouldner, "Reciprocity and Autonomy in Functional Theory," in Llewellyn Gross (ed.), *Symposium on Sociological Theory*, Harper & Row, 1959, p. 246.

[31] The belated return of sociological attention to poverty is yet another instance of the tendency in sociology to be behind the times regarding "issues of the day." For a critique of contemporary sociological writing on poverty, see Jack L. Roach, "Sociological Analysis and Poverty," *American Journal of Sociology*, July, 1965, pp. 68–75.

[32] It is difficult even to raise the issue with the typical sociologist of the possibility that economic deprivation entails something more than the "meaning" of deprivation, that material deprivation is also involved, and that such factors cannot be adequately dealt with simply by resorting to the social-

study of poverty today compared to times past is the emphasis on what is called the "culture of poverty"—an application of the orthodox conception that values and meaning are the causal forces in the behavior of the poor.[33]

Sociological analysis will contribute little toward understanding the behavior of the poor until proper attention is given to the effects of the material conditions of poverty. Essentially, this means that the determinants ordinarily given causal emphasis in sociology—e.g., meaning, social relations, status needs—must be treated as variables which intervene between material conditions of poverty and the behavior of the poor. In such a scheme causal primacy is ascribed to material conditions, not to the intervening variables.[34] Material conditions are treated as affecting behavior directly as well as indirectly through their effects upon social relations and the meaning of poverty.

There are substantial empirical and theoretical grounds for the above views. Descriptions of poverty in industrial societies have a remarkable similarity, be they concerned with Victorian England, America at the turn of the century, America today, or other contemporary Western lands. The similarities exist whether the observer is a social reformer, historian, novelist, or one of the poverty-stricken.[35] Despite great variations in cultural settings there is a striking correspondence in descriptions of personality impoverishment and severe sociocultural deprivation of the poor. The misery of an Italian family eking out an existence in the middle of a Naples slum resembles that of a Negro family living in squalor in a New York City tenement, and the misery of a family in Appalachia trying to wrest a living from a barren countryside. The poor of Charles Booth's London could as well be the Brazilian children of the favela, physically and mentally stunted, their parents old

psychological concept of "relative deprivation." For a recent statement of orthodox thinking on the relationship between "poverty and behavior," see Marshal Clinard, *The Sociology of Deviance*, Holt, Rinehard and Winston, 1963, pp. 101–105.

[33] Jack L. Roach and Orville R. Gursslin, "A Critique of the Culture of Poverty Thesis," presented at the 35th Annual Meeting of the Eastern Sociological Society, April, 1965 (mimeo).

[34] Most sociologists would agree with Goode that, "we need not escape into the simplicist versions of 'economic causation' any more than those of personality causation. . . . Both are different abstract levels, and if we are to use either type of data we must look for the processes by which they take on social meanings, and thus become converted into variables with sociological significance." William J. Goode, "Economic Factors and Marital Stability," in Robert F. Winch and Robert McGinnis (eds.), *Selected Studies in Marriage and the Family*, Holt, Rinehart and Winston, 1953, p. 543.

Too often this emphasis on intervening processes (i.e., meaning) is carried to extreme lengths. Some investigators engage in mental gymnastics in their ascription of primacy to mediating influences. Leighton, *et al.*, for example, in describing the etiology of mental disorders in a poverty-stricken region, hypothesize that, "Sociocultural disintegration fosters psychiatric disorders by interfering with phsycial security—e.g., needs for adequate food, shelter, clothing, sleep and care of physical ailments." Dorothea C. Leighton, *et al.*, *The Character of Danger*, Basic Books, 1963, p. 371.

[35] For a review of literature on poverty—primarily non-sociological sources—see Jack L. Roach, "Economic Deprivation and Lower-Class Behavior," unpublished Ph.D. dissertation, State University of New York at Buffalo, February, 1964, pp. 85–94.

and spent long before their time. Over and again the same picture emerges of the humanity being ground out of the poor, of family life fraught with fear and violence, of exhausted mothers unable to give warmth and affection, and above all, of a grim apathy.

These descriptions of poverty strongly suggest that, whatever else is involved, the physical conditions of poverty play a central role in the characteristic deterioration of behavior and social life of the poor. It is here that a major difference exists between most sociological contributions to the literature on poverty and non-sociological works. Because of their conviction that the causes of the behavior of the poor are to be found in the meaning of poverty or the value system of the poor, sociologists not only ignore the effects of material deprivation, but often dismiss suggestions that oppressive conditions of life in themselves have a significant influence upon behavior. Since the poor suffer from a double burden of physical as well as social-psychological deprivation the effects of *both* types of deprivation must be assessed in explaining their behavior.

AN EXPLANATORY SCHEME

OF LOWER-CLASS BEHAVIOR

A substantial theoretical basis exists for giving primacy to the physical conditions of poverty in developing an explanatory framework for lower-class behavior. Especially relevant as a point of departure is Maslow's scheme of a "hierarchy of prepotent needs."[36] Maslow postulates a motivational system consisting of *physiological needs, safety needs, love needs, self-esteem needs*, and *self-actualization needs* which are organized in a hierarchy of priority or potency. "The chief dynamic principle animating the organization is the emergence of less potent needs upon gratification of the more potent ones. The physiological needs, when unsatisfied, dominate the organism, pressing all capacities into their service . . ."[37]

In Maslow's theory physiological needs are the most prepotent of all needs. For persons seriously lacking in all need levels, ". . . it is likely that the major motivation would be the physiological needs rather than any other . . ."[38] In general, according to Maslow, the higher the position of the need in the hierarchy, the weaker it is. Gratification of higher needs can be postponed longer, they are less urgent subjectively, and require more "external conditions" for their emergence.[39] Expressed

[36] Abraham H. Maslow, *Motivation and Personality*, Harper & Row, 1954, chaps. 5–8.
[37] *Ibid.*, p. 107.
[38] *Ibid.*, p. 82.
[39] *Ibid.*, pp. 147–149.

as a general proposition, the principle suggested by Maslow is that: *1. If the organism's physical needs are inadequately met then higher level needs will be restricted.*

Since its appearance over two decades ago Maslow's scheme has been widely accepted. Whether influenced directly by his formulations or not, a number of other social scientists have expressed comparable views on the consequences for behavior when vital needs are not met or are continually threatened. Sherif, for example, states that, "When an individual cannot meet the demands of biogenic motives . . . their deprivation has major psychological effects on his entire functioning."[40] Similarly, Redfield holds that, "We see extreme contractions in samples of mankind reduced for long periods to hunger and weakness or exposed to persisting exploitation and abuse . . ."[41]

Other investigators have attempted to describe more fully the effects of physical deprivation upon *mental processes*. Schachtel[42] and Scheerer[43] speak of "primitivization" of thinking and cognitive disorders occurring in persons who lack freedom from anxiety over physical needs. Foote and Cottrell[44] suggest that inadequate meeting of physical needs can lead to an impairment of empathic functioning; and the contributions of Sarbin,[45] Plant,[46] and Sorokin,[47] among others, indicate that physical deprivation is disorganizing to the self-system. These observations which generally follow the path initiated by Maslow can be summarized as follows: *2. If the organism's physical needs are inadequately met then higher mental processes will deteriorate.*

Findings on the consequences of deprivation of physical needs have been supported in laboratory experimentation on the effects of various kinds of physical deprivation on human functioning. Studies of experimental starvation, for example, report incidents of perceptual and cognitive distortion, impairment of reasoning processes, and normative breakdown.[48] Similar effects have been observed in research on fatigue

---

[40] Muzafer Sherif, *An Outline of Social Psychology*, Harper & Row, 1956, p. 377.

[41] Robert Redfield, *Human Nature and the Study of Society*, University of Chicago Press, 1962, p. 467.

[42] Ernest Schachtel, *Metamorphosis*, Basic Books, 1959, pp. 252–253.

[43] Martin Scheerer, "Cognitive Theory," in Gardner Lindzey (ed.), *Handbook of Social Psychology*, Addison-Wesley, 1954, pp. 114–115; Boyd R. McCandless, "Relation of Environmental Factors to Intellectual Functioning," in Harvey A. Stevens and Rick Heber (eds.), *Mental Retardation*, The University of Chicago Press, 1964, pp. 175–209.

[44] Nelson Foote and Leonard Cottrell, *Identity and Interpersonal Competence*, University of Chicago Press, 1955, p. 71.

[45] Theodore Sarbin (ed.), *Studies in Behavior Pathology*, Holt, Rinehart and Winston, 1961, p. 113.

[46] James Plant, *Personality and the Cultural Pattern*, The Commonwealth Fund, 1937, pp. 227–228.

[47] Pitirim Sorokin, *Man and Society in Calamity*, Dutton, 1942.

[48] Harold S. Guetzkow, *Men and Hunger*, Brethren Press, 1946. For a review of a number of studies of this nature, see Sherif, *op. cit.*, pp. 420–424.

and sleep deprivation.[49] These findings can be expressed as follows: *3. If the organism is subjected to severe physical deprivation then behavioral disorders will ensue.*

While social scientists have long been interested in the effects of sociocultural isolation upon human behavior,[50] only in relatively recent years can one point to a substantial body of literature on this topic. Noteworthy are the increasing number of empirical studies showing that an adequate level of sociocultural stimulation is as vital to the development of the human organism as adequate physical nurturance. In a broad sociological vein many writers speculate on the general implications of life in an isolated, culturally impoverished milieu.[51] Social isolation is seen as reducing an individual's effectiveness and eventually leading to personality disorders. Protracted existence in unstimulating surroundings may result in "wants being 'cut down to size' to fit the impoverished want-arousing potential of his environment."[52] Other theorists have focused on the effects of experiential (sociocultural) deprivation in early life. Reports describe, for example, the "occurrence of serious and irreversible disruptions of normal development and behavior," as a result of inadequate early environmental experience.[53] From the most extensive analysis to date of relevant evidence Hunt concludes that, "impoverishments of experience during the early months . . . may result not only in a permanently reduced I.Q. but in a failure of the basic criterion capacities of individuals to develop to the degree that they might have developed."[54]

These theoretical speculations and empirical generalizations on the effects of experiential deprivation can be summarized as follows: *4. If the organism's experiential (sociocultural) needs are inadequately met then mental development will be retarded.*

Laboratory research on sensory deprivation complements studies of the effects of sociocultural deprivation.[55] Similar anomalies in behavior

---

[49] S. Howard Bartley and Eloise Chute, *Fatigue and Impairment in Man*, McGraw-Hill, 1947; Joe Kamiza, "Behavioral, Subjective, and Physiological Aspects of Drowsiness and Sleep," in Donald W. Fiske and Salvatore Maddi (eds.), *Functions of Varied Experience*, Dorsey Press, 1961, pp. 145–174; A suggestive account of the effects of general physical deprivation is also given in Arnold Rose, "Social Psychological Effects of Physical Deprivation," *Journal of Health and Human Behavior*, Winter, 1960, pp. 285–289.

[50] See, for example, Martin Matthews, *Experience Worlds of Mountain People*, Columbia University Press, 1937.

[51] For a general presentation of these findings, see Sherif, *op. cit.*, chap. 20.

[52] David Krech *et al.*, *Individual In Society*, McGraw-Hill, 1962, p. 87.

[53] Philip E. Kubzansky, "The Effects of Reduced Environmental Stimulation on Human Behavior," in Albert Biderman and Herbert Zimmer (eds.), *The Manipulation of Human Behavior*, Wiley, 1961, pp. 54–55.

[54] J. McV. Hunt, *Intelligence and Experience*, Ronald, 1961, p. 346.

[55] Yarrow suggests that, "Social deprivation probably acts in a similar way as deprivation of sensory stimulation, leading to disturbances in social functioning, such as social apathy and social hyperresponsiveness . . ." Leon J. Yarrow, "Maternal Deprivation: Toward An Empirical and Conceptual Re-evaluation," *Psychological Bulletin*, November, 1961, pp. 480–481.

have occurred which are also comparable in many ways to the deterioration of behavior induced through experimental physical deprivation. Such effects have been reported as cognitive disorders, impairments of reasoning, severe anxiety, disorganization of the self-system, and psychotic-like states.[56] The following proposition summarizes typical findings from sensory deprivation research: *5. If the organism is subjected to severe sensory deprivation then personality disorders will ensue.*

A recapitulation

A number of theoretical conclusions and empirical generalizations have been presented on the consequences for human functioning when basic needs are not met. This material has been summarized by five propositions:

From general psychology theory:

1. If the organism's physical needs are inadequately met, then higher needs will be restricted.
2. If the organism's physical needs are inadequately met, then higher mental processes will deteriorate.
3. If the organism's experiential (sociocultural) needs are inadequately met, then mental development will be restricted.

From experimental deprivation research:

4. If the organism is subjected to severe physical deprivation, then behavioral disorders will ensue.
5. If the organism is subjected to severe sensory deprivation, then personality disorders will ensue.

The referents of these statements overlap considerably, yet certain distinctions are sufficiently present to warrant separate presentation. For example, statements 1, 2, and 4 refer to inadequacies of physical needs, but the consequences of this condition are described respectively as a restriction of functioning at higher levels, a deterioration of higher mental processes, and behavioral disorders. As with statement 2, statement 3 is concerned with mental functioning, but deprivation of experiential needs rather than physical needs is designated as the antecedent condition. Further, statements 1 and 3 refer to restriction of the organism's potential functioning, while 2, 4, and 5 refer to deterioration or disorders in the functioning of the organism.

Despite variations in terminology and the fact that through summarization the language of these statements necessarily diverges from the

[56] Philip Solomon (ed.), *Sensory Deprivation*, Harvard University Press, 1961; I. E. Farber *et al.*, "Brainwashing, Conditioning, and DDD," in Sarbin, *op. cit.*, pp. 106–115; Donald W. Fiske, "Effects of Monotonous and Restricted Stimulation," in Fiske and Maddi, *op. cit.*, pp. 106–144.

expressions of the source materials, some basic commonalities in conditions of deprivation and their effects are discernible. These commonalities appear to be manifestations of an underlying process which, in its most general form, can be expressed as follows:

Under varying conditions of severe deprivation of basic human needs, behavioral disorders will occur.

Basic-need deprivation and the lower class

Most theories of the lower class are essentially attempts to account for the high degree of personal and social disorganization in this segment of the population. As alluded to previously, a widely used sociological explanation of the lower-class deviant behavior is the status-frustration hypothesis. According to this interpretation lower-class persons are motivated to attain success values, as are all members of American society. However, lower-class persons are blocked in their ambitions by socially structured barriers. They perceive that legitimate access to high status positions is restricted by external forces beyond their control. The combination of frustration due to thwarted ambition and a sense of injustice leads to deviant adaptations. This explanation has a ring of plausibility yet its applicability to the lower class is open to serious doubt. Specifically, the key assumptions of the status-frustration hypothesis—presence of a high level of aspiration, perception of external barriers to success, and presence of intense status frustration—are contradicted by empirical evidence on the lower class.[57]

To be sure, lower-class persons experience frustration stemming from status deprivation, but is this type of deprivation at the core of their behavior? Virtually all relevant stratification literature depicts lower-class persons as living under conditions of poverty throughout their lives.[58] Moreover, most accounts of the poor describe them in terms closely resembling the socioeconomic characteristics of the lower class.[59] In short, there is sufficient basis for treating the lower class as synonymous with the poor. To be sure, there is much controversy on what is meant by poverty and on the degree of economic deprivation that must be present in order for persons to be classified as poor.[60] Whatever else poverty

[57] Roach and Gursslin, "The Lower Class, Status Frustration, and Social Disorganization," *op. cit.*

[58] Additional identifying indices are also employed, such as lack of job skills and limited education, but economic deprivation is almost always referred to as a central characteristic of the lower class.

[59] For a profile of the "poverty group" showing characteristics comparable to those of the lower class, see *Economic Report of the President and the Annual Report of the Council of Economic Advisers*, U.S. Government Printing Office, 1964, pp. 61–66.

[60] Kahl asserts, for example, that, "we simply do not have enough information to decide what proportion are actually suffering from poverty." Joseph A. Kahl, *The American Class Structure*, Holt, Rinehart and Winston, 1957, p. 99.

connotes, at a minimum it refers to a chronic insufficiency of basic physical needs such as food and shelter.[61] In keeping with Maslow's scheme, and its elaboration as presented above, status deprivation can be seen as a secondary motivational force in persons who are deprived of physical needs or who live under constant threat of such deprivation.

A second basis characteristic of the poor is a marked degree of sociocultural deprivation.[62] Although a much more complex phenomenon to assess than physical deprivation, studies of poverty also note extensive social isolation and cultural improverishment of the poor. Not only are they isolated from the general community, but they interact only minimally with each other. Their experiential worlds are circumscribed and deficient as learning milieus.

Some writers claim that the physical and sociolcultural deficiencies in the everyday life of the poor play an important part in the personality impoverishment and behavioral disorganization so commonly reported in studies of poverty. But only nominal attention is given to the nature of the causal linkages between these forms of deprivation and behavior.[63]

The theoretical scheme presented below rests upon the premise that physical and sociocultural deprivation are causally related to the behavior of the poor and that the processes of causation are explainable by subsumption under the principle, *under varying conditions of severe deprivation, behavioral disorders will occur*. The application of this principle to the lower class is as follows:

1. If organisms are subjected to severe economic deprivation, then they will be subject to severe (a) physical deprivation, (b) sociocultural deprivation, and (c) behavioral disorders.
2. Since lower-class persons are organisms subjected to severe economic deprivation, they are subject to severe (a) physical deprivation, (b) sociocultural deprivation, and (c) behavioral disorders.

[61] Some measures of poverty based upon this dimension are available. A commonly used scheme is the "emergency budget" constructed by the Bureau of Labor statistics. (An appraisal of this measure of poverty is given in Gabriel Kolko, *Wealth and Power in America*, Praeger, 1962, pp. 96–99.) According to one of the foremost students of public welfare, "The emergency budget . . . represents the lowest level of living that would provide minimum requirements for adequate nutrition . . . It is generally held that families forced to live at this level for an extended period of time would be subject to serious health hazards." Eveline M. Burns, *The American Social Security System*, Houghton Mifflin, 1951, p. 22. In today's America at least 25 million persons exist under conditions of poverty determined in this way. As Kolko puts it, "their expenditures are not guided by social norms of well-being but by the demands of survival." *Op. cit.*, p. 97.

[62] Sociocultural deprivation is inclusive of status deprivation, the type most sociologists focus upon. As discussed previously, not only is there a preoccupation in sociology with a narrowly defined status motive, but as Himelhoch suggests, the sources and expressions of this motive are oversimplified. Jerome Himelhoch "Delinquency and Opportunity: An End and a Beginning of a Theory," in Alvin Gouldner and S. M. Miller (eds.), *Applied Sociology: Opportunities and Problems*, Free Press, 1965, especially pp. 195–197.

[63] Michael Harrington, *The Other America*, Macmillan, 1962; Edward B. Banfield, *The Moral Basis of a Backward Society*, Free Press, 1958; Robert W. Kelso, *Poverty*, Longmans Green, 1929; Cora Kasius, "Family Disorganization and the Multi-Problem Family," *Golden Anniversary White House Conference*, 1960, pp. 233–241; Helen L. Witmer and Ruth Kotinsky, *Personality in the Making*, Harper & Row, 1952.

This set of statements is the foundation for an expanded explanation of lower-class behavior. The line of causation is: economic deprivation ———→physical deprivation———→sociocultural deprivation———→behavioral disorders.[64] In this scheme sociocutural phenomena mediate between the physical world (conditions of physical existence) and man. This is consonant with a basic tenet in social science which holds that culture and social relations are adaptations to the physical conditions of existence.[65] Sociocultural phenomena are therefore treated as intervening variables[66] which effect behavior, but the degree and nature of these effects are strongly determined by the conditions of physical existence. There are other points at which one could cut into this causal sequence. An important focus, for example, might be the causal relationship of sociocultural deprivation and social-psychological functioning. There remains, however, the problem of the origins of sociocultural deprivation. In addition to other causal linkages the scheme proposed attempts to explain these origins. Three general sets of determinants—material, biological, and sociocultural variables—are handled in a framework which is expressed in a form midway between single-factor determinism and "theoretical orientations that lose all sense of causality in a cloud of particulars."[67]

The elaboration of the basic framework attempts to take account of the variety of empirical findings available in the social science literature on the lower class. Although these findings may be classified into broad categories such as sociocultural phenomena and personality processes, the research upon which they are based generally deals with lower-level concepts in circumscribed areas of investigation. For example, studies have been carried out on the ability of lower-class persons to handle abstractions, on their role-taking skills, on child-rearing practices, and on specific types of social disorganization. Clearly, in many instances these are arbitrary divisions. What one researcher treats as an aspect of personality, for example, another may describe as an intellectual function. However, it does seem desirable to elaborate the general propositions of the theory in a language approximating the conceptual level and language of the source documents.

64 In keeping with the general principles governing behavior under conditions of deprivation, the basic characteristic of economic deprivation is treated as the "initiating variable" in this causal sequence.

65 See the excellent statement by Gellner in which social scientists are reminded that man, their object of study, is fundamentally a physical animal existing in a physical as well as social environment. Ernest Gellner, "Nature and Society in Social Anthropology," *Philosophy of Science*, July, 1963, pp. 236–251.

66 It is recognized that the problem of "intervening variables" is a highly controversial topic in social science. As Lynd suggests, what is treated as an intervening variable by one investigator is another's hypothetical construct. And for others, intervening variables are used interchangeably as independent variables. Helen Lynd, "Thinking from Parts to Wholes," in Bartlett H. Stoodley (ed.), *Society and Self*, Free Press, 1962, p. 626. More generally see Hubert M. Blalock, *Causal Inferences in Nonexperimental Research*, University of North Carolina Press, 1964, Chaps. 1 and 2.

67 Walter R. Goldschmidt, foreword to Alvin W. Gouldner and Richard A. Peterson, *Technology and the Moral Order*, Bobbs-Merrill, 1962, p. xii.

To facilitate understanding of the structure of the theoretical scheme and to indicate more clearly the connections among its components, the framework itself is first set forth in its entirety. Following this an empirical interpretation is presented. Each of the four propositions on the lower class (designated by 1.3, 2.3, 3.3, and 4.2) is deduced as a particular instance of four central generalizations (1.1, 2.1, 3.1, and 4.1) describing the consequences of basic deprivation for human functioning.

1.1 Persons who exist under temporally extended conditions of physical deprivation have a deficient sociocultural milieu.

1.2 Lower-class persons exist under temporally extended conditions of physical deprivation.

1.3 *Therefore*, lower-class persons have a deficient sociocultural milieu.

2.1 Persons with a deficient sociocultural milieu have a deficient group life and role system.

2.2 Lower-class persons have a deficient sociocultural milieu.

2.3 *Therefore*, lower-class persons have a deficient group life and role system.

3.1 Persons with a deficient group life and role system have a deficient personality system.

3.2 Lower-class persons have a deficient group life and role system.

3.3 *Therefore*, lower-class persons have a deficient personality system.

4.1 Persons who exist under temporally extended conditions of physical deprivation with a deficient (1.1) sociocultural milieu, (2.1) group life and role system, and (3.1) personality system, have severe behavioral disorders.

4.2 *Therefore*, lower-class persons have severe behavioral disorders.

EMPIRICAL BASIS

Proposition 1.3: Lower-class persons have a deficient sociolcutural milieu.

Lower-class persons are only peripherally affected by influences from the general culture.[68] They exist in an impoverished experiential world.[69]

---

[68] James West, *Plainville USA*, Columbia University Press, 1945, p. 131; Arthur Vidich and Joseph Bensman, *Small Town in Mass Society*, Doubleday, 1958, p. 296; Charles Willie, *The Structure and Composition of "Problem" and "Stable" Families in a Lower Income Population*, Youth Development Center, Syracuse Housing Authority, 1962, Mimeo.; Hylan Lewis, "Child Rearing Practices Among Low-Income Families in the District of Columbia," Paper presented at the National Conferences on Social Welfare, Minneapolis, May 16, 1961.

[69] Frank Riessman, *The Culturally Deprived Child*, Harper & Row, 1962, p. 57; Martin Deutsch, *Minority Groups and Class Status as Related to Social and Personality Factors in Scholastic Achievement*, The Society for Applied Anthropology, 1960, pp. 28–29; Madeline Kerr, *The People of Ship Street*, Routledge & Kegan Paul, 1958, *passim*; Richard L. Masland, *et al.*, *Mental Subnormality*, Basic Books, 1958, p. 224.

Lower-class homes are inadequate settings for learning.[70] Typically, the life-span of lower-class children is confined to their own immediate surroundings.[71]

Proposition 2.3: Lower-class persons have a deficient group life and role system.

Lower-class persons are almost completely isolated from community activities whether these be formal organizations or loosely knit cliques.[72] This isolation from others extends to those of their own kind. Lower class persons have few friends; neighboring is at a minimum.[73]

Lower-class persons have a restricted repertory of roles. Lower-class men, in particular, often have no clearly defined role due to their lack of a definite occupational role and frequent unemployment.[74]

Proposition 3.3: Lower-class persons have a deficient personality system characterized by:

Impaired intellectual functioning

A large proportion of the lower-class population is intellectually impaired. Conceptual performance is limited.[75] They have difficulty in handling abstractions, relationships, and categories.[76] In general,

[70] Suzanne Keller, "The Social World of the Urban Slum Child," Paper presented at the Annual Meeting of the American Orthopsychiatric Association, March, 1962; Reissman, *op. cit.*, p. 84.

[71] Patricia C. Sexton, *Education and Income*, Viking Press, 1961, p. 144; Robert Havighurst and Bernice Neugarten, *Society and Education*, Allyn and Bacon, 1957, pp. 161–162.

[72] Nicholas Babchuk and C. Wayne Gordon, *The Voluntary Association in the Slum*, University of Nebraska Press, 1962, p. 116; Earl H. Koos, *Families in Trouble*, Kings Crown Press, 1946, p. xiii; August Hollingshead, *Elmtown's Youth*, Wiley, 1949, p. 219; In general, see the resume of studies showing marked social isolation in the lower class given in John Spencer, "The Multi-Problem Family," in Benjamin Schlesinger (ed.), *The Multi-Problem Family*, University of Toronto Press, pp. 27–28.

[73] Daniel Wilner et al., *The Housing Environment and Family Life*, The Johns Hopkins Press, 1962, p. 164; David Caplovitz, *The Poor Pay More*, Free Press, 1963, pp. 133–134; Jerome Myers and Bertram Roberts, *Family and Class Dynamics in Mental Illness*, Wiley, 1959, pp. 178–179; Robert S. Lynd and Helen M. Lynd, *Middletown*, Harcourt, Brace & World, 1929, p. 272; Jane Jacobs, *The Death and Life of Great American Cities*, Random House, 1961, pp. 66–67; Leighton et al., *op. cit.*, p. 384.

[74] Thomas McPartland and John R. Cumming, "Self-Conception, Social Class and Mental Illness," *Human Organization*, Fall, 1958, p. 28; Leighton et al., *op. cit.*, p. 384; Kerr, *op. cit.*, *passim*; Myers and Roberts, *op. cit.*, p. 176; Sexton, *op. cit.*, p. 108.

[75] Masland et al., p. 392; A review of studies consistently showing poor performance of lower-class subjects on I.Q. tests is given in P. E. Vernon, *Intelligence and Attainment Tests*, University of London Press, 1960.

[76] Lee Rainwater, "A Study of Personality Differences Between Middle and Lower Class Adolescents," *Genetic Psychology Monographs*, First half, 1956, p. 17; Reissman, *op. cit.*; Leonard Schatzman and Anselm Strauss, "Social Class and Modes of Communication," *American Journal of Sociology*, January, 1955, p. 330. Psychological studies have generally demonstrated an inverse correlation between social class and ability to perform on an abstract, conceptual level. See Eugene S. Gollin, "Organized Characteristics of Social Judgment," *Journal of Personality*, June, 1958, pp. 139–153; Donald Findley and Carson McGuire, "Social Status and Abstract Behavior," *Journal of Abnormal and Social Psychology*, January, 1957, pp. 135–137.

lower-class persons find mental activity arduous and have little energy for, or interest in, new thoughts and ideas.[77]

Cognitive restrictions

The cognitive process of lower-class persons is relatively unstructured.[78] Knowledge of the outside world is hazy; critical decisions are made with little comprehension of alternatives or implications.[79]

Inadequate verbal skills

Lower-class persons have numerous language handicaps. Reading and writing abilities are at a low level.[80] General linguistic retardation is common.[81] Their lacks in verbal facility restrict verbal expansion of thought.[82]

Defective self-system

The self-system of lower-class persons is poorly integrated and characterized by weak ego controls.[83] Lower-class persons are not inclined toward introspection and are deficient in ability to conceptualize the self.[84]

Limited role-behavior skills

Lower-class persons are restricted in their ability to take the role of the other. They lack subtleties in role-playing and have difficulties in shifting perspectives.[85]

[77] Ralph Mason Dreger and Kent S. Miller, "Comparative Psychological Studies of Negroes and Whites in the United States," *Psychological Bulletin*, September, 1960, p. 394; Koos, *op. cit.*, p. 25; Deutsch, *op. cit.*, p. 3; Lee Rainwater and Karol Weinstein, *And the Poor Get Children*, Quadrangle Books, 1960, pp. 50–53.

[78] B. W. Spinley, *The Deprived and the Privileged*, Routledge and Kegan Paul, 1958, p. 170; Martin Deutsch, "The Disadvantaged Child and the Learning Process," Paper prepared for Ford Foundation Work Conference on Curriculum and Teaching in Depressed Urban Area, Columbia University, New York, July 10, 1962, p. 9; Vera P. John, "The Intellectual Development of Slum Children," Paper presented at the Annual Meeting of American Orthopsychiatric Association, 1962.

[79] Lloyd G. Reynolds and Joseph Shister, *Job Horizons*, Harper & Row, 1949, pp. 51, 64; Gabriel A. Almond, *The American People and Foreign Policy*, Harcourt, Brace & World, 1950, pp. 123–130; Hollingshead, *op. cit.*, pp. 359, 365; West, *op. cit.*, p. 78; Caplovitz, *op. cit.*, pp. 175–176.

[80] Joseph Veroff, *et al.*, "The Use of Thematic Apperception to Assess Motivation in a Nationwide Interview Study," *Psychological Monographs*, 1960, p. 12; Sexton, *op. cit.*, pp. 31–35.

[81] Masland *et al.*, *op. cit.*, p. 227; Keller, *op. cit.*

[82] Basil Bernstein, "Some Sociological Determinants of Perception," *British Journal of Sociology*, June, 1957, pp. 159–174; Riessman, *op. cit.*, p. 74; Schatzman and Strauss, *op. cit.*, p. 337.

[83] Leo Srole *et al.*, *Mental Health in the Metropolis*, McGraw-Hill, 1962, p. 355; Plant, *op. cit.*, pp. 227–228; Myers and Roberts, *op. cit.*, p. 261; Spinley, *op. cit.*, p. 116; Rainwater, *op. cit.*, p. 72.

[84] George Gurin *et al.*, *Americans View their Mental Health*, Basic Books, 1961, chap. 3; Albert K. Cohen and Harold M. Hodges, "Characteristics of the Lower-Blue-Collar Class," *Social Problems*, Spring, 1963, p. 317; Riessman, *op. cit.*, p. 70; Deutsch, "The Disadvantaged Child and the Learning Process," *op. cit.*

[85] Schatzman and Strauss, *op. cit.*, *passim*; Cohen and Hodges, *op. cit.*; Kerr, *op. cit.*, pp. 9–11. A speculative account of role-playing, with some relevance to the lower class, is given in Howard E.

Proposition 4.2: Lower-class persons manifest severe behavioral disorders characterized by high rates of:

Mental disturbance

The highest rates of mental disturbance including most forms of neuroses and psychoses are found in the lower class.[86] The most severe forms of psychoses are concentrated in this range of the population.[87]

Suicide and homicide

Unskilled laborers and the unemployed have high suicide rates[88] and the highest rate of homicide.[89]

Delinquency and general crime

The highest rates of delinquency[90] and adult crime[91] occur in the lower class.

Family disorganization

The highest rate of family dissolution is found in the lower class.[92]

Freedman and Gene G. Kassebaum, "The Illiterate in American Society," *Social Forces*, May, 1956, pp. 371–375. Also suggestive are experimental studies which show an inverse relationship between role skills and variables of social class. See Leon H. Warshay, "Breadth of Perspective," in Arnold Rose (ed.), *Human Behavior and Social Processes*, Houghton Mifflin, 1962, pp. 148–176; Bela O. Baker and Theodore R. Sarbin, "Differential Mediation of Social Perception as a Correlate of Social Adjustment," *Sociometry*, March, 1956, pp. 69–83.

[86] August Hollingshead and Frederick Redlich, *Social Class and Mental Illness*, Wiley, 1958; Charles C. Hughes *et al.*, *People of Cove and Woodlot*, Basic Books, 1960; Raymond G. Hunt, "Sociocultural Factors in Mental Disorders," *Behavioral Science*, April, 1959, pp. 96–106; Edward A. Rundquist and Raymond F. Sletto, *Personality in the Depression*, University of Minnesota Press, 1936, p. 366; William H. Sewell, "Social Class and Childhood Personality," *Sociometry*, August, 1961, p. 350.

[87] Robert E. Clark, "Psychoses, Income, and Occupational Prestige," in Reinhard Bendix and Seymour Lipset (eds.), *Class, Status and Power*, Free Press, 1953, pp. 333–340; Robert M. Frumkin "Occupation and the Major Mental Disorders," in Arnold Rose (ed.), *Mental Health and Mental Disorder*, Norton, 1955, pp. 136–160; Robert J. Kleiner and Seymour Parker, "Goal-Striving, Social Status, and Mental Disorder," *American Sociological Review*, April, 1963, pp. 189–203; Srole *et al.*, *op. cit.*

[88] Elwin H. Powell, "Occupation, Status, and Suicide; Toward a Redefinition of Anomie," *American Sociological Review*, April, 1958, pp. 131–139. This work summarizes similar findings from a number of other studies. See also Jack P. Gibbs, "Suicide," in Robert Merton and Robert Nisbet (eds.), *Contemporary Social Problems*, Harcourt, Brace & World, 1961, p. 244; Warren Breed, "Occupational Mobility and Suicide," *American Sociological Review*, April, 1963, pp. 179–188.

[89] Gerhard J. Falk, "Status Differences and the Frustration Aggression Hypothesis," *The International Journal of Social Psychiatry*, Winter, 1959, pp. 214–222; Robert C. Bensing and Oliver Schroeder, *Homicide in an Urban Community*, Thomas, 1960, chap. 2.

[90] Orville Gursslin, "The Formulation and Partial Test of a Class Linked Theory of Delinquency," Unpublished Ph.D. dissertation, University of Buffalo, 1961. In addition to the provision of more recent data this study reviews a number of investigations pointing to the concentration of delinquency in the lower ranges of the population.

[91] On general crime, see Donald Cressy, "Crime," in Merton and Nisbet, *op. cit.*, p. 42.

[92] A review of research demonstrating the high incidence of family disorganization in the lower class is given in William Goode, *After Divorce*, Free Press, 1956, chap. 4.

A majority of lower-class homes that remain intact are ridden with marital strife and bitter feelings among siblings and parents.[93]

CONCLUSION

Modern sociology is overly influenced by a type of sociocultural determinism which precludes the possibility that non-social factors play a causal role in behavior. While this orientation may generally be of heuristic value it creates barriers to the understanding of important ranges of human behavior. A conspicuous example exists in orthodox sociological explanations of lower-class behavior. Most sociologists would agree that, "A social scientist is free to employ any model of man he chooses so long as it is capable of ordering empirical data and so long as he is willing to relinquish it when it can be shown that some other image orders the data in a superior fashion."[94] Since it is questionable that the model of man dominant in sociology adequately orders the available knowledge on the lower class, alternative models are required. A theory of lower-class behavior has been presented based upon an image of man and his motives which significantly departs from usual sociological conceptions.

---

[93] E. Franklin Frazier, *Negro Youth at the Crossways*, The American Council on Education, 1940, p. 24; Myers and Roberts, *op. cit.*, pp. 66–71; Allison Davis, "Child Rearing in the Class Structure of American Society," in Marvin Sussman (ed.), *Sourcebook in Marriage and the Family*, Houghton Mifflin, 1963, p. 230. For descriptions of the nature of lower-class family disorganization, see Allison Davis, "The Motivation of the Underprivileged Worker," in William F. Whyte (ed.), *Industry and Society*, McGraw-Hill, 1946, pp. 84–106; Hollingshead, *op. cit.*, pp. 432–436.

[94] William L. Kolb, "Images of Man and the Sociology of Religion," in Stoodley, *op. cit.*, p. 630.

LLEWELLYN GROSS

A transactional
interpretation
of social problems

This essay assumes that much of the "descriptive" vocabulary of social problems can be restated to fit the scientifically familiar language of "conditions," "operations," and "results." It further assumes that the choice of "descriptive" vocabulary and its translation in scientific language rests upon the usefulness of both forms of expression for achieving human goals. In Dewey's words, "There is always a field in which observation of *this* or *that* object or event occurs. Observation of the latter is made for the sake of finding out what that *field* is with reference to some active adaptive response to be made in carrying forward a *course* of behavior."[1] Taking Dewey as a guide, interpretation of the language of conditions, operations and results follows from the behavior adapted by scientist and citizen in evaluating the field of social problems.

Criticism of the approach can be anticipated on the grounds that it emphasizes syntax and neglects semantics—that it is concerned more with the relation between concepts than it is with their relation to "things"

[1] John Dewey, *Logic, The Theory of Inquiry*, Holt, Rinehart and Winston, 1938, p. 67.

315

or "events." Though pertinent, this criticism is offset by the transparent circumstance that the "things" and "events" alluded to have questionable factual status when taken as existing independently of the "descriptive" vocabulary of sociology. Up to now, few, if any, successful attempts have been made to define semantic rules for governing the interpretation of sociological concepts. The closest equivalents to such rules are conventions of symbolic reference which obtain without the technical capacity to provide semantic verification. In this respect they are not unlike widely accepted rules of measurement which are retained despite the failure to apply them with complete success as, for instance, in determining the dimensions of a table. Thus, although the syntactical definition of the yardstick is a necessary condition for the semantic interpretation of length, the yardstick's definition is unaltered by the results of its application. With sociology, only the most general categories of syntax, detached from specific semantic referents, seem to approach universality. In the absence of rules for identifying such referents, this essay offers a heuristic symbolism for ordering the "descriptive" vocabulary of social problems, a vocabulary reflecting partisan shifts in "values" and "actions."[2]

As a beginning step, the "values" and "actions" of scientist and citizen are translated into the language of conditional sentences. Simply expressed, conditional sentences state that certain phenomena behave in certain ways under certain conditions.[3] By treating values as subclasses of conditions and restricting actions to the felicitous terminology of operations, specializing forms of the conditional sentence can be stated. When these forms are generalized they imply that certain valued (or disvalued) results are produced by certain valued (or disvalued) operations together with certain valued (or disvalued) conditions. In this context, the distinction between "conditions" and "operations" draws upon the commonsense difference between "given" conditions and "added" conditions. The principal advantage of the distinction is twofold: First, to articulate the broad assumption that the destiny of many social problems results from human intervention in processes of social change; and secondly, to call

---

[2] Despite considerable work on operational definitions, coordinating definitions, epistemic correlations, and correspondence rules, little has been done to explicate the semantic dimensions latent in the common language of social science. That uncertainties abound even in the physical sciences is indicated by Nagel: "It is a familiar fact that theories in the sciences (especially though not exclusively in mathematical physics) are generally formulated with painstaking care and that the relations of theoretical notions to each other (whether the notions are primitives in the system or are defined in terms of the primitives) are stated with great precision. Such care and precision are essential if the deductive consequences of theoretical assumptions are to be rigorously explored. On the other hand, rules of correspondence for connecting theoretical with experimental ideas generally receive no explicit formulation; and in actual practice the coordinations are comparatively loose and imprecise." Ernest Nagel, *The Structure of Science*, Harcourt, Brace & World, 1961, p. 99.

[3] For a discussion of conditional sentences see L. Gross, "Theory Construction in Sociology: A Methodological Inquiry" in L. Gross (ed.), *Symposium on Sociological Theory*, Harper & Row, 1959, pp. 531–564.

attention to the widespread discrepancy between what scientists and citizens find social conditions to be in fact and what they attempt to do about them.

Stated more formally, conditional sentences delineate the scope of a social problem by designating categories of (1) conditions or antecedents, (2) operations or modes of action, and (3) results or consequences. A table may be used to present a schematic summarization of their principal forms.

	Conditions	Operations	Results
First Form	*If* C's, a given set or pattern of neutrally valued conditions obtains	*And* certain acts or operations, O's, be initiated (which produce successively more accurate descriptions of the conjunction of C's with R's).	*Then* neutrally valued R's either singly, in series or patterns, will probably be found to occur.
Second Form	*If* C's, a given set or pattern of positively valued conditions obtains	*And* certain acts or operations, O's, be initiated (which together with C's produce successively nearer approximations of R's)	*Then* positively valued R's either singly, in series or patterns, will probably be found to occur.
Third Form	*If* not-C's, a given set or pattern or negatively valued conditions obtains	*But* certain acts or operations, O's, be initiated (which produce successively greater departures from not-C's, and, correlatively, nearer approximations of R's)	*Then* positively valued R's either singly, in series or patterns, will probably be found to occur.

In the *First Form*, O's are merely observation reports descriptive of the conjunction of C's with R's. Operations of this kind are usually thought of as functioning in an independent way with respect to the occurrence or non-occurrence of positively valued C's and R's. In the *Second Form*, O's are designed to implement positively valued C's by reinforcing them with new C's which will maximize the probable occurrence of positively valued R's. In the *Third Form*, O's are designed to restrict negatively valued

C's by substituting new C's which will maximize the probable occurrence of positively valued R's.[4]

Conditional sentences of the *First Form* are hypotheses which attempt to reveal how certain empirical phenomena are related "in nature," without in any way disengaging or reshaping them to meet the goals of men. As such they seek to determine what is probably true knowledge. Conditional sentences of the *Second* or *Third Forms* are hypotheses which attempt to reveal how certain empirical phenomena may be employed, altered, or transformed to serve the goals of men. They are prompted by some conception, implicit or explicit, of what should or ought to obtain in the realm of events. Ideally, they provide both citizens and scientists with instrumental principles for remaking social reality.[5]

The conceptual differences separating the three forms of sentences are not absolute. When changing contexts are specified, most conditional sentences will be found to contain mixtures of both positively and negatively valued elements. The variables, C's, O's, and R's, may be conceptually interchangeable; O's become C's, C's are transformed into R's, and earlier R's are sometimes equivalent to the C's of a later phase of the "same" social problem. Inevitably, the evaluation of each variable is determined by the particular kinds of interests predominant in its formulation.

APPLICATIONS TO WHITE-COLLAR CRIME

To exemplify the usefulness of conditional sentences we turn to an examination of E. H. Sutherland's *White Collar Crime*.[6] On the well-founded assumption that Sutherland's primary interest was to provide a scientific description of the conditions within which violations of corporation law occur his acts are partially reducible to the sentence:

> *If* conditions (C's) of differential association, social disorganization, restraint of trade, etc. obtain *and* operations (O's) including unbiased observations, systematic classifications, etc., be initiated, *then* consequences (R's) involving violation of corporation laws will probably be found to occur.

[4] Otherwise expressed, positively valued C's are those conditions which contribute toward or support a desired result; negatively valued C's are those conditions which interfere with or are opposed to a desired result.

[5] Perhaps the reader will find it helpful to hold an analogous terminology in mind: conditional sentences of the *First Form* include "identifying" operations only; conditional sentences of the *Second* and *Third Forms* include both "identifying" and "prescriptive" operations. "Identifying" operations represent relationships between conditions and results within a problematic situation. "Prescriptive" operations represent instrumentally altered relationships between conditions and results within a problematic situation. When first introduced, they may be viewed as *added* conditions or results; after they become an integral part of the situation they may be viewed as belonging to, or acting in concert with, the *given* conditions or results of that situation. That all sentences are in one sense "identifying" and in another sense "prescriptive" is not at issue here.

[6] Holt, Rinehart and Winston, 1949.

Here we have an example of a conditional sentence of the *First Form*. Since its O's are largely descriptive it differs from the O's of the *Second* and *Third Forms* which are largely instrumental in character. The latter assume descriptive O's at the initial stage of inquiry.

By replacing descriptive O's with instrumental O's in the *First Form* of the conditional sentence, the problem of white-collar crime can be stated to conform with Sutherland's actual findings:

> If conditions (C's) of differential association and social disorganization obtain *and* operations (O's) including restraint of trade, etc. be initiated, *then* consequences (R's) involving violation of corporation laws, will probably be found to occur.

In this statement C's and R's are not explicitly asserted as positively or negatively valued. If corporation executives positively value social disorganization (C's) and legal violations (R's) they may do so only as necessary conditions for the maximization of profits, a highly valued goal.[7] By substituting this goal for R's in the context of the conditional sentence above, the C's and O's supported by corporation executives can be expressed as follows:

> *If* conditions (C's) of differential association and social disorganization obtain *and* operations (O's) including restraint of trade, etc. be achieved, *then* consequences (R's) involving the maximization of profits will probably be found to occur.

This is a conditional sentence of the *Second Form* since the majority of C's are positively valued. It may be contrasted with a conditional sentence of the *Third Form* in which the majority of C's are negatively valued. The following example is a conceivable reconstruction of the problem from the point of view of a group of citizen-reformers.

> *If* conditions (not-C's) of differential association and social disorganization obtain *but* operations (O's) including public control of corporate industries, etc. be achieved, *then* consequences (R's) involving obedience to federal laws will probably be found to occur.

In the preceding example, not-C's may be displaced by O's which eventually function as C's.

Although the conditional sentences described herein are of similar abstract form, each applies to concretely dissimilar elements. Moreover, their empirical content is of such a character as to pose a basic ethical dilemma. Assuming the absence of operations for implementing the *Third Form*, accurate description of the *First Form* will contribute toward the

---

[7] Various interpretations of executive behavior may be appropriate. For instance, "violation of corporation laws" (R's) may be construed as negatively valued C's which corporation executives seek to supplant by positively valued O's directed toward "legalization of restraint of trade." Such an interpretation can be represented as follows: "*If* conditions (C's) of differential association and social disorganization obtain *and* operations (O's) including legalization of restraint of trade, etc., be achieved, *then* consequences (R's) involving the maximization of profits will probably be found to occur."

solution of problems of the *Second Form*. This conclusion follows from the closer similarity of content found in the *First* and *Second Forms* when both are compared with the content of the *Third Form*. Since the content of the *First Form* offers descriptive knowledge of white-collar crime, it will be most useful to those disposed to act upon the information it provides. If, in addition, this information suggests suitable operations for implementing the content of the *Second Form*, utilization by such a group is even more likely.[8] Therefore, it must be concluded that any scientist unwillingness to accept the problem of the *Third Form* unwittingly aids corporation executives and forestalls solution of the problem as viewed by citizen-reformers.

As previously indicated, sentences of all forms except the *First* are explicitly predicated on the assumption that the consequences (R's) predicted by scientists are outcomes of modes of action proposed for purposes of achieving, altering, or ameliorating human goals. Indeed, it may be contended that no scientifically meaningful consequence is so unqualifiedly inevitable or inalterable as to be devoid of all practical significance. Every meaningful consequence must make some difference in the activity of the scientist and such a difference is subsequently reflected in altered outcomes.[9] Of course, when conditions and modes of action require sacrifices of values beyond those realized from proposed outcomes, the problem must be restated in new terms.[10]

OTHER FORMS

OF THE CONDITIONAL SENTENCE

The three forms of conditional sentence described thus far are among the simplest and most familiar to be found in sociology. They are based

---

[8] It is, of course, true that the *First Form* of the conditional sentence could be used with equal facility to describe law-abiding operations. But such operations are not usually taken as problematic by social scientists.

[9] If this assumption is granted perhaps the most fundamental questions for research become: Which (sets of) conditions are problematically relevant, i.e., determinable *and* alterable, in the light of modes of action known from past experience to be appropriate for realizing a desired result? Which modes of action, O_1, O_2, O_3, O_n, should be given test priority at successive stages of information about alternative conditions and results? Or, how can the efficacy of possible modes of action for producing a desired result be assessed prior to their implementation in concrete situations? No doubt, the relationships which bind conditions, modes of action, and results together are inferences drawn from generalizations of experience and ordered in terms of rough estimates of probable association. As long as the reality from which these generalizations are derived is believed to exist, inferences concerning the reliability of previously tested modes of action will seem warranted.

[10] One such value that some pragmatists believe must not be sacrificed is the ideal of continuously closer approximations to truth. For instance, if the suggested solution to a particular problem is presented in terms of conditions and operations which would prevent the continuance of scientific research, then it must be rejected even though these conditions and operations would guarantee, for the present time, a maximum degree of predictability. From this position it follows that "authoritarian" resolutions to social problems like crime, which would be inimical to the continuance of criminology, should not be fostered.

primarily upon an elementary distinction between positive and negative
C's. The introduction of parallel distinctions for O's and R's would
permit the construction of a wider variety of forms. If, for instance,
subclasses of C's and not-C's, O's and not-O's, R's and not-R's, were
specified, innumerable combinations and permutations of the conditional
sentence could be derived. Quite obviously, a full exploration of these
possibilities cannot be made in a brief paper. However, partial testimony
to the latitude of conditional sentences can be provided by attempts to
describe some commonly recognized types of social problems. A summary
list of ancillary definitions for variables and connectives precedes the
detailing of general cases, illustrations, and corresponding logical forms.

Ancillary definitions

Let C's, O's, and R's signify variables of either positive or neutral
value. Let not-C's, not-O's, and not-R's signify variables of negative value.
Let the subscripts 1, 2, 3 signify different types of C's, O's, and R's.
Let "and" signify the conjunction of compatible variables. Let "but"
signify the conjunction of incompatible variables.

General cases[11]

1. The case in which negative conditions lead to joint positive action
that produces positive results.
   Illustration: If state administration opposes programs of penal reform
but community councils promote objective studies of public needs and
local newspapers publicize their conclusions, then penal reforms will
come into being.
   Logical Form: If not-C but O_1 and O_2 then R[12]

2. The case in which incompatible conditions lead to positive action
that produces positive results.
   Illustration: If citizens of the state support a program of penal reforms
but state legislators promote probationary measures, then newspapers
will sponsor "objective" studies of prison life and penal reforms will come
into being.
   Logical Form: If C_1 but C_2 then O and if O then R

[11] These cases are simplified archetypes of situations depicted not only in newspaper and
magazine literature but in the writings of professional criminologists. Although their constituent
elements are recurrent in political communities their frequency of appearance is unknown.
[12] Since the positive values of one group may be equivalent to the negative values of another
group, a separate set of subscripts could be provided for each. Subscripts of this kind are omitted
because they are cumbersome in an elementary treatment. Moreover, the reader can easily determine
which group interest is accented from the context of the statement. In our first case the group interest
of those who support penal reform is accented. The cognate form for those who oppose penal
reform is: If C but not-O_1 and not-O_2 then not-R.

3. The case in which positive conditions and positive action produce positive results of one type accompanied by negative results of another type.

Illustration: If citizens of the state support a program of penal reforms and newspapers publicize such reforms, then they will come into being but state taxes will be raised.

Logical Form: If C and O then R_1 but not-R_2

4. The case in which under positive conditions one or another alternative to positive action produces its corresponding positive result.

Illustration: If citizens of the state support a program of penal reforms and newspapers publicize the advantages of occupational training for prisoners, then occupational training will come into being; but if, in the absence of this publicity, a government commission supports group therapy for prisoners, then group therapy will come into being.

Logical Form: If C_1 and O_1 alone then R_1 but if C_1 and O_2 alone then R_2

5. The case in which positive action prevents negative conditions from producing negative results.

Illustration: If citizens of the state support a program of penal reforms but state legislators fosters interminable "studies" of public needs, then penal reforms will come into being.

Logical Form: If O but not-C then R[13]

6. The case in which research operations describe negative conditions productive of negative results thereby contributing to positive conditions productive of positive results.

Illustration: Prison research in criminal behavior describes "make work" as conditions productive of prisoner dissatisfaction and consequently fosters creative work productive of prisoner satisfaction.

Logical Form: If O then "not-C then not-R" and if "not-C then not-R" then C and if C then R

7. The case in which invalid operations show that positive conditions are productive of negative results whereas valid operations show that negative conditions are productive of negative results.

Illustration: Unrepresentative samples show that ethnic membership is a general determinant of delinquency whereas representative samples show that gang association is a general determinant of delinquency.

Logical Form: If not-O then "C and if C then not-R" but if O then not-C and if not-C then not-R

---

[13] The partial interchangeability of C's and O's described in earlier paragraphs of this paper becomes evident when positive conditions are stated as operations.

8. The case in which invalid operations show that negative conditions are productive of positive results whereas valid operations show that positive conditions are productive of positive results.

Illustration: Informal observations show that strict discipline is productive of orderly behavior whereas controlled experiments show that group rewards are productive of orderly behavior.

Logical Form: If not-O then "not-C and if not-C then R" but if O then C and if C then R[14]

Additional forms of the conditional sentence could be constructed from finer discrimination in meaning or word usage. Following upon an inventory of forms, descriptive of the role of social innovators in major problem areas, principles of administrative policy, action rules and theories of scientific control could be stipulated. Responsible "social engineering" might then become an integral part of sociology.

THE QUESTION OF UNIFORMITY

Any attempt to provide an adequate account of uniform association among variables—in this case, C's, O's, and R's—is bound to give rise to some of the most difficult issues in the methodology of theory construction. The customary view holds that uniform association is dependent upon establishing the necessary and sufficient conditions for the occurrence of a given result. Applied to our variables, a *necessary* condition is any C or O without which a given R does not occur. In other words, if C or O does not occur then R does not occur and if R occurs then C or O occurs. A *sufficient* condition is any C or O with which a given R does occur. In other words, if C or O occurs then R occurs and if R does not occur then C or O does not occur. Thus, the establishment of uniform association between C's, O's, and R's can be said to depend upon the discovery of all those C's and O's that are together necessary and sufficient for the occurrence of R's. This interpretation assumes, however, that there is no plurality of conditions, no independent sets of sufficient conditions. If plurality of conditions is assumed there can be no sure way of determining whether other C's and O's will be found, on future occasions, to be sufficient for the occurrence of R. On the assumption of plurality of conditions, uniform association is no longer certain and the important

---

14 I am grateful to William T. Parry for proposing that logical distinctions between belief and knowledge be introduced. The latter cases may then be written as follows:

    6. If O then "if not-C then not-R" is known and (if this is known then) C and if C then R.

    7. If not-O then "C and if C then not-R" is believed but if O then "not-C and if not-C then not-R" is known (i.e., believed and true).

    8. If not-O then "if not-C then R" is believed but if O then "if C then R" is known (i.e., believed and true).

question becomes, "What level of *probable* association among variables is sufficient to meet criteria of theoretical significance?

Acceptable "replies" to this question appear to depend upon the precise degree of association among variables which is believed necessary for either defining or resolving particular problems. For instance, if the association between "restraint of trade" and "misrepresentation in advertising" is found to occur in at least 75 percent of the cases examined, and this frequency represents the degree of association believed necessary to justify reformative measures of a certain kind (O's), then such association may be taken as significant. In subsequent cases, absence of uniformity will then be defined as frequencies of association below the seventy-fifth percentile. In these cases, it is not specific C's and R's but specific proportions in certain samples of C's and R's which constitute exceptions and hence disconfirming evidence of significant uniformity. For illustration, assume that R's are constant and C's and O's are gradually introduced until an acceptable degree of probability (P) is achieved. Taking the latter as P_6 and assuming a simple notational correspondence between the introduction of successive units of C's and O's on the one hand, and additional increments of P on the other hand, note that:

$$\text{If } C_1 \text{ and } O_1, \text{ then probability } P_2 \text{ that } R$$

and

$$\text{If } C_1 \ C_2 \ C_3 \ C_4 \text{ and } O_1 \ O_2, \text{ then probability } P_6 \text{ that } R$$

Accordingly, $C_1 \ C_2 \ C_3 \ C_4$ and $O_1 \ O_2$ are, in combination, the sufficient conditions for predicting the occurrence of R. They could not, however, be regarded as the necessary conditions for R, unless it could be established (with acceptable degrees of probability) that these and only these conditions in their particular arrangement give rise to R.

Although it is always possible that other C's and O's than those initially found may be sufficient to bring about a desired result, there is some antecedent probability that as sets of C's or O's are multiplied the necessary conditions for a particular R can be more clearly established. The possibility that the familiar principle "same causes, same effects" (whenever certain C's and O's, then certain R's) will be confirmed for any problem is a function of the degree to which all possible kinds and combinations of C's and O's have been tested for their efficacy in producing R's.

Nevertheless, for pragmatic reasons not all possible kinds and combinations of C's and O's may be viewed as equally significant. Concern for practical application may dictate the expediency of regarding only those C's which are most easily observable (i.e., noticeable because dynamic), or most amenable to operational control (i.e., alterable by O's), as relevant. In this sense the customary distinction between precipitating and dispositional causes can be quite useful. Moreover, if the relation between sets of C's, or between sets of C's and sets of R's, is regarded as one of functional correlation, the question of temporal priority is irrelevant and all that can be said of one set of C's can be said of other sets of C's and R's; the designation of C's and R's is entirely a matter of practical expediency.

The added consideration, that C's, O's, and R's may vary in degree of generality-specificity, is not without pragmatic consequences. The more general (widespread in occurrence) the R to be predicted, the greater the antecedent probability of its appearance following upon the introduction of amost any C or O. Given a narrower range of phenomenal instances which can be taken as exceptions to it, there are fewer occasions for disconfirming the relation in question. If, however, the problem at hand calls for the prediction of highly particular (infrequent) instances of R, the antecedent probability of any C or O contributing to their occurrence decreases with every increase in the instances which can be taken as exceptions to it.

From a methodological standpoint, the uniform association of C's, O's, and R's is a generalization of the observed conjunctions of specific c's, o's and r's wherein a repetition of the latter leads, by inference, to construction of the former. Despite the errors which may ensue from "jumping levels," i.e., in connecting C's with c's, O's with o's, or R's with r's, there are heuristic advantages. New kinds of associations may be discovered and if precautions are taken to search out disconfirming instances social problems may be clarified with economy in time and energy.

FROM INTERACTION TO TRANSACTION

The previous analysis suggests that conditional sentences arise from a framework of interacting variables—"separated components allotted irregular degrees of independence." Within this framework C's are interpreted as antecedent states or processes, R's as consequential states or processes, and O's as conceptual or manual manipulations of such states or processes. But to insist on construing conditional sentences in this way is to lose sight of the truism that all such variables are artifacts of analysis. Motivated by considerations of convenience or simplicity, we often attempt to handle phenomena as if they appeared before us in readily distinguishable units. We fail to realize that even though our concepts must remain relatively stable the phenomena symbolized by them are constantly undergoing change. Once, however, we accept the necessity of adapting concepts to phenomena, procedures can be sought for increasing their flexibility. A preliminary step in this direction is taken when we begin to handle C's, O's, and R's as reciprocal phases of a continuous process, as occurrences or events which interpenetrate *transactionally*.[15] Then any given variable, C, O, or R, can be viewed in the perspective of one moment of time as condition and in the perspective of some other moment of time as operation or result.

The following stipulations attempt to clarify what has just been said about the changing phases of a social problem. The fixity of meanings connoted by interactional concepts is not eliminated by reduced and transactional meanings are emphasized. A complete transactional interpretation would probably admit of greater circularity within definitions than is provided below:

I. *Transactional Conditions*
   1. Positive, C's sustaining or producing valued R's
   2. Negative, C's impairing or preventing valued R's
   3. Controllable, C's amenable to alteration by valued O's
   4. Uncontrollable, C's not amenable to alteration by valued O's

II. *Transactional Operations*
   1. Positive, O's sustaining or producing valued R's
   2. Negative, O's impairing or preventing valued R's
   3. Controllable, O's amenable to alteration by valued C's
   4. Uncontrollable, O's not amenable to alteration by valued C's

III. *Transactional Results*
   1. Positive, R's sustaining or producing valued C's
   2. Negative, R's impairing or preventing valued C's
   3. Controllable, R's amenable to alteration by valued O's
   4. Uncontrollable, R's not amenable to alteration by valued O's

Insofar as C's, O's, and R's elicit latent dispositions in one another or supply the situational requirements for organizing social problems, they are "conditional" in quality. Insofar as they direct activity in selected ways or actualize the potentialities of one another they are "operational" in quality. And insofar as each determines the factual admissibility and relevance of the others for resolving social problems they are "resultant" in quality. Even so-called "final" R's are never final in the sense that they may have no remote connection with future events fraught with problematic issues. There is at least a small probability that they will perform the role of C's or O's in some unforeseen situation. Briefly, then, since each variable circumscribes the functions which each performs, indicates ways of actualizing the potentialities of each, and contributes toward a

---

[15] The basic reference for the concept of transaction is J. Dewey and A. F. Bentley, *Knowing and the Known*, The Beacon Press, 1949.

settled appraisal of the evidential outcome of each, they are one and all "conditions," "operations," and "results."

Toward a transactional definition of uniformity

Although the difficulties of formulating a generalized transactional definition of uniformity are great there is no a priori reason for believing they are altogether insurmountable. With the addition of two new terms, approximations to a transactional account can be proposed. To our previous repertory of symbols we add E's (Entities) and S's (Situations).

E_1, E_2, E_3, E_n	Entities or things, phenomenal or hypothetical elements which are assumed to remain constant within limited situations.
C_1, C_2, C_3, C_n	Conditions, states, aspects, phases or reactions of any E, which when empirically described, express the actual range of its dispositions, and when hypothetically derived, express the potential range of its dispositions.
S_1, S_2, S_3, S_n	Situations, fields or complexes of entities and conditions in the environment, i.e., all recognized but unspecified E's and C's bordering upon or in transaction with specified E's and C's.
O_1, O_2, O_3, O_n	Operations, modes of action, overt performances (manual manipulations) made upon E's, C's, or S's in such a way as to elicit or produce new alterations (changes) in the C's of one or more E's.
Generalized Transactional Definition	If E_1, a thing in state C_1, is continuous with E_2, a thing in state C_2, then the introduction of operations O_1 will produce a change in E_1 to C_3 together with a change in E_2 to C_4.
Empirical Illustration	If a "victim" of established gullibility associates with a "criminal perpetrator" habituated to successful cheating, then the operation of card playing will produce change in the victim toward financial depletion, together with change in the perpetrator toward financial repletion.[16]

[16] Adapted from an incident cited by Hans Von Hentig, *The Criminal and His Victim*, Yale University Press, 1948, p. 389. Von Hentig's analysis of the "subject-object relation" in the form of the criminal and his victim is suggestive of the potential fruitfulness of this kind of formulation. He writes: "In a sense the victim shapes and moulds the criminal. The poor and ignorant immigrant has bred a peculiar kind of fraud. Depressions and wars are responsible for new forms of crimes because new types of potential victims are brought into being. It would not be correct nor complete to speak of a carniverous animal, its habits and characteristics, without looking at the prey on which it lives. In a certain sense the animals which devour and those that are devoured complement each other. Although it looks one-sided as far as the final outcome goes, it is not a totally unilateral form of relationship. They work upon each other profoundly and continually, even before the moment of disaster. To know one we must be acquainted with the complementary partner." Pp. 384–385.

The accompanying illustration simplifies reality since it assumes that certain environmental E's and C's (that is, S's) are not undergoing change. Thus, alterations in the relationship of variables in time and place are not made explicit. Still, the illustration suggests that analysis of a social problem may feasibly begin with two or more entities found to be in mutual transaction. Granting such a possibility, the transactions subsumed under the generalized definition may be stated in several forms. By introducing positively and negatively valued S's, E's, and C's and interpreting predicted R's as equivalent to C's or E's which occur with varying probabilities, this definition can be restated to conform with the *Second* and *Third Forms* of the conditional sentence:

Second Form

If S_1, E_1, C_1 and O_1, then P_i that R_1

If S_1, E_2, C_2 and O_2, then P_j that R_2

If S_1, E_3, C_3 and O_3, then P_k that R_3

Third Form

If not-S_1, not-E_4, not-C_4, but O_4, then P_i that R_4

If not-S_1, not-E_5, not-C_5, but O_5, then P_j that R_5

If not-S_1, not-E_6, not-C_6, but O_6, then P_k that R_6

In addition to these forms of conditional sentence two others are implied by sociologists who emphasize the unanticipated consequences of operations which are meant either to reinforce positively valued conditions or to counteract negatively valued conditions. The following forms are descriptive of the negatively valued results of such operations:

Fourth Form

If S_1, E_7, C_7 and O_7, then P_i that not-R_7

If S_1, E_8, C_8 and O_8, then P_j that not-R_8

If S_1, E_9, C_9 and O_9, then P_k that not-R_9

Fifth Form

If not-S_1, not-E_{10}, not-C_{10}, but O_{10}, then P_i that not-R_{10}

If not-S_1, not-E_{11}, not-C_{11}, but O_{11}, then P_j that not-R_{11}

If not-S_1, not-E_{12}, not-C_{12}, but O_{12}, then P_k that not-R_{12}

Within the above forms, those operational hypothese which symbolize the persistent tendency of selected aspects of phenomena to hang together are represented by the same numerical subscripts. It is assumed that positively and negatively values S's, E's and C's are, with certain degrees of probability, typically conjoined with positively and negatively valued R's. The question of uniformity is in principle determinable from P. Simplicity of forms is maintained by not combining positively and negatively valued notations within statements.

Quite obviously, these forms of the conditional sentence do not exhaust the full range of theoretical possibilities. More combinations of E's, C's, O's, R's, and S's, than those listed may be found to apply to a particular problem. For example, it is not unlikely that in some concrete situation "S_2, E_5, C_3, and O_2" may be equivalent to, say, "Not-S_3, E_4, C_8 but O_4," insofar as both are found to produce the same R or not-R.

General applications

Regardless of linguistic preferences the study of social problems requires consideration of positive and negative R's. Should criminologists specify R's and not-R's by referring to the presence or absence of common offenses: Criminal Homicide, Rape, Robbery, Aggravated Assault, Burglary, Larceny, and Auto Theft? Should they specify R's and not-R's by referring to a typology of political, ordinary, white-collar, and professional criminals?[17] Should the specification of not-R's point to the violation of conduct norms rather than the violation of law?[18] In this case, criminal action would be treated as an aspect of nonconforming behavior within society. How should O's, the means of "treating" juvenile delinquents and adult criminals, be specified? By discovery and control of "predelinquents" through child guidance clinics? By "character education" in the public schools? By organization of neighborhood clubs or area projects? By probationary or parole supervision? By establishing institutional communities? Or through some portion or combination of these?

Not unlike R's and O's, the specifications of C's and S's are fraught with numerous difficulties. If C's are taken as states or reactions of the potential criminal and S's as patterned aspects of environmental transactions, then, again, a number of crucial questions can be posed. Should C's be used to specify "heredity"; physical traits and pecularities; mental deficiency and abnormality; endocrine functioning, or others? Should S's be used to specify family factors; urban, rural, and regional differences; migration and social mobility; economic deprivation, ethnic and class status, cultural values or others?

Perhaps a workable choice of analytic categories can be developed out of new departures in semantics and the psychology of language. On the claim that all criminogenic situations and conditions are either immediately or remotely continuous—in transaction with one another[19]— it may be assumed that such partitioning and organization of phenomena

[17] Cf. Walter C. Reckless, *The Etiology of Delinquent and Criminal Behavior*, Social Science Research Council, Bulletin No. 50, 1943, p. 91.
[18] See Thorsten Sellin, *Culture Conflict and Crime*, Social Science Research Council, Bulletin No. 41, 1938, pp. 32 ff.
[19] There is substantial support for the contrary assumption of gaps or discontinuities "in nature." However, the loci of such discontinuities are often discoverable through painstaking efforts to dispose of them via operations which are based upon the assumption of continuity.

as occur in science are outcomes of goal-oriented perceptual frameworks. This being the case, sociological theorists should experiment ingeniously with the symbolization and ordering of phenomena which come under their purview. If they made greater effort to undercut the surface phenomena described by conventional categories with the end in view of delineating hypothetical entities of high constancy and wide operational utility, they might come closer to realizing scientific objectives. For instance, in place of conventional definition of intelligence this variable might be redefined in such a way as to establish its relevance for the context of conditions in which the criminal behaves. If intelligence is a function of cultural conditions, and the criminal learns his behavior through "differential association" or "subcultural differentiation," then perhaps some items in the standard tests should be omitted and new content added. Likewise, differential performance tests might be constructed to measure the specialized skills of the criminal.

The same line of thought may well apply to personality characteristics. Which portions of the customary measures of aggression or "psychopathic personality" are constant and which changing? The changing portions may reflect psychiatric or cultural biases and be inoperative within the context of the delinquent gang or criminal community. Following this line of thought, perhaps the construct "delinquency area" should be reconstituted as new variables joined to one another through hypotheses standing as logical nexus between S's, C's, O's and R's. If "area" were defined in terms of cognitive and material conditions of life it is conceivable that more useful operational hypotheses for controlling criminal behavior would ensue. These hypotheses would, of course, have to be linked with a corps of fundamental assumptions from which deductions of conditional sentences could be made.[20]

Apart from the issue of designating appropriate conceptual categories, there is the practical difficulty of finding appropriate occasions for directing operational hypotheses toward the confluence of C's, S's, O's, and R's. Usually the selection and application of such hypotheses are made without reference to their place in an analytic scheme of situational and explanatory conditions. Innocent of theoretical knowledge, representatives of reformative institutions and social service agencies are given responsibility for rehabilitating criminals. When the social scientist is called upon to contribute it is often assumed that the cultural and communal conditions of criminal action cannot be changed. As a consequence, conceptual categories are not balanced and adjusted to one another; ill-fitting *operations* are conjoined with inappropriate *conditions* to produce *results* of questionable scientific value.

[20] For an overview of current assumptions consult M. E. Wolfgang, L. Savitz, and N. Johnston, *The Sociology of Crime and Delinquency*, Wiley, 1962.

What is required are large-scale efforts at testing various forms of S's, C's, O's, and R's under the auspices of socially responsible agencies with this singular purpose in mind. Heretofore, the major source of resistance against such efforts has come from persons in public life who do not believe that scientists should make ethically directed attempts to alter the goals of men.[21] Because criminologists have not been altogether free to uncover crucial conditions by means of scientific operations conducive to the concrete transformation of such conditions, they (the criminologists) have had to confine their analyses to plausible conjectures about the etiology of crime. Of course, in many cases social scientists cannot be held responsible for the limitations under which they work. But this they can do, viz., to assume that any examination of the conditions of criminal behavior without a corresponding assessment of the operations and goals (results) they wish to pursue is scientifically unsatisfactory. If they are not free to introduce concrete O's and R's, they should devote at least as much time to formulating plausible O's and R's as they have given to conjecturing about plausible S's and C's.

[21] For discussion of this issue see L. Gross, "Values and Theory of Social Problems," in A. Gouldner and S. M. Miller, *Applied Sociology: Opportunities and Problems,* New York: Free Press, 1965, pp. 383–397.

Theory and Values

The sociology of

BENJAMIN WALTER *knowledge and the*

problem of objectivity

O f treatises on the sociology of knowledge there is no end. The
catalogued list of scholarly books, articles, and monographs is
already immense and the conclusion is not yet in sight. Nor is there any
irrefragable consensus as to what the subject is all about; what its
distinctive "scope and method" is, to borrow the bland and evasive cliché
academic officials use in compiling college curricula. After an exhaustive
survey of the field, one student felt constrained to assert that it deals
with ". . . any exterior symbolic manifestation of an activity of the mind"
as it is related to ". . . social or cultural factors."[1] In statesmanlike fashion,
Robert K. Merton acknowledged the indistinct boundaries and indefinite
content by concluding that ". . . (the sociology of knowledge) . . . is
primarily concerned with the relations between knowledge and other
existential factors in society and culture . . . a more specific statement
will not serve to include the diverse approaches which have developed."[2]

[1] Jacques Maquet, *The Sociology of Knowledge: Its Structure and Its Relation to the Philosophy of Knowledge*, trans. John F. Locke (Boston: Beacon Press, 1951), pp. 4–5.
[2] Robert K. Merton, "The Sociology of Knowledge," in *Social Theory and Social Structure* (New

The admission is more illuminating than the description. Almost any succinct specification of the content of a given discipline is bound to be vague; I doubt that an economist would dare do the job for his field in fifty words. But although one economist may think that a second is doing some very bad economics, he will not deny that he is trying to be an economist. All use the same battery of techniques: the familiar supply and demand curves, national income accounts and the like. There are disputes, of course; but they concern the applicability of certain techniques for the analysis of specific problems, not the logical merit of the devices themselves. It is the common conception as to the method, content, and frontiers of such fields as economics and history that suffuses discussions about the sociology of knowledge with such an oddly apologetic air. There is no common core that serves as a point of reference, only a diffuse agglomeration of orientations huddled together and marching along under one ambiguous emblem in the disorderly manner of irregular soldiers rather than as a well-disciplined troop. All that binds the disparate approaches is a desire to account for the inter-relations between intellectual life and the "harder" aspects of the social order.[3] This labile declaration of intent, almost needless to say is hospitable to much diversity in analytic strategy. What is more, within its vague precincts no narrow academic specialty enjoys a proprietary monopoly: technical philosophers, speculative epistemologists, ethicists, economic historians, sociologists, anthropologists, historians, and political scientists—all these and more have made their contributions, some unwittingly.

York: Free Press, 1957), p. 456. Merton's essay was originally published in Georges Gurvitch and Wilbert E. Moore (eds.), *Twentieth Century Sociology* (New York: The Philosophical Library, 1945).

[3] A lengthy terminological note. To render *Wissenssoziologie* in conversational or even pedantic English is apparently a very awkward matter, according to those able to read Mannheim in German. It is clear the noun "science" cannot be translated as "*Wissens*" without leaving behind a sediment of unabsorbed residue. "*Wissens*" evidently embraces the speculations of the philosopher as well as the positive knowledge of the scientist, the creative art of the poet as well as the dull musings of the professor. Throughout this essay I shall use an idiomatic translation that does not appear to deal treacherously with the term as Mannheim uses it. I shall regard *Wissenssoziologie* as equivalent to the sociology of the intellectual. This proposal makes it clear that the actions of individuals, or collections of individuals, are the primary data for sociologists of knowledge. This gets rid of any metaphysical adhesions right off the mark, for we begin with actions, which have a comforting solidity, rather than with "Idea-systems" and "structures of thought," conceptions which are preternaturally ethereal and abstract.

We still of course have to define "intellectual." Let me stipulate that an intellectual is someone engaged in the production and distribution of controversial thought as set down in the written or spoken word. The key element is "controversial." A scientist who runs the same test over and over is not controversial; an Einstein is. The sociologist who grinds out the results of a sample survey is not controversial; his colleague who takes on Russell Kirk in the pages of *The New York Times* is. A general practitioner is not; the head of the American Medical Association is. Baudelaire is; the lady from Des Moines who would like to have a whirl at writing quatrains is not.

One more convention: "Intellectual" refers indifferently to all manner of men whose thought provokes controversy; "thinker," to controversial people in the arts and letters; and "scientists," to men in physics, biology, sociology and the like. This convention permits me to distribute my emphases without becoming tedious or unnecessarily ambiguous.

Small wonder, then, that the sociology of knowledge is such a Protean inquiry. Within it, we can detect remarkable differences in levels and styles of analysis to testify to its lability. It spans a continuum marked at the one end by fastidious biographical accounts of a single intellectual feat, and at the other by dazzling historical syntheses which encompass whole eras in their majestic sweep. A brief sketch, done with broad brush strokes, may help to fix the topography of the range, to give some idea of its profile and silhouette. We start with the individual intellectual. As a "discovery machine,"[4] he receives inputs of information from other actors in society. He communicates with workers within his chosen field; he receives encouragement from his sponsors or is frustrated by them; he absorbs, whether critically or unthinkingly, various systems of cosmological belief and supposition; and he has access to the funded positive and speculative knowledge of previous generations. At the same time he retains exclusive title to one component of experience which is at best only partially and imperfectly available to others: knowledge of his own past discoveries and failures. Some sociologists and historians of knowledge deal only with the individual thinker; they lift him from the nexus of social relations as though he represented a perfectly self-contained particle of human intellective activity. Others place him at the center of the web or close to it. But, apart from the tacit conviction that intellectual activity cannot be intelligibly explained as the singular acts of singular men, a unity of assumption gives way to a diversity of theories. In the resulting melange, some stress the influence of religion; others emphasize the political and economic currents which alternately propel and retard intellectual activity; and a third band discovers the antecedents of scientific progress in a state of mind that spurns any allegiance to mystical and non-rational values. Other scholars, perplexed by the implicit tension among all these points of view and alert to the incompleteness of each, anxiously attempt to pick out the separate strands, draw them together, and finally weave them into a synoptic theoretical tapestry.

However drastically they may vary in postulate and explanation, these schemata subscribe to a set of orientations that loosely tie them together in a common enterprise. At one level of concern, their aim is to explain the origins and diffusion of systematized knowledge by referring the entire process of intellectual activity to some exterior existential plane: class, party, the dominant mode of economic relations. In a less ambitious context, the sociology of knowledge becomes intellectual biography with a sociological twist, little different, let us say, from *Native Son*. It illuminates

---

[4] I borrow this mechanical metaphor from Edwin G. Boring. See his splendid article, "The Dual Role of the *Zeitgeist* in Scientific Activity," in Phillip G. Frank (ed.), *The Validation of Scientific Theories* (New York: Collier Books, 1961), pp. 187–198.

the way the mind of a thinker is molded by his social habitat. The pungently self-conscious autobiographies recounted in *The God That Failed* lie squarely within the sociology of knowledge tradition. So intellectual activity is seen, as it were, as the joint effect of a thinker's genetic endowment and the social forces that shape it.

Let us guard against some childish misinterpretations. No assumption of the sociology of knowledge compels the adoption of a feeble and contentious reductionism, the fatuous assumption that ethical systems, criteria of verification, political philosophies and notions of artistic excellence are *nothing but* pathetic reflexes set in motion by existential factors. The thinker is of course influenced by the currents that ebb and flow about him, but the products and by-products of his thought provide a bend and an impulse to the historical pattern itself. As soon as they enter the stream, they become part of the social stock of ideas that will influence other minds, even whole historical movements, later on. What is largely a dependent variable at one stage becomes part of a configuration that may be viewed as an independent variable at some future phase in history. In the grand academy of science, after all, the dead easily make up a majority.

No meretricious "group mind" or hypostasized *Zeitgeist* has to be confected in order to endow an empirically vacuous theory with specious coherence. Scientists, philosophers, and ordinary folk select alternatives, and these alternatives are not directly forced upon them by the social structure they inhabit. But they make their choices from an ensemble of techniques and suppositions available within their immediate social environment. If this makes humans something less than gods, it leaves them as something more than beasts. To chide the sociology of knowledge as though it were a piece of scholastic metaphysics is both vulgar and irrelevant, for no irresolubly metaphysical point of view is entailed by it. To be sure, sociologists of knowledge are infatuated by some extravagant metaphors—the *Zeitgeist* is one—but one may in principle effect a translation of such bits of metaphorical shorthand into an unequivocally descriptive vocabulary. Further, the sociology of knowledge takes no position on the so-called "determinism *vs.* free will" issue, unless "predictability" is mistakenly regarded as the conceptual equivalent of "logically necessitated," and everybody pretends that David Hume never lived.

Schematically, the sociology of knowledge begins with such facts as:

1. *X* believed that planets move in circular orbits around the sun,

or

2. *Y* believed that planets move in elliptical orbits with the sun at a focus.

The first sentence is true if X, an anonymous logical pronoun, is replaced by any one of a long series of names, Aristarchus of Samos being one. It is made false by replacing X with Ptolemy and Kepler. But if Kepler is inserted in place of Y in the second sentence, we now have a true statement. It is like the first proposition in one respect: it can be made false by inserting Ptolemy as the first word. These two sentences are only specimens. Actual work in the sociology of knowledge is rather more likely to begin with such statements as: "Edmund Burke believed in the existence of a mystical compact that bound current generations to those dead and gone," or "German trade unionists rejected the revolutionary strategy of Marx for a policy of social meliorism." The first of these sentences makes an assertion about the behavior of a discrete human being. We know much about his life, both from his own writings and those of his contemporaries. Records of his behavior are abundant. The second sentence is rather more like a chronicle than a statement. Under a little logical probing, it becomes a conjunction of a large number of separate facts that are analytically its constituents. It is an economical way of describing the average behavior of many obscure people about whom not much can accurately be known. Though the fact is much easier to validate than the chronicle, both are data for the sociologist of knowledge. Whether the strategic datum concerns the behavior of men prominent or obscure; of heroes or of scoundrels; of crackpots or of geniuses; of individuals or of aggregations—all this is of no logical concern. What is important is the fact of a man's belief, not its objective truth or error. How men come to err is no less important a matter than how men come to see things clearly. Both matters, as Bergmann has lucidly argued, are susceptible of casual explanation.[5]

The sociologist of knowledge, then, begins with facts that prick his interests. But he makes himself a job that is more ambitious than piecing together a compendious collection of statements that express facts, established and validated according to the canons of all reliable inquiry. Science is more than a summary. The sociologist of knowledge aims at providing an objective account of why and how human beings come to believe as they do. Substantive explanations do differ in content, as I tried to indicate above, but all of them proceed by means at the command of empirical science. This sketch is so piteously brief as to be almost a parody, and I do not wish to belittle the practical problems of marshalling sufficient data to sustain a particular theory against its rivals. However fragmentary, the sketch does indicate that there is nothing objectionably metaphysical about the sociology of knowledge. It deals with matters as

---

[5] Gustav Bergmann, "Ideology," *Ethics*, *LI* (April, 1951), 205–218.

factual as a baked potato on one level, or the second law of thermodynamics on the other.

These, cruelly abbreviated, are the positive theses of the sociology of knowledge. But there is more. In the long sweep of human history, ideas cherished and revered by the intellectuals of one generation have been derided and scorned by those of another. Not only do substantive theories vary between one generation and another and within the same historical period, but also divergent are the standards socially accepted for establishing truth: agreement with Scripture; revelation; the inspired word of seer, scribe, and prophet; the correspondence of statement with publicly observed fact, and whatnot. An exacting catalogue would require the labor of many scholars and fill many pages of print. Observation of this lush variety of criteria led many scholars, though not in any straightforward logical fashion, to an austere and uncomproming epistemological relativism. The premise of the epistemological thesis is the variability of criteria; its conclusion, the outright dismissal of all. As an oak grows from acorn, all ideas rise out of the social setting in which they take hold. It is therefore both puerile and arrogant to hold up a transcendant standard as though it could be valid for time. Each system of criteria for judging between truth and error springs up in its own time and place in a manner dictated by its own unique set of structural circumstances. The notion of scientific objectivity is itself an arbitrary emulsion of social conditions, regarded as proper in its time as soothsaying was by the Greeks who once stood before the gleaming towers of Troy.

I have confined this introduction to a small number of incontestable and noncommittal observations, for they are all I need to get down to the business at hand. In what follows, I will say next to nothing about the positive aspects of the sociology of knowledge. On this score, Merton's notes are still unsurpassed.[6] But I do wish to deal with two closely interrelated matters. First of all, I want to address the problem of objectivity, largely through a critique of Karl Mannheim. I single out Karl Mannheim because of the relentless and courageous way he reasons, even if the reasoning becomes only quixotically heroic at times. He is never willing to betray logic to polemical enthusiasm. If his reasoning manages to propel sensible premises toward odd consequences, he does not refrain from drawing them by washing his inconsistencies in a flood of impassioned rhetoric. To a practical man or to a fanatic trying to win general acclaim for his proposals, this is proof of sheer insanity. The professor is, after all, only a learned *Luftmensch*; what counts are results. Mannheim seldom resorts to *tu quoque* arguments, as vulgar Marxists are inclined to do. None of this will do for Mannheim, above all a philosopher

---

[6] Merton, *op. cit.*, pp. 439–455.

willing to wrestle with his own perplexity. His words are better than mine:

> If there are contradictions and inconsistencies . . . (it) . . . is not so much due to the fact that I overlooked them but because I make a point of developing a theme to its end even if it contradicts some earlier statements. . . . in this marginal field of human knowledge we should not conceal inconsistencies, so to speak covering up the wounds, but our duty is to show the sore spots in human thinking in its present stage.[7]

He would paint himself as honestly as Cromwell, warts and all. Mannheim states his case fully and often with incandescent clarity. Seldom does he seek refuge in ambiguous tricks. If all of this has redounded to his credit, it has also added to his pain. It is always the fate of definitive exposition to be staked out as a definitive target.

Secondly, there is a kindred matter, the so-called value problem. It runs like a red thread through the texture of Mannheim's argument, now partially hidden, now breaking visibly to the surface. But what was only tangential for Mannheim becomes central and distinct in the poignantly self-conscious and often touching methodological ruminations of social scientists. Their doubts, let it be noted, grow honorably from the knowledge they have accumulated about the behavior of man in society. Men, their study tells them, have willfully deluded themselves into believing their values and preferences and then hold that they view the world as it really is, entire and clear. Men kick dust in their own eyes and so far from complaining that they cannot see, obdurately insist that their vision is unimpaired. Then the social scientist, so to speak, gives himself over to an empathic identification with the objects in his scholarly field. The doubt this process inspires eventually gives rise to a pair of self-critical questions. They are: (1) Is it possible for a social scientist to select problems (2) Can the social scientist furnish objectively warranted explanations of social events?

I shall argue that the negative answer commonly given to the first question is true, but only tautologically or vacuously so. Therefore it cannot support the wholesale skepticism of, let us say, a Carl Becker[8] or a Charles A. Beard.[9] As for the second, I will reason that a negative answer would force a paralyzing self-contradiction, and therefore cannot be consistently maintained.

---

[7] Quoted from a letter sent to Professor Kurt Wolff. The letter is printed in full in Kurt H. Wolff, "The Sociology of Knowledge and Sociological Theory," in Llewellyn Gross (ed.), *Symposium on Sociological Theory* (New York: Harper & Row, 1959), pp. 571–572.

[8] Carl L. Becker, "What Are Historical Facts," *Western Political Quarterly, VIII* (September, 1955), 327–340. The article has been reprinted in an ingenious little reader edited by Hans Meyerhoff. See Hans Meyerhoff, *The Philosophy of History in Our Time* (Garden City, N.Y.: Doubleday Anchor, 1959), pp. 120–137.

[9] Charles A. Beard, "Written History as an Act of Faith," *The American Historical Review, XXXIX* (January, 1934), 219–229. The essay also appears in Meyerhoff, *op. cit.*, pp. 140–151.

KARL MANNHEIM: POSITIVE SOCIOLOGY
AND EPISTEMOLOGICAL RELATIVISM

First, there is the job of exposition. I shall not strain for any comprehensive or perfect coverage of Mannheim's writings, a task that is in any case impossible to accomplish within the compass of a few pages. All that I can sensibly attempt is to provide a selective inventory or recapitulation of some of Mannheim's crucial arguments. Since my ambitions are so limited, I am under no compulsive obligation to pursue his arguments over every dogleg and follow them into each cranny and crevice. The matter at hand is much less arduous: merely to stay on the main track and resist the temptation to be diverted by Mannheim's innumerable and often fascinating digressions.

Mannheim's analyses of the connections between social structure and knowledge have at least two components: one epistemological and the other empirical. In this epitome, I shall slight the latter and emphasize the former, by far the more important of the pair. To grant the epistemologicol thesis the center of the stage is not to make the claim that Mannheim's theory of knowledge and the substantive problems of the sociology of knowledge are unrelated. Quite the contrary: they are related; but in a very odd way. If the epistemological thesis is controverted, then and only then may one proceed to tackle the empirical issues of the sociology of knowledge with a clear head and an untroubled methodological conscience. The converse also holds. If Mannheim's epistemological doxies may in some sense receive justification, the sociologist of knowledge has no business whatever undertaking any positive inquiry. Investing the sociology of knowledge with a royal epistemological function would, if taken seriously, make the *empirical* sociology of knowledge a transparent absurdity. Mannheim's epistemological tenets, as I shall hope to show, interdict an empirical sociology of knowledge and, with it, all positive science whatever.

Our point of departure lies on familiar ground. Like Marx before him, Mannheim held that thought is largely epiphenomenal, froth on the water churned up by deeper currents flowing unperceived beneath.[10] We may vary the metaphor in a way that will show the distant precursors

---

[10] Mannheim leaves the relationship between social structure and thought strategically ambiguous. As he says, "Here we do not mean by 'determination' a mechanical cause-effect sequence: we leave the meaning of 'determination' open . . ." *Ideology and Utopia: An Introduction to the Sociology of Knowledge*, trans. Louis Wirth and Edward A. Shils (New York: Harcourt, Brace & World, 1936), p. 239.

Marx and Engles also equivocated. In a letter to Joseph Bloch written in 1890, Engels remarked, "According to the materialist conception of history the determining element in history is *ultimately* the production and reproduction in real life. More than this neither Marx nor I ever asserted. If therefore somebody twists this into the statement that the economic element is the *only* determining one, he transforms it into a meaningless, abstract and absurd phrase. . . . I cannot exempt many of the more recent 'Marxists' from this reproach, for the most wonderful rubbish has been produced from this quarter too." The emphasis is Engels', as is the sarcastic embrace of the quotation marks in the last sentence.

of Mannheim's position. The ideas men use to interpret their social existence are no more than flickering shadows cast up on the wall of the cave by the light of the fire burning unobserved outside. Those who have chained themselves within the cave are distracted by spectral images, and the hallucinated inmates impute to them a specious autonomy. But in this tenacious assumption they are cruelly received, for the phantasms they passionately affirm as real are nothing but insubstantial reflections of hidden casual agents, puffs of smoke a locomotive has left behind.

Mannheim's argument proceeds from a corpus of assumptions more or less current among German intellectuals of his time. By, so to speak, drawing aside the curtain of words in which his conceptions were draped, we can trace the pedigree and status of his suppositions. Mannheim joined Kant, Hegel, and Marx in taking for granted a dynamic dualism or polarity between the sentient observer and the world outside, between knower and known, between subject and object.[11] The word "and" in each pair does more than grammatically connect the words that flank it. The conjunction is material and existential. Although it is in principle impossible for any knowledge to transcend experience, a certain ir-resoluble portion of human knowledge is not directly inferred from experience. The external world, which includes other human beings in its ambience, is responsible for the primary or aboriginal data of sensation, but that is all. But this external world is radically unintelligible. The perceiver imposes order upon it through his categorial apparatus, the suppositional system he uses, sometimes reflectively but more often reflexively, to make sense of the world as it is presented to his senses. One sees through his eyes, but with his head. Hegel and Marx received this doctrine from Kant and infused it with a sort of historical dynamism. The human mind, both philosophers held, changes its suppositions through an endless dialectical interaction with the world outside. As historical circumstances change, so do the axioms men take for granted in inter-preting and adjusting to the social world about them. Patterns of thought poorly suited to the age are ridiculed, wither and finally disappear. Marx many times over records the way the rationalistic, calculating, anti-metaphysical thought of the ascendant bourgoisie first rubbed the super-natural glamor from the mystical ideas of feudalism and then erased them entirely. What thought cannot keep pace with the exigencies of living is bound to be destroyed, burst asunder by the social forces it cannot confine.[12]

---

[11] *Ibid.*, pp. 12 ff.

[12] The compatibility of these points of view with Dewey's "instrumentalism" "or pragmatism" is apparent. Mannhein, in fact, pays Dewey his homage. "Indeed we may say that for modern man pragmatism has, so to speak, become in some respects, the inevitable and appropriate outlook, and that philosophy in this case has simply appropriated this outlook and from it proceeded to its logical conclusion." *Ibid.*, p. 65. Mannheim seems also to have absorbed the pragmatists' criterion for judging between true propositions and false: "A theory is then wrong if in a given practical situation it uses concepts and categories which, if taken seriously, would prevent man from *adjusting himself at that historical state*" (p. 85, italics supplied). The historicist overtones are apparent.

In Mannheim's case, it is important to emphasize that the world outside the mind is never regarded as a sheer creation of the mind. The data of the external world are not formless or utterly insubstantial, like wisps of ectoplasm. Rather, what the external world presents to the mind is like a piece of statuary not yet hardened in the kiln. Since it retains its plasticity, it can be further shaped according to the predilections of the artisan. Nonetheless the clay is not infinitely malleable. The sculptor is forever impeded by certain refractory characteristics he is powerless to alter: the sheer size of the lump of clay, its frangibility or its brittleness, and the like. These intrinsic characteristics of the raw material enforce limitations upon his reconstructions, and he cannot completely evade them. Within similar limits, the inquiring mind imposes order, coherence, and systems of relations and relevancies upon the raw material presented in conceptually uninterpreted streams of experience. In Mannheim's words:

> All knowledge is oriented toward some object and is influenced by the nature of the object with which it is preoccupied. But the mode of the approach to the object is dependent upon the nature of the knower . . . since in order to be transmuted into knowledge, every perception is and must be ordered into categories. The extent, however, to which we can order and express our experience in such conceptual forms is, in turn, dependent upon the frames of reference which happen to be available at a given historical moment.[13]

Thus the mind is active, even creative. It does more than notice and register impressions; it has an unequivocally constitutive function, one of conferring structure and of imposing value. The "categories" that differentially filter and shape perception are the sedimentary deposits of social existence. There is no such thing as an abstract contemplating mind knowing only immaculate perceptions. Like Marx and Pareto before him, Mannheim is scornful of men who would interpret networks of social relationships by categories and theories presented as valid for all times and places. Such calm Olympian detachment, says Mannheim, is delusory and pitiable. The thinker is, willy-nilly, bound by frames of reference that are determined by his social location. Mental contents are related to social structure as branch is related to root. We find that:

> Every epoch has its fundamentally new approach and characteristic point of view, and consequently sees the "same" object from a new perspective.[14]

and that:

> . . . it is no accident that today the *Gestalt* theory of perception, and the theories of morphology and characterology, etc., which constitute a scientific counter attack against positivistic methodology, are coming to the fore in an atmosphere which derives its *Weltanschauung* and its political outlook from neo-romanticism.[15]

[13] *Ideology and Utopia*, pp. 76–77.
[14] *Ibid.*, p. 243.
[15] *Ibid.*, p. 148.

The entire surge and thrust of Mannheim's position can be summed up in his own words:

> We must realize once and for all that the meanings which make up our world are simply an historically determined and continuously developing structure in which man develops, and are in no sense absolute. . . . Knowledge . . . is by no means an illusory experience, for ideology in its relational concept is not at all identical with illusion. Knowledge arising out of our experience in actual life situations, though not absolute, is knowledge none the less. . . . [A]ll the elements of meaning in a given situation have reference to one another and derive their significance from this reciprocal interrelationship in a given frame of thought.[16]

If, so to speak, we lift to one side Mannheim's baroque and ponderous vocabulary—noological, transvaluation and the rest of it—we can unearth the pivotal scrap of principle on which his entire epistemology turns. Mannheim makes much of a distinction between "particular" and "total" ideologies. Social life is intermittently disrupted by open strife among various groups based on party, guild, or class allegiances. These antagonistic divisions, and the factors that engender them, are not the creations of intellectuals. They result from fundamentally exogenous sources: the rise of the trading and manufacturing bourgeoisie; the displacement of human labor by machines, and whatnot. But the intelligentsia invade the warring camps and become their advocates and pamphleteers, placing their intellectual skills in the service of a secular vision. They supply their clients with ostensibly impersonal and disinterested justifications for their tangible ambitions, with slogans and rhetoric to incite indignation and outrage, and, most important of all, with a pungent sense of historical mission.[17]

Since they bend their intellectual talents to hostile causes, one wing of the intelligentsia is bound to conflict with another. When they do, each band will accuse its opponents of being stalking horses, of weaving a tissue of deceitful abstractions to mask the goals they advance and the grudges they bear. At this stage, the "particular ideology" has been exposed.[18] The function it performs is essentially one of rationalization, and to puncture one is to bring to light the interests it shelters. The disclosure of particular ideologies is, of course, a venerable strategy in political and ethical disputation. Thrasymachus, a Sophist from Chalcedon,

---

[16] *Ibid.*, p. 76.

[17] *Ibid.*, pp. 141–143. Joseph A. Schumpeter offers a parallel analysis in his *Capitalism, Socialism and Democracy*, 3rd ed. (New York: Harper & Row, 1950), pp. 153–154. Both Schumpeter and Mannheim note the tendency for radicalized intellectuals, many of them of unmistakably bourgeois origin, to become more strident and zealous than their host group. In one sense they are trying to live down their previous social affiliations, a sort of inverted social-climbing.

The word "client" should not be mistaken for "patron." On the contemporary scene, university-based intellectuals enlist their skills in behalf of groups that do not provide them with livelihoods. In the past century, reformist labor leaders sneered at the nebulous *Kathedersozialismus* of the college professors who urged them to forego expediential compromises for the final victory of socialism.

[18] *Ideology and Utopia*, pp. 49–50.

rebuked the affable Socrates by claiming that what men affect to call justice is no more than the "interest of the stronger," and that all ethical discussions are an interminable series of highblown irrelevancies that conspire to evade this elemental fact. The discovery and delineation of a particular ideology serves two closely intertwined goals; one urgent and practical, the other more distant and academic. The immediate aim is to abuse and discredit an opponent by pointing to his suppressed motivations; the more academic, to trace varieties of social thought to their existential correlates.

At this stage, rational criticism is still possible. However mordantly intellectual adversaries disagree, however sharply they accuse the other side of dissembling, they do not renounce shared criteria for recognizing truth and for stigmatizing error. They strive to win over their opponents by superior logic and fact; this failing, to convince a broader audience they are correct and their opponents wrong. It is essential that the opponents adhere to the objectivity and neutrality of a set of standards that transcend factional dispute. Otherwise disputation can never rise above obloquy and all argument becomes an ugly display of febrile name-calling. When these criteria themselves are shown to be the ideational partners of social conditions, we have, in Mannheim's terms, hit upon the conception of a "total ideology." "The simple theory of ideology," writes Mannheim,

> develops into the sociology of knowledge. What was once the intellectual armament of a party is transformed into a method of research in social and intellectual history generally. To begin with, a given social group discovers the "situational determination" (*Seinsgebundenheit*) of its opponents' ideas. Subsequently the recognition of this fact is elaborated into an all-inclusive principle according to which the thought of every group is seen as arising out of its life conditions.[19]

The sociology of knowledge strives to show how the categorial frames of reference, the suppositions and postulates men use to impress order and coherence on the external world, are themselves rooted in social conditions. These postulates, especially the criteria for judging propositions, are regarded as logically unproblematic by those who cleave to them. Each socially generated system of postulates, each total ideology, is proclaimed by its adherents as indefectible, even truistic. Men unconsciously guided by radically divergent total ideologies are destined always to talk past one another, for their perspectives are incommensurable. They cannot speak the same language. The total ideology is the sociological equivalent of Kant's stock of privileged synthetic premises held to be true a priori, taken for granted without test or question. The components of the total ideology are for the most part implicit. Except in the recondite writings of a very few great men, they are seldom set

[19] *Ibid.*, p. 69.

forth in black and white for all to examine and criticize, but together they form an inescapable matrix for all discussion and criticism. Just as Kant held that all knowledge of the physical world had to be compatible with Euclidian geometry in order to be valid, so does the total ideology of any group insist that all lesser propositions be consistent with it.

It is at this juncture in his argument that Mannheim supplies the sociology of knowledge with its decisive epistemological function. Its task is nobler than the discovery of the existential correlates of disparate modes of thought and cognition. No matter how ingenious and informative, these correlations can never aspire to more than purely casual significance. They can tell us *only* that the emergence of different intellectual perspectives can be empirically traced to different social milieux. Mannheim correctly sees that establishing these correlations would be utterly irrelevant to validating the truth-value of the derivative propositions. To say that a bundle of propositions can be correlated with a definite configuration of social conditions produces no evidence whatever bearing on the truth of falsity of those proprositions. On a psychological rather than a sociological level, who would defend the audacious thesis that the state of Galileo's mind ought to be used as pertinent evidence in deciding the truth-claims of the heliocentric hypothesis? The heliocentric hypothesis may be casually related to Galileo's brain-states, but it is in no way implicated by anything that went on within his head. To separate the context of discovery from the context of justification is a critical principle Mannheim will not tolerate on the sociological level. Far from being extrinsic to any configuration of social conditions, standards of truth and justification, Mannheim affirms, are themselves implicated by the specific social conditions leading to their formulation. Positivism, to choose one example of many, represents nothing more than the technical refinement of perspectives inherent in the bourgeois-liberal outlook then dominating Europe. For positivism to claim some sort of privileged transcendence is a sign of invincible sociological arrogance.[20] Throughout, Mannheim insists there are no universal and perspectivally neutral standards that can be used to adjudicate the truth-claims of rival theories. There are no impartial criteria because:

> . . . every theory of knowledge is itself influenced by the form which science takes at the time and from which alone it can obtain its conception of the nature of knowledge. . . . it claims to be the basis of all science but in fact it is determined by the condition of science at any given time. The problem is thus made the more difficult by the fact that the very principles, in the light of which knowledge is to be criticized are themselves found to be socially and historically conditioned.[21]

[20] *Ibid.*, pp. 147–148. In this connection it might be noted that Hitler's professors asserted that positivism was little more than an insidious attempt of the Jews to demolish European culture by mocking its non-rational and profoundly anti-rational suppositions.

[21] *Ibid.*, p. 259.

This, in turn, propels us inexorably toward the conclusion that "the concept of truth itself is dependent upon the already existing types of knowledge."[22] Thus, we are enjoined to "reject the notion that there is a 'sphere of truth in itself' as a disruptive and unjustifiable hypothesis,"[23] and to revise "the thesis that the genesis of a proposition is under all circumstances irrelevant to its truth."[24]

CRITIQUE

Mannheim's epistemological thesis suffers from its failure to be sufficiently drastic in applying its own principles. Indeed, Mannheim's skepticism is so unremitting that he was well advised not to maintain it in practice. We are better off that he never tried. Had he rid himself of his generous capacity for blinking at inconsistencies, we would have been deprived of his brilliant investigations into the existential correlates of diverse thought systems, an enterprise his epistemological tenets arraign as untenable. I do not wish to thrash him with his own words, for that is unmannerly polemics. But it is acceptable, though somewhat rough-handed, methodological justice to oblige a set of conclusions to contra-dict without remorse the premises from which they arise.

Mannheim, as has been shown in the preceding pages, in principle denies the objectivity of all knowledge about social affairs through his asseveration that all propositions can be at best perspectivally valid. The propositions and theories of social scientists and ordinary men fall indifferently under his corrosive skepticism. Our knowledge of the social world stems from observation. But between the aboriginal observation and the interpretation imparted to it by the inquiring mind there lies a screen of whose mediating influence and properties the thinker himself is normally unaware. This partition blocks some obser-vations entirely in the sense that they never register on the mind and tints the remainder with the tacit biases caused by the thinker's own social perspectives. Even the standards of validation, the whole cumbersome apparatus of rules and criteria for certifying knowledge, are all of them uniquely determined by the social settings from which they spring. The social habitat is primal, the categories of analysis and interpretation merely supervenient.

Argumenti causa, let me compress Mannheim's cardinal epistemological thesis into one abbreviated sentence:[25]

22 *Ibid.*, p. 274.
23 *Ibid.*, pp. 262–263.
24 *Ibid.*
25 I use this compressed form because it is convenient. To cram all of Mannheim's involved and subtle argument into one sentence may appear somewhat disrespectful at best, and at worst, to

S-1 : All empirical propositions about social life are (a) perspectivally conditioned, and (b) therefore lack objectivity.

But it is also the case that:

S-2 : S-1 is an empirical proposition about social life.

S-1 cannot be said to be analytic. No self-contradiction is forced by asserting that propositions about social life are *not* perspectivally conditioned. Therefore S-1 is not tautologous since it can claim no logical warrant for its certainty. It is not a command or an injunction, either. Since it is neither a logical truth nor a recommendation, it must therefore be synthetic; speaking more strictly, an empirical generalization. But, if S-1 is a proposition about social life, it must be perspectival and therefore cannot secure the slightest measure of objectivity. This, to be sure, is not Mannheim's intention. But whoever proposes any principle whatever must agree to be bound by its logical implications.

Thus do the epistemological claims of the sociology of knowledge collapse in one inescapable and baffling contradiction. As Karl R. Popper notes, the self-contradiction Mannheim's cardinal principle must encounter if consistently pursued is a perfect analogue of the tantalizing conundrum professors of philosophy have used from time immemorial to bedevil students enrolled in Logic I.[26] The riddle goes: "Epimenides, who is a Cretan, says 'All Cretans lie.'" If Epimenides speaks truly, then at the very least one Cretan tells the truth and the sentence as a whole is self-contradictory, that is, false. If, on the other hand, Epimenides has set out with the playful intention of deceiving his audience by an outright falsehood, it must necessarily be the case that every Cretan (apart from Epimenides) is as relentlessly veracious as old Diogenes. And that, too, indicts the sentence as self-contradictory. No matter what the facts happen to be, the sentence is false. It is a vicious circle. Any sentence that implicates others cannot be part of the body of statements it implicates.[27]

It is patent that the sentence formed from the logical conjunction of S-1 and S-2 is another instance of the vicious circle. If all propositions about social life are perspectival, then the sentence that affirms this

---

court the disaster of distorting Mannheim's thought by wantonly lopping off qualifications and reservations. That is the reason for the lengthy introduction to a brief critique. Anyone who suspects that I have butchered Mannheim even in that very lengthy abridgment can refer to his own argument, presented in its entirety in *Ideology and Utopia*.

[26] Karl R. Popper, *The Open Society and Its Enemies*, Vol. 2 (London: Routledge & Kegan Paul, 1962), notes 7 and 8, pp. 353–354, and note 53, p. 361.

[27] A less picturesque way of presenting the poser makes the self-contradiction transparent. "It is both the case that Epimenides, the Cretan, tells the truth and that all Cretans lie." Removing the opacity of the original formulation also eliminates the fun of discovering the self-contradiction. It is now clear that the sentence is of the form *p* and *not-p*, which has to be false, necessarily.

Another famous teaser of the same logical structure: "The village barber shaves all those in the village who do not shave themselves."

contention is also perspectival and hence must be invalid. There is no way I can see for the argument to break out of the vicious circle, except perhaps to enter the very queer contention that statements referring to the existential determinants of knowledge are, in some odd sense, themselves not empirical statements about social affairs. To do this, of course, would be to negate S-2. But if they are so construed, it is difficult to imagine what cognitive status they might possess. Waiving that objection might allow Mannheim's epistemology to elude the circle, but only at the cost of making it tendentious. If it is postulated that some knowledge about social affairs is objectively ascertainable without the mediation of socially determined categories, there is no special reason I can see to grant S-1 the exclusive exemption. Any other statement would have at least as good a claim as S-1. But if all thought is perspectival, as S-1 affirms, then it is entirely mischievous to speak of the objective truth of any doctrine, even of the perspectival character of knowledge about social affairs.[28]

Carrying the argument one step further will show why the positive sociology of knowledge must remain paralyzed until it intellectually severs all connections with Mannheim's untenable animadversions to the possibility of objective knowledge. We start, as before, with:

S-1 : All empirical propositions about social life are (a) perspectivally conditioned, and (b) therefore lack objectivity.

But we will replace S-2 with an alternative set of sentences, this time specimens drawn from the substantive sociology of knowledge, say:

S-2 : (a) Human beings do not theorize about the actual conditions in which they live so long as they are well adjusted to them.

(b) Political movements are generally more bellicose to closely related factional opponents than they are to distant enemies. As evidence, Communists are harsher towards revisionists and meliorists then they are towards Conservatives.[29]

---

[28] I cannot resist appending Arthur Child's wicked and brilliant commentary to this paragraph. He points out that no amount of jejune scoffing about "Eternal Truths" can rescue Mannheim's logic by juxtaposing it with sententious phrases. See Arthur Child, "The Problem of Truth in the Sociology of Knowledge," *Ethics*, LVIII (October, 1947), 18–34.

To coax your audience into emitting a loud guffaw has always been a useful rhetorical stratagem for getting rid of an uncomfortable inconsistency. It may amuse the crowd but it has no magic to charm away miscarried logic.

[29] Both S-2 (a) and S-2 (b) are, of course, lifted from *Knowledge and Utopia*; the first sentence from p. 206 and the second from p. 215. This apparently is at sixes and sevens with my declared intentions not to abuse Mannheim with impolite and irrelevant arguments *ad hominem*. I use these hypotheses as exemplars for two reasons. First, I think they are brilliant, having great explanatory potential. Second, they show that it is possible for a person to argue for a self-stultifying epistemology and still do the good empirical work that his "philosophical" doctrines argue is impossible.

Whether S-2 (a) and S-2 (b) will stand empirical test without severe modification, I do not know. Their logical texture is coarse and they are excessively fertile; but they are certainly empirical propositions. It is therefore unarguable on the basis of S-1 that they are perspectivally con-ditioned and therefore lack objectivity, incorrigibly proscribed as they are by the interdictions set down in S-1. Indeed, it is inevitably the case that the positive sociology of knowledge, like any other body of scientific information, will consist of empirical statements of greater or lesser generality, presented singly or interrelated in theories of great scope and beauty. But, *ex hypothesi*, all of it merges into one vast and imponderable chimera. Who seeks scientific knowledge, vainly pursues fools' fire. There is no resting place. To choose one pair of examples, Mannheim asserts the material truth of S-2 (a) and S-2 (b). These are clearly empirical generalizations, and Mannheim evidently believes in their truth indepen-dent of his own social perspective and commitment. But a first anonymous critic will always be within his rights in using Mannheim's own hypothesis S-1 against him, to call both S-2 (a) and S-2 (b) perspectival, and a second critic equally so in rendering the same judgment of the first. This spiralling series of *tu quoque* rebuttals can have no end. The regress is infinite, a desperate conclusion inescapable on Mannheim's own principles.[30]

In respect of logic, it is no longer admissible to speak of the truth of any proposition whatever, for "truth" is one predicate the apostle of a consistent relativism must necessarily forswear.[31] He is in the very curious predicament of the philosopher who tries to persuade a skeptical audience that all that appears to be matter is really incorporeal. For, on his own hypothesis, he does a thing no more sensible than wage verbal battle with his own hallucinations. Similarly, the consistent relativist, after announcing that all standards of truth are perspectival, tries to convince his audience that the perspectivistic hypothesis is true. But this is a kind of performance already ruled absurd by the very doctrine he strives to propound.

[30] As A. I. Melden argues in greater detail in his " Judgments in the Social Sciences," in George P. Adams, William R. Dennes and Stephen C. Pepper (eds.), *Civilization*, Volume XXIII of the Uni-versity of California Publications in Philosophy (Berkeley, California: University of California Press, 1942), pp. 147–148. Melden further points out that it will not do for the sociologist to socioanalyze himself. Even the most sincere self-conscious criticism is carried on in the unperceived light of the thinker's own *Weltanschauung*. Thus the thinker's analysis of himself can be analyzed by another thinker, and so on *ad infinitum*. It is this endless procession of analyses that the doctrine of pers-pectivism invites.

[31] See Everett W. Hall's fine criticism, "Truth would then be a function of sentences and not at all of facts. This is objectionable because, first, it gives us a redundancy. To assert that a sentence asserting *f* is true is to say no more than to say that the sentence asserts *f*. Second, it takes away a perfectly good usage of 'true' which would have to be replaced in any adequate language (the relativist's language just omits this usage). I refer to the usage whereby 'the sentence asserting *f* is true' requires, when correctly used, that *f* be in the world, not merely asserted in the sentence." *What is Value? An Essay in Philosophical Analysis* (London: Routledge & Kegan Paul, 1952), p. 78.

Like Hall, I do not see how any language can function well for science if it absolutely forbids the semantic predicate "true" to be ascribed to any sentence formulated within the language.

SELECTIVITY AND BIAS

It is hard to say how much of Mannheim's thought is genuinely original. An acute and irreverent historian of ideas would probably find it child's play to pull Mannheim's thought to pieces and find little of it that had not been foreshadowed in the works of his earlier contemporaries and of men who died long before he was born: Protagoras, Bacon, Nietzsche, Marx. What distinguishes Mannheim is the enormous depth and breadth of his learning and his almost obsessive talent for relating his erudition to the problems of the sociology of knowledge as he conceived them. He searched out and absorbed every pertinent fact previous generations of scholars and his own contemporaries placed within his grasp. But he was more than a sedulous encyclopedist mechanically spinning out all the data that had lodged in his copious notebooks; he sorted out and recombined these bits of information into new and arresting patterns. The result is that his works have never accumulated dust on library shelves. Their animating spirit has fanned the fires of the *Methodenstreiten* that have since raged in history, political science, economics, and sociology. The debt is too profound to be cast up and reckoned only in footnotes, which are the professional scholar's ledgerbooks and memororials. Mannheim's arguments were deft, judicious, and learned, but it remained for later generations of scholars to particularize his doctrines and apply them to the specialized problems of each social science, often in such a way that their antecedents appeared only in shadow. The questions Mannheim posed and answered have given shape and outline to the protracted and virulent methodological debates that have divided scholars ever since. These confrontations, as ubiquitous as they have been, are never *psychologically* conclusive. They leave each of the warring camps convinced that in its own ranks lies wisdom and in the other only confusion and worse. The same battles are fought over and over again with hastily disguised acrimony in our professional journals and, as one might expect, are annually renewed in our graduate schools where the veteran troops train their combat replacements. It is no irrelevant measure of the power and importance of Mannheim's thought that links it with its extraordinary vitality.

Of the many questions Mannheim raised, two have achieved great prominence. The first is the issue of selectivity. Social scientists of a strongly antipositivistic inclination often charge that the distinction their adversaries draw between matters of fact and matters of value is purely illusory. For even the very act of choosing topics for inquiry is conditioned by criteria of relevance that are indelibly tinged by the values of the social scientist, his paymaster, or the social movement to which he owes his (often unconscious) allegiance. The second deals, not unsurprisingly, with the way social scientists gather and appraise empirical evidence. The allegation, to express it somewhat picturesquely, is that the social scientists, a human being observing other human beings, cannot attain that measure of cold clinical detachment the biologist (supposedly) achieves when he peers at microbes through a microscope. The social scientist is no more than a special pleader however sincerely he professes to put his value involvements behind him. Rather, they run on ahead, sublimated, repressed, so well masked that they were not recognized for what they are. They appear once again in his conclusions in so magisterial a role that the answers often seem prior to the problems. I will treat each matter in its turn.

The argument from suspicious origins

It is often contended that the social sciences are unable to attain more than a modicum of dispassionate objectivity because the individual scholar is psychologically unable to part head from heart. In his selection of topics for investigation and analysis, the argument runs, the social scientist is guided by an ensemble of culturally generated values and dominant preconceptions. Emergent in some sort of social setting, these criteria, which are value-impregnated, possess more than biographical or even causal significance. On the contrary, they pervade and vitiate his results, which are logically as well as psychologically informed by his values and inseparable from them. Because values or ideology put him on the track of certain problems, his conclusions must bear the indelible thumbprint of their origins. What begins in values, must necessarily end in values. The critical allegation has been levelled by scholars in each of the social science disciplines. In sociology, proponents of structural-functional analysis have been castigated for their subconscious cravings in behalf of the status quo. Similar charges reverberate in political science, and scholars who critically examine the operations of the American party system can expect to be chided for their reforming zeal. Summing up the case, Harry V. Jaffa, an American political philosopher, asserts "(Professor David) Easton has argued, and argued very soundly, that a value-free social science is a delusion. Values have a determining influence on everything humans do, and political scientists are human beings. Research interests are determined by values, criteria of relevance are so determined; the ways in which we select our data are so determined."[32]

[32] "The Case Against Political Theory," *The Journal of Politics*, *XXII* (May, 1960), 267. Emphasis supplied.

See Charles A. Beard's similar indictment, "Every student of history knows that his colleagues have been influenced in their selection and ordering of materials by their biases, prejudices, beliefs, affections, general upbringing, and experience, particularly social and economic; and if he has a sense of propriety, to say nothing of humor, he applies the canon to himself, leaving no exceptions to the rule." In Meyerhoff (ed.), *op. cit.*, p. 141.

Such arguments derive their rhetorical appeal from the tacit assumption that there must be some sort of structural isomorphism between cause and effect; that effects, so to speak, are logically bound to resemble their causes. It is, of course, undeniable that choice of problems is affected by a scholar's values: his reforming zeal, his affinities for things the way they are, the bundle of analytic techniques that fall to his hand, worship of his teachers, or whatnot. The assumption is undeniable because it verges on a tautology. To choose a topic is to prefer one line of action to all those theoretically available, from opening a bicycle repair shop all the way to discovering the vocational aspirations of Negro high school students. To say that the latter is preferred to the former is to say that it has greater value for him. And this statement is necessarily true of any pair of alternatives whatever. If values are revealed in choice then it is certain that values are operative in the choice of problems for analysis.

That much is certainly true; for it is a tautologous proposition, and tautologous propositions are irrefutable. But the pathetic conclusion follows the premise only by a sleight of hand, not by fidelity to rules of logic. Let me sacrifice needless generality for the benefits of a pointed example. I present two sentences:

(P-1) Marx chose to analyze unemployment in free markets because he wanted to show the inherent fragility of capitalistic economic systems.

and

(P-2) In capitalistic economic systems, the rate of unemployment varies directly with the introduction of labor-saving technologies.

P-1 is an element of that set of propositions which account for the behavior of social scientists on motivational grounds. P-2 is an element of that set of propositions advanced by social scientists which purport to explain the behavior of social institutions or organizations. Palpably, P-1 and P-2 are logically independent of one another. P-1 can be true and P-2 false; P-2 false and P-1 true; both can be true and both can be false. Whatever the combination, no contradiction occurs. The behavior of capitalistic economic systems has nothing whatever to do with the state of Marx's mind, the values he affirmed and the values he denied, his outrage or his joy. P-1 asserts something about Marx, and perhaps his biographer will be able to tell us whether the inference is true or not. But the findings of the biographer or of the psychoanalyst have nothing to do with the material truth or falsity of the economic hypothesis. Rhetorically, of course, the biographical data will tell more against P-2 than the nicer economic evidence, but social scientists, who do not have to appeal to the crowd, are in no way obliged to play the sophist.

Persistently argued, the confounding of *P*-1 and *P*-2 explanations can be used to discredit and raze the objectivity of mathematics and the natural sciences as well. The Pythagorean cult had many bizarre beliefs. Among other things, the devout refrained from eating beans, and sitting on a quart jug was held to be the blackest impiety. But the proposition that asserts that the square of the longest side of a right triangle must be equal to the sum of the squares of the adjacent sides is not derivable from Pythagorean ritual taboos. Pythagorean mathematicians may have imbibed inspiration and incentive from their outlandish cultic beliefs, but that is all. The validity of the Pythagorean theorem is a matter of mathematics, and not of social psychology. For all we know, Charles Darwin may have been driven by a frenetic impulse to make life miserable for Fundamentalist ministers. But this putative bias I ascribe to Darwin *argumenti causa* is neither evidence for nor evidence against his biological explanations. And, seriously, who inquires into Jenner's motives when he takes his children to be vaccinated? The psychological or sociological basis of a man's intellectual concerns is one thing, and the truth of the opinions he affirms quite another.

The argument from spurious conclusions

As with origins, so with conclusions. The claim is perennially made that no one who writes about controversial issues can possibly divest himself of all traces of local or temperamental bias: his political loyalties, his allegiance to a particular sector of society, his tender regard for underdog or topdog as the case may be. Into his conclusions the social scientist imports his prejudices—for they are literally prejudgments or decisions already made before any appraisal of the evidence—most often surreptitiously as contraband, less frequently as cargo correctly labelled. Whether or not he declares his values on the manifest, they are bound to tamper with if not compel his conclusions.

Often, one suspects, bias is something we are generously disposed to find in our opponents and never see in ourselves. So viewed, bias is opposed to modesty, whose absence we are inclined to lament only in others. In the practical sense, mutual distrust takes care of itself and poses no problem at all for the logical analysis of scientific discourse. The antagonists who perfervidly assault each other's good faith are destined to talk past one another eternally in a dialogue of the deaf, or the forced amity of the debate will eventually succumb to countervailing dogmatism; in either case, any appeal to the logic they both renounce is completely disingenuous. Paradoxically, the radical claim is the more tractable. The immoderate asseveration that all conclusions bear the gravamen of the scholar's value involvements is amenable to analysis, and not only for its gracious egalitarianism.

The word "bias" is a contrast word; it earns significance totally from the sharp way it differs from "neutral" or "warranted." If every conclusion is in some way "biased" by the way the data have been collected and interpreted, then the word has been drained of any stable meaning whatever. To assert that a conclusion has been "biased" would be in a roundabout way to say only that it is a conclusion. Indeed, a sociological explanation of why a scholar went wrong is logically defensible only after it *has been shown where he went astray*, and to do this presupposes standards whose objectivity cannot be impugned. Otherwise, not only has the cart preceded the horse, but all rational criticism is submerged in the tyranny of name-calling.[33] To be sure, objectivity is more aspiration than attainment, for the research methods of the social sciences generally permit some leeway for the play of values. But the discovery that some scholars have tricked up their data, or have omitted disconcerting facts from their accounts, or have used a deficient sampling frame or improper standards of measurement, does not compel the conclusion that all social scientists are either unwitting partisans or outright mountebanks. To find that some *A* are *X* does not necessitate that every *A* is an *X*. And, in any case, to show that the canons of reliable and objective inquiry have been violated or are hard to approximate no more proves their debility than violations of the Seventh Commandment clinch the case for adultery.[34]

SUMMARY

I have argued that adherence to the enigmatic epistemological claims of the sociology of knowledge would logically entail the absurdity of a positive sociology of knowledge and, with it, the utter futility of obtaining any warranted knowledge whatever. Traced to its logical conclusion, the epistemological doctrine is self-refuting and cannot be consistently maintained.

[33] See Ernest Nagel, "Some Issues in the Logic of Historical Analysis," reprinted in Edward H. Madden (ed.), *The Structure of Scientific Thought* (Boston: Houghton Mifflin, 1960), p. 193.

[34] To counsel someone to renounce standards simply because they are trying is the sophistication of the gutter. In a similar connection, Arnold Brecht quotes Valentin of Goethe's *Faust* as he remonstrates with Margarete, "*Du bist doch nun einmal eine Hur', so sei's auch eben recht.*" (You are a whore now anyway, so why not go all the way.) My translation is not the same as Brecht's, but it is more faithful to the American idiom. See Arnold Brecht, *Political Theory: The Foundations of Twentieth-Century Political Thought* (Princeton, N.J.: Princeton University Press, 1959), p. 299.

Bibliography

Beard, Charles A., "Written History as an Act of Faith," *The American Historical Review*, 39 (January, 1934), 219–229.

Becker, Carl L., "What Are Historical Facts?" *Western Political Quarterly*, 8 (September, 1955), 327–340.

Bergmann, Gustav, "Ideology," *Ethics*, 51 (April, 1951), 205–218.

Boring, Edwin G., "The Dual Role of the *Zeitgeist* in Scientific Activity," in Phillip G. Frank (ed.), *The Validation of Scientific Theories*, New York: Collier Books, 1961, pp. 187–198.

Brecht, Arnold, *Political Theory: The Foundations of Twentieth-Century Political Thought*, Princeton, N. J.: Princeton University Press, 1959.

Child, Arthur, "The Problem of Truth in the Sociology of Knowledge," *Ethics*, 58 (October, 1947), 18–34.

Hall, Everett W., *What Is Value?: An Essay in Philosophical Analysis*, London: Routledge & Kegan Paul, 1952.

Jaffa, Harry V., "The Case Against Political Theory," *The Journal of Politics*, 22 (May, 1960), 259–277.

Mannheim, Karl, *Ideology and Utopia: An Introduction to the Sociology of Knowledge*, trans. Louis Wirth and Edward A. Shils, New York: Harcourt, Brace & World, 1936.

Maquet, Jacques, *The Sociology of Knowledge: Its Structure and Its Relation to the Philosophy of Knowledge*, trans. John F. Locke, Boston: Beacon Press, 1951.

Melden, A. I., "Judgments in the Social Sciences," in George P. Adams, William R. Dennes, and Stephen C. Pepper (eds.), *Civilization*, Vol. XXIII of the University of California Publications in Philosophy, Berkeley, California: University of California Press, 1942, pp. 136–169.

Merton, Robert K., "The Sociology of Knowledge," in *Social Theory and Social Structure*, New York: Free Press, 1957, pp. 456–488.

Nagel, Ernest, "Some Issues in the Logic of Historial Analysis," reprinted in Edward H. Madden (ed.), *The Structure of Scientific Thought*, Boston: Houghton Mifflin, 1960, pp. 189–197.

Popper, Karl R., *The Open Society and Its Enemies: Hegel, Marx*, Vol. 2, London: Routledge & Kegan Paul, 1962.

Schumpeter, Joseph A., *Capitalism, Socialism and Democracy*, New York: Harper & Row, 1950.

IRVING LOUIS HOROWITZ

*Mainliners and
marginals:
the human shape of
sociological theory*

" **A** science which hesitates to forget its founders is lost." With these proud words culled from the philosopher A. N. Whitehead, the sociologist Robert K. Merton introduces his justifiably famous collection of papers on *Social Theory and Social Structure*.[1] One is tempted to make a quick retort to this sentiment by recalling the words of Soren Kierkegaard, to the effect that the man who would forget the past "has condemned himself and deserves nothing better than what is sure to befall him, namely, to perish."[2] Both positions have avid, not to mention livid, followers in sociological ranks. And in the hands of its supreme practitioners, there is, and has been for many years, a forceful effort to get

[1] Alfred North Whitehead, *On Understanding Education*. Quoted by Robert K. Merton in the Preface to *Social Theory and Social Structure*. New York: Free Press, 1957.
[2] Soren Kierkegaard, *Repetition: An Essay in Experimental Psychology*. Princeton, N. J.: Princeton University Press, 1946, p. 5.

beyond the apparent contradictions involved in these two philosophic standpoints, and at the risk of a nasty word, try to *synthesize* them.[3]

If we drive the contradictions between Whitehead and Kierkegaard far enough, or examine the differences between modern sociological titans such as Samuel Stouffer and C. Wright Mills, what remain are the basic questions and root metaphors of contemporary sociological theory: Should sociology concern itself with its own history as part of theory, or should sociology, like medicine, view its history as part of a humanistic hubris which is better flushed out and forgotten? To what extent can self-awareness be considered part of scientific understanding? And to what degree is self-consciousness a literary intrusion upon the vigorous and rigorous character of all true science? From these questions we can clearly perceive the importance which the choice of sociological stylings has for the character of sociological theory.

To sharply demarcate boundaries between men who fundamentally share the same universe of scientific discourse may be viewed as a cursed scholastic inheritance—a navel-picking exercise out of proportion to the actual worth of the differences which obtain. While there can be no quarrel with those who would caution against drawing the internal differences of sociology too exactly, too tightly, to grab hold of the opposite intellectual pole and refuse to make any distinctions in the name of an engineered consensus, is surely no answer. The carefully drawn ambiguities with which the word sociology is modified—"field," "craft," "profession," "occupation," "convention," etc.—indicate just how sensitive the man of sociological learning can be to his hard-won efforts. Let us therefore try to overcome the false option between exclusive self-reflection and its infantile rejection of its own history. This we will do by treating problems of sociological theory as basically responses to the emergence of the field of sociology as an organizational framework and more decisively, as a human enterprise.[4]

---

[3] We may take the current raft of books on the subject of sociological self-analysis as being precisely concerned with this task of synthesis. See in particular the following: Arthur J. Vidich, Jospeh Bensman, and Maurice R. Stein (eds.), *Reflections on Community Studies*. New York: Wiley, 1964; Phillip E. Hammond (ed.), *Sociologists at Work: Essays on the Craft of Social Research*. New York: Basic Books, 1964; and Gideon Sjoberg (ed.), *Politics, Ethics, and Social Research*. Cambridge, Mass.: Schenkman Publishing Company, forthcoming.

[4] While the treatment of sociological theory from the viewpoint of the organization of sociologists is not a commonplace, certain forceful antecedents to such a perspective should not go unnoticed. For good examples, see the following: Pitirim Sorokin, "Some Contrasts of Contemporary European and American Sociology," *Social Forces*, Vol. 8, No. 1, September, 1929, pp. 57–62; Robert K. Merton, "The Role of the Intellectual in Public Bureaucracy," *Social Forces*, Vol. 27, No. 4, May, 1945, pp. 405–415; Talcott Parsons, "The Professions and the Social Structure," *Social Forces*, Vol. 17, No. 4, May, 1939, pp. 457–467; C. Wright Mills, "Two Styles of Research in Current Social Studies," *Philosophy of Science*, Vol. 20, No. 4, October, 1953, pp. 266–275; and most recently but on a more general level, Walter Hirsch, "Knowledge, Power, and Social Change: The Role of American Scientists," *Explorations in Social Change*, G. K. Zollschan and W. Hirsch (eds.), Boston, Mass.: Houghton Mifflin, 1964; Everett C. Hughes, "Professional and Career Problems of Sociology," *Men and Their Work*, New York: Free Press, 1958, pp. 157–168.

I

What we must concern ourselves with is the evolution of a language which will permit a description of the organization and the ideology of sociology within a single framework. To do this means, first of all, to describe four types and two pairs of sociological styles. Those who conceive of sociology as a profession in contrast to those who conceive of it as an occupation constitute the particular pairing we will call *mainliners*, those who are in the center of sociological activities and disputes. The second coupling of sociologists is less easily defined. At their extremes they are the unsociologist, the individual trained in the discipline but whose fundamental allegiance is to the institution for which he works; and the antisociologist who, while likewise trained in sociology, has a fundamentally different allegiance, to the intellectual horizons which inform all the social sciences. This pairing can be called, with some qualms, to be sure, the *marginals*.[5]

To those who feel that science is some sort of monolithic enterprise performed by marching soldiers given their orders by an elite corps of knowers, these pairings will appear to slash at the very flesh of sociology. But for those less given to a romantic view of science as the virgin birth of knowledge, the pairings will be perfectly understandable. Thus far, the most incisive contribution to this concept is Merton's evidence that norm inconsistency is characteristic of all social systems, and certainly characteristic of science in the form of the growth of "contradictory pairs of norms."[6] For the purpose of this study we will explore each pairing separately, and then see how they connect up to each other in the actual conduct of sociological theory.

Toward the close of the fading fifties, in 1958 to be precise, an organizational confrontation took place. The formal issue before its membership was this: Should the American Sociological Society (ASS) be rechristened the American Sociological Association (ASA)? The results of the vote conclusively demonstrated that for a majority of the participants it was preferable to be known as a group of ASA's rather than a collection of ASS's. But frivolity aside, the debate on nomenclature introduced matters of deep substance, which have increasingly come to disturb the sociological community. It became evident that underlying

[5] This formulation owes a profound intellectual debt to the paper by Alvin W. Gouldner, "Cosmopolitans and Locals: Toward an Analysis of Latent Social Roles," *Administrative Science Quarterly*, Vol. 2, December, 1957 and March, 1958, pp. 281–306, 444–480. This debt is herewith acknowledged.

[6] See Robert K. Merton, "The Ambivalence of Scientists," *Bulletin of John Hopkins Hospital*, No. 112, February, 1963, pp. 79–97. And for a creative application of this concept, see Marvin B. Sussman, "The Social Problems of the Sociologist," *Social Problems*, Vol. 11, No. 3, Winter, 1964, pp. 215–225.

the manifest problem of bureaucratic nomenclature is the more serious choice of scientific images and ethical guidelines. For the big question continued to be unresolved: Should the practitioner of sociology be considered primarily as a member of a scientific profession or is he to be viewed as associated with a scientific discipline? It does little good to say that profession and occupation are not incompatible. This mediating formula leaves open exactly the issue which must be settled: whether profession is a more meaningful sociological designation than occupation; or indeed, if these concepts are at all scientifically relevant or simply represent strategies for upward mobility.

Actually, what has taken place in sociology represents in a most acute form the basic rift *within* empirical modalities, between pragmatism and positivism. It is not an argument *between* the empirical and the non-empirical, for that discussion has been resolved, with rare exceptions, in favor of empirical techniques and definitions. We might say that the pragmatic currents supply the intellectual cement for occupationalism; while the positivistic currents supply the same sort of support for professionalism—with the "machine runs" and the "machine room" providing the web of data justifying a heuristic approach to sociology.

But even within such a common modality, profound differences obtain. The professional is concerned with developing a picture of the world, a model of the universe, which to all intents and purposes jumps up at him from the data. A good example of this is the account by James A. Davis of his work, "Great Books and Small Groups." His concluding remarks reveal an almost mystic reverence for the self-revealing properties of data. "Those few moments when a new set of tables comes up from the machine room and questions begin to be answered; when relationships actually hold under controls; when the pile of tables on the desk suddenly meshes to yield a coherent chapter; when in a flash you see a neat test for an interpretation; when you realize you have found out something about something important that nobody ever knew before—these are the moments that justify research."[7] The occupationalist, for his part, has a more affective approach toward the object of his study, and his disposition is towards developing theories of behavior, which are more likely to be imposed upon the data than jump up from the data. In describing Riesman's attitude toward a project on sociability, a project that could just as well have been conducted in the circumstances of Davis' Great Books groups, we find out that "his own forte lay in the more anthropological methods of observation and description. His approach to the study of parties was to ask what a whole party was like: what were its major, often concurrent themes; what were its blockages, frustrations, liquidities, accomplishments?"[8] This is not simply a distinction between statistical and ethnographic information, but between differing notions of what constitutes the starting and terminal points of research, as well as what constitutes the proper relationship between investigator and informant.

Pragmatism supplied the intellectual ammunition for two wings of the famed "Chicago School"—the educationists as well as the sociologists. Men like Mead, Dewey, Morris, and Veblen insisted upon an orientation in the social and behavioral sciences towards values of ameliorating and understanding the plight of the poor. It was this picture of the world which had a large part in the drive behind the sociological wing. While it is true that the Chicago type of sociologist makes a posture out of appearing "hard," "tough," and "unsentimental," this is partially due to the easy sentimentalism that has been popularly associated with those kinds of human materials with which he works. The pragmatism of men like Louis Wirth, Robert E. Park, Walter Reckless, and Everett C. Hughes not only consists of the fact that they wrote about urbanization, but on how crime can be minimized or channelized; not only about Negro-White relations, but on how such relationships can be humanized. Their commitment then, sociologically, was strongly influenced by their belief in reform. The occupationalist emphasizes the connections of the social problem to the social program and in so doing defines the core tasks of sociology in a unique way.

The idea of sociology as an occupation squares well with the "good craftsman" view of the field. Style, literary "punch," publicity are genuine values for the pragmatic mind; as they are for the occupationalist. Both want to provide not just "hard data," but much more than that— sociological awareness of social marginality. Only a sophistication about the world could save the sociologist from falling into the square mold. And such sophistication is integrally linked to sociology as doing, as exposure. Active knowing, implying action programs, made for a pragmatic fusion of theory and practice in the best populist manner. Living was its own reward; action generated its own further consequences. Sociology thus acquired an open-ended property in their hands. It meant informed policy, easy movement between the scholar and the policy-maker. It meant making the sociologist aware of himself as a social actor in the very act of making sociology. The Chicago School product attempted to develop a "package" which contained not only hard data but also ethnographic observation and value orientations.[9] And in its most recent and most sophisticated form, it is an approach which readily

[8] David Riesman and Jeanne Watson, "The Sociability Project: A Chronical of Frustration and Achievement," in *Sociologists at Work, op. cit.*, esp. pp. 278–279.
[9] See Irving Louis Horowitz, "Max Weber and the Spirit of American Sociology," in *The Sociological Quarterly*, Vol. 5, No. 4, Autumn, 1964.

grants, and indeed insists upon, the positive value of facing up to the "irreconcilable conflict between the interests of science and the interests of those studied."[10]

Within empirical sociology a new strategy of research has evolved. The positivistic wing, with its emphasis on observation independent of action, nomological laws apart from real laws, logical stipulations apart from ontological status, and above all, criteria of verification apart from standards of valuation, has come along to challenge older holistic conceptions of the field. It is clear that for this positivist tendency, the control of variance is far more important than an impressionist understanding of social problems. The dilemma then becomes that the control of variance rules out examination of a whole range of variables which might impede or impinge upon the experimental situation. It might well be that the tendency of this group to lean toward social psychology is not so much a reflection of intellectual preferences as it is of methodological pressures for exactitude.

To speak of the professionalist as a positivist should not conjure up memories of August Comte and the "engineering of the soul" attitude to social science. For the Columbia School would be most vociferous in its denial of offering recipes for social change. It deals in "implications for action" rather than actual policy recommendations. By positivism is meant the development of a total portrait of man derived from the combination of discrete questionnaires, surveys, and other "atomic" facts. Professionalism is a sociological ideology emanating from the sharp distinction between facts and values. It considers sociology as a positive science in the special sense that the ends for which it is used are independent of the findings as such, and which views professional expertise something apart from intellectual luster. If the pragmatic Chicago School was defined by the particular problems which sociology should at least confront, the Columbia School is no less clearly defined by the emphasis on the universal and scientistic values of sociology. Indeed, it views with contempt "social dilettantism" and is hostile to any notion of sociology that would deprive it of its "systematic," "serious," or "austere" characteristics.[11]

On a different plane, professionalization, by virtue of its grim fight for status, ironically permits a kind of irresponsibility with respect to the future of the social world. The professional can, by virtue of his professionalism, exempt himself as a scientist from responsibility for the ends to which his scientific findings are put. It is not that the positivists are politically more conservative than the pragmatists. Perhaps the very reverse is the case. The positivists were in all likelihood more radical

10 See Howard S. Becker, "Problems in the Publication of Field Studies," *Reflections on Community Studies*, *op. cit.*, pp. 276–277.

11 See the most interesting "Acknowledgment" to Paul F. Lazarsfeld in Robert K. Merton, *Social Theory and Social Structure*. New York: Free Press, 1957.

in their political beliefs, more dedicated to the idea of socialist change, more convinced of the corruptness of the bourgeois social order than were the pragmatists—who at the most were (and remain) "worldly" men in a limited *demimonde* setting. Therefore, the main difference is not in the beliefs held, but in what is expected in the way of sociological reinforcement of such beliefs.

The positivist methodologically oriented sociologist has a compartmentalized view, in which the quality, the formal elegance of the sociology performed counts for more than the quantity, or the purposes for which sociology is employed. The European positivist tradition gave a special warrant for a sociology which could be considered scientific without at the same time outraging the sensibilities of other scientists. The pragmatists, for their part, developed a series of intellectual networks—groups of people responsive to larger pressures—and in turn they sought to act as a pressure group on the larger society.[12] The positivists, on the other hand, developed a series of "circles"—and like a circle, the people included were responsive only to one another's pressures, and acted as insulating material against the general pressures of society. The extreme intellectualism of the professional ideology is thus, in an American context, either akin to, or a direct response to, the kinds of positivism brought to America from Vienna, Berlin, and from Warsaw.[13] The actionism of the occupational ideology tends to be more of a response to immediate situations and to "nativistic" tendencies in social thought. The positivist wing in sociology desires logical coherence, firm rules, and the kinds of inner directed rituals geared to satisfy collegial standards. The pragmatist wing in sociology desired connection, guidelines to action, and the kinds of outer directed experiences geared to satisfy recipients of service and information.

This point may be summed up by noting that the sociologist who emphasizes professionalism tends to have as his main reference group other working sociologists. While the sociologist emphasizing an occupational orientation has as his main reference group a directly concerned public, whether real or imaginary. The positivist wants *to know* as an end; the pragmatist wants *to act* as his end. This distinction is clearly typical of attitudes expressed in writings emanating from traditional centers of graduate education, and evident in such works as *Sociology Today* and *Sociologists at Work*, in contrast to work being done at the newer centers of graduate training, and evident in such works as *The New Sociology* and *Reflections on Community Studies*.

---

[12] C. Wright Mills, *Sociology and Pragmatism: A Study in the American Higher Learning*, Irving Louis Horowitz (ed.). New York: Paine-Whitman Publishers, 1964, pp. 35–83.

[13] See Ernest Nagel, "Impressions and Appraisals of Analytic Philosophy in Europe," *Logic Without Metaphysics and Other Studies in the Philosophy of Science*. New York: Free Press, 1956, pp. 191–246.

In the forties, at a time when sociology had to choose between humanist and scientist affiliations, positivism offered an incredible opportunity to justify the latter. The positivists provided the fundamental critique; humanism provided a series of emotions; science provided facts. Humanism was dialectical; science was cumulative. Humanism was brilliant but got nowhere; science was prosaic but got somewhere. It was easier to sell government agencies, private business, and foundation funds information which was cumulative and went somewhere, than emotions which were woven into a fine mosaic but not into a saleable package. The rhetoric of "hard" science eased the path toward El Dorado. The gold rush was on. Professionalism served to keep the grubby amateurs and dilettantes out of the picture. The occupationalists, with their touching faith in the practicality of sociological activities, could not offer a systematic critique to this process of the bureaucratization of sociology. The spill-over in accoutrements and advantages from the professionalization process was large enough for the entire field to prosper. And no ideal argument can overcome material affluence. For every sociologist prepared to put his discipline "on trial," there were a hundred others prepared to put the sociologist-turned-apostate "on trial." Robert Lynd's *Knowledge for What?*, for example, remained an isolated outburst—tolerated because his *Middletown* studies helped to professionalize the field of sociology, but thunderously ignored by the new breed of sociological positivists who had been taught that Lynd's sort of queries could be fashionably (and profitably) ignored.

The good sociological Schweiks of the fifties assumed their professionalism poses with a disconcerting naturalness. The sociological institute or bureau became a way of life, on a par with the college or university. Sociology was more than a discipline; it offered work, jobs, careers. An uncomfortable argument by analogy arose which somehow established an equation between non-academic work routines and scientific substantiation.[14] But the routinization of sociological work entailed something more profound, namely, the assumption that any second- or third-rate person, particularly if his young mind was uncluttered by knowledge or cultivated opinion, could be transformed into a first-rate methodologist. This fact was to provide a demonstration effect that sociology had little to do with humanistic learning.[15] Actually, a

[14] The first person to note the illicit character of this equation between career patterns and science was John Dewey, in "Liberating the Social Scientist: A Plea to Unshackle the Study of Man," *Commentary*, Vol. 4, No. 4, October, 1947, pp. 378–385. But at that time, few sociologists were ready to pay attention to such "logic chopping"; particularly not in the vast laboratory at Columbia University.

[15] The most forceful advocate of this position was Samuel Stouffer. See his paper on "Some Observations on Study Design," *American Journal of Sociology*, Vol. 55, No. 3, November, 1950, pp. 355–361. Ironically enough, Stouffer's work on *The American Soldier* and on *Loyalty and Disloyalty in Post-War America* obviously could not be done without a man who retained a criterion of brilliance and not simply competence.

reverse Pygmalion effect took over. The bright-eyed student, direct from the undergraduate schools and a world of sociological classics, found himself confronted with a concerted effort to disabuse him of "inherited" styles of thought. Indeed, the basic measure of his "successful adjustment" to graduate school was exactly his capacity to be liquidated as a "theorist" and resurrected as a "methodologist."

The present period in sociology reveals a rising tide of discontent and self-criticism that may well foreshadow the *Gotterdamerung* of professionalization as such. After a full generation of domination and control, after establishing a sociological rhetoric that has been parlayed into a universe of "soft money," the professionals find that training and precision can be purchased at the price of objectivity itself. Such phenomena as the Cold War come to be viewed as "stable states," so that one comes to analyze "alternative future states of affairs of the Cold War," rather than the sort of "intervention research" needed to show how to finally end the Cold War. As Lazarsfeld has recently made plain:

> There are a number of important problems which are not being studied at all because there just doesn't exist an interested client. Some of the more obvious social evils like juvenile delinquency do find their tie-up with organized research, but how about studying the conditions under which a desirable political candidate wins out over a well-heeled political hack? Who makes studies as to how participation among workers in factory management could be organized, overcoming resistance of management as well as apathy among workers? What is really known about the victory of manifestly corrupt union leaders in union elections or about the informal relations between businessmen and members of Congress? It has repeatedly been pointed out that applied social research in this country is especially handicapped by our general *laissez-faire* philosophy. If we had more social planning there would be more opportunity to study its effectiveness and shortcomings.[16]

While this does not exhaust the problems of bureaucratic research technique, it is indicative of the new role that sociological theory must play in the future development of the field. For example: What is the relation between government agencies' expectations and the design of sociological research projects? How does the canon of secrecy affect the character of sociological findings? When should an individual cooperate or not cooperate with federal decision-making units? Where should the intellectual lines be drawn?[17]

The rush is now on to prove that everyone can really do important things no less than the trivial; big-range sociology no less than two-person group analysis. It is at this point that self-reflection must be converted into substantial theoretical gains and not simply applaud

16 Paul F. Lazarsfeld with the collaboration of Sydney S. Spivak, "Observations on the Organization of the Empirical Social Research in the United States," Information Bulletin of the *International Social Science Council*, No. 29, December, 1961, p. 26. (Reprinted by Bureau of Applied Social Research, Reprint No. 351.)

17 See Gilbert Shapiro, "Social Science Research and the American University," *The American Behavioral Scientist*, Vol. VIII, No. 2, October, 1964, pp. 29–35.

"big range" efforts because of their bigness. What needs to be established in sociology is some recognition that the grounds of the field still rest on people no less than powers, masses no less than elites, spontaneity no less than equilibrium, revolution no less than reaction, conflict no less than consensus. And for this a dialectical sociology must be brought into force, whatever may be the number of people or the size of the organization being studied. Whether it be called thinking in pairs, thinking triadically, concretely, or what you will—the full scientific weight of sociology will not be realized unless the present "two sides" to every story becomes transformed and elevated into one whole with many sides.[18]

Sometimes the occupational orientation is thought to be earlier in time than the professional orientation; namely, occupationalism is a less sophisticated, more primitive version of the same thing—the drive toward the specialization and bureaucratization of learning. While it is true that in certain fields, such as sociology, the occupational orientation as symbolized by the Chicago School gained preeminence earlier than the professional orientation as symbolized by the Harvard and Columbia styles of work, this is by no means a general rule. In such spheres as engineering, for example, occupational orientations are relatively recent, and have come into being as responses to the dysfunctional aspects of professionalization.

We might say that occupationalism is itself something of a professional ideology, since it rests not simply on a critique of professionalization, but more profoundly, on a defense of the "field" against amateurs and dilettantes. A recent instance of this irony is Martin Rein's blistering "insider" critique of professionalism among the social service and social workers. He points out several major shortcomings in professionalization that hold not only for social work but for social science in general. "When a group of persons who perform a service band together to control the body of persons who may legitimately perform that service, certain inevitable consequences follow: a striving to raise their own prestige and rewards; a tendency to overdefine the skills needed to do the work; a limit on those who may do it, and to whom it may be done; and an increasing concern with 'professional standards,' personal satisfaction, and income. The danger is that the interests of the recipients can easily become subverted to serve the interests of the dispensers."[19]

[18] See Reinhard Bendix and Bennett Berger, "Images of Society and Problems of Concept Formation in Sociology," in *Symposium on Sociological Theory*, Llewellyn Gross (ed.). New York: Harper & Row, 1959, pp. 92–118; and also, Llewellyn Gross, "Preface to a Metatheoretical Framework for Sociology," *The American Journal of Sociology*, Vol. LXVII, No. 2, September, 1961, pp. 125–136.

[19] Martin Rein, "The Social Service Crisis," *Trans-Action*, Vol. 1, No. 4, May, 1964, pp. 3–6. Similar statements by sociologists and political scientists have also been recorded. See Peter Townsend, "A Society for People," *Conviction*, Norman MacKenzie (ed.). London: MacGibbon E. Kee, 1958; and William A. Robson, *The University Teaching of Social Sciences: Political Science*. Paris: UNESCO, 1954.

The core of the occupationlists ideology is in the last analysis determined by his belief in the primacy of the interests of the "recipients" over those of the "dispensers." The occupationalist sees his role as determined, in the long haul, by the needs of the recipients. Hence, his view of the field must be by definition more flexible and fluid than that of the professionalist—whose prime concern is building up organizational security against the vagaries of the future. Indeed, the occupationalist views the drive to build up security as in fact a move toward bureaucratization—a direction which is at the same time a violation of the scientific ethos.[20]

II

Thus far, we have presented illustrative material to support the thesis that the mainliners within sociology have been divided between two styles of empirical work. Only when one turns to an examination of marginality do we encounter non-empirical or even anti-empirical tendencies. Clearly, what is being said here in the rough requires careful documentation and clarification. But such tests are eminently possible. Career lines can be traced. Publishing habits can be examined. Mobility among sociologists can be charted.[21]

What I herein want to content myself with is a formalization of the inner sociological disputes as they now exist. Whether this will yield some "higher synthesis" is problematic. Nonetheless, the forthright presentation of the dilemma, as it works its course in a scientific field, provides powerful case material for the view that while theoretical issues may be sidetracked, they can scarcely be permanently outflanked. Theoretical principles are embedded in the core of research strategies. This may prove small comfort for those who take sociological theory to be a device for ordering the world, but for those who take a more modest view of it, a formal inventory of available postures and policies may be of some utility.

Any effort at systematic account of a field, particularly when framed in terms of polar opposites, is justifiably open to the charge of over-simplification. Yet, the need to formulate the lines of division between sociologists, no less than between sociological styles, is pressing enough to chance erring on the side of simplicity. Further empirical probing, research techniques to test propositions, and simple reflections on the issues raised may all serve as essential correctives. For our purpose, it will be sufficient to make plain just what undergirds present sociological cleavages.

[20] See Alfred McClung Lee, "Annual Report for 1963–1964 of the SSSP Representative to the ASA Council," *Social Problems*, Vol. 12, No. 3, Winter, 1965, pp. 356–360.
[21] See Elbridge Sibley, *The Education of Sociologists in the United States*. New York: Russell Sage Foundation, 1963.

Several precautionary measures are in order prior to a review of the forces upholding the integrity of the profession on one side, and defending the honor of the occupation on the other.

The first precaution is to bear in mind that by a professional we do not imply a bigoted upholder of any one concept of sociology, nor by an occupationalist do we imply an intellectualist posture in general. The professional may be of any political persuasion and have any number of interests. He may be connected with non-academic agencies, but he is largely affiliated with colleges and universities. His commitment to the idea of professionalism, however, forms an ideological set of beliefs which may be said to produce a sociological ideology, but which nonetheless has a line of development independent of other ideological strains in the field of sociological theory. The occupationalist, for his part, is also obliged to justify himself in terms of the field, and, unlike a "freelance" intellectual, he cannot make "ideas" as such his frame of reference. The terms profession and occupation are not directly transferable to denote narrow specialist and broad intellectual. However, there does seem to be some rationale for believing that the professionals see themselves in a physicalist image, while the occupationalists are more likely to seek an image based on political and even literary sophistication.

The second precaution is to avoid assumptions about the professional and the disciplinarian either preceding or following each other in time. The question of chronological evolution is a difficult one, and worth pursuing, but not subject to simple answer. The serious rifts between members of the Royal Society about this question make clear that even in former centuries, divisions existed between professionals and occupationalists (sometimes called *dilettantes*) within a professional organization.[22] Similarly, even within a dedicated occupational and intellectualist chore such as the *Encyclopédie*, men like D'Alembert upheld the notion of professional standards. In effect, (a) when dilettantism is replaced by some sort of formal organization of a field, (b) when it becomes sanctified as a science, and (c) when findings become serviceable to purchasers, at that point "hard-line" divisions between professionals and occupationalists tend to emerge. The growth of a science is not a straight-line phenomenon, but one which proceeds "dialectically"—through a conflict of different tendencies and orientations. Science itself can be viewed as a struggle for a style of work—with the victors crowned as the epitomizers of truth by the every present epigone.

The third precaution is to avoid any assumptions that popularization is a unique property of occupational or professional types. The mainline

---

[22] See M. Ornstein, *The Role of Scientific Societies in the Seventeenth Century* (revised second edition). Chicago: The University of Chicago Press, 1938; and Richard S. Westfall, *Science and Religion in Seventeenth Century England*. New Haven: Yale University Press, 1958.

members of a scientific community embrace both those who believe in sociology as an eight-hour day profession and those who believe in it as a twenty-four hour occupation. They are united by a roughly common educational background (although emphasis on different "minor" subjects may provide a revealing distinction) and by a set of personal relations and associations in common. From this the marginalist is often excluded. This is not to deny the role of popularization; the work of social science journalists like Dan Wakefield, Michael Harrington, Thomas Morgan, and Vance Packard represents a significant dent in the public consciousness of the role of sociology in public affairs. Yet, this role is performed from the outside. One need simply compare the above-named "outsiders" to such occupationalists as C. Wright Mills, David Riesman, and Erving Goffman; or to such professionals as Talbott Parsons, Robert K. Merton, or Kingsley Davis to see how thoroughly marginal the popularizers remain.[23]

The fourth precaution is to guard against ignoring the powerful kinship ties between sociologists. They have a shared emphasis on standards of quality, on the need for formal educational requirements, and a common attitude concerning the worth of sociology as such. In a real sense, both professionals and occupationalists are "professional" in their fundamental connections with a university, and both are "occupational" in that the criteria for such appointments and promotion are often contingent on originality, brilliance, and intellectual productivity.[24] Thus, the differences described take place within the same "interior." This stands in marked contrast to conflicts between the various social sciences which appear to stimulate "worldly" conflicts, that is, competition for public approval and policy domination. Intradepartmental struggles also differ from interdepartmental struggles in that the conflict between professional and occupational positions are ultimately supplementary rather than antagonistic to one another. Each must check its activites against the other so that a mutual dialogue continues openly which can give vitality to the field of sociology.

Several additional points must be stressed. Both professional and occupational types represent fully elaborated tendencies *within* the main line of sociological activity. They are "ideal types" which, however logically consistent, do not imply their extreme crystallization in any one person or among any one group of practitioners.

Nor should it be imagined that this model can be mechanically assigned

---

[23] One test for the extent to which "mainliners" and "marginals" are subject to differential treatment are the reviews of their work in the sociological journals—the respect accorded the most extreme "insider" of the sociological community in contrast to the rejection accorded the latter.

[24] Despite the monstrous abuses of universalistic criteria, "professional judgment" is based on performance and is as equitable as conflicts of viewpoint permit. See Theodore Caplow and Reece J. McGee, *The Academic Marketplace.* New York: Basic Books, 1958, pp. 87–93.

to any particular research method or general philosophic orientation. Functionalism, for example, may be used by both in professional and in the occupational styles. Naturally enough the emphasis will be different. The same holds true for believers in the "natural history" theory. In some sense the differences between these two groups seem to be directly connected to the social-academic position and to the goal orientations of the sociologist. They are related to the attitudes of the individual sociologists about the utility of varying methodologies only indirectly and in a mysterious "long run." The work of a sociologist can center on the "small group" and still fall within an occupationalist orientation. If this were not the case, the problem of "styles" in sociology would be considerably simplified. "Mind" would no longer stand as a specific factor to be examined on its own terms, since "behavior" could be directly inferred from "interests."

This brings us to a major question mark: What exactly is the relationship between style of work and the quality of results? After all, both professional and occupational types have as their ultimate court of appeal the utility and longevity of their work. And both mainliner sectors have come to appreciate the weaknesses in past sociological theory. But for the professional such weaknesses were a function of the relative scarcity of time and funds to think about theory. The retort of the occupationalists is that since there is, at least in the present, sufficient time and funds, why is there no corresponding improvement in sociological theory? Perhaps sound theoretical development is a consequence of the seriousness with which problems are thought about, rather than a simple function of available material resources at the disposal of the scholar.[25]

To complicate the problem, there is the stark and ever-present fact that there may be first-rate professionals and second-rate occupationals (and vice versa). We have then to explain whether or not there is a relationship between styles of work and qualities of results. But this deserves the full attention of a separate study. It is sufficient to say that there is a *prima facie* value in making this distinction between believers in an occupational orientation and believers in a professional orientation with such clarity as the field of sociology permits. But it is no less important to indicate that this *prima facie* value may be far more limited than is here stated. It might turn out that challenges from outside forces— political critiques, other social science encroachments, widespread withdrawals of foundation support, etc.—may turn out to be more cohesive elements in sociology than any legislated consensus or "gentleman's agreement" to withhold criticism.

[25] On this whole set of issues, the reader might compare and contrast Paul F. Lazarsfeld, "Reflections on Business," *The American Journal of Sociology*, Vol. LXV, No. 1, July 1959, pp. 1–31; with Dennis H. Wrong, "The Oversocialized Conception of Man in Modern Sociology," *American Sociological Review*, Vol. 26, No. 12, April, 1961, pp. 183–193.

Professionalism

1. Sociology is defined by the people who have been educated in the field and who go on to work and earn their living in the same field. A heavy premium is placed on the "boundedness" of sociology. This usually comes attached to a highly socialized attitude, or set of attitudes, e.g., problems of priorities in research discoveries resolved in bureaucratic terms.

2. The professional tends toward an esoteric attitude toward his activities. He believes in the need for a special language (jargon). He places a high premium on professional associations, and upon special status awards and rewards. He further tends to insist upon an early choice in specialization. In short, the professional operates within a theory of *exclusivity*.

3. Professionalism tends to accept the effective working of institutions as a norm not to be impeded, and indeed, to be aided. It is an assumption of the right of public institutions to define the character of their actions and the consequences of such acts. (The defence of social myths.)

4. There is a strong emphasis on the "team", on not breaking the "consensus", and on the testability of the propositions used in research reports. A premium is placed on reliability and on measurability. (The classical image of perfection.)

5. The assumption made about sociological information is that it is derived basically from informants. The field is held to be a series of generalizations derivable from a public. Emphasis on questionnaire design and model building. There is a further assumption that methodology and training techniques can compensate for original differences in levels of ability between sociologists. Professionalism implies standards of competence.

6. Either on the grounds of belief or utility, the professional holds that there is a

Occupationalism

1. Sociology is defined more in terms of the contents of the field and much less by its practitioners. The occupational type has a greater interest in intellectual activities taking place in adjacent or even distant disciplines. This usually comes with a linkage to an "individualistic" attitude toward such matters as primacy in discovery, e.g., problems resolved in terms of personal identity.

2. The occupationalist has an esoteric attitude toward his activities. He believes the common language is good. He places a high premium on associations outside of the profession—reward system based on some sort of public acclaim or policy utilization of efforts. Membership in professional organizations is often considered as peripheral. In short, the occupationalist operates within a theory of *inclusivity*.

3. Occupational orientations tend to an irreverence for authority and established institutions. It is a tendency not to treat public institutions as sacred, or to accept their self-definitions of the social situation. (The populist frame of mind.)

4. There is a strong emphasis on individual uniqueness which in turn is accompanied by varying intensities of disaffection and disaffiliation. A premium is placed on "quality of mind" and not doing the quality or kind of work which may not be subject to standard forms of measurement. (The romantic image of innovation.)

5. The assumption made about sociological information is that it is derived basically from the investigator. The field is held to be essentially a dialogue between the present generation of disciplinarians and the inheritance of the field. There is a further belief that while methodology can produce a minimal level of competence, it cannot and it does not eliminate different levels of insight and talent. Occupationalism thus implies standards of excellence.

6. The occupationalist feels entitled to examine questions of value, i.e., ethical

clear and distinct separation between factual commitment and valuational consequences. Thus, part of a definition of the field includes the proposition that research findings are neutral with respect to those who may use such findings. They are neutral in themselves, values being added by those who apply the findings.

7. For the professional the question is: For whom is sociology useful? The answer is usually made in terms of whoever can utilize the information. (The marketplace conception of knowledge.) For the professional utility is heightened insofar as technique and efficiency have reduced the area of intellectual conflict and increased the capacity to anticipate conflict. Method is held to lead to intellectual resolution of doubt.

8. The "image" or chain of associations instilled is of other professions, usually of a high prestige standing. In the case of sociology: physics, mathematics, and sometimes engineering. Images are often linked to those areas which have achieved a high grade of systematization and qualification, and no less a clear and distinct separation of theory-building from historical antecedents.

9. Professional emphasis is on the institutes which act as clearing agents for the dissemination of sociological information. The sociologist has some rationalized authority, with a high degree of work routinization. He considers the field as a job rather than a calling.

10. The professional often operates within a framework which assumes the existence of a clear understanding of the rules of research rites of passage, and stability of the social order. He is more concerned with problems of mobilization. That is to say, his concern is the maintenance of set standards that have been agreed upon by the elite within the profession. This leads to a general downgrading of novelty and individuality.

questions, insofar as they are intrinsically entailed in sociology. Sociology is defined in its interplay of fact and value, and of description and prescription. Thus, the findings of sociology are held to imply values which have proper and improper application. Those who apply the findings also draw their value implications.

7. For the occupational the question is: What are the values of sociology? The answer is usually made in terms of integrity of the field, i.e., rejecting sociology as marketable service in favour of sociology as knowledge. (Humanistic conception.) For the occupationalist the intellectual "dialogue" is valued above the canon of efficiency; these being mere evasions from position taking in the area of conflict. Technique and efficiency are not seen as assurance that the resolution of debate is either possible or desirable.

8. The "image" or chains of associations instilled is of other fields, usually of high prestige but low systematization. In the case of sociology: history, biography, and sometimes fiction. Images are often linked to those areas which have a high degree of interest relevance and which resist systematization. There is an emphasis on auto-consciousness, on an awareness of the historical continuities of social problems and social forces.

9. Occupationalists, because of their departmental emphasis, rely heavily on the sociologist as teacher and writer. There is a disinterest in, or a disavowal of, agencies which impersonally disseminate information. He views the field as a calling rather than as a job. The sociologist is a charismatic figure who defies routinization.

10. The occupational often operates within a framework which assumes a high degree of social conflict and a low degree of social cohesion. He tends to transfer from this image of reality an image of the field which is also basically unstructured. There is a pragmatic view of roles, and a looser view of academic roles. Under such conditions, novelty, generalization, and new modalities of relations to the general public are countenanced if not encouraged.

11. Professionalism involves an emphasis on technique, on the formal elegance of a presentation, and on approval from peer groups. The professional thinks in partialities, in terms of adjusting, correcting, and ameliorating. (The reformist imagination.)

11. Occupationalism involves an emphasis on critique, on the deftness of presentation, and on approval from an amorphous but relatively large-sized public. The disciplinarian thinks in totalities, in terms of overhauling and transforming. (The revolutionary imagination.)

III

The concept of marginality has many meanings and avenues of expression. One can infer from it a person living in limbo, between intellectual worlds as it were. It might be used to signify a self-conscious alienation, a feeling of the positive values being outside the mainstream. It may also be employed as a concept going against the mainstream, so that marginality becomes a function of a belief system rather than of the social systems.[26]

This last strikes closest to my use of the notion of marginality. The anti-sociologist employs marginality, whereas the unsociologist simply lives out this process in his institutional environment. In a sense, marginality is a response to traditionalism, the critique of present trends in terms of past achievements, and therefore will always be required. However, as it is herein used, marginality is a response to mainliner behavior, a belief that in some sense, nuclear membership in an organization or a profession is destructive of some major value which is in itself more social than sociological. For the anti-sociologist the power necessary to maintain oneself in a central organizational position violates the scientific and/or ethical need for the maintenance of principles and scruples.

However that elusive word "knowledge" is evaluated, there is a sense in which the assertion of marginality is a demand for the sociologist to concern himself with action programs, with intervention in social affairs, and with value considerations. The marginal man is concerned with immortality—differentially conceived by the unsociologist as a remembrance for services rendered to the alma mater, and by the anti-sociologist as the supreme critic combining poetry and science into a universal synthesis. Hence, to deal with marginality is to deal with powerful and contradictory forces motivating men toward extremes of self-sacrifice and self-centeredness.

[26] The notion of marginality is sometimes used to express the relationship of the "immigrant scholar" to his new environment. I shall not be dealing with this kind of marginality. Nonetheless, several interesting observations of marginality in general were made in this special immigrant connection. See Franz Adler, "The Marginal Man on the Faculty," and John Kosa, "The Immigrant Scholar in America," both in *Arena*, No. 17, January, 1964, pp. 33–34, 7–32.

In discussing the marginal sectors within sociology it should be emphasized that the anti-sociologist has certain functional similarities with the unsociologist. Both have standards of professional judgment which are determined not so much by sociological performance as by patterns extrinsic to such performance. The anti-sociologist for his part penetrates the field with a series of aesthetic judgments and often adopts a critique of sociology from the point of view of consciously applied literary techniques.[27] The unsociologist for his part has an entirely different starting point. He reflects a collegiate set of values, the point of view of practical judgment. His framework and frame of reference is not sociology but what is good or what is perceived to be good for the university or the college with which he is affiliated. The irony is that the profoundly alienated sociologist shares with the thoroughly integrated unsociologist a virtual abandonment of sociology as a system of strategy for engaging in social research.

Keeping in mind both the dissimilarities in starting points, and the similarities in terminal points, let us work up a diagrammatic profile of the relationship which obtains between the anti-sociologist and the unsociologist.

Anti-sociologist

1a. The anti-sociologist owes a functional allegiance to a source of authority, or to a set of ideas which is outside the control system of sociology. This may at times carry over into a critique of academic life as such, but it does not have to. It may be restricted to a critique of sociology as such, using criteria of judgment generally found in either mathematics or the humanities.[28]

2a. The anti-sociologist by virtue of his ideological orientation does a considerable amount of writing. He generally adopts a polemical style in his work. He sees these writings as transcendental, in contrast to most sociological writings, which he sees as transient in value and temporary in significance. As a writer, he "converses" with the classical figures—both dead and alive.

Unsociologist

1b. The unsociologist has his primary allegiance not so much to "main line" attitudes, or alternative forces which are contesting for pre-eminence in sociology, as a profound sense of obligation and loyalty to the institutional agency (usually a college or university) which employs him. The unsociologist has a perception of himself as a defender of an educational institution even at the risk of negating sociology as such.

2b. The unsociologist tends to do very little writing beyond the requirements for graduate training. Writing is not a value for the unsociologist; since the terms of promotion and advancement depend upon institutional loyalty and perhaps on teaching ability. When the unsociologist does write, he tends to do so more as an educationist than as a social scientist.

[27] For a fine essay developing this, see Maurice R. Stein, "The Poetic Metaphors of Sociology," *Sociology on Trial*, Maurice Stein and Arthur Vidich (eds.), Englewood Cliffs, N. J.: Prentice-Hall, 1963, pp. 173–181.

[28] One finds among the anti-sociologists such diverse types as the methodological model builder who uses formal logical criteria rather than empirical criteria for the judgment of sociological work or, at the other end of the spectrum, the anti-sociologist who employs literary or metaphysical judgments. The singular unifying trend is that the judgment about sociology is generally made from the point of view of another discipline.

3a. Anti-sociologists tend to be drawn from the pool of cosmopolitans. They have a view of sociology as placing arbitrary limits to debate and discussion. In this way, sociology comes to be considered an essentially parochial activity, having dubious scientific merits.

4a. Anti-sociologists tend to be messianic. They see themselves as men with a mission. They make an effort to proselytize; but the proselytization process is not so much of the heathen as it is one of the orthodox and the entrenched. They apply the pressures of the cultivated to the organization men of the field.

5a. The anti-sociologist is usually located at major universities, and in large departments of sociology. In this role he functions as a critical pivot addressing himself to the larger dilemmas of the profession. He is also able to connect up with the main intellectual currents either of the university or the community.

6a. The anti-sociologist starts with a critical ideological posture, generally well thought out, and not infrequently involving radical political premises. As a matter of fact, oftentimes the anti-sociologist can be found arguing not so much against sociology as for politics.

7a. The anti-sociologist adopts an alienated view of the world. In the very act of identifying with marginal groups of society, he often considers himself as part of the breakdown in sociological solidarity. He tends to picture his own role as being alienated with respect to the work processes of sociology as such.

8a. It can be surmised that the anti-sociologist has his personal background in a big city, prefers urban life, and works on a set of problems which derive in part from the big issues in world affairs. He tends to view sociology as good when it addresses itself to total issues in a total way and bad when it ignores such issues, or delves into them from a "social problems" or partial way.

3b. Unsociologists tend to be local. They are concerned with a small range of problems, generally those kinds of problems which deeply affect the administrative apparatus of college life and in consequence their attitudes towards sociology are conventional and non-emotive. They see it in terms which are value-neutral.

4b. Unsociologists do little to win adherents. Instead, they function in such a way as to lessen the desires or the drive to engage in fundamental sociological effort. They are organizational men. Their power within the profession largely derives from administrative sensitivities. They are more interested in administration than in intellect.

5b. The unsociologist is usually located at small colleges where his administrative prowess is appreciated and needed; and also where the demands for his continued professional achievement are at a minimum. The unsociologist may be "cultivated" in a general sense, but unlike the anti-sociologist he has no need of performing critical catharsis.

6b. The unsociologist generally adopts a consensualist posture, one based on organizational agreement and one oriented towards getting the job done whatever the task may be. He tends to be, therefore, politically indifferent and mildly conservative in his "outlook".

7b. The unsociologist takes a gentleman's view of the field. He tends to be pleased with sociological activities insofar as they create a "halo effect"—an image which is respectable and can create an additional "line" to the school he is at. He is sometimes enmeshed with the creation of sociological rituals—which are neither offensive nor innovative.

8b. The unsociologist tends to be from a small town and rural background. He therefore is interested in the utilization of sociology only as it addresses itself to small or middle range problems; problems which are susceptible to immediate control and problems which can be resolved without raising theoretical issues having much of a "cutting edge".

9a. The anti-sociologist has a well-worked out philosophical system, or is at least pro-philosophy. He may draw upon a network of doctrines such as dialectical materialism, neo-thomism, existentialism, intuitionism, etc. He sees empiricism as a philosophically crude system which "mystifies" the terms of ordinary language, by leaving them in a "repressive" universe of discourse.

9b. The unsociologist tends to be an anti-philosopher. His theoretical premises rarely move beyond the doctrine of common sense. He is willing to forgo philosophic implications of scholarship if this impedes bureaucratic development. He is a "pragmatist" only in the sense of being discontent with "European ideologies" or systems of thought which impede direct access to the materials of course work in sociology.

IV

With this set of characterizations now completed, we might summarize the relationship between our broad sociological types by means of a chart. This chart, hopefully, illustrates what I take to be the core relationships which are found between the four types of sociologists herein dealt with. It can be seen that from the viewpoint of the ethos (the vertical line) professionals and unsociologists tend to "line up" together, as do occupationals and anti-sociologists on the side of the diagram. This factor of "ethos," "ideology," "world outlook"—or what you will—has been the victim of neglect in these pages for two reasons: First is my belief that immediate "organizational" relations shape the ideology, and not the other way about. Second is the admittedly personal reason of wanting to draw the lines between sociological types in such a way as to perhaps ease tensions between competing styles, by showing how such styles are keyed to organizational developments of science in general, and to the social sciences in particular.

Rather than suggest an outcome to this analysis which would be a beatific vision of the sociological horizons, deprived of the creative tensions which make sociology one of the more dynamic social sciences, I propose a reading of those elements in the occupation-professional orientation, and in the anti-sociological-unsociological orientation which can serve to increase the value of the research done and the theories devised.[29]

---

[29] The reader should be apprised of the fact that this study represents one chunk of an ongoing effort of mine to develop a sociology of sociology. For other related aspects of this effort, I should like to draw attention to my following papers: "Establishment Sociology: The Value of Being Value Free," *Inquiry: An Interdisciplinary Journal of Philosophy and the Social Sciences*, Vol. 6, No. 2, 1963, pp. 129–140; "Consensus, Conflict and Cooperation: A Sociological Inventory," *Social Forces*, Vol. 41, No. 2, December, 1962, pp. 177–188; "Social Science Objectivity and Value Neutrality: Historical Problems and Projections," *Diogene: International Review of Philosophy and Humanistic Studies*, Vol. 39, Fall, 1962, pp. 17–44; "Professionalism and Disciplinarianism: Two Styles of Sociological Performance," *Philosophy of Science*, Vol. 32, No. 2, July, 1964, pp. 275–281; "Max Weber and the Spirit of American Sociology," *The Sociological Quarterly*, Vol. 5, No. 4, Autumn, 1964, pp. 344–354; and "Anthropology for Sociologists: Cross Disciplinary Research as Scientific Humanism," *Social Problems*, Vol. II, No. 2, Fall, 1963, pp. 201–206.

A Double Interchange System for the Study of Sociological Types

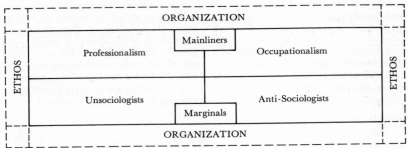

Although professionalism provides an organizational basis to sociology, it also contains dysfunctional elements, degenerative devices for enforcing early career decisions, ensuring consensual indoctrination, and crystallizing conventions into dogma. Professionalism does indeed provide mechanisms for the increase of public awareness and acceptance of sociology; but it too often does so at a cost of hindering scientific openness and experimental innovation among sociologists. Its demands for universalism, for competence at the expense of excellence, too often spill over into an attack on heterodoxy—the very charge which the sociological tradition has consistently addressed to the European ideologies from which it broke away.[30]

The person who views sociology as an occupation has the distinctive advantage of being central to the development of the field without losing sight of the connections between sociology and allied disciplines. He has a vested interest in the idea content rather than the bureaucratic norms of a field. Of all the strategies the sociologist is eligible to adopt, occupationalism offers maximum intellectual flexibility. He can function both "inside" and "outside" professional confines with equal ease. He can maintain a critical posture without reducing his position to sheer negative demands for the self-liquidation of the field. And finally, the occupationalist can appreciate the fact that the word society is larger and more embracing than the word sociology.

This statement of optimal outcomes, however, leaves much to be desired. The occupationalist too often suffers from a ready default of sociological effort. His cultural concerns are at times misanthropic,

30 For critique of professionalism along these lines, see Ralf Dahrendorf, "Out of Utopia: Toward a Reorientation of Sociological Analysis," *American Journal of Sociology*, Vol. 64, No. 2, September, 1958, pp. 115–127; Robert W. Habenstein, "Critique of 'Profession as a Sociological Category." *The Sociological Quarterly*, Vol. 4, No. 4, Autumn, 1963, pp. 291–300; E. C. Hughes, "Professional and Career Problems of Sociology," *Men and Their Work*. New York: Free Press, 1958, pp. 157–168; and most recently, David J. Gray, "Sociology as a Science: A Dysfunctional Element," *The American Journal of Economics and Sociology*, Vol. 21, No. 4, October, 1962, pp. 337–346.

since they entail an unwillingness to state clearly the basis of judgment and the grounds of action. The occupational orientation has grown content with being part of a sprawling discipline, a sort of "loyal opposition" too ready to condemn and too slow to correct. Occupationalists have too frequently mistaken their intellectual orientation with a need to avoid organizational involvement and participation—as if the critique of professionalism necessarily carries with it a mandate to frown upon organizational solidarity.[31] This in turn stems from a long tradition in which ideas and power were considered not just as different, but as antagonists.

The anti-sociologists in the sociological ambient provide a necessary reminder that a totalist critique of the field is a necessary stimulant to serious work. It is a constant reminder that sociology is a human science, and as such is intimately connected to human foibles. The anti-sociologist at his best is the outsider within. He reminds us how many of our grants are due to the conservatizing needs of a welfare establishment. How many of our positions on standards and measures are really postures taken defiantly in the absence of firm standards. How much of our insistence upon the appropriate rites of passage rest on primitive puberty rites—oftentimes designed to weed out the different rather than the deviant.[32]

But this does not preserve the anti-sociologist from overreacting to an admittedly difficult cultural environment. How much weight can someone who disbelieves in either a professional or occupational view of sociology pull? Isn't anti-sociologism a reactionary view of social change disguised as super-revolutionism? Isn't it a contempt for social problems and social adjustment in much the same way as the old-fashioned nineteenth-century revolutionism which was dismayed with every attempt at reform lest it weaken the revolutionary "impulses" of the people? The anti-sociologist may drift into the higher irresponsibility. He takes seriously only his criticism of the field; and not the need to do something about the society he studies. The anti-sociologist is metaphysically proper and right—since in fact every attempt at social amelioration must fall short of the mark. But in the concrete, profane sense,

[31] The literature which is either critical or positively disposed towards an occupational orientation remains surprisingly slim. This in part may be a reflection of its "emergent" status. And it may also be, as I have elsewhere indicated, a consequence of an absence of a self-conscious, well-articulated strategy on the part of the professionals. The best single exposition which seeks to defend an occupational orientation, in the "classical tradition," is C. Wright Mills' *The Sociological Imagination*. New York: Oxford University Press, 1959; and along roughly similar lines, see Jrving L. Horowitz, *The New Sociology*, New York: Oxford University Press, 1964. While no single sustained attack on occupationalism has yet been made, one may take the olympian statement in *Sociology Today: Problems and Prospects*, as typical. Edited by Robert K. Merton, Leonard Broom, Leonard S. Cottrell, Jr., New York: Basic Books, 1959.

[32] See, for example, Herbert Marcuse, *One Dimensional Man: Studies in the Ideology of Advanced Industrial Society*. Boston: Beacon Press, 1964; and from a different perspective, Daniel J. Boorstin, *The Image, or What Happened to the American Dream*. New York: Atheneum, 1962.

an anti-sociologist is always wrong, since his totalist critique never gets us nearer the utopia the anti-sociologist so clearly craves. He can only "possess" the future in poetic imagery; unfortunately he can never work for a realization of that future with perhaps a prosaic imagery that gets us one step nearer to a meaningful future.[33] The drive to possess the future *en bloc* usually comes out fitted with garments inherited from the past. What is celebrated is not so much that which is to come, but an idyllic past which has already been. That is why the reactionary-revolutionary pendulum has more than surface attitudes in common.

The unsociologist is the most difficult to categorize of our four types. He is least likely to articulate his position in an intellectually convincing way. Yet, there is much to be said for the unsociologist who at least takes his duties as a teacher and a member of the faculty seriously. He can, under optimal circumstances, provide the kind of elementary grounding in sociology from which careers are launched. He can prove to be innovative with respect to academic needs. He can employ his sociological skills to constructive ends in the university-college establishments. He can provide the link between the personalized student and an impersonal college administration.

However personally attractive the marginal type may be, he is involved in an objective default. In his accommodation for functional tasks, in his gentlemanly search for local power independent of sociological tasks, or in his assiduous avoidance of power as such, he represents the kiss of death—the man who can do more to destroy student interests in *sociology* than to stimulate such interests. His passions are for administration and college gentility. His discomfort with intellectual brilliance, with sociological effort, makes him intolerant of those dedicated to sociology. Thus, throughout the small colleges of America are to be found elder statesmen who feel more threatened by sociological talents than inspired by them. Like his anti-sociologist compatriot, he reveals the repressed fear of the demands that sociology as a science makes on the time, the energy, and the talents of the sociologist.

There is no single answer to the problems herein posed. Obviously each of the four sociological types in our profile-in-diagram form has points of utility as well as inutility. Insofar as the social position and perspective of the sociologist determine the quality of the work done, it remains an empirical task to figure out which of the four types does indeed lead to greater sociological creativity. But we should not overlook the fact that there is an autonomous element involved in sociological creation and that we are just as likely to get the brilliant work from an unexpected

---

[33] Sociological "anti-sociology" has a long and honorable tradition within the field (which is perhaps the most difficult phenomenon of all which the anti-sociologist has to account for). The best recent symposium on this position is *Sociology on Trial*, Maurice Stein and Arthur Vidich (eds.), Englewood Cliffs, N. J.: Prentice-Hall, 1963.

marginal source as we are from an expected mainliner context. There is a functional autonomy between individual creativity and organizational connections. Were this not the case, the size of the university and the quality of creation would be perfectly correlated. If it were indeed possible to establish a definite correlation between professionalism and maximum creativity, the dispute would be settled then and there. It is precisely because this cannot be done that it becomes useful to develop profiles of various sociological types and insist upon refinements and changes in various forms of sociological norms.

For example, at the most elemental level, the unsociologist, one who is willing to subordinate his entire interest to the teaching apparatus, is most unlikely to be in a functional position to make any sort of theoretical breakthrough. On the other hand, it might with equal assurance be said that a professionally oriented sociologist might be inhibited from making any breakthrough at the level of educational methods, if for no other reason than a fear of alienating any possible lines of "worldly" organizational support. At the extremes, the problem is capable of a general formalization. But it is unlikely that the sociological dilemmas will be broken out of, independent of a general resolution of academic and university affairs.

Without wishing to minimize the contributions of the "marginal," it must be said in all frankness that the main struggle for the emergence of a new sociology can only be engaged in by those willing and capable of entering the arena, that is, by the "mainliners." In this competition between sociological styles, the unsociologists and the anti-sociologists confine themselves to the role of spectator, so that at least in the present period, the struggle over the kind of theories and methods sociology should have is directly proportional to the institutional questions—what kind of agency should the sociologist have and what kind of man should the sociologist be? Indeed, in the very process of fashioning institutions appropriate to the solution of these concrete questions, we will travel some distance on the road to answering ethical questions. But to lose sight of the fact that institutions are responses to moral demands is to build castles in the air which cannot be defended intellectually, or inhabited practically.

Perhaps the most damaging aspect of marginality is that it encourages premature expressions of cynicism and resignation about the organization of sociology and the strategies of its practitioners. However, at the present period in American sociology, the responsibility for fostering this premature futilitarian attitude also belongs to the professionals. It is the organizational kingpins who, after all, have insinuated the ideology of homogeneity, and not their critics. They have urged the sorts of monolithic organizational identities which make a heterodox sociology difficult to bring about. Thus the problems created by professionalism require the most immediate concern.

The idea that once a science becomes "professionalized" it is "lost" in terms of any radical transformations is simply an erroneous and dangerous myth. Just as we have found that bureaucracy has many "irrational" and dysfunctional features, so too professionalism has been found, by many of the sciences, to be likewise dysfunctional, and in much the same way as any complex organization is something more and something less than rational.[34] (1) Professionalism leads to great stress because of its overstructuring the field of sociology—its ritualistic demands for codification gradually slip over into demands for consensus and finally cohesion, having little to do with scientific standards. (2) Professionalization tends to reduce experimentation to a minimum, by setting arbitrary definitions of sociological activities, and by circumscribing the kinds of positions found acceptable. (3) Professionalization sets up a bureaucratic chain of command, and for that very reason, endures the same complex of pains that all other bureaucratic structures undergo. (4) Professionalization is an ideological posture which, insofar as it removes the sociologists from the social problems he writes of, tends to weaken his stature in the research efforts to the degree that he becomes professionalized.

These conditions have evolved more fully in other sciences, particularly those not engaged in the process of image-building. Hence, the revolt against professionalism as an ideology of science (or at least against it obvious dysfunctional elements) is at a more advanced stage in physics and engineering than in sociology or social work. We may take the following sharply critical statement on the reduction of knowledge to information, as characteristic of the present vigorous assertion of the anti-bureaucratic concept of scientific man as expressed among contemporary natural scientists.

> The huge "think factories" of our time are the equivalent of the Lancashire cotton mills of the industrial revolution. The scientists are many, and they are very busy producing staggering quantities of "knowledge." Their product, however, is increasingly taking on the character of a mere commodity: and their work takes on the alienated character of assembly line production, with no rhyme or reason or discernible relation to a meaningful whole. To call this mushrooming mass-production of information a flowering of science, makes only a little more sense than to call the booming output of television commericals a flowering of poetry and dramatic art. Without integrative understanding, without theory, science is not really possible. All the electric computers in the world, both those present and those to be built, storing and analyzing all the myriad pieces of detailed information, produced by countless technical workers, do not constitute science, because they cannot provide

34 See, for example, Herman D. Stein, "Administrative Implications of Bureaucratic Theory," *Social Work*, Vol. 6, No. 3, July, 1961, pp. 14–21.

effective knowledge and understanding *for us*, for human beings. They cannot make a meaningful, humanly livable world *for us*.[35]

The enormous increase in experimental programs, in cross-disciplinary research, in demands for humanistic preprofessional training in such areas as medicine and engineering, by leading graduate schools are strong indicators that a narrowly conceived professionalism can no longer hold the day in the court of ideas. The emergence of different styles and strategies in sociology can only augur well for the future development of what is after all a public body of information produced by scientific men and not a mystic sect interested in sealing off knowledge from action.

[35] Paul R. Zilsel, "The Mass Production of Knowledge," *Bulletin of the Atomic Scientists*, Vol. XX, No. 4, April, 1964, p. 29; also see C. Wright Mills, "The Bureaucratic Ethos," *The Sociological Imagination*. New York: Oxford University Press, 1959, pp. 100–118.

Index